The African American Experience in Texas

D1564716

The African American
Experience in Texas

AN ANTHOLOGY

★

EDITED BY

Bruce A. Glasrud

AND

James M. Smallwood

TEXAS TECH UNIVERSITY PRESS

This book is typeset in Trump Mediaeval. The paper used in this book meets the
minimum requirements of ANSI/NISO z39.48–1992 (R1997). ∞

Book design by Mark McGarry,
Texas Type & Book Works

Library of Congress Cataloging-in-Publication Data
The African American experience in Texas : an anthology / edited by
Bruce A. Glasrud and James M. Smallwood.
p. cm.
Includes bibliographical references and index.
ISBN-13: 978-0-89672-609-3 (hardcover : alk. paper)
ISBN-10: 0-89672-609-6 (hardcover : alk. paper)
1. African Americans—Texas—History.
2. African Americans—Texas—Social conditions.
3. African Americans—Civil rights—Texas—History.
4. Texas—Race relations. 5. Texas—History—19th century.
6. Texas—History—20th century. I.
Glasrud, Bruce A. II. Smallwood, James M.
E185.93.T4A38 2007
976.4'00496073—dc22
2006103020

Printed in the United States of America
07 08 09 10 11 12 13 14 15 | 9 8 7 6 5 4 3 2 1

Texas Tech University Press
Box 41037
Lubbock, Texas 79409–1037 USA
800.832.4042
ttup@ttu.edu
www.ttup.ttu.edu

For Lawrence L. Graves and Alwyn Barr,
professors and mentors, whose pivotal and dedicated
efforts in developing and continuing the study of African American
history produced "The Texas Tech School of Black History"

Contents

PART TWO

The Twentieth Century Experience

Tables

Preface

As HISTORIANS measure time, only recently did Texas historians begin to focus on the historical experience of African Americans in their state. In the past thirty to forty years, research into the subject has burgeoned, and now, by the first years of the twenty-first century, an appreciable body of scholarship has accumulated on the different eras and topics of black Texas history circa 1820 through contemporary times. The literature is uneven; in the introduction to this anthology, we describe some of the work that remains to be done, but these gaps continue to be explored—we see additions to the history of black Texans in the form of articles, books, theses, and dissertations contributing to our further understanding virtually every year.

The African American Experience in Texas is meant to provide students, teachers, and the general public with a book that uses meaningful research and writing on black Texans to offer insight into a previously neglected part of our history. The thrust of this collection focuses on the lives and contributions of blacks in Texas history. This anthology will be of good use to high school teachers, college professors, and students, supplementing general course materials in United States history surveys, Texas history courses, black history offerings, and graduate-level courses in African American, Texas, Western, and Southern history. Historians, students, and other individuals interested in the broader Southwest, South, and West will also be able to learn from and appreciate better the history of black Texans.

The coeditors of this volume believe that a selection of the best previously published material illustrates the development and evolution of the research and writings on African Americans in Texas and serves to correlate the achievement to date. As important, it also becomes a repository of the lives, history, and accomplishments of African Americans in white-dominated Texas. It is an exciting history of the events, people, ideas, and communities of this significant segment of Texas society. Since so many works of quality have been published, these articles offer in their arguments and in their citations a sense of new directions that future researchers may wish to explore.

This volume provides under a single cover access to the finest historical research and writing on Texas African Americans from the 1960s to the present. It also includes a representative selection of the scholarly literature on Afro-Texas history. It is fortunate that the scholarship on black Texans also maps the changing and divergent scholarly trends across the years as noted in the introduction. The collective contributions succeed in portraying episodes of African American history in the state, and in showcasing the best studies which have been done on black Texans. We chose to limit the survey to journal articles because book excerpts and chapters from monographs seldom stand alone. We also believe that it is in their journal articles that many historians introduce their original thought-provoking theses and themes and as a result journal articles tend to be on the cutting edge of research.

We have limited the chronology to cover the period from 1820 to the late 1970s. We begin in 1820 for two reasons: first, this is the time when Mexico gained its independence and allowed Anglos (e.g., Stephen F. Austin and followers) with their black servants to enter the northern province, now Texas, and second, there remains a void in the journal literature on the role of blacks in Spanish/Mexican Texas. We stop in the late 1970s because again there is a void in the journal literature. Most historians are reluctant to write on recent events because of problems with sources and perspective. This means that there are few published journal articles that focus on the last thirty years of African American history in Texas.

On the other hand, since a considerable number of solid, scholarly articles have been published on African American history in Texas choosing the particular selections for this volume has been a difficult albeit fascinating and rewarding task. After an extensive search, we began with a list of approximately seventy articles, which we then organized chronologically and topically. We sought a chronological framework but felt it imperative also to cover the critical issues of Afro-Texas history and experience. We arranged the articles in chronological order, and then proceeded to place each of the articles within one of six chronological divisions. We cut down the number of articles carefully, keeping in mind our original goal of developing a supplemental text for classroom use. Articles were eliminated on the basis of readability, topics, and scholarship.

This first round of elimination left us with a total of thirty articles—a strong group that we then worked into an outline. This material was sent to our publisher on an exploratory basis and to scholars in the field to solicit their input. From that thirty we reduced the list to the current seventeen and reduced the chronological divisions from six to two: one covering the nineteenth century, the other the twentieth century. The final collection represents a group of articles that allow a teacher or a reader to gain more depth from and understanding of new and significant topics and individuals in Afro-Texas history than can be accomplished with more general textbooks. A few essays were retained for their wider scope and their clear significance beyond Texas (see especially the selections by Alwyn Barr, W. Marvin Dulaney, and Paul D. Lack). The anthology contains two articles not previously published, whose authors focus on subjects not well represented in the published literature—Michael Searles on black cowboys and Robert Fink on the emergence of separate black baseball leagues and teams during the 1920s. Both emphasize more than just the topic indicated by their title; they also investigate the social and cultural milieu of African Americans working and playing in Jim Crow society. Articles by Gregg Cantrell, Darlene Clark Hine, Merline Pitre, and Martin Kuhlman illustrate the commitment of black Texans to create a better, more equitable place for themselves as blacks in white Texas society. The remaining articles were selected because of their chronological period, focus, scholarship, readability, and/or contribution to and understanding of the African American story in the Lone Star State.

As a result of the above decisions, we arrived at an easy-to-use, readily available collection that explicates the lives, experiences, communities, organized protests, and contributions of African Americans in and to Texas history, one that can expose readers to a range of enjoyable, readable, and penetrating perspectives on the African American experience in Texas. The articles are significant and original. They are also inclusive and revisionist; that is, they foster the important and significant role that black Texans played in the development of Texas and in the formation of the black community in Texas.

In studying, and referring to, groups in the United States, terminology is important. For the purposes of this anthology, we have used the terms African American (without a hyphen), black, and Afro-Texan interchangeably in the editors' writings and in the selections. We also corrected what are clearly typographical errors, as well as errors or language we are certain the author would have corrected, in the selections used in our collection.

Throughout their history Afro-Texans have been in the vanguard of protest and challenge to their second-class status and to the ravages of racism and Jim Crow laws. We hope that all readers, from the casually interested to the professional, will find themselves engaged and enlightened within these pages.

BRUCE A. GLASRUD

JAMES M. SMALLWOOD

Acknowledgments

In dedicating this anthology to the late Lawrence L. Graves and to Alwyn Barr, professors of history at Texas Tech University, we wish to acknowledge the appreciation we have for their support and encouragement as we struggled with the intricacies of becoming historians of the black experience. Glasrud studied with Dr. Graves, a University of Wisconsin PhD, and Smallwood with Dr. Barr, who took his PhD from the University of Texas. Both editors of this volume are products of the "Texas Tech School of Black History," and along with Paul Lack, Lawrence Rice, Neil Sapper, and Martin Kuhlman, we charted in our dissertations the course of black history in Texas from slavery through the Civil Rights movement. Since then, numerous other scholars have studied at and graduated from the "Texas Tech School of Black History."

This book would not have been possible without the keen insight and editorial skills of Judith Keeling, Editor in Chief at Texas Tech University Press. She aided us, pushed us, and consoled us as the need arose. Her suggestions and assistance went well beyond the call of duty; thanks, Judith. Noel Parsons, Director of the Press, also provided help and encouragement. Karen Medlin took the manuscript, polished it, and produced a book.

The numerous contributors to this anthology have waited with us for its completion; we thank them for their patience and trust that the finished product is everything they thought it could be. Journal editors and the authors gave us publishing permissions and support, and many colleagues made suggestions and comments that led to the improvement of the manuscript.

George Ward and Ron Tyler, past officers of the Texas State Historical Association, supported our effort and generously allowed us permission to reprint six articles originally published in the *Southwestern Historical Quarterly*. We also wish to acknowledge the debt we owe to two anonymous readers who supported this work but asked for revisions that ultimately strengthened the volume; we appreciate their diligence and encouragement as the project came to fruition. Even though we mentioned him earlier, it would be impossible not to heartily thank Alwyn Barr for his help in recommending useful selections, in reading and rereading the manuscript, and in general being an extraordinary and committed scholar and colleague.

One cannot complete a work of history without aid and support from librarians. We especially wish to acknowledge the library staff at Sul Ross State University. To further our effort, Monte Monroe, at the Southwest Collection of Texas Tech University, helped us locate computer specialists who could help with the most difficult of tasks—scanning the manuscript. Those specialists are on the staff of Tech's Vietnam Archives: archivist Steve Maxner and digital coordinator Justin Saffel provided us with an excellent disk copy of all the articles included in this work. Thanks!

Occasionally, Murphy's Law prevails; if so, any errors found in the volume are our own.

The African American Experience in Texas

Introduction

African American History in the Lone Star State

BRUCE A. GLASRUD
AND JAMES M. SMALLWOOD

THE HISTORY OF African Americans in Texas can be traced back almost five hundred years. In 1528 a black man, Estevan, landed with the Spanish explorer Cabeza de Vaca on Galveston Island near the coast of Texas. After six years they moved into the interior, and from around San Antonio they crossed Texas to Pecos before turning to Mexico. Other blacks entered the state at various intervals over the succeeding centuries. Some, especially under Spanish and Mexican control, arrived as free people; others, once Anglos began to dominate the area, came as slaves; and once the Civil War put an end to slavery, still more blacks sought a life in Texas.

Over time the African American population of Texas has increased mightily. As late as 1792 only 450 blacks and mulattos called the future state home, but the number grew to 5,000 by 1836. The count stood at 182,566 on the eve of the Civil War, and the growth continued. By 1900 620,722 blacks, composing 20.4 percent of the population, resided in the state, but by 1960 the 1,187,125 people of African descent composed a declining 12.4 percent of the Texas population. In 1990 2,000,000 blacks formed only 12 percent of the population, and the percentage decline continued through the 2000 census—the total population in Texas reached nearly 21 million, but the 2,404,566 Afro-Texans constituted a reduced 11.5 percent of that population. Current census projections indicate a continuing decline. This declining percentage of African Americans in Texas is one of the most significant developments of the late twentieth and early twenty-first centuries. Despite the fact that African Americans have resided in the state for more than five hundred years and despite their substantial portion of the population, studies of black Texans were lacking up until the last quarter-century, and African American history has only recently become an integral part of the curriculum.

Since at least the 1930s, historians, critics, and teachers have deplored the lack of research on black Texans and have called for the inclusion of African American history courses in state schools. In 1935 L. V. Williams argued that black history ought to be taught in both the white and black schools in Texas. The following year Ira B. Bryant Jr. wrote a pamphlet on *The Texas Negro Under Six Flags* "to clearly indicate to those who write Texas history in the future that such a history is incomplete if the past and present accomplishments of Texas Negroes are omitted." Florence O'Brien concluded in 1939 that "it is obvious from the evidence given that the Negro does not receive the proper recognition in the texts used in Texas." In 1952 Westerfield T. Kimble noted that history instruction in black schools taught "that which life does not confirm." J. Reuben Sheeler underscored the importance of African American efforts to develop an interest in black history when he asked in 1955: "If the Negro does not support the promulgation of the history of the Negro, who else can he expect to do it?" Writing more than twenty years after his earlier pamphlet, Bryant still found in 1957 that "for the most part, the contributions of the Negro to the history of Texas do not appear in the textbooks."[1] Nor, he might well have concluded, in any other publishing venue.

But some historical writing had accrued over the years. In 1898 Lester G. Bugbee wrote an article for the *Political Science Quarterly* entitled "Slavery in Early Texas." In this article he described the back-and-forth skirmishing over the emergence of the institution of slavery in Texas during the years from 1821 to 1836. Although he did not discuss African Americans themselves, his was the first article by an academic to cover the topic of African American history in the Lone Star State. Four years later, the transportation of slaves into Texas was the topic of Eugene C. Barker's "The African Slave Trade in Texas" published by the *Texas Historical Association Quarterly.* Such white academicians were not the only ones writing about black Texans at this time. In 1885 African American author H. T. Kealing published a *History of African Methodism in Texas;* in 1900 R. L. Smith published two articles discussing the Farmer's Improvement Society; and in the following year (1901) the eminent W. A. Redwine published a *Brief History of the Negro in Five Counties.*[2]

Although not trained historians, two fiction writers, one black and one white, published works that are invaluable depictions of black society at the turn of the twentieth century. Black Texas-born author Sutton E. Griggs published a novel in 1899 entitled *Imperium in Imperio*, in which African American Texans, tired of how they had been treated by whites in the state, joined an organization—the Imperium in Imperio—bent on claiming the state, either peaceably or violently, for blacks. The same year, white author John Wesley Carhart, a Texas physician, published a series of short stories about the black community in the state. One of the very few turn-of-the-century white racial liberals, Carhart, in his book *Under Palmetto and Pine*, presents sensitive portraits of black Texans struggling against discrimination and poverty. Two of his powerful short stories are "Lynchers Foiled" and "The Black Man's Burden," the latter a poignant depiction of sharecropping for a white owner.

There were other sources for understanding the history of black Texans by the turn of the twentieth century. Reports depicted the life and meandering of Estevan, who, as mentioned earlier, was the first black to reach Texas.[3] The poem and song, "The Yellow Rose of Texas," alludes to the perils facing a free black woman during a time of revolutionary strife.[4] Folktales and folklore helped explain the lives and community of black Texans during and after slavery.[5]

Mostly, however, documenting the history of African Americans in Texas and their roles in building the state has been a twentieth-century effort. Even as late as 1965, writings about African Americans had not developed into a special focus for any group of historians. Publications and studies remained scattered.

In the years between 1900 and 1940, for example, academically trained (read white) scholars produced only a few articles or books concerned with the history of black Texans. Charles William Ramsdell published "Presidential Reconstruction in Texas" in the *Quarterly of the Texas State Historical Association* (1908), followed two years later by his monograph, *Reconstruction in Texas*. Ramsdell's studies emphasized an anti-black stance, and neither, in a strict sense, could be considered African American studies. Both works deplored Reconstruction's impact on white Texans while deprecating the black experience. During the 1920s, Abigail Curlee pursued her interest in slavery and finished a master's thesis and an article, "The History of a Texas Slave Plantation, 1831–1863," in 1922. She followed those studies with her dissertation, "A Study of Texas Slave Plantations, 1822–1865," a decade later at the University of Texas at Austin. Curlee provided an overall assessment of plantation management and life, but her evaluation of the slave community followed the now discredited traditional-ist Ulrich B. Phillips's interpretation that slaves enjoyed their entrap-ment, loved their masters, and understood that they would not be suc-cessful as free men and women. Curlee, as did Ramsdell and Phillips, started from the belief that African Americans were inferior. Similar views were developed in Johanna Rosa Engelking's, "Slavery in Texas." The slave trade itself intrigued writers such as W. J. Carnathan in "The Attempt to Re-Open the African Slave Trade in Texas, 1857–1858," published in the journal of the *Southwestern Political and Social Sci-ence Association*. Another investigation, by Karl E. Ashburn, "Slavery and Cotton Production in Texas," reviewed the relationship of that in-stitution with cotton production. Yet there were also free blacks in early Texas, and they, too, interested a scholar. In 1936 and 1937, Harold Robert Schoen published articles on "The Free Negro in the Re-public of Texas" in the *Southwestern Historical Quarterly*. Schoen completed his dissertation on that topic at the University of Texas at Austin in 1938.

Most of the work that was favorably disposed toward African Amer-icans during the first part of the twentieth century and that considered both individuals and the black community, was written by black histo-rians. Not surprisingly, their published output was limited because few were economically or educationally advantaged. In 1920 Monroe Work published "Some Negro Members of Reconstruction Legislatures: Texas," in the *Journal of Negro History*. Two biographies were also pro-duced on key black Texas political leaders: Maud Cuney Hare's *Norris Wright Cuney* (1913) and William Oliver Bundy's *Life of William Madi-son McDonald* (1925). A biography of a black minister written by his son also serves the student of black Texans. Theodore Sylvester Boone wrote *"Old Chief," Alexander Lorenza Boone, D.D., LL.D.; A Biogra-phy by His Son*. A pastor and an attorney, Theodore Sylvester Boone was easily the most prolific black Texas writer of the first half of the twentieth century. By the time he left the state for Detroit in 1941, he had published at least fifteen books, and by 1952 he had published twelve more. Among his other works are *The Philosophy of Booker T. Washington, Paramount Facts in Race Development, Feet Like Pol-ished Brass*, and *From George Lisle to L. K. Williams: Short Visits to the Tombs of Negro Baptists*.

An astute and enlightening autobiography by a slave-born attorney, J. Vance Lewis's *Out of the Ditch: A True Story of an Ex-Slave*, provides another indication of life in the African American community, especially on the relationships between white and black people in the judicial setting. For a time in Texas, the Democratic party refused to allow African Americans to vote in its primary elections; as a result, blacks were ultimately unable to decide who would represent them. An important work portraying the dramatic and ultimately successful struggle against this "white primary" was J. Alton Atkins's *The Texas Negro and His Political Rights*. Two additional histories of the period prior to 1940 were J. Mason Brewer's *Negro Legislators of Texas and Their Descendants: A History of the Negro in Texas Politics from Reconstruction to Disfranchisement* (1935) and his *An Historical Outline of the Negro in Travis County* (1940). One other noteworthy study, compiled by Walter Cotton, was *History of Negroes of Limestone County from 1860 to 1939* (1939). These works by blacks about blacks are invaluable to the study of the black community in white Texas.

Other writers covered additional aspects of black Texas culture. Especially important were J. Mason Brewer's collection of black Texas poetry, *Heralding Dawn*; William R. Davis's *The Development and Present Status of Negro Education in East Texas*; and the account of African American contributions to the 1936 Texas Centennial celebration in Jesse O. Thomas's *Negro Participation in the Texas Centennial Exposition*. The prewar era closed with A. W. Jackson's invaluable publication of *A Sure Foundation and a Sketch of Negro Life in Texas*, a book filled with biographical information covering the black Texas community, unfortunately rendered somewhat difficult to use because of an incomplete index.

As noted earlier, in the mid-thirties critics and teachers began discussing in publications the limited nature of research into black history in the Lone Star State. Unfortunately, conditions did not improve much over the next twenty-five years. Rayford W. Logan set the stage for the 1940s with his analysis of "Estevanico, Negro Discoverer of the Southwest: A Critical Reexamination." During the remainder of the 1940s other historians continued to show interest in black history in Texas, especially in topics such as education, family, free blacks, and slave insurrections. Andrew Forest Muir published four articles on free blacks in five Texas counties—Fort Bend, Galveston, Harris, Jefferson, and Orange—in *Journal of Negro History*, *Southwestern Historical Quarterly*, and *Negro History Bulletin*.

William W. White covered slave insurrection scares in his "The Texas Slave Insurrection of 1860" (1949). The next year Wendell C. Addington brought out "Slave Insurrections in Texas" (1950). During

World War II Henry Allen Bullock discussed "Some Readjustments of the Texas Negro Family to the Emergency of the War," and in 1947, as segregated schools for blacks became a major social and political issue, Bullock wrote on "The Availability of Education in the Texas Negro Separate School" in the *Journal of Negro Education.* A sociologist, Bullock taught at Prairie View A&M from 1930 to 1949 and at Texas Southern University from 1950 to 1969. At that time he became the first black professor hired in Arts and Sciences at the University of Texas at Austin. He won the Bancroft Prize for his *A History of Negro Education in the South* in 1968.

Historians, including scholars from across the United States, continued throughout the 1950s to look at black Texans in varied ways. These investigations included Kenneth W. Porter's "The Seminole Negro-Indian Scouts, 1870–1881" (1952) and his "Negroes and Indians on the Texas Frontier, 1831–1876" (1956); Jack Abramowitz's "John B. Rayner: A Grass Roots Leader" (1951); Claude Elliott's unfavorable assessment of "The Freedmen's Bureau in Texas" (1952); Billy Bob Lightfoot's "The Negro Exodus from Comanche County, Texas" (1953); George R. Woolfolk's "Cotton Capitalism and Slave Labor in Texas" (1956) and his "Sources of the History of the Negro in Texas, with Special Reference to Their Implications for Research in Slavery" (1957); Earl W. Fornell's "The Abduction of Free Negroes and Slaves in Texas" (1957) and "Agitation in Texas for Reopening the Slave Trade" (1957); and Conrey Bryson's "El Paso and the Poll Tax" (1959). Although the published output of the 1950s on black Texans was sparse compared to the large number of white-based Texas history items, the publications pointed the way to such issues as the black Seminole scouts, African American leaders, white discriminatory actions, and the key role of the slave trade in Texas. The 1960s witnessed a proliferation of these trends.

Reflecting the influence and attention generated by the national civil rights struggle, which in many respects began in and then permeated Texas, an article by Harry Holloway entitled "The Negro and the Vote: The Case of Texas" was published in the early 1960s. The Holloway article, replete with new ideas and research, followed long-standing interest in black voting by scholars such as Robert W. Hainsworth in "The Negro and the Texas Primaries" (1933); Dick Smith's "Texas and the Poll Tax" (1955); Donald S. Strong's "The Poll Tax" (1944) and "The Rise of Negro Voting in Texas" (1948); and O. Douglas Weeks's, "The White Primary" (1948). The civil rights movement–influenced scholarship led to the publication of mono-graphs on other topics as well. Among the book-length studies are George R. Woolfolk's history *Prairie View: A Study in Public Con-science, 1878–1946*; Hettye Wallace Branch's biography of her father, *The Story of "80 John": A Biography of One of the Most Respected Negro Ranchmen in the Old West*; and John Upton Terrell's biography *Estevanico the Black*. Article-length studies include George R. Wool-folk's "Turner's Safety Valve and Free Negro Westward Movement" (1965); Ralph A. Wooster's "Notes on Texas' Largest Slaveholders, 1860" (1961); Kenneth Wiggins Porters's "Negro Labor in the Western Cattle Industry, 1866–1900" (1969); and Erwin N. Thompson's "The Negro Soldiers on the Frontier: A Fort Davis Case Study" (1968). The changes set in motion during the 1960s indeed played a prominent part in the blossoming of African American studies and the study of blacks in the Lone Star State.

Beginning in the mid-sixties, pressure from individuals and scholars who understood that all cultures and people should be studied with equal enthusiasm brought about a greater emphasis on topics that re-lated to black Texans in universities throughout the state. The late 1960s and early 1970s witnessed the birth of what would eventually be referred to as the "Texas Tech School of Black History." This group of historians studied and produced works on black history; Bruce A. Glas-rud and James M. Smallwood in "The Texas Tech School of Black His-tory—An Overview" explored the history and significance of this excit-ing development. Students began studying and researching African American history at other Texas institutions as well, including the University of Texas at Austin. Alwyn Barr produced an excellent syn-thesis of 1960s and early 1970s works on black Texans in *Black Texans: A History of Negroes in Texas, 1528–1971* (1973). Barr's work, revised in 1996, remains the classic general survey text on the African Ameri-can experience in Texas.[6]

To understand the background of the study of African American history in Texas, it is undoubtedly illustrative to outline what we per-ceive to be the general chronological groupings of black history study: (1) the pioneers—beginning with the late nineteenth century and con-tinuing through the second World War; (2) the contributors—who wrote about the accomplishments of the black community, including those of black explorers, soldiers, cowboys, and politicians from 1945 to 1965; (3) the discrimination interpreters—who wrote about the prob-lems people of color faced in Texas society, their survival skills, and the influence of race as a critical factor in determining the possibilities and limits of black life from 1965 to 1990; and (4) the multiculturalists or pluralists—who wrote in the 1990s and early twenty-first century about the diversity of peoples in Texas, establishment of communities, and relationships of African Americans to other peoples in the Lone Star State.

As has been indicated, during the first sixty-five years of the twentieth century, black and white authors produced a scattered number of studies on African Americans in Texas. But for the past quarter century or so, the state has witnessed a tremendous increase in both the quality and quantity of publications on black history. *The African American Experience in Texas: An Anthology* focuses on this boom and provides an excellent sense of the quality and wide range of works published in the past thirty-five years.

As a result of the tremendous increase in black history publications, an important question emerges: where were the materials published? The journals most often likely to include something on black Texans were the *Red River Valley Historical Review*, the *Journal of Negro History*, the *Southwestern Historical Quarterly*, the *East Texas Historical Journal*, *The Houston Review*, *Phylon*, *The Journal of Big Bend Studies*, *The Journal of South Texas*, and the *West Texas Historical Association Year Book*. However, these titles are increasingly limited in availability. The *Journal of Negro History* has been on shaky ground, with recent publication suspended several times; however, supporters have been able to keep it alive. Quite recently, with a name change to *Journal of African American History*, some issues have been published. Both *Phylon* and the *Red River Valley Historical Review* published numerous articles on African Americans in Texas, but those two journals have now ceased publication. Also problematic, *The Houston Review* was sporadic for a couple of years, but it underwent a successful transfer from the Houston Public Library to the University of Houston. Hopefully, it will reemerge as an important force in publishing new research about black Texans. The *West Texas Historical Association Year Book*, the *Journal of South Texas*, and *The Journal of Big Bend Studies* are published only once a year, and the *East Texas Historical Journal* is issued just twice per year, so they cannot be expected to carry a major load. However, articles on black Texans normally appear in these journals each year.

That leaves the *Southwestern Historical Quarterly*. Although the *Quarterly* was not actively engaged in publishing materials on black

Texans prior to the mid-1980s (in fact, a number of scholars submitted their work, were summarily rejected, and were then published in other regional and national journals), it has since played a significant role in disseminating research on black Texans. The largest number of articles used in this book come from that journal. The Texas State Historical Association has also been supportive by including black history sessions at its annual meeting and by publishing works such as *Black Leaders: Texans for Their Times*, edited by Alwyn Barr and Robert A. Calvert. The association's *New Handbook of Texas* is replete with articles on various aspects of the black experience in Texas.

One of the reasons for such an overwhelming amount of scholarly production regarding black Texans during the past quarter-century is the uniqueness of the history of the African American community in white Texas. The following list of unique themes and concepts indicate why investigating black Texas is important:

- *Proximity to the west* gave credence to freedom, space, opportunity, hope
- *Proximity to Mexico* provided black Texans with an alternative homeland plus the knowledge of a society that was not as racially biased as Texas; Mexican antislavery sentiment was an important force in early Texas history, including the reasons for the Texas Revolution
- *Exposure to Spanish culture,* including early black involvement with Spanish
- *The experience of slavery* and its concomitant Southern relationships
- *The experience of "Juneteenth"* and its special meaning (African Americans in most states now celebrate Juneteenth even though the original celebration pertained to Texas only)
- *A long tradition of social and political protest,* continuing through the civil rights movement to today
- *A growing Tejano population* and its intermingling with whites and blacks; the intermingling has created key economic, social, and political dynamics
- *Key demographics* that include out-migration—to Mexico, Kansas, Oklahoma, California—but greater in-migration overall; the rural-to-urban shift within the state; and the fact that often more blacks came into the state from the Deep South than left, thereby preserving Texas's claim to be a land of opportunity

- *Political party participation*—after Republicans gained control during Reconstruction, at no time in Texas history were blacks completely excluded from the political process (not as in Mississippi and Alabama, for instance); black Texans also led the national struggle to acquire complete voting rights
- *Vicious white antiblack violence*—from slavery to Reconstruction to Waco (1916) to the Sherman Riot (1930) to Jasper (1999), white opposition to the black community was as drastic in Texas as in any other state and greater than in most
- *Wide variety in job opportunities,* such as being cowboys, rodeo competitors, soldiers, teachers, ball players
- *Educational opportunities*—numerous preparatory schools and colleges existed for black Texans, although black education was segregated, and potential professionals were forced to leave the state for an education until the 1960s
- *The role of music,* as demonstrated by artists such as Leadbelly and in jazz or folksongs; the use of music for community involvement
- *Caliber of leadership*—the strong line runs from Estevan through Rayner and McDonald to Sweatt to Jordan to key political and educational leaders of today
- *Vital roles of women*—in a Texas society where black men could be and were incarcerated in jail or killed, or denied employment opportunities, black women were forced to develop unique and effective survival skills

As a result of this uniqueness, the interest in black Texas history persists, and the list of publications seems to grow every day. Over the past thirty-five years the topics investigated have been widespread, ranging from chronological (slavery to the recent) as well as social, economic, cultural, and political venues.

As most historians realize, slavery was firmly entrenched in Texas, and this practice led white Texans to join their southern counterparts in a war to maintain the institution. Randolph B. Campbell, the foremost historian of Texas slavery, investigated extensively the nature of slavery in Texas in a wide-ranging series of articles as well as in his seminal work *An Empire for Slavery: The Peculiar Institution in Texas, 1821–1865.* Additional studies of antebellum Texas that explore slavery include Elizabeth Silverthorne's *Plantation Life in Texas,* T. Lindsay Baker and Julie P. Baker's *Till Freedom Cried Out: Memories of*

Texas Slave Life, Ron Tyler and Lawrence R. Murphy's *The Slave Narratives of Texas,* James M. Smallwood's "Blacks in Antebellum Texas: A Reappraisal," and Paul D. Lack's "Urban Slavery in the Southwest."

Before 1970 the period of Reconstruction in Texas history was either neglected or filled with white-biased studies deploring freedom for blacks; but more recently, solid, scholarly efforts have been produced that depict blacks and whites in Reconstruction Texas. This change is due especially to five authors: James M. Smallwood, Barry A. Crouch, William L. Richter, Carl H. Moneyhon, and Randolph B. Campbell. Smallwood, in a series of well-conceived articles and his book-length study, *Time of Hope, Time of Despair: Black Texas during Reconstruction,* focused on the role and status of Afro-Texans during Reconstruction. Crouch searched the archives and showed the prowess of the Freedmen's Bureau in Texas with several articles and a book entitled *The Freedmen's Bureau and Black Texans.* Richter was less favorably disposed toward black Texans or to the Freedmen's Bureau, but his works, such as *Overreached on All Sides: The Freedmen's Bureau Administrators in Texas, 1865–1868* and *The Army in Texas during Reconstruction,* opened up additional avenues. Moneyhon's *Texas after the Civil War: The Struggle of Reconstruction* provided a thought-provoking and compelling revision of Reconstruction history in Texas. Campbell's contribution also proved significant. His *Grass-Roots Reconstruction in Texas, 1865–1880* provides a thorough and enlightening analysis of Reconstruction Texas.

During the latter nineteenth century, Afro-Texans adapted to freedom, entered politics, established communities, engaged in economic enterprises and employment, and survived. The starting point for studies of this period is Lawrence Rice's significant work, *The Negro in Texas, 1874–1900.* Three other authors reported on black leadership during these years—Merline Pitre in *Through Many Dangers, Toils, and Snares: Black Leadership in Texas, 1868–1900,* Gregg Cantrell in *Kenneth and John B. Rayner and the Limits of Southern Dissent* as well as in *Feeding the Wolf: John B. Rayner and the Politics of Race, 1850–1918,* and Douglas Hales in *A Southern Family in White and Black: The Cuneys of Texas.* Alwyn Barr and Barry Crouch also added to the politics of the period; Barr with "Black Legislators of Reconstruction Texas" and Crouch with "Hesitant Recognition: Texas Black Politicians, 1865–1900." Black Texans in the late nineteenth and early twentieth centuries pursued varied means to survive and to counter discrimination; Bruce Glasrud focused on these means in two articles,

"Early Black Nationalist Movements in Texas" and "Black Texas Improvement Efforts."

Although Bruce A. Glasrud, Melvin James Banks, Neil G. Sapper, and William Joseph Brophy produced dissertations covering the period in black Texas history from 1900 to 1954, no book-length monograph covering these years has yet been published. On the other hand, important studies have been completed. These include Ernest Obadele-Starks's *Black Unionism in the Industrial South*, Merline Pitre's *In Struggle Against Jim Crow: Lulu B. White and the NAACP, 1900–1957*, and Darlene Clark Hine's *Black Victory: The Rise and Fall of the White Primary in Texas*. Journal articles especially have been an avenue for adding to the historical evaluation of this period; Glasrud, for example, published "Child or Beast? White Texas' View of Blacks," "Enforcing White Supremacy in Texas, 1900–1910," and "Blacks and Texas Politics during the Twenties." Authors such as William J. Brophy, Michael L. Gillette, Neil G. Sapper, and James M. SoRelle also have investigated aspects of these important years in black Texas history.

The period from 1954 to the present is now beginning to receive consideration and study by historians, although one expects the next decade to witness a much greater explosion of publications than we have so far noticed. Important studies of these years include Chandler Davidson with *Race and Class in Texas Politics* and Michael R. Botson Jr.'s *Labor, Civil Rights, and the Hughes Tool Company*. Prominent black politician Barbara Jordan has begun to receive academic attention. Study should begin with her autobiography with Shelby Hearon, *Barbara Jordan: A Self-Portrait*, and also Ira B. Bryant Jr.'s *Barbara Charline Jordan: From the Ghetto to the Capitol*; Mary Beth Rogers's *Barbara Jordan: American Hero*, and Mary Ellen Curtin's "Reaching for Power: Barbara C. Jordan and Liberals in the Texas Legislature, 1966–1972." Broader works on the civil rights struggle in Texas can be found in Carolyn Jones's *Volma, My Journey: One Man's Impact on the Civil Rights Movement in Austin, Texas* and in Thomas R. Cole's *No Color Is My Kind: The Life of Eldrewey Stearns and the Integration of Houston*. The successful integration of one Texas city can be noted in Robert Goldberg's "Racial Change on the Southern Periphery: The Case of San Antonio, Texas, 1960–1965." Gail Beil contributed an insightful article as well, "Four Marshallites' Roles in the Passage of the Civil Rights Act of 1964." For this period as for the prior chronological eras, other works have been published that more appropriately will be included in one of the following five topical areas that have been of particular interest to historians over the past few decades: women, violence, urbanism, education, and Buffalo Soldiers and black cowboys.

As noted previously, one of the exciting avenues of research in Texas concerns the lives, work, and roles of black Texas females. Although other works have been published, the most significant step toward elucidating the black female experience in Texas took place with the publication in 1994 of Ruthe Winegarten's *Black Texas Women: 150 Years of Trial and Triumph*. Winegarten followed that work two years later with *Black Texas Women: A Sourcebook*. With Winegarten's work, knowledge of and research on African American women in Texas followed apace. Other studies of note of black Texas women included Sherilyn Brandenstein on the *Sepia Record*, Barry Crouch on black marriages during Reconstruction, Trudier Harris on "The Yellow Rose of Texas," Scott S. Keir on middle class black families, Merle Yvonne Miles on black families, Ruth C. Schaffer on black midwives, Julia Kirk Blackwelder on twentieth century beauty culture as reflected in the Franklin School of Beauty, and James M. Smallwood on black women and families during Reconstruction. Bernice Love Wiggins, a 1920s poet from El Paso, had *Tuneful Tales*, her book of poems, republished by editors Maceo C. Dailey Jr. and Ruthe Winegarten. On black women more generally in El Paso, see Maceo C. Dailey Jr. and Kristine Navarro's *Wheresoever My People Chance to Dwell: Oral Interviews with African American Women of El Paso*. For an overview of African American women during a particular period, see LaVonne Roberts Jackson's "Freedom and Family: The Freedmen's Bureau and African-American Women in Texas in the Reconstruction Era." Although not specifically on black Texas women, books by Rebecca Sharpless, *Fertile Ground*, *Narrow Choices*, and Angela Boswell, *Her Act and Deed*, contain much about African American women. In 2008 Texas A&M University Press will publish a monograph edited by Bruce A. Glasrud and Merline Pitre, *African American Women in Texas: A History*.

Some years ago, African American scholar George Wright moved from Kentucky to Texas and soon voiced his concern that not much had been written about his field of specialty, violence and discrimination, in Texas. Writers have taken him at his word and have now produced path-breaking studies of white-black violence in Texas. Among these studies are Ricardo C. Ainslie's *Long Dark Road: Bill King and Murder in Jasper, Texas*; Monte Akers's *Flames after Midnight: Murder, Vengeance, and the Desolation of a Texas Community*; Patricia Bernstein's *The First Waco Horror: The Lynching of Jesse Washington and the Rise of the NAACP*; William D. Carrigan's *The Making of a Lynching Culture, Violence and Vigilantism in Central Texas, 1836–1916*; and Nick Davies's *White Lies: Rape, Murder, and Justice Texas Style.* These books point to a vicious and sadistic practice of brutality in the Lone Star State. For two other examples, turn to James M. Smallwood, Barry A. Crouch, and Larry Peacock's *Murder and Mayhem: The War of Reconstruction in Texas* and to Rebecca A. Kosary's Southwest Texas State University thesis, "Regression to Barbarism in Reconstruction Texas: An Analysis of White Violence against African-Americans from the Texas Freedmen's Bureau Records, 1865–1868."

A major feature of twentieth-century African American life in Texas has been a migration into cities, both from within the state as well as from other southern states such as Louisiana and Arkansas. This urban growth has been well covered for some Texas cities, less well for others. Studies of Houston have been the most plentiful as well as qualitatively sound. Consider Howard Beeth and Cary D. Wintz's *Black Dixie: Afro-Texan History and Culture in Houston,* a collection of first-rate essays by individual scholars. Sociologist Robert D. Bullard's *Invisible Houston: The Black Experience in Boom and Bust* is also significant. Dwight David Watson's *Race and the Houston Police Department, 1930–1990* and Roger Wood and James Fraher's *Down in Houston: Bayou City Blues* further capture that city's African American experiences. Migration to Houston is thoroughly explained by Bernadette Pruitt in "Exodus: the Movement: People of African Descent and Their Migrations to Houston, 1914–1945." Also on Houston, two other path-breaking dissertations have been recently concluded: Alice K. Laine's "An In-Depth Study of Black Political Leadership in Houston, Texas" and James M. SoRelle's "The Darker Side of 'Heaven': The Black Community in Houston, Texas, 1917–1945."

An example of what can be accomplished for other cities is Kenneth Mason's *African Americans and Race Relations in San Antonio, Texas, 1867–1937*; also see Charles Christopher Jackson's "A Southern Black Community Comes of Age: Black San Antonio in the Great Depression." Lubbock is examined in Katie Parks's *Remember When? A History of African Americans in Lubbock, Texas* (with a foreword by Alwyn Barr); Julius Amin's "Black Lubbock: 1955 to the Present"; Robert L. Foster's "Black Lubbock: A History of Negroes in Lubbock, Texas, to 1940"; and Robert L. Foster and Alwyn Barr's "Black Lubbock." Increasingly, students and scholars are turning to the study of African American topics in other Texas cities, including Austin, Dallas, and Marshall. For example, see the remarkable *Behold the People: R. C. Hickman's Photographs of Black Dallas, 1949–1961* and Alan B. Govenar and Jay E. Brakefield's *Deep Ellum and Central Track: Where the Black and White Worlds of Dallas Converged.*

During the time of slavery black Texans were denied an education, but immediately upon emancipation, they flocked to Texas schools. Recent studies of African American education in Texas indicate the effort to change the educational system from a second-class, segregated one into a respected, integrated one. Works on black education in Texas include Michael R. Heintze's *Private Black Colleges in Texas, 1865–1954;* David Alvernon Williams's "The History of Higher Education for Black Texans, 1872–1977"; Vernon McDaniel's *History of the Teachers State Association of Texas;* Amilcar Shabazz's *Advancing Democracy: African Americans and the Struggle for Access and Equity in Higher Education in Texas;* Almetris Marsh Duren and Louise Iscoe's *Overcoming: A History of Black Integration at the University of Texas at Austin;* and William Henry Kellar's *Make Haste Slowly: Moderates, Conservatives, and School Desegregation in Houston.*

Scholars and writers also have turned their attention to two distinct and fascinating groups in late nineteenth-century Texas: the Buffalo Soldiers and the black cowboys. On the Buffalo Soldiers, an overall assessment can be discerned in "Black Regulars on the Texas Frontier, 1866–1885" by William H. Leckie. Other studies of the Buffalo Soldiers in Texas include Harold Ray Sayre's *Warriors of Color;* Paul H. Carlson's *"Pecos Bill": A Military Biography of William R. Shafter* and *The Buffalo Soldier Tragedy of 1877;* Garna L. Christian's *Black Soldiers in Jim Crow Texas, 1899–1917;* and James N. Leiker's *Racial Borders: Black Soldiers along the Rio Grande.* On violence and the infamous Brownsville incident, see Ann J. Lane's *The Brownsville Affair* and John D. Weaver's *The Brownsville Raid;* on a later episode see Robert V. Haynes's *A Night of Violence: The Houston Riot of 1917.* On a related group of Buffalo Soldiers, see Thomas A. Britten's *A Brief History of the Seminole-Negro Indian Scouts.* Black cowboys in Texas can be discovered in Sara R. Massey's collection *Black Cowboys of Texas.* For two essays not included in Massey, read Douglas Hales's fine study, "Black Cowboy: Daniel Webster '80 John' Wallace" and Michael N. Searles's recent and illuminating "Taking Out the Buck and Putting in a Trick: The Black Cowboy's Art of Breaking and Keeping a Good Cow Horse."

As it is possible to notice, even in this brief overview of black Texas historiography, much has been written since 1970 about the African

American experience in Texas. Recently published articles further illustrate this reflection and provide a window on the future. Recently published articles include Elizabeth R. Rabe's "Slave Children of Texas: A Qualitative and Quantitative Analysis"; Paul E. Sturdevant's "Black and White with Shades of Gray: The Greenville Sign"; Milton H. Williams III with "Romeo M. Williams: Tuskegee Airman and Civil Rights Lawyer"; Alwyn Barr's "The Impact of Race in Shaping Judicial Districts, 1876–1907," Roger D. Cunningham's "'A Lot of Fine, Sturdy Black Warriors': Texas's African American 'Immunes' in the Spanish-American War"; Francine Sanders Romero's "'There Are Only White Champions': The Rise and Demise of Segregated Boxing in Texas"; Charles F. Robinson II with "Legislated Love in the Lone Star State: Texas and Miscegenation"; Bernadette Pruitt's "'For the Advancement of the Race': The Great Migrations to Houston, Texas, 1914–1919"; and Bruce A. Glasrud's "From Griggs to Brewer: A Review of Black Texas Culture, 1899–1940." Also of significance, and certainly a must-read for any student of black Texas history, is the informative and stimulating *Freedom Colonies: Independent Black Texans in the Time of Jim Crow* by Thad Sitton and James H. Conrad. As a final effort, readers ought to peruse Alan Govenar's *Portraits of Community: African American Photography in Texas*.

The uniqueness and the richness of the history of Texas black culture and community become clearer with study, but questions remain. Where are we now? Where do we go in the twenty-first century? In particular, what topics remain to be explored? The list, though long, is shrinking and includes:

- Free blacks in the antebellum era
- The importance of the underground railroad that helped slaves in Texas reach Mexico or the Indian Territory
- Literature and the arts—for example, the relationship between the Harlem Renaissance, which eventually spread nationwide, and black Texans (as a start, look at Bruce Glasrud's "The Harlem Renaissance in Texas and the Southwest")
- Religion, from antebellum times to the present (a beginning is available; see Clyde McQueen, *Black Churches in Texas: A Guide to Historic Congregations*)
- A comprehensive history of the Texas civil rights movement
- The importance of fraternal groups in building cohesiveness in the black community

- The need to examine the critical impact of changing and declining population statistics on African Americans in Texas
- Studies relating to economic and business interests
- A thorough study of the years from 1954 to 1974
- A path-breaking study of the years from 1975 to 2005; also needed are investigations of numerous aspects of black life in Texas during these years (as we prepared this anthology we especially noticed the dearth of such studies)
- More study of blacks in urban areas such as Abilene, Beaumont, Fort Worth, Galveston, and Waco
- More research on blacks in West Texas, especially in the Trans-Pecos.

It is obvious to us as the study of African American history increases in Texas, especially in such schools as Texas Tech University, the University of Houston, Texas Christian University, the University of North Texas, Texas Southern University, Baylor University, and Texas A&M University, that the above topics will be explored. Undoubtedly, increasing interest certainly may precipitate new studies that revise interpretations of previously explored topics.

The richness of the study of black history in Texas can be noticed by the large number of sessions on black history at the TSHA's annual meeting as well as at meetings of the Southwestern Social Science Association, the Center for Big Bend Studies, the West Texas Historical Association, and the East Texas Historical Association. Perusing Bruce A. Glasrud and Laurie Champion's bibliography, *Exploring the Afro-Texas Experience: A Bibliography of Secondary Sources about Black Texans*, provides further evidence of the growth of the study of black Texans.[7] The prospects for continued exploration of the history of African Americans in Texas during the twenty-first century indeed look good and follow a pattern begun more than a century ago, though, as this book indicates, explored most heavily during the past thirty-five years.

Notes

1. L. V. Williams, "Teaching Negro Life and History in Texas High Schools," *Journal of Negro History* 20 (1935): 13–18; Ira B. Bryant Jr., *The Texas Negro Under Six Flags* (Houston: Houston College for Negroes [1936]): 3; Florence Bradshaw

O'Brien, "Adequacy of Texas History Texts in Reporting Negro Achievements" (Master's thesis, Stephen F. Austin State Teachers College, 1939): 15; Westerfield T. Kimble, "An Analysis of the Methods of Teaching History in the Seventeen High Schools for Negroes in Texas Accredited by the Southern Association of Colleges and Secondary Schools" (Master's thesis, Prairie View University, 1952): 32; J. Reuben Sheeler, "Negro History Week in the Houston Area," *Negro History Bulletin* 19 (October 1955): 2, 21; Ira B. Bryant Jr., "The Need for Negro History in the Schools of Texas," *Negro History Bulletin* 20 (January 1957): 77–78.

2. Footnote citations for each of the works mentioned in the text will not be used; rather, turn to "Black Texas History: A Selected Bibliography," located near the end of the book, for complete bibliographic information.

3. Studies of Estevan, based on these reports, include Carolyn Arrington, *Estevanico—Black Explorer in Spanish Texas* (Austin: Eakin Press, 1986); Weldon F. Heald, "Black Pathfinder of the Deserts," *The Crisis* 57 (1950): 703–708; Jeannette Mirsky, "Zeroing in on a Fugitive Figure: The First Negro in America," *Midway* 8 (June 1967): 1–17; Elizabeth Shepherd, *The Discoveries of Esteban the Black* (New York: Dodd, Mead, 1970); and John Terrell, *Estevanico the Black* (Los Angeles: Westernlore Press Publishers, 1968). Estevan, or Esteban, frequently is referred to pejoratively as Estevanico, or "Little Stephen."

4. On the "Yellow Rose of Texas" see Trudier Harris, "'The Yellow Rose of Texas': A Different Cultural View," in *Juneteenth Texas: Essays in African-American Folklore,* edited by Francis Edward Abernethy, Carolyn Fiedler Satterwhite, Patrick B. Mullen, and Alan B. Govenar (Denton: University of North Texas Press, 1996): 315–333. Also, Anita Bunkley has written a fascinating novel, *Emily, the Yellow Rose: A Texas Legend* (Houston: Rinard Publishing, 1989).

5. Investigations of the folklore and folktales from early Texas include Natalie Taylor Carlisle, "Old Time Darky Plantation Melodies," in *Rainbow in the Morning,* edited by J. Frank Dobie (Hatboro, Pa.: Folklore Association, 1965): 137–143; John Michael Vlach, "Afro-American Folk Crafts in Nineteenth Century Texas," *Western Folklore* 40 (1981): 149–161; Mary Virginia Bales, "Negro Folk-Songs in Texas, Their Definition and Origin" (Master's thesis, Texas Christian University, 1927); and J. Mason Brewer, *Dog Ghosts and Other Texas Negro Folk Tales* (Austin: University of Texas Press, 1958).

6. Bruce A. Glasrud and James M. Smallwood, "The Texas Tech School of Black History: An Overview." *West Texas Historical Association Year Book* 82 (2006): 102–119; Alwyn Barr, *Black Texans: A History of Negroes in Texas, 1528–1971* (Austin: Jenkins Publishing Company, 1973); Alwyn Barr, *Black Texans: A History of African Americans in Texas, 1528–1995,* 2nd ed. (Norman: University of Oklahoma Press, 1996). See the "Preface to the Second edition" for a valuable overview of the books on black Texas history that were published between 1973 and 1995.

7. Bruce A. Glasrud and Laurie Champion, eds., *Exploring the Afro-Texas Experience: A Bibliography of Secondary Sources About Black Texans* (Alpine, Tex.: SRSU Center for Big Bend Studies, 2000). For additional information about the quality and quantity of writings on black Texans during the past thirty-five years see Alwyn Barr, "African Americans in Texas: From Stereotypes to Diverse Roles" in *Texas Through Time: Evolving Interpretations,* ed. by Walter L. Buenger and Robert A. Calvert (College Station: Texas A&M University Press, 1991): 50–80; Alwyn Barr, "Black Texans," *A Guide to the History of Texas,* ed. by Light Townsend Cummins and Alvin R. Bailey Jr. (Westport, Conn.: Greenwood Press, 1988): 107–121; Paul M. Lucko, "Dissertations and Theses Relating to African American Studies in Texas: A Selected Bibliography, 1904–1990," *Southwestern Historical Quarterly* 96 (1992): 547–573. For primary sources on studying black Texas history see Alwyn Barr, "Advancing from History's Hollow to History's Mountain: Sources on African American History in Texas," *East Texas Historical Journal* 38.1 (2000): 28–34.

PART ONE

The Nineteenth Century Experience

★

The Nineteenth Century Experience
An Introduction

It happened a long time ago. The year was 1527. A storm was blowing through the Gulf of Mexico. Along with a handful of Spaniards, he endured the vicious weather and fought to keep the craft afloat, but all efforts failed. The makeshift boat went down. Along with everyone in the party, he was shipwrecked near the Texas coast. His name was Estevan. He became the first black man to leave a recorded history in Texas. He was from Azamor in Morocco, and he was an actor on the Lone Star stage almost three centuries before white Americans and their slaves began their migration to modern Texas.

Estevan belonged to Captain Andres Dorantes, one of the leaders of the Panfilo de Narvaez expedition that explored the Floridas before the party was shipwrecked. Along with other survivors—Dorantes, Alonzo de Castillo, and Cabeza de Vaca—Estevan was first enslaved by Indians but later escaped. He was valuable to the little Spanish party as they traversed Texas because he studied Native American languages, was apparently good at the task, and could translate for the Spaniards. After a number of exciting, if dangerous, adventures, Estevan and his cohorts finally reached the safety of a Spanish settlement in Sonora in March of 1536. Although the Zuni Indians killed Estevan in 1539 because he was leading Spanish conquistadors who were invading their lands, the black man from Azamor had already won his place in Texas history.

People of African descent have been in Texas since Estevan's era. Later Spanish expeditions not only brought more blacks into the area, but they also found some who already lived among the Indians. Those blacks had villages on the Rio Grande near its mouth. Surviving records indicate that they may have had contacts with a larger colony of Africans who lived on an unnamed island in the Caribbean, a colony that may have predated Columbus. Blacks were with Domingo Teran when his expedition entered Texas in 1691. Founded in 1718, early San Antonio became the home of several of the sons and daughters of Africa. When Gil Antonio Ybarbo established Bucareli on the Trinity River in 1776, black people were with him. By 1792, Texas had approximately 450 blacks and mulattoes out of a total population of 2,992.

From the beginning, then, blacks helped build the Lone Star State—first Hispanic Texas, then American Texas. Once Stephen F. Austin and other whites began settling the region in the 1820s, African Americans were among their number. Like Jean Baptiste Marturia, some came as free farmers, but most came as slaves. By 1825 69 slave holders owned 443 chattels, whose number grew to five thousand by 1836. They helped build early Texas even as it was still under Mexican rule.

Some people of African descent fought in the Texas Revolution. Their number included Samuel McCullough, who was probably the first casualty of the violent conflict. He received a severe shoulder wound in the Battle of Goliad in 1835. Clearly, black people helped create the Republic of Texas. Then they helped develop it, as slave numbers grew to 11,323 by 1840 and to 58,161 by 1850. In the 1850s the number exploded to 182,566 as Texas quickly grew to resemble the states of the Deep South. Conversely, only 355 free blacks called the Lone Star State home in 1860, a very small number compared to other states.

Although they did much to build Texas and to create wealth for the white community, the bondspeople, of course, received almost nothing in return. Because Texas was born in Dixie, slavery in the state mirrored the system as it functioned in the Deep South. Most bondsmen (about 80 percent) were field hands who worked on plantations and farms that yielded cotton and assorted food crops. They worked from "can see to can't see." Artisans and house servants may have had a better work life, but they numbered only about 10 percent of the slave population, as did urban chattels who also had a better material life than field hands. Living in crude cabins, with inadequate clothing and only enough food for subsistence, the people of color continued to toil, while harsh Slave Codes regulated their behavior. Many slaves had cruel owners. Some masters beat and whipped their bondspeople unmercifully. Many surviving ex-slave accounts mention cruelty and outright barbarism on the part of overseers and owners. Such treatment increased the number of runaways, always a problem in Texas, but the majority of slaves knew not where to go or what to do. They remained locked in the South's "Peculiar Institution" until 1865.

Although slavery bred cruelty, there were exceptions. For example, the great Sam Houston held slaves, but he and his family treated them well. Two of them, Jeff Hamilton and Joshua Houston, left accounts that stressed the benevolence of the Houston family. A family member taught Joshua to read and write, and all of the Houstons treated him as a family member—almost. Joshua became a politician during the Reconstruction era and was wealthy enough to offer loans to General Houston's widow when she faced difficult financial times. Slaves had complex experiences that often reflected the cruelty or benevolence of their owners, but under any guise, slavery was an affront to humankind.

When the Civil War began approximately 182,000 slaves lived in Texas, where they toiled and created wealth for their masters. As the war increasingly turned against the South, owners in other Southern states—fearful that their land would fall behind Union lines—"ran" their chattels to the Lone Star State, hoping to therefore save their human property. Slave owners saw Texas as a safe, relatively secure place, for it was never successfully invaded during the conflagration. By the end of the war, Texas was the home of up to 400,000 bondspeople. Only after the Civil War would the freedpeople return to their former homes to look for lost kin or just to start over in familiar environs.

White Texas was fortunate in another way: ample slave labor was available to till the fields of the eastern region and to supply the Confederacy with workers in various government installations. A military complex in Tyler that included an armory, a medical facility that included pharmaceutical laboratories and a hospital, an ordnance works, a shoe factory, a transportation department, a prisoner-of-war camp, and other facilities were all potential places of work for slaves during the war. Wherever they were, collectively the slaves did massive amounts of labor, so much so that General Ulysses S. Grant said that one slave was worth two free workers. Even so, the Confederacy collapsed after Robert E. Lee's surrender at Appomattox. Occupation of the South soon began in earnest.

Union general Gordon Granger and his small force of eighteen hundred men arrived in Galveston on June 19, 1865. Almost immediately, the general read the official Emancipation Proclamation for the Texas chattels—the date is still celebrated in Texas and elsewhere as "Juneteenth." Yet not all owners freed their slaves in 1865. In isolated areas that the army and the Freedmen's Bureau were slow to reach, some owners held their human property as late as 1868. Moreover, the ex-slaves soon realized that physical freedom did not guarantee political and civil rights. The Constitution of 1866, drawn up mainly by former Confederates and their sympathizers, denied the new freedpeople the right to vote, to serve on juries, or to testify against whites. That same year, the Black Codes replaced the Slave Codes, although the restrictions were much the same. Many researchers use the term "semi-slavery" when evaluating the effects of the Black Codes. The purpose was to control the ex-slaves and continue the South's feudal system. Segregation developed rapidly in Reconstruction Texas in all places of public accommodations, including common carriers (such as railroads) and schools.

As if the Black Codes were not enough to guarantee that whites would control the new freedpeople, terrorist groups sprang up in Texas almost immediately after the war. According to available data, the first two such organizations coalesced in Limestone and Freestone counties and then quickly spread throughout eastern and northeastern Texas. The Lone Star State soon had Klan-like groups in at least seventy-seven counties. Usually organized at the county level, individual groups went by many names, such as the Ku Klux Klan, the Knights of the White Camellia, the Knights of the Rising Sun, and the Palefaces. Despite the different names, all the terrorist groups had the same goal—complete subjugation of the black community—and they did their work very well. Almost as important, outlaws and outlaw gangs flourished. They wrapped themselves in the flag of the "Lost Cause," as they bedeviled, robbed, beat, and killed freedpeople and their white Unionist allies. Many of them—like Ben Bickerstaff, Bob Lee, and Cullen Baker—became "enforcers" for conservative ex-Confederates and accumulated easy money in return.

To offset the wrath of former Rebels and to help the ex-slaves make their transition to freedom, Congress created the Freedmen's Bureau in 1865 and renewed it annually until 1870. Bureau agents helped blacks establish schools and assisted them in finding missionaries, mostly young white women from the North, as their first teachers. Agents were authorized to take legal jurisdiction away from civil authorities if those authorities appeared prejudicial, and bureau men were able to void many of the Black Codes. Agents supervised labor contracts to ensure fairness, and they performed a number of other functions as well. Perhaps most important, though, the bureau tried to help freedpeople find kinsmen who had been torn from their families during slavery. However, the bureau had only limited effectiveness because of ex-Confederate resistance and because the bureau was greatly understaffed and underfunded. At the height of bureau expansion in Texas, only sixty-eight local agents worked in the entire state. Thus, there were far fewer agents than there were massively manned Klan groups.

Even as bureau agents worked to help the recently freed Afro-Texans, by late 1866 it was clear that presidential Reconstruction had failed as a result of massive Southern white resistance, and Texas—like all Confederate states except Tennessee—was reorganized under congressional Reconstruction beginning in early 1867. With blacks given the right to vote, federal army commanders in Texas supervised elections for a constitutional convention that wrote a new constitution. Among other provisions, it accepted the Fourteenth Amendment and called for a free (but segregated) public school system. Then, with overwhelming support from the African American community, the Republican E. J. Davis won the governor's chair and other Republicans captured a majority in the legislature. Two blacks, George T. Ruby and Matt Gaines, served in the Texas Senate, while nine others served in the House.

Two of the most noted, and most controversial, acts of the Davis administration created the state police and the state militia. Among other instructions, Davis demanded that the two forces control the inordinate amount of racially motivated violence in the Lone Star State. From 1865 to 1868, whites committed fifteen hundred recorded acts of violence against blacks, including 350 recorded murders. The actual totals were undoubtedly much higher, for many such acts were likely never reported to authorities—both the freedpeople and white Unionists feared ex-Confederate retaliation.

As blacks were widely recruited to serve in the new agencies, Davis's goal was partially realized. Racially motivated violence began to decline. Such progress was short-lived, however. In 1874, Davis suffered a landslide defeat when he ran for re-election. By that time federal forces—soldiers who had offered some protection for black and white Unionists—had been withdrawn from the state. With its Klansmen and outlaws as enforcers, the Democratic party suppressed Unionist voters be they black or white. The African American Texans then entered an era (1874 to circa 1900) that some authors called the "nadir" of their existence. Whites suppressed them politically, socially, and economically. Simply put, the death of the African Americans' political and civil rights represented the failure of American democracy, the failure of the Republican ideal.

During the nadir of the black experience in the United States, some

African American leaders continued to fight for true freedom, to re-
verse the trends leading to second-class citizenship for the freedpeople.
From 1868 to 1900, for example, forty-three black Texans served in the
Texas Legislature, where they strove for real democracy. Norris Wright
Cuney and later William Madison McDonald helped lead the Republican party, and dozens of African Americans were elected to local offices
even as outbreaks of lynching grew in number.

Lynching and other forms of murder obviously affected the black
community legally, politically, socially, and economically. In Texas
there were about five hundred recorded lynchings of African Americans
in the late nineteenth century, but the actual number was much
higher—as with the other acts of violence and murder mentioned previously, many lynchings in isolated areas were never recorded by the authorities. Further, killing by extra-legal mob violence continued into
the new century. The reforming Democrat-Populist governor James
Hogg sought a statewide antilynch law in 1892 after a Paris mob took a
black man accused of raping a white woman from jail and mutilated
him before burning him alive. Although Hogg failed to get his law, a
similar 1897 lynching in Tyler was so brutal that the legislature finally
responded with a law requiring the dismissal of all public officials who
permitted "Judge Lynch" to rule and also called for prosecution of
lynchers.

Meanwhile, the focus of the state's black community was on simple
survival. Economically, about 63 percent of the African Americans labored in some aspect of agriculture. Of that group, about 69 percent
were sharecroppers and tenants who battled grinding poverty every
day; only 31 percent managed to buy small farms. Black men also
worked in the expanding East Texas lumber industry. Of the state's
6,500 lumberjacks in 1890, 42 percent were African Americans. Several
thousand more worked on railroad construction or labored as longshoremen in coastal towns like Galveston and Indianola. A valued
number served in the United States Army, both in the infantry and in
the cavalry, and became known as the Buffalo Soldiers. Somewhat better off economically were the black cowboys, who constituted about 20
to 25 percent of all the stockmen in Texas. An integral part of the expanding Cattle Kingdom, they had more freedom and made more
money than their brothers and sisters who were locked into agricultural peonage.

Black urban dwellers may also have had a better time of it than
their country cousins. By 1900, of all employed people of color, 28 per-

cent worked in towns and cities. They were barbers, saloon keepers, restaurant workers, laundresses, midwives, and domestic help as well as teamsters, nurses, and day laborers. As Texas continued to industrialize, African American workers added much to the labor pool. They helped build railroads, they manned machines in factories, they helped build modern Texas. A number of African Americans entered the professions of law and medicine while others joined the teachers' ranks. Some made a transition to the business class: they owned restaurants, funeral parlors, barbershops, grocery stores, boarding houses, blacksmith shops, and dairies. Black-owned newspapers in the state, such as the *Dallas Express* and *The Houston Informer*, numbered twenty-three by 1900.

Many working African Americans who struggled through the nadir pinned their hopes on the education of the next generation. But educational problems abounded. Black schools never shared state money equally when white legislators distributed the tax-driven school funds. By 1900 fully two-thirds of all black public schools met in churches or rented buildings. Some met in barns or out-of-doors. Despite such problems, observers noted great success. Between 1880 and 1900, illiteracy among the people of African descent fell from 75.4 percent to 38.2 percent and advances were also made in higher education. Created in 1878, Prairie View A&M became a premier institution, the flagship of colleges for blacks. Organized along the Hampton-Tuskegee model, its administrators stressed industrial training along with scientific agriculture. Private colleges grew in number and were perhaps best represented by Wiley College in Marshall. Overall, the number of black colleges grew from two in 1875 to eleven in 1905.

Although the state's black community had increasing educational opportunities, white Democrats reversed much of the limited political progress that had been made during Reconstruction. Blacks were gradually reduced to political impotence. Democratic "clubs" continued to intimidate potential Afro-Texas voters. Despite attempts to quell their participation, more than one hundred thousand African Americans still voted in various elections in the early 1890s. To solve that "problem," Democrats adopted the "white primary" and effectively prevented black constituents from voting in primary elections, and thus selecting their representatives. Next, the Democratic legislature secured a constitutional amendment in 1902 that levied a poll tax for voting. After the adoption of the new tax, the number of black voters declined to about five thousand by 1906.

White politicians also undermined the African Americans' legal status by excluding them from jury selection and by ignoring their testimony in court if whites were involved. Further, many whites assumed that blacks were prone to criminal activity. Racist judges and juries handed down stiffer sentences for African Americans than for whites—all of this while blacks had difficulties securing competent legal counsel. Soon, the sons and daughters of Africa numbered more than 50 percent of all prison inmates.

Further, the white drive for segregation—a trend that developed during Reconstruction—intensified in the latter part of the century. Increasingly, blacks were set apart in churches, schools, and public accommodations, including restaurants, theaters, public transportation, and the like. In 1882 the legislature even enacted a law forbidding interracial sexual relations. In all, calling the late nineteenth century the "nadir" of the black experience may not miss the mark by much.

Urban Slavery in the Southwest

PAUL D. LACK

*In the following essay, Paul Lack examines urban slavery and how it dif-
fered from bondage in the countryside. In many ways, Lack follows the lead
of two of the pioneers in the study of urban slavery: Richard B. Wade, who
penned* Slavery in the Cities, *and Claudia Dale Goldin's* Urban Slavery in
the American South: A Quantitative History. *Lack's conclusions largely re-
inforce the views of Wade and Goldin. For example, he finds that bondsmen
who lived in cities and towns had much more personal freedom than their
countryside cousins. They created a "quasi-separate black world" complete
with more control over their own lives. They had more social outlets, including opportunities to attend their own religious services; greater recreational outlets; and more freedom to come and go as they pleased. Some
even went to makeshift schools where they learned the rudiments of the "3
Rs." Lack also discusses the hiring-out system that was prevalent in urban
areas and the employer/owner's habit of allowing chattels to find separate
housing, despite local ordinances in some cities that prohibited the practice. The opportunity to live away from the owner/employer was a natural
springboard to increased freedom.*

*

THE URBAN EXPERIENCE of blacks in the Southwest began under
slavery. Thus the motives of the earliest black migrants into the cities
of the area require little elaboration: they came under force of compul-
sion. Because of their status, no one at the time bothered to record how
the slaves reacted to their new homes, but certainly many features of
life on the urban frontier of the Old South must have seemed primitive
even to those unaccustomed to a refined society. Whether their owners
brought them to Austin, Galveston, Little Rock, or Shreveport, the
bondsmen encountered many similar conditions. All of the towns were
young and relatively small even by southern standards. The oldest, Little Rock, dated its existence from 1819, but the capital city developed

too slowly to warrant incorporation until 1831 and contained only
1,500 people in 1840, the year after the other towns came into being.
Only Galveston with its fine harbor grew rapidly, to over 7,000 in 1860;
the others "boasted" between 3,000 and 4,000 residents on the eve of
the Civil War. These communities existed primarily to serve the commercial needs of sparsely settled but developing agricultural regions.
Most of the oceanic trade of Texas passed through Galveston; likewise,
Little Rock was a river port and convenient point of departure on a
westward migration route. Although Shreveport had to struggle with
the difficulties of navigation on the Red River, it tapped a rich cotton
economy. Even Austin, which owed its existence to government, derived much of its unspectacular growth from the expansion of farming
in Travis County. All of the towns faced such frontier problems as Indian threats, competition from other aspiring towns, primitive transportation facilities, and lawless groups in their populations. None developed a significant industrial component in its economy.[1]

Despite the factors which retarded urban development, the town
slaves forged a way of life that differed measurably from that of their
rural counterparts. From the first the young southwestern cities thrust
slaves into contact with a variety of people and social opportunities,
and masters had difficulty in restricting the experiences of their bondsmen. Slaves frequently gained the freedom to provide their own jobs
and housing. They met with other slaves at dances, congregated for religious purposes, and held other celebrations. Urban blacks also found
many whites willing to provide liquor and to engage in clandestine social activities. These daily events of city life made the slave less a chattel and more a free person. As a result many bondsmen assumed an air
that whites considered inappropriate to their slave status.

Soon after their creation the town governments recognized the
special nature of urban bondage and made regulation of slaves a public
responsibility.[2] An Austin ordinance of 1855 granted to "the Council
generally and the Marshal and his assistants particularly control and
supervision" of "the conduct, carraige [sic], demeanor and deportment
of any and all slaves living, being, or found within the city limits."[3]
The urban slave codes varied according to time and place, but certain
restrictions on blacks remained constant. The law forbade the purchase of liquor, possession of weapons, unsupervised congregations,
gambling, and any form of disorderly conduct. Each southwestern
town also established a curfew for slaves and restricted interracial
social contact.[4]

On two issues basic to the welfare of urban slaves and their owners—housing and hiring—the town governments vacillated or hesitated
in asserting their authority. City masters frequently found it profitable
or convenient to allow bondsmen to find their own jobs and living
quarters. Slaves usually sought these privileges as a means of gaining
greater independence. On the other hand advocates of social order
charged that these "quasi-free negroes" had acquired and spread dan-
gerously unservile habits. The local authorities at first sought to reconcile these disparate interests and attitudes. All the town governments
except Shreveport acted quickly and steadfastly to prohibit owners
from allowing slaves to hire their own time but demonstrated greater
tolerance of separate housing arrangements. For years Austin and Little
Rock ignored the housing issue while Galveston attempted to curtail
"living out" through taxes and bonds. During the middle and late
1850s each town prohibited slaves from living "separate and apart"
from their owners. Shreveport had enacted this law a decade earlier but
allowed slave self-hiring until 1861.[5]

Each town lived in a state of flux regarding its rules governing
bondsmen. Almost biennially local governments added and deleted
laws, changed penalties, and experimented with the manner of enforcement in an effort to extend the coverage and to plug loopholes in the
ordinances. In general the regulations grew more realistic and flexible,
while punishments became increasingly harsh for both master and
slave. Yet none of the towns succeeded in creating a comprehensive
and workable slave code because enforcement procedures remained
primitive. During their infancies each community relied on a single
town constable with responsibilities for tax collection and street maintenance as well as police. Throughout the antebellum period overbur-
dened marshals functioned with only one or two assistants supplemented by an unreliable and unpaid city patrol. Local residents fulfilled
their policing obligations sporadically in spite of the heavy fine provided by city ordinances.[6] Enforcement of town laws also suffered because officials had to rely on state courts for prosecution of many offenders. Especially in cases of selling liquor to slaves, the county court
records reveal a pattern of non-prosecution, disappearing witnesses, extended litigation, and non-conviction.[7]

Inadequacies of law enforcement resulted in continuous criticism
of local government, with blame being cast alternately on the officials,
the laws, and the owners of slaves. Alarmed at the weakness of "the
control of our negroes," "A Citizen" of Austin wrote, "it is a moral

shame, it is superlatively degrading, that at the seat of government of a large and prosperous State we have such a *farce* of a city government." Occasionally the critics seemed resigned to failure. A Shreveport journalist concluded in 1843 that "Our police is inefficient and the abatement of the evil [of slave] drunkeness if accomplished at all must be done by the masters themselves." More often public concern took the tone of a reform movement, as in Galveston in 1856 when a number of residents petitioned city officials on the sale of liquor to blacks and eventually forced a major revision of the slave code.[8] Leaders of local government also noted imperfections. A Little Rock mayor and city council in 1856 won office on a promise to establish an effective night police, but here as elsewhere intentions of reform and invigoration seldom yielded significantly improved enforcement. Only a few years earlier another mayor had concluded his analysis of the problem of liquor-dispensing "groceries" with the vigorous assertion "that the laws had better be repealed at once, or fairly enforced."[9]

It appears that town authorities attempted to punish violators of the slave code but that general institutional weaknesses, underpaid police, and conflicting public interests led only to intermittent application of the law. Certainly neither whites nor blacks violated the slave code with impunity. Newspapers that condemned non-enforcement also at times praised energetic officials. City records indicate that many residents sought to comply with regulations and that slaves sometimes received severe punishments.[10]

The testimony of former slaves from the urban Southwest suggests a spirit of jubilation in confuting attempts to regulate black social life but also a recognition of the power of the "Patrollers."[11] In practice the law exercised the power to harass slaves, not to command cowering obedience. From the white perspective slave violations of legal restraints were, in the words of a Galveston reporter, "flagrant and disgraceful."[12] Thus the urban slave codes may be read as catalogue descriptions of slave social life.

Slaves in the towns of the Southwest, by asserting a relative independence from legal and other disciplinary restraints, developed a complex and vital social environment that most bondsmen preferred to a rural setting. The rural hirer of a group of town slaves wrote of their hatred for farm life. One slave in particular, according to this employer, "has sworn not to work on any plantation & says he will not live out of a city or town." The slave made good his oath by persistently running away from the farm.[13] The urban destination of many southwestern slave runaways provide clear evidence of this preference. Advertisements of slave owners frequently indicated a belief that runaways "skulked" around the towns, apparently seeking momentarily the pleasures of city society or hoping to avoid apprehension through the aid of friends and relatives.[14]

Explanations of this slave preference for urban conditions have often centered on the treatment of bondsmen by their town masters. In writing of the "indulgence" of urban owners for their black "retainers" and of the resulting cheerfulness and polite mannerisms of the slaves, historians have but reflected the conclusions of antebellum travelers and even of former slaves.[15] Though patterns of work in the towns offered considerably more variety than did the normal rural environment, not all town bondsmen escaped the drudgery of hard manual labor. Many toiled in the fields adjacent to the towns or performed rough day labor, but most labored at domestic work or found employment in skilled capacities. Even in their dress city bondsmen directed attention to their apparently luxurious manner of living. On Sundays slaves displayed lavish silks and satins that they had purchased or acquired from the castoff garments of their owners.[16] However, analysis of the slave clothing described in runaway advertisements suggests that town bondsmen typically wore suitable amounts of "good clothing" usually described as "common," "home-made," "coarse," or "good stout" rather than "genteel."[17] The dearth of information on the diet of urban slaves suggests its commonality. The frequency of hiring must have added to the number of slave families that underwent forcible destruction. Hired slaves often found too that a temporary master had less concern than their owner for questions of material welfare or state of mind. For example, two slaves rented out in Little Rock not only expressed "disappointment with their present homes," but complained bitterly of overwork and abuse. After the slaves had been returned to their owners the spectre of hiring became a means of discipline. "I could not make Charlotte hush," the owner once explained, "until I told her I would send her off the place; she is so much opposed to being hired out that I suppose that frightens her."[18] The health of town slaves also suffered from hazardous labor and exposure to epidemic diseases.[19]

The availability of greater liberties, rather than the kind treatment of benevolent masters, best explains slave preference for the urban setting. For example, slaves in the urban Southwest frequently lived in makeshift housing. Many found lodging in the residences where they worked, but most lived in "negro quarters" or outbuildings adjacent to the main dwelling. Although some structures were sturdy and commodious, most of these facilities served multiple functions as outside kitchens, carriage houses, or stables, with slaves occupying the upper story or some corner of the buildings.[20] Other slaves[21] occupied dwellings completely separate from their owners that offered no real improvement in quality other than being independent of white supervision. In fact these residences may have presented even poorer physical surroundings than the housing normally provided by owners. Some Galveston slaves rented what a committee of the city council described as "wretched hovels or huts."[22] However poor these housing arrangements, blacks flocked to them in search of de facto segregation from the master class. Whites in turn often feared the subculture that developed around the back buildings, suburban dwellings, or other quarters occupied by "quasi-free" slaves who hired their own time and "lived out." Reports of these "pest houses" described the occupants as disorderly and perhaps even rebellious. Even if no revolutionary movement developed, "this 'worse than free' class exercises an exceedingly pernicious influence upon servants who are kept at home in their proper places—where all negroes ought to be," wrote an Austin journalist.[23]

The most significant institutional development within the urban slave community—the growth of the black church—also reflected the drive toward autonomy. In the earliest years of the southwestern towns blacks normally joined white congregations, frequently comprising one half or more of the total membership. The churches provided special seating arrangements or afternoon meetings for their black members,[24] but the loyalty-to-master message delivered by white preachers repelled most slaves. A few renounced religion altogether, but more often blacks turned to their own meetings led by "native" preachers. These gatherings functioned in either open or underground fashion depending on place and circumstance. With the somewhat reluctant approval of many whites, the slaves of Little Rock and Galveston each formed separate Baptist and Methodist churches. The slaves of the Texas port created the most substantial buildings—each denomination could seat three hundred and fifty persons—and engaged in active fund-raising. The black churches of the Arkansas capital suffered greater financial woes but sponsored more far-reaching activities. William Wallace Andrews established in the Wesley Chapel in Little Rock a Sunday school that taught reading, writing, and spelling to other slaves.[25]

When denied organized religion of their own direction, bondsmen often sought worship at the outdoor revivals of the white churches or withdrew to the woods near town for their own "prayer meetings." Some of the slaveowners who attended these gatherings reacted with amused toleration; others attacked what they interpreted as meaningless religious pantomimes or insane emotionalism.[26] Amidst growing tensions over slavery in the late antebellum period both Shreveport and Austin attempted to repress independent slave religion. Vigilantes in the Texas capital in 1854 agreed on severe restrictions on black-led prayer meetings. Two years later another vigilance committee condemned them as "the great rendezvous for bad negroes" who concocted "thievish" and "incendiary" plots. Though temporarily "put down," within a few months slaves once again began holding nightly religious meetings in and around Austin.[27] Shreveport experienced less upheaval on slave spiritual matters until the Civil War when it expelled a free black Baptist preacher.[28] The Austin and Shreveport cases indicate the strength of the slaves' quest for religious autonomy even where whites refused to accommodate themselves to separate black churches.

Town life offered slaves a wide range of recreational opportunities, and masters customarily allowed a substantial amount of leisure, especially on weekends and during the Christmas holidays. Frequently slaves from neighboring farms swelled the ranks of the black population. Dances, the favorite activity, usually had the benefit of black musicians like the Shreveport Ethiopian Band, which played for both white and black audiences.[29] Slaveowners and city officials normally permitted slave dominated functions that had approved white supervision, though they sometimes commented warily on the noisy and expansive nature of the frolics.[30] Regardless of their masters' disapproval or concern about the need for supervision, the urban blacks demanded a certain amount of diversion as their right. As a Little Rock resident wrote, local slaves "claimed the week of Christmas as their own and acted accordingly."[31] In the pursuit of their social freedoms the urban slaves frequently violated both the law and the prevailing understanding of race relations. The presence of firearms and existence of literacy among so many bondsmen especially provoked alarm over the potential for revolution.[32]

In their moments of leisure town slaves usually sought the company of other blacks—they sometimes gathered in small groups on the streets or in front of stores and engaged in uproarious conversation. Since these open displays of freedom incurred the ire of whites, bondsmen more often assembled on the sly at night when they could temporarily escape from the control of their owners. The sparsely populated southwestern towns afforded little opportunity to submerge into secret rendezvous; therefore, slaves often journeyed into nearby wooded enclaves. Galveston, with a larger and more complex street system and social composition, offered greater numbers of whiskey shops and slave-run houses where blacks often congregated.[33] In all the towns slaves purchased liquor with minimal fear of apprehension—a typically frustrated newspaper editor charged that "a nigger can get drunk in our town as easily as a white man." Four years after a major revision of the municipal code, the Galveston *News* admitted that "this negro traffic [in liquor] is carried on most systematically."[34] Slaveowners exhibited the greatest alarm over the habits that their bondsmen acquired while hanging around the groceries or other suburban meeting places. In addition to drinking, slaves discovered such pleasures as smoking, gambling, thieving, and amorous carousing, sometimes with "low, unprincipled white" men and women. The slaves and their companions also held unlicensed "balls" that the authorities suppressed into secrecy but failed to abolish. Concluding his description of one of the biracial dances, an Austin editor wrote that "the observer almost imagines himself in the land of *amalgamation, abolition meetings, and women's rights conventions.*"[35]

Implicit in these social activities was the essentially unservile attitude of the slaves. Slaveowners and nonslaveowners alike noted the dignified bearing and growing self-esteem of the slaves and labeled this demeanor "impudent." In particular slaves commonly disregarded the groveling courtesies demanded by "polite" racial etiquette, used "insulting," loud, and profane language, and engaged in what the aldermen of Galveston described as "insubordination and disorderly conduct."[36]

Explanations for this behavior generally centered around the indulgence of individual owners; however, the relations of individual town masters and their slaves suggest that the problem of control stemmed largely from urban conditions. Former Texas Governor Elisha M. Pease owned a slave named Maria who worked mostly as a nurse for the children. Her many endearing attributes—youth, good looks, cheerful attitude—pleased her owners until they hired her out in Galveston. The agent in charge of Maria reported, "I cannot give a very flattering Account of the Negro Girl you left in my charge. She cuts up all sorts of rustics . . . it seems impossible to keep her in of night and She will not please anyone—but takes Special pains to displease them." A year later Mrs. Lucadia Pease wrote, "I am quite out of patience with Maria, and her many derelictions of duty. . . . [She] is really a very capable servant . . . but has so many vices, that she will never be worth anything except on a plantation."[37]

The dynamics of urban life created an environment that owners could not dominate, but at the same time the role of individual slaves in seeking the quasi-freedoms cannot be ignored in accounting for the breakdown of social controls. For example, the bondsmen of the Fulton family of Little Rock constantly probed for disciplinary weaknesses and took advantage of any lapses of authority. The family complained of the surliness of their servants, worried over their thieving proclivities, and yet found it impossible to stifle their recreational enterprises. While in Washington Senator William S. Fulton personally chose one slave and sent him to Little Rock, "confident," he explained to his wife Matilda, that "you will be pleased with him." After being hired to a local hotel the slave acquired a taste for alcohol, proved to be a disastrous carriage driver, and eventually ran away.[38] Another slave named Manuel, despite verbal promises to the contrary, asserted by his actions that on certain matters he would govern himself. He disliked living on the country estate and therefore maintained sleeping quarters with his wife in Little Rock where he spent most of his considerable free time. Manuel came into frequent conflict with the man who owned his wife, threatening arson against his house and stealing from him. As a result of these incidents local authorities barred Manuel from the city limits, whipped him, and for a time had him placed in prison. Undaunted, "Old General Manuel" lived up to his military nickname by waging a kind of guerrilla war against property in Little Rock. His mistress struck the major theme in his life when she wrote: "he is indeed his own man."[39]

Whatever the causes of the weakened authority of the masters, critics of the urban slave life style believed the problem to be of serious proportions. Many slaveowners feared that the contagious nature of freedom would not only ruin valuable servants but also lead to a more fundamental form of rebellion. Thus the most common form of overt resistance, running away, could "be traced to the unusual liberties which slaves in Texas seem to exercise in our towns, when out of the control of their masters," concluded an Austin newspaper.[40] Other observers attributed violent acts of slave resistance to this same factor— the "almost unlimited scope allowed negroes in our midst." Throughout the latter 1850s, slave revolt panics led to continual condemnation of the freedoms available to town bondsmen.[41] Although the conditions in southwestern towns may not have threatened the continued existence of slavery, certainly many city slaveowners believed they were witnessing the breakdown of the institution.[42]

The social life of slaves in the urban Southwest paralleled conditions in the larger cities of the Old South, differing only slightly in manner and degree. The anonymity of the great urban areas lessened in the uncrowded cities west of the Mississippi, resulting in decreased chances for bondsmen to meet on the sly in the houses of free blacks or "living out" slaves. Yet, the quest for separation existed as strongly as in the older communities, with bondsmen in the Southwest also seeking their own living quarters, establishing independent churches, and finding unsupervised recreation in suburban grog shops or in nearby wooded areas. The essential flavor of urban slave life, described by historian Richard C. Wade as a world of "variety, diversity, and fluidity," which sprang up "beyond the master's eye," characterized the institution in both the older, larger, eastern cities and the newer, smaller, western towns of the antebellum South.[43]

Wade concludes that these manifestations of black freedom caused the disintegration of urban slavery; the southwestern towns reproduced the basic social patterns but not the other evidence of decay. The city governments of the Old South, Wade points out, responded to their inability to curtail slave liberties by passing laws providing for racial segregation, thus tacitly admitting the failure of traditional controls.[44] In the towns of the Southwest the impetus for separation came from the slaves alone, with municipal authorities retaining laws which forbade blacks from meeting together outside of white supervision. The most important evidence of disintegration cited by Wade is statistical. Unable to discipline their bondsmen satisfactorily in an urban setting, masters sold slaves away from the cities, and the relative size of urban slave populations declined precipitously. In 1820, at the peak of the growth of urban bondage, slaves made up 22 percent of all urban inhabitants; by 1860 a mere 10 percent of city dwellers were chattels.[45] Tables[46] (1 and 2) indicate that numerical stability rather than deterioration characterized urban slavery in the Southwest. In every case except Shreveport[47] the numbers of slaves grew at approximately the same rate as the whole population; the total figure for all four southwestern towns in 1860 (22 percent) equaled that of the Old South during what Wade considers the boom period of urban slavery. At the same time it should be noted that urban slavery in the Southwest grew in an unspectacular fashion. In none of the towns did slaves compose a larger percentage of the population in 1860 than in 1850. Nor did the urban variety of bondage develop more rapidly than slavery in the surrounding countryside—the ratio of slaves to total population in the towns either just equaled or fell below that of their respective states.[48] The incidence of slave ownership also suggests neither rapid growth nor alarming decline in the southwestern cities. In both census years a sizable and basically stable minority of free heads of household had a direct stake in the system through ownership of slaves.[49]

Social characteristics help explain the comparative vitality of slavery on the western urban frontier of the Old South. Despite the essential similarity of the disciplinary problems of slaveowners in both sections, the environment of the towns of the Southwest was in some ways less provocative than in other cities of the South. The southwestern communities, with relatively small and homogeneous populations, presented somewhat fewer opportunities for slaves to escape their mas-

Table 1

Slave Population in the Urban Southwest

City	1850		1860	
	Total Pop.	Slave Pop.	Total Pop.	Slave Pop.
Austin	854	226 (27%)	3,500	973 (28%)
Galveston	4,177	678 (16%)	7,328	1,186 (16%)
Little Rock	2,178	532 (24%)	3,736	856 (23%)
Shreveport	1,731	597 (35%)	2,966	899 (30%)
	8,940	2,033 (23%)	17,530	3,914 (22%)

Table 2

Incidence of Slave Ownership

City	1850		1860	
	# Free Heads of Family	# Slave-owners	# Free Heads of Family	# Slave-owners
Austin	122	57 (48%)	499	175 (35%)
Galveston	682	147 (22%)	1,259	263 (21%)
Little Rock	299	108 (36%)	454	143 (32%)
Shreveport	257	99 (39%)	335	137 (41%)
	1,360	411 (30%)	2,547	718 (28%)

ter's oversight.[50] The restrictive features of the social milieu resulted from more than just the smallness of the towns—slaveowners in the urban Southwest demonstrated considerable militance in combating what they considered to be undesirable elements of the population.

From their founding the southwestern towns created formidable barriers to prevent the development of a sizable community of free blacks. This class, according to prevailing fears, mingled with slaves and stirred up discontent both by the example of freedom and by active encouragement of the pursuit of illicit social liberties.[51] State laws that forbade immigration and denied permanent residence allowed non-slave blacks only a tenuous place in society, even though authorities enforced the restrictions spasmodically. The municipal governments of the Southwest further harassed free blacks with prohibitive taxes, bond securities, and other requirements. Those who resided in the towns either by meeting or by somehow evading these laws faced the regulations of the urban slave codes that governed blacks in basically the same manner regardless of free or chattel status.[52] These legal hostilities limited the growth of the "free colored" population to a small group in all the towns at all times; in the latter 1850s Arkansas and Texas moved to eliminate the "free negro nuisance" altogether. Galveston applied a series of Texas laws to reduce its free black contingent from a high of thirty-eight in 1848 to only two by the 1860 census. Little Rock led the expulsion movement that triumphed in Arkansas in 1858 and applied the legislation so sternly as to eliminate all free blacks from the city within two years.[53] The free blacks may have been scapegoats whose removal merely relieved the anxieties of frustrated slaveowners, but the masters had at least acted decisively against a perceived social problem.

Austin had the smallest free black population of all the southwestern towns, but in the early 1850s local slaveholders responded to what they regarded as a most disconcerting situation when several Mexican families moved into the vicinity. According to predominant local opinion, this group escaped the legal constraints imposed upon free blacks but had an equally corrosive effect on the "proper governance" of slaves. Newspapers charged that the Hispanic Texans aided slave runaways and intermingled in a spirit of equality with bondsmen, thus stirring up "insubordination." In the fall of 1854 citizens' meetings, dominated by the local slaveholding elite, adopted and enforced extralegal methods of ridding the community of "rascally peons" as well as curbing the freedoms of Austin slaves. The vigilance committee created by these meetings warned all "transient Mexicans" to leave the area within ten days unless they could obtain the sponsorship of some "responsible American citizen." The vigilantes summarily ejected about twenty families, and other Mexican Texans received equally rough treatment the next year.[54]

Although vigilantism proved unsuccessful in permanently curbing other types of slave liberties such as unsupervised "prayer meetings," Austin turned to it again to investigate a suspected slave revolt scheme in 1856. This form of extra-legal community pressure seemed to invigorate local government, which adopted quick and decisive measures of police both in this year and again during the insurrection panic of 1860.[55] The Texas capital, like city governments throughout the Southwest, lacked the complex machinery and intricate modes of punishment of eastern urban areas,[56] but the combined activities of vigilantes and the regular authorities provided it with at least minimally acceptable measures protecting order and property.

Another explanation for the viability of urban slavery in the Southwest is that the town economies offered a sound base for employment of slave labor. As elsewhere more town bondsmen worked as domestics than in any other capacity. Most masters owned or hired only a few slaves and sought versatile laborers rather than those with specialized but limited abilities. Town residents often became exasperated in their search for a suitably skilled and energetic servant, and the demand for slaves as domestic workers seems to have been unrelenting.[57] In comparison to other southern cities, the southwestern towns provided little industrial employment[58] but were small and uncrowded enough to allow for the use of town slaves in agriculture. In Shreveport, Austin, and Little Rock slaves toiled in the fields either in or near the city while maintaining town residences. Other slaves alternated their labor between the town and country properties of their owners; rural employers also occasionally hired town bondsmen.[59] The number of slaves who had jobs in farming cannot be calculated accurately except in the case of the capital city of Texas.[60] The U.S. census for Austin in 1860, compiled in an unusually careful and detailed manner, suggests that many city slaves spent at least part of their work days in farm labor. The agricultural schedule of the census includes the names of two-thirds of all Austin slaveholders. Most owned land and a small amount of livestock only, but others were extensively involved in agriculture. Approximately one-third of the slave workforce in Austin labored mostly in agricultural activities. Others spent parts of their days gardening, tending animals, and working at related jobs.[61]

The expanding urban areas of the Southwest also provided labor for a sizable number of slave artisans. A Little Rock native whose slave father came to the town during the 1840s exaggerated somewhat in writing that "Few of the trades workers were white. [Blacks worked as] brick makers and brick layers, stone masons, lathers, plasterers,—all types of builders. . . . Slaves were the only ones who did this work."[62] White workers objected both to the degradation of laboring alongside slaves and to the economic losses resulting from this competition, but free labor made only sporadic efforts to deal with this grievance. The white artisans of Little Rock organized the most serious movement against slave mechanics in 1858, urging the defeat of all candidates who hired out skilled black workers and threatening to strike all projects that employed black tradesmen. The labor movement backed off from this proposed militance in the face of newspaper claims that such actions too closely resembled northern abolitionist fanaticism. In the other southwestern towns slaveowners also heard occasional faint whimpers of protest from white labor, but nowhere did they face any serious impediment in hiring out their slaves.[63] A Shreveport ordinance that levied a prohibitive tax on slave mechanics lasted only two weeks before being repealed.[64] City councils enacted no licensing law or badge system that might have restricted the employment of slave labor; even laws preventing slaves from hiring their own time seem to have been largely ineffectual.[65]

Perhaps in part because organized labor failed to limit the employment opportunities of slave labor, the southwestern towns attracted relatively few free laborers, and bondsmen formed the core of the working class. Only Galveston, a major center for the disembarkation of immigrants, attracted a large number of foreign-born residents. Table 3[66] indicates a clear relationship between the size of immigrant and slave populations.

Whether or not they undersold native white and slave labor,[67] immigrants swelled the total size of the labor pool. In a recent quantitative study, Claudia Dale Goldin argues that the demographic decline of urban slavery in the Old South occurred because cities generally had more elasticity in their demand for slave labor. Rural areas, unable to find suitable substitutes to fill the field gangs, thus pulled bondsmen out of the cities even though the urban demand for slaves remained high. This pull process resulted in urban slave demographic patterns that differed considerably from rural areas. Goldin's statistics suggest that city owners retained older, presumably more skilled, slaves and sold younger

Table 3

Foreign-Born and Slave Population, 1860

City	Total Population	Slaves	Total Free Population	Foreign-born
Galveston	7,328	1,186 (16%)*	6,142	2,698 (44%)**
Austin	3,499	982 (28%)	2,517	424 (17%)
Little Rock	3,736	846 (23%)	2,890	544 (19%)
Shreveport	2,966	899 (30%)	2,067	392 (19%)

* percentage of total population

** percentage of free population

bondsmen.[68] The data in Tables 4 and 5[69] indicate the make-up of the slave populations in the southwestern towns resembled the South as a whole more nearly than the other southern urban areas. In Little Rock, Shreveport, and Austin the percentage of children was greater than in the three representative southern cities, and the percentage of older slaves (aged 36 and over) was substantially smaller. In these inland towns, where employers had few alternatives to slave labor and substantial need for agricultural workers, the marketplace phenomenon of rural areas siphoning off large numbers of urban slaves did not occur. In contrast Galveston closely reproduced the normal demographic patterns of the urban South because it had little demand for exclusively slave labor. That urban slavery in the Southwest displayed both weakened social controls and demographic stability suggests the primary importance of economic factors in determining the size and character of urban slave populations. This conclusion thus reinforces the idea that slavery and urbanization were compatible.

The strength of urban slavery in the Southwest received a final test during the Civil War, an experience that added new pressures and accentuated the existing problems of city bondage. The war disrupted essential economic routines—especially in blockaded Galveston and militarily vulnerable Little Rock where normal patterns of hire, sale, and employment broke down to be replaced by unhealthy enterprises hazardous to the life of the slave and thus to the investment of the owners.[70] Socially the wartime cities developed environments even more corrosive of "proper" slave behavior than the already troubled atmosphere of antebellum years. Critics of slave behavior asserted that the

Table 4

Percentage of Male (Female) Slave Population in Various Age Categories

1850

	Charleston	Mobile	Richmond	Little Rock	Shreveport	Austin	Galveston	Total U.S.
0–9	20 (17)	20 (24)	15 (20)	24 (27)	28 (24)	31 (24)	26 (22)	32
10–23	31 (27)	25 (29)	36 (34)	38 (37)	33 (36)	34 (39)	33 (33)	
24–35	21 (21)	31 (23)	25 (20)	23 (20)	24 (23)	15 (20)	26 (28)	
36–54	19 (23)	20 (18)	19 (18)	12 (11)	10 (15)	17 (15)	9 (14)	
over 54	9 (12)	4 (6)	4 (8)	4 (5)	4 (2)	3 (2)	6 (3)	5

1860

	Charleston	Mobile	Richmond	Little Rock	Shreveport	Austin	Galveston	Total U.S.
0–9	20 (20)	23 (21)	13 (21)	24 (28)	30 (29)	33 (31)	23 (24)	31
10–23	29 (29)	25 (29)	40 (32)	35 (34)	15 (37)	31 (36)	31 (37)	
24–35	23 (20)	26 (25)	27 (21)	24 (24)	49 (29)	18 (18)	28 (20)	
36–54	21 (22)	20 (19)	16 (20)	13 (11)	6 (3)	15 (12)	13 (11)	
over 54	7 (9)	6 (6)	4 (6)	4 (3)	1 (2)	3 (2)	5 (5)	5

Table 5

Percentage of Slaves 10–54 Years Old (Labor Force Percentages)

	Charleston	Mobile	Richmond	Little Rock	Shreveport	Austin	Galveston	Total U.S.
1850	71	73	76	70	71	70	72	64
1860	72	72	79	70	68	65	71	64

presence of impressed bondsmen, soldiers, and other transients added to the volatility of city life and emboldened slaves to what a Little Rock writer called "evils and immoralities . . . attaining huge proportions." Corporate authorities in Galveston asserted that "our negro population . . . has become demoralized and almost worthless"; similar complaints echoed in editorial pages throughout the war.[71]

Each town had a different form of social unrest about which it appeared most concerned. In Little Rock drinking and prostitution seemed on the increase. Authorities in Galveston battled an outbreak of burglaries that many residents blamed on slaves. Shreveport also worried about these thieving "depredations" but faced a more dangerous problem from the growing number and militance of runaway slaves, some of whom gathered in gangs near the town in 1864.[72] These breakdowns in slave controls occurred despite the availability of additional police forces in the form of Confederate troops, expansion of the regular police in Little Rock, creation of a vigilance committee in Shreveport, and toughening of the slave codes everywhere.[73]

Yet despite the dislocations wrought by the Civil War, in the final analysis these years presented further evidence that town slavery was not a naturally dying institution in the trans-Mississippi area. In none of the towns did the war-time experience alone impart irreparable damage to slavery. The will to preserve the social characteristics of slavery endured even after Appomattox, as evidenced by post-war city ordinances that, in both terminology and specific provisions, duplicated antebellum black codes.[74] Given the tenacity with which whites held to the institution during this era of stress and unrest, it appears that only force could have wiped out slavery, whatever weaknesses it may have experienced in the urban setting. Many bondsmen used their wits and legs to find freedom, but since no large, organized slave revolt arose, it took the armed might of the Union to bring about the demise of slavery.

For urban slaves in the Southwest the Civil War brought both hardship and exaltation. The scarcities of the wartime economy resulted in varied forms of material deprivation, including poorer food, clothing, and health. These physical maladies applied especially to the bondsmen impressed by Confederate authorities to labor on fortifications or in war-related industries.[75] The war also undermined the status of many town slaves who found themselves sold or hired out to plantations because of disrupted city economic patterns or the threats of invading armies. But overall the war increased the number of slaves who contacted urban conditions, and, regardless of when they lived there, slaves generally came to prefer the town to the country. City life offered both greater recreational opportunities and withdrawal into a quasi-separate black world; in either case it thrust slaves into contact with a variety of folk willing to share experiences and convivialities. Whether the slave emerged from these encounters embittered by an awareness of the inequities of slavery, inspired by economic incentives, enlightened by knowledge of the printed word, inebriated by strong drink, enamored with a new acquaintance, embroiled with the law, shorn of hard-earned possessions, or in any number of other moods or conditions, he or she came away with broadened horizons. The growth of black populations in all the southwestern towns between 1865 and 1870 suggests that to the slave the city had become a symbol of opportunity and freedom.

Notes

1. Ira Don Richards, *Story of a Rivertown, Little Rock in the Nineteenth Century* (Benton, Arkansas, 1969), pp. 9–26, 38–39; Kenneth W. Wheeler, *To Wear a City's Crown: The Beginnings of Urban Growth in Texas, 1836–1865* (Cambridge, Massachusetts, 1968), pp. 25–35, 70–78, 119–124, 160–165; J. Fair Hardin, "An Outline of Shreveport and Caddo Parish History," *Louisiana Historical Quarterly* 18 (Oct. 1935), pp. 769–779.

2. Little Rock *Arkansas Gazette*, Feb. 7, 1826; Minutes of the Meetings of the Mayor and Board of Trustees of the Town of Shreveport, Book A, p. 8, Division of Tax Office, City Hall, Shreveport; *Austin City Gazette*, Feb. 12, 1840; Charles Waldo Hayes, "The Island and City of Galveston," Typescript, Rosenberg Library, Galveston, 334.

3. Austin *Texas State Gazette*, Feb. 24, 1855.

4. *Charter, Amendments and Revised Ordinances of the City of Galveston* (Galveston, 1855), pp. 52–54; William Wallace Wood, ed., *The Charter, Ordinances Police Regulations and Laws of the Corporation of the Town of Shreveport* (Shreveport, 1849), pp. 26–28; *Ordinances of the City of Little Rock* (Little Rock, 1848), pp. 80–82; *Charter and City Ordinances of the City of Austin* (Austin, 1859), pp. 42–45.

5. Austin *Texas State Gazette*, Oct. 12, 1850, Sep. 10, 1859; *Charter and Ordinances of Austin*, pp. 42–44; Minutes of Trustees of Shreveport, B, pp. 434–435; Wood, ed., *Ordinances of Shreveport*, 26; Little Rock *Arkansas Gazette*, Feb. 1, 1832; Little Rock City Council Records, Book B, Oct. 27, 1856, Office of the City

Clerk, City Hall, Little Rock; Proceedings of the Mayor and Board of Aldermen for the City of Galveston, July 17,1851, May 1, July 14, 21, 1854, Office of the City Secretary, Municipal Building, Galveston.

6. Little Rock *Arkansas Gazette,* Jan. 12, 1836, June 24, 1850, Feb. 25, 1854; Little Rock City Council Records, B, Jan. 19, 1861; Austin *Texas State Gazette,* Nov. 2, 1850, Sep. 10, 1859; Wood, ed. *Ordinances of Shreveport,* pp. 23–25; Minutes of Trustees of Shreveport, A, pp. 14, 104–105, 142–143, 254–256; Proceedings of Aldermen, Galveston, March 14, 1850, Sep. 1, 1851; Earl W. Fornell, *The Galveston Era: The Texas Crescent on the Eve of Secession* (Austin, 1961), p. 65.

7. Pulaski County Circuit Court, Criminal Record, B, Dec. 12, 1849, Feb. 26, Dec. 3, 1850, Jan. 5, July 17, 21, 1852, June 23, Dec. 13, 1853, Dec. 9, 1854, C, May 6, 1859, May 16, 1860, Oct. 22, 1862, County Clerk's Office, Pulaski County Court House, Little Rock; District Court of Galveston, Minutes, May 24, 1847, June 12, Nov. 27, 1848, May 28, Nov. 27, Dec. 7, 1849, June 9, 1853, June 12, 1856, July 9, 1858, Jan. 9, June 13, 1860, Jan. 16, 1861, Galveston County Court House, Galveston.

8. Austin *Texas State Gazette,* June 25, 1853; Shreveport *Caddo Gazette and De-Soto Intelligencer,* Nov. 22, 1843; *Galveston News,* June 10, Oct. 2, Dec. 30, 1856.

9. Little Rock *True Democrat,* May 20, 1856; Little Rock City Council Records, A, April 2, 1850.

10. *Civilian and Galveston Gazette,* April 16, 1842; Austin *Texas State Gazette,* Oct. 3, 1857; Little Rock *Arkansas State Gazette and Democrat,* April 24, 1858; *Galveston News,* March 6, 1860; Minutes of Trustees of Shreveport, B, 103; Proceedings of Aldermen, Galveston, March 30, 1850, July 14, Dec. 1, 1854.

11. J. Mason Brewer, ed., *An Historical Outline of the Negro in Travis County* (Austin, 1940), p. 14; The Story of J. N. Gillespie in Federal Writers' Project, "Slave Narratives: A Folk History of Slavery in the United States from Interviews with Former Slaves," Arkansas, No. 3, pp. 34–37. Typescripts on microfilm, Texas Tech University Library, Lubbock.

12. *Galveston News,* March 6, 1860.

13. Aaron Coffee to William P. Ballinger, Jan. 9, Feb. 16, March 2, 1863, William P. Ballinger Papers; Ballinger Diary, March 4, 1863, Archives, University of Texas Library, Austin.

14. Little Rock *Arkansas Gazette,* Feb. 21, 1838; Little Rock *Arkansas Times and Advocate,* May 15, 1843; Little Rock *Arkansas Democrat,* Sep. 25, 1846; Austin *Southwestern American,* Nov. 3, 1852; *Galveston Weekly News,* April 8, 29, 1856; Shreveport *Caddo Gazette,* Feb. 5, 1855; Shreveport *South-Western,* Jan. 10, March 21, Aug. 22, 1855, July 9, 1856, July 8, 1857; Little Rock *Arkansas True Democrat,* March 16, 1858, May 25, Sep. 7, 1859; *Shreveport News,* July 1, 1864.

15. Fornell, *Galveston Era,* pp. 115–117, 241; Wheeler, *City's Crown,* pp.

147–148; Willis W. Pratt, ed., *Galveston Island, or A Few Months Off the Coast of Texas: The Journal of Francis C. Sheridan 1839–1840* (Austin, 1954), 89; Charles Hooton, *St. Louis' Isle, or Texiana; with Additional Observations Made in the United States and in Canada* (London, 1847), pp. 138–141; The Story of Charlotte E. Stevens, Federal Writers' Project, "Slave Narratives," Arkansas, No. 6, pp. 226–228.

16. Little Rock *Daily National Democrat,* Jan. 9, 1865, quoted in Richards, *Rivertown,* 78; Fornell, *Galveston Era,* pp. 116–117; Walter Lord, ed., *The Fremantle Diary: Being the Journal of Lieutenant Colonel James Arthur Lyon Fremantle, Coldstream Guards, on His Three Months in the Southern States* (Boston, 1954), pp. 58–60.

17. Little Rock *Arkansas Advocate,* May 9, 1832; Little Rock *Arkansas Gazette,* April 12, May 17, 1836, Aug. 8, 1838, Oct. 30, 1839, Nov. 10, 1841; *Civilian and Galveston Gazette,* Aug. 14, 1847; *The Caddo Gazette,* Feb. 6, 1850; Austin *Texas State Gazette,* Jan. 5, 1856; *Little Rock Arkansas True Democrat,* June 30, Oct. 27, 1857, Dec. 15, 1858, June 29, 1859.

18. John F. Fulton to William S. Fulton, Jan. 9, 1842; David Fulton to William S. Fulton, April 17, 1842; Matilda Fulton to William S. Fulton, Aug. 14, 1842, William S. Fulton Collection, Arkansas History Commission, Little Rock.

19. Little Rock *Arkansas Gazette,* June 5, 1833; Austin *Southwestern American,* Jan. 7, 1853; Marshall *Texas Republican,* July 2, 1853; *Galveston Weekly News,* Oct. 12, 1858.

20. Orville W. Taylor, *Negro Slavery in Arkansas* (Durham, 1958), pp. 112, 149; [Anonymous], "The William E. Woodruff Home," *Pulaski County Historical Society Review* 10 (Dec. 1962), pp. 53–55; The Story of Julia A. White, Federal Writers' Project, "Slave Narratives," Arkansas, No.7, p. 123; *Civilian and Galveston Gazette,* Nov. 20, 1847; *Galveston Weekly News,* April 17, 1855, Oct. 28, 1856, Nov. 24, 1857, March 20, 1864.

21. Most observers made only general estimates of the number of slaves who hired their own time and had independent residences: "Many" in Galveston, "Nearly half" in Austin, and a "settled Practice" in Little Rock. Ben C. Stuart, Scrapbook, Rosenberg Library, Galveston, Texas, 233; Austin *Texas State Gazette,* July 19, 1851; Little Rock *Arkansas State Gazette and Democrat,* Oct. 16, 1858.

22. Proceedings of Aldermen, Galveston, April 1, 1854.

23. *Civilian and Galveston Gazette,* July 22, 1851; Austin *Texas State Gazette,* July 19, 1851; Little Rock *Arkansas State Gazette and Democrat,* Oct. 16, 1858.

24. T. H. Thurmond, "History of the First Baptist Church," in Maude Hearne O'Pry, ed., *Chronicles of Shreveport* (Shreveport, 1923), p. 203; Macum Phelan, *A History of Early Methodism in Texas 1817–1866* (Nashville, 1924), pp. 369–427.

25. The Story of John Williams, Federal Writers' Project, "Slave Narratives," Arkansas, No. 7, p. 174; Taylor, *Slavery in Arkansas,* pp. 196–197; Little Rock *Arkansas Gazette,* Nov. 7, 1851; Wheeler, *City's Crown,* p. 132; Stuart, Scrapbook,

pp. 185–186; Fornell, *Galveston Era*, pp. 84–86; *Galveston Civilian*, March 23,1858; Clara B. Kennan, "The First Negro Teacher in Little Rock," *Arkansas Historical Quarterly* 9 (Autumn 1950), pp. 194–204.

26. Frank Brown, Annals of Travis County and the City of Austin, typescript, Austin Public Library, 1954, X, pp. 62–63, XIX, p. 30; Austin *Southwestern American*, Aug. 27, 1853; Austin *Texas Sentinel*, Aug. 29, 1857; Austin *Southern Intelligencer*, Aug. 17, 1859; Brewer, ed., *Negro in Travis County*, p. 12.

27. Austin *Texas State Gazette*, Oct. 14, 1854, March 14, 1857.

28. Mrs. R. M. Sibley, *History of the First Baptist Church, Shreveport, Louisiana* (Shreveport, 1945), p. 13.

29. The Story of John Sneed, Federal Writers' Project, "Slave Narratives," Texas, No. 4, p. 48; Taylor, *Slavery in Arkansas*, p. 112; Minutes of Trustees of Shreveport, A, p. 235.

30. Little Rock *Arkansas State Gazette and Democrat*, Dec. 30, 1853; Proceedings of Aldermen, Galveston, Dec. 1, 1854.

31. John T. Fulton to William S. Fulton, Dec. 31, 1854, William S. Fulton Collection.

32. Little Rock *Arkansas Gazette*, March 21, 1838; *Galveston Civilian and Gazette*, Nov. 2, 1844; Austin *Texas State Gazette*, July 22, Oct. 14, 1854, March 8, 1856, Oct. 3, 1857; Little Rock *Arkansas State Gazette and Democrat*, April 4, 1857.

33. Galveston *Civilian and Gazette*, Nov. 2, 1844; Little Rock *Arkansas State Democrat*, Sep. 14, 1849; *Galveston Weekly News*, Jan. 21, 1850; Austin *Texas State Gazette*, June 25, 1853, July 22, 1854; Shreveport *South-Western*, Nov. 8, 1854.

34. Austin *Texas State Gazette*, March 8, 1856; *Galveston Weekly News*, March 6, 1860.

35. Little Rock City Council Records, A, April 2, 1850; Shreveport *Caddo Gazette and De-Soto Intelligencer*, Nov. 22, 1843; Little Rock *Arkansas State Gazette and Democrat*, Oct. 20, 1854; *Galveston Weekly News*, June 10, July 29, 1856, June 30, 1857; Austin *Texas State Gazette*, July 22, 1854.

36. Little Rock *Arkansas State Gazette and Democrat*, July 19, 1851; Austin *Texas State Gazette*, Oct. 10, 1857, June 30, 1860; Corporation Court Records in the Little Rock City Council Records, A, May 19, 1841, March 21, 1842; *Galveston Weekly News*, Sep. 30, 1856.

37. [Mr. Hunt] to E. M. Pease, June 17, 1856; Lucadia Pease to "My dear Sister [Juliet]," Jan. 21, 1854, July 20, 1857, Pease-Graham-Niles Family Papers, Austin Public Library.

38. William S. Fulton to Matilda Fulton, May 18, 1840, David Fulton to William S. Fulton, Feb. 2, 1842, Matilda Fulton to William S. Fulton, Jan. 1, Feb. 6, 10, 1843, William S. Fulton Collection; Little Rock *Arkansas Banner*, May 22, 1849.

39. Matilda Fulton to William S. Fulton, Nov. 17, 1839, March 15, Dec. 29,

1840, Jan. 1, 1843, D. F Shall to William S, Fulton, Feb. 8, 1842, William S. Fulton Collection; Corporation Court Records in Little Rock City Council Records, A, Aug. 28, 1841.

40. Austin *Texas State Gazette*, Sep. 23, 1854.

41. Shreveport *South-Western*, Sep. 11, 1861.

42. Little Rock *Arkansas Whig*, March 2, 1854; Austin *Texas State Gazette*, June 16, 1855, Nov. 22, 1856; *Galveston Weekly News*, Feb. 17, 1857.

43. Richard C. Wade, *Slavery in the Cities: The South, 1820–1860* (New York, 1964), p. 143.

44. *Ibid.*, pp. 258–278.

45. *Ibid.*, pp.16–19, 243.

46. The figures in these tables were compiled from the manuscript census returns. U.S. Seventh Census, 1850, Schedule I: "Free Inhabitants," Schedule II: "Slave Inhabitants," Travis County, Texas, Galveston County, Texas, Pulaski County, Arkansas, Caddo Parish, Louisiana; U.S. Eighth Census, 1860, Schedule I: "Free Inhabitants," Schedule II: "Slave Inhabitants," Travis County, Texas, Galveston County, Texas, Pulaski County, Arkansas, Caddo Parish, Louisiana, Microfilm at Texas Tech University Library, Lubbock.

47. A careless census taken in Caddo parish in 1860 failed to differentiate clearly between urban and rural-dwelling slaves. The figure 899 was computed by eliminating from the Shreveport totals the 771 slaves who belonged to farmers listed as living just inside the city limits. Since this method is inexact, the 5 percent decline in Shreveport slaves should be considered with caution.

48. The ratio of slaves to total population in 1860 was 30 percent in Texas, 23 percent in Arkansas, and 47 percent in Louisiana, U.S. Eighth Census, *Population of the United States in 1860* (Washington, 1864).

49. In a recent study Randolph Campbell and Richard Lowe, using sampling techniques, seriously underestimate the incidence of slave ownership in Texas towns. These scholars conclude that only 15.9 percent of the urban family heads in 1850 and 11.7 percent in 1860 owned slaves. *Wealth and Power in Antebellum Texas* (College Station and London, 1977), pp. 97–99. The figures in Table 2 are based on a comprehensive tabulation of the census data. In the Texas towns (including Houston and San Antonio) the actual percentage of heads of family owning slaves remained constant at just over 20 percent in both 1850 and 1860.

50. Wade recognized that slavery in newer and smaller cities did not decline, but he conjectured that attrition would have come as the cities expanded. *Slavery in the Cities*, 243. Of the four cities in this study Galveston came closest to reproducing the social milieu of the older urban areas. Yet no attrition set in during the last antebellum decade; the slave population continued to grow at the same rate as the free population.

51. Little Rock *Arkansas Gazette*, Nov. 17, 1835, April 14, 1841, March 16, 1842; Galveston *Civilian and Gazette*, Nov. 2, 1844, Aug. 27, 1858; *Galveston Weekly News*, Dec. 23, 1856, Jan. 11, 1859; Austin *Southern Intelligencer*, Jan. 5, 1859.

52. Harold Schoen, "The Free Negro in the Republic of Texas," *Southwestern Historical Quarterly* 40 (Oct, 1936), pp. 93–95; Taylor, *Slavery in Arkansas*, pp. 247–252; H. E. Sterkx, *The Free Negro in Ante-Bellum Louisiana* (Madison, 1972), Chapters I–III; Hayes, "Galveston," pp. 344, 349; Minutes of Trustees of Shreveport, A, pp. 8, 177, 233–234, B, p. 167; *Ordinances of Little Rock*, pp. 80–82; *Charter and Ordinances of Galveston*, 1855, pp. 52–54.

53. Fornell, *Galveston Era*, pp. 232, 237; *Galveston Weekly News*, Dec. 23, 1856; Galveston *Civilian and Gazette*, Aug. 4, 1857, June 29, 1858; H. P. N. Gammel, ed., *The Laws of Texas*, 1822–1897 (Austin, 1898), IV, pp. 466–467, 947–949; Thomas Law Nichols, *Forty Years of American Life* (London, 1874), pp. 146–147; Taylor, *Slavery in Arkansas*, pp. 256–258; Little Rock *Arkansas State Gazette and Democrat*, Dec. 27, 1856, Sep. 25, Nov. 13, 1858, Jan. 15, Feb. 19, March 5, 1859.

54. Austin *Texas State Gazette*, July 15, Sept. 2, 9, 23, 30, Oct. 7, 14, 21, 1854.

55. *Ibid.*, Nov. 15, 22, 29, Dec. 6, 16, 1856, March 14, 1857, Aug. 4, Oct. 6, 1860; Austin *Southern Intelligencer*, Oct. 10, 1860.

56. In addition to the absence of sizable professional police forces, the southwestern towns also failed to employ penalties like workhouses, irons, branding, and treadmills which eastern slave cities adopted. Wade, *Slavery in the Cities*, pp. 80–110, 180–208.

57. Lucadia Pease to "Sisters Ju and Gusty," April 15, 1854, Elisha M. Pease to Lucadia Pease, June 12, 16, 1856, Pease-Graham-Niles Family Papers; Ballinger Diary, Jan. 13, 19, 25, Aug. 11, 12, 1860; Fornell, *Galveston Era*, pp. 120–121; *Civilian and Galveston Gazette*, Oct. 27, 1835; *Shreveport Daily News*, April 30, 1861.

58. Wheeler, *City's Crown*, p. 120; Shreveport *Caddo Gazette*, Feb. 6, 1850; Little Rock *Arkansas State Gazette and Democrat*, Aug. 2, 1850, March 26, 1852; Austin *Texas State Gazette*, July 1, 1854.

59. Taylor, *Slavery in Arkansas*, pp. 53–54, 143; Brown, Annals of Travis County, X, p. 54.

60. The Shreveport census schedules make an unclear differentiation between urban and rural residents, but the agricultural economy of the area suggests that a fairly large number of town slaves worked in agriculture. The Pulaski County agricultural schedules are scanty and omit the names of some local farmers. Based on the occupations of their owners, 15 percent of the Little Rock slaves in 1860 labored primarily in farm jobs.

61. These statistics were compiled from the manuscript census returns by comparing the list of Austin slaveholders with the persons enumerated in the agricul-

tural schedule. The slave work force, here defined as slaves between the ages of 10 and 54, totaled 676 for Austin, of whom 222 belonged to owners who produced agricultural commodities. This latter figure does not include slaves of owners engaged only in small-scale livestock production. U.S. Eighth Census, 1860, Schedule I: "Free Inhabitants," Schedule II: "Slave Inhabitants," Schedule IV: "Productions in Agriculture," Travis County, Texas, Microfilm at Texas State Library, Austin.

62. The Story of Charlotte E. Stevens, Federal Writers' Project, "Slave Narratives," Arkansas, No. 6, p. 227.

63. Little Rock *Arkansas State Gazette and Democrat*, July 31, Sep. 25, Oct. 16, 1858; Little Rock *Arkansas True Democrat*, Sep. 29, 1858; Frederick Law Olmsted, *A Journey through Texas* (New York, 1857), p. 114.

64. Minutes of Trustees of Shreveport, A, pp. 337, 345–346, 351.

65. The most recent study of urban slavery suggests that these taxes were actually too light to affect the economic viability of city slavery. Claudia Dale Goldin, *Urban Slavery in the American South: A Quantitative History* (Chicago, 1976), pp. 36–39, 50.

66. Ralph A. Wooster, "Foreigners in the Principle Ante-Bellum Towns of Texas," *Southwestern Historical Quarterly* 46 (Oct. 1962), pp. 217–218; the figures for Shreveport and Little Rock were compiled from the manuscript census returns. U. S. Eighth Census, 1860, Schedule I: "Free Inhabitants," Pulaski County, Arkansas, Caddo Parish, Louisiana.

67. Fornell, *Galveston Era*, p, 130.

68. Goldin, *Urban Slavery*, pp. 115, 120, 123–129.

69. The data for the southern cities and total U.S. came from *ibid.*, pp. 56–57. The statistics for the southwestern towns were compiled from the manuscript census returns. U. S. Seventh Census, 1850, Schedule II: "Slave Inhabitants," Travis County, Texas, Galveston County, Texas, Pulaski County, Arkansas, Caddo Parish, Louisiana; U.S. Eighth Census, 1860, Schedule II: "Slave Inhabitants," Travis County, Texas, Galveston County, Texas, Pulaski County, Arkansas, Caddo Parish, Louisiana.

70. Galveston *Civilian and Gazette*, July 2, 1861; Houston *Tri-Weekly News*, July 22, Sep. 24, 1862, Feb. 4, March 14, 1863, Jan. 11, 24, 1864; Ballinger Diary, Jan. 6, April 14, Dec. 15, 1863; Richards, *Rivertown*, p. 73; Ted R. Worley, ed., "At Home in Confederate Arkansas: Letters from Pulaski Countians, 1861–1865," *Pulaski County Historical Society Bulletin* 2 (Dec. 1955), pp. 36–42.

71. Little Rock *Arkansas State Gazette*, July 4, 1863; Galveston Ordinance Book, 1857–1866, March 13, 1865, Office of the City Secretary, Municipal Building, Galveston; *Shreveport News*, April 20, 1865; Shreveport *South-Western*, Sep. 11, 1861; *Shreveport Weekly News*, Feb. 23, 1863.

72. Richards, *Rivertown*, p. 64; Little Rock City Council Records, C, No. 17, 1862; Houston *Galveston News*, July 2, 1862, Jan. 2, May 6, Oct. 28, Nov. 2, 1864;

Shreveport *South-Western*, Sep. 25, 1861, Oct. 21,1863; Robert L. Kerby, *Kirby Smith's Confederacy: The Trans-Mississippi South, 1863–1865* (New York, 1972), p. 256; *Shreveport News*, Sep. 6, 20, 1864.

73. Little Rock City Council Records, B, Jan. 19, 1861, C, Nov. 17, 1862; Kerby, *Kirby Smith's Confederacy*, pp. 256–257; Minutes of Trustees of Shreveport, B, pp. 434–435, 566, 571; Shreveport *South-Western*, Jan. 9, June 12, 1861; *Shreveport Daily News*, June 18, 1861; Hayes, "Galveston," pp. 615–616; Records of the Mayor's Office and Board of Aldermen of Austin, Nov. 20, Dec. 1, 4, 5, 1862, March 2, April 6, July 6, 1863, Office of the City Clerk, City Hall, Austin.

74. Records of Aldermen, Austin, June 27, 30, 1865; Galveston Ordinance Book, June 28, 1865.

75. Houston *Tri-Weekly News*, Feb. 12, 18, April 21, 1863, Oct. 24, 1864; Worley, ed., "At Home in Confederate Arkansas," pp. 36–41.

Human Property
The Black Slave in Harrison County, 1850–1860

RANDOLPH B. CAMPBELL

In the selection below, Randolph B. Campbell presents a well-researched local investigation of slavery, a microstudy that tests broad generalizations by delving into the primary sources of Harrison County, an area where slavery flourished. Indeed, by 1860 the chattels composed 58 percent of the county's population. About 60 percent of the white families in Harrison owned at least one slave. Such figures showed that the county was an atypical one in both Texas and in the larger South, but Campbell chose Harrison for that very reason—he had large numbers of owners and bondsmen who interacted, and he had many local primary sources to use in examining slavery at the local level, at the grassroots level. Above all, Campbell finds complexity in the chattels' work life and in their social utility. He asserts that the slave's humanity was the great flaw of the South's Peculiar Institution but that the slave's very humanness in some ways increased his or her worth as property.

*

HARRISON COUNTY provides an excellent setting for a study in microcosm of the black slave's role in antebellum Texas society. The federal censuses of 1850 and 1860 reported a larger population for this East Texas county than for any other in the state. There were 599 slaveholders in 1850 and 650 in 1860, which meant that in both census years approximately 60 percent of Harrison's white families owned at least one slave. There were 6,100 slaves reported in the first federal census of Harrison County taken in 1850. Ten years later the number stood at 8,726, an increase of 41 percent during the decade before the Civil War. Black slaves made up 52 percent of the county's total population of 11,822 in 1850 and 58 percent of the 15,001 people living there in 1860.[1]

Thus a majority of antebellum Harrison County's free families were slaveholders and a majority of its population were black slaves. This situation was not typical of either Texas or the South in the 1850s. Only 20 percent of families in the Lone Star State and 25 percent of all southern families held slaves in 1860. In the same year, slaves composed 30 percent of Texas's population and 32 percent of the population of all fifteen slave states and the District of Columbia.[2] Harrison County's advantages for a study of slavery in microcosm do not, therefore, depend on its being "typical." Instead, the large numbers of slaveholders and slaves in a limited area and the availability of good county records provide an opportunity to combine federal census materials and local government documents in a study small enough to be exhaustive in the use of statistical information and yet large enough to test significant ideas about slavery. Quantitative information from the federal censuses establishes the broad framework of slaveholding in Harrison County and provides evidence of the importance of slave labor there, while local records illustrate the social utility of the institution.[3]

Obviously slavery was a central fact in the existence of Harrison County before the Civil War. But what can be said of the slave's position and role in this society? In the first place, African American bondsmen in Harrison County were property, chattels personal whose conduct was subject to the discipline of their owner just as their labor and services were at his disposal. Slaves were given a few civil rights by Texas law—such as the right to trial by jury when charged with a crime greater than petty larceny—but they had no religious rights, no right to lawful marriage, and virtually no property rights. State law in the 1850s declared it illegal for an owner to make a contract with a slave allowing the latter to "hire his time" by paying a set price and then be free to negotiate his own labor contract with another employer. Under no circumstances could one slave be hired to another slave or to any "free person of color." In general slaves had no legally prescribed way to earn or otherwise win their freedom.[4]

Clearly Harrison County's slaves were property, and the laws of Texas provided definitions and guarantees in this area. Nevertheless, slaves were much more than simple chattels personal; they were also human beings with human intelligence and abilities. African American bondsmen represented a unique combination of the qualities of property and humanity, and this created a complexity in their role in slave society that must not be underestimated.

David Brion Davis's study, *The Problem of Slavery in Western Culture,* points out that the contradiction involved in holding men as things is believed to have produced tension in virtually all slave societies. Charles G. Sellers Jr. has argued that the conflict between slave-holding in the South and the liberal and Christian ideals for humanity espoused by most free Americans constituted the "travail of slavery." Indeed a major part of the Civil War crisis was the "suggestible" psychological state produced in southerners by the tensions of holding humans as property. Their struggle was not a clear-cut contest between slaveholders and nonslaveholders or proslavery and antislavery forces, but rather a more subtle internal conflict for those who faced the problems of conscience and belief involved in owning and controlling human beings defined as property. Ralph E. Morrow contended that much of the proslavery argument was not really aimed at its apparent targets such as the abolitionists and antislavery people. Instead it was intended to reassure those people who had no hostility to slavery and were committed to its preservation. For the South as a whole there is much evidence to support the argument that the contradictions of holding men as things resulted in internal psychological strain for many individual slaveholders.[5] Did the slave's peculiar situation as property and humanity create similar tensions for the free citizens of Harrison County?

Harrison County's slaveholders could not avoid the contradictions of their "Peculiar Institution." The slave's humanity was a fact not easily denied, and the constitution and laws of the state directed all Texans to remember it. The Constitution of 1845 called on the legislature to pass laws "which will oblige the owners of slaves to treat them with humanity." In fact, a new law was not necessary because "An Act Concerning Slavery" which had been passed in 1840 under the Republic of Texas was simply continued in effect after statehood. It outlawed unreasonable or cruel treatment and made the murder of a slave, or deliberate action causing a bondsman's death, a felony comparable to a similar act perpetrated against a white man. The Texas Supreme Court in the cases that came before it in the antebellum period, several of which began in Harrison County, was careful to read this law with emphasis on the slave as humanity rather than as property. Legislation, of course, also called for punishing the slave's criminal offenses as though committed by whites. Punishment, however, was either whipping or death, and eventually the legislature came to enact the ultimate legal recognition of the slave as humanity and property when in 1852 it passed "An Act to Indemnify the Owners for the Loss of Slaves Executed for Capital Offenses." The slave was human enough to be tried for his crimes and property enough to be paid for if destroyed.[6]

Many slaveholders in Harrison County did not need constitutional or legislative reminders that their slave property differed significantly from their other chattels personal such as cattle and horses. The county's estate and probate records from the antebellum period provide evidence of this fact in the many wills that conferred special status on individual slaves or groups of bondsmen. John P. Thompson's will of August 11, 1849, for example, referred to an "old favorite Negro man . . . whom I desire to maintain on the place with his mistress and to perform easy labor, but I do not wish him to be regarded as the property of anyone." J. M. Saunders directed his wife to provide five dollars per month to a black man named Henry, "said Negro at no time nor under any circumstances to be subject to sale." In 1853, J. J. Webster requested "that my Negroes be so distributed as to allot the families by families in the partition [of his estate] that members of the same family may remain together."[7] When William T. Weathersby's will freeing three of his slaves was contested by would-be heirs, his brother-in-law and executor, John L. Sherrod, successfully defended Weathersby's recognition of human dignity all the way to the Texas Supreme Court in 1854.[8]

Although the cases of Thompson, Saunders, Webster, and Weathersby were probably more typical than unusual, not every slaveholder in Harrison County was concerned with the humanity of his slaves.[9] Many wills directed the division and sale of slave property without any apparent regard for the African American family or individual. Agnes McKay, for example, directed in 1853 that her boy Andrew be reserved to serve her daughters until they were grown, at which time he was to be sold and the proceeds divided among the girls. The laws protecting slaves undoubtedly were not enforced to the letter, especially since bondsmen were hardly in a position to bring charges against their masters and could not testify in criminal actions except against other slaves and free blacks.[10] Yet the fact remained—the black slave was a human being and there is evidence that many slaveholders were very aware of that fact.

Did the slave's humanity, however, serve only to make him a property troublesome to the consciences of many owners, and ultimately of course, a property unacceptable in the civilized world? Perhaps slave property was valuable and socially useful in some ways precisely because it was human. This proposition may seem obvious at first glance, but it is not often considered.[11] If true, it adds a dimension to the story of the African American as a member of his society. He made the plantation system work, but he contributed much more than muscle for farm work. To provide evidence to support this idea, it is necessary to examine the variety of ways in which the slave was involved in the day to day economic affairs and social arrangements of antebellum Harrison County and the degree to which the slave's many roles depended on his humanity, and finally to consider what it meant to the master and the slave that the latter was recognized as a human in many aspects of the same institution that defined him as property.

The slave's most obvious role in the 1850s was as a supplier of labor for Harrison County's thriving agricultural economy ruled by King Cotton. It is difficult to imagine in the 1970s when there is only one gin operating in the county, but Harrison was among the major cotton producing areas in the Southwest in the years before the Civil War. According to the census of 1850, the 1849 crop of 4,560 bales was the second largest grown in any Texas county that year. Harrison's 1859 crop showed an increase of 366 percent to 21,231 bales. (Even then the county fell one spot to third in the state's cotton production.) While cotton was the main crop, it was not the sole concern of Harrison's farmers. The county's production of corn, for example, 377,902 bushels in 1849 and 647,732 bushels in 1859, ranked her first in the state in both years.[12]

Other statistics drawn from the censuses of 1850 and 1860 demonstrate how important the black slave was to agricultural production in Harrison County. Plantations and farms using slave workers controlled more than 90 percent of the improved acreage and represented approximately 90 percent of the cash value of the county's farms in 1850 and 1860. They produced 96 percent of the cotton in 1849 and 94 percent in 1859. The corresponding figures for corn production were 91 percent in 1849 and 88 percent in 1859. These figures are especially significant because slaveholding plantations and farms constituted only 76 percent of the county's agricultural units in 1850 and 68 percent in 1860. Nonslaveholding farmers owned a disproportionately small share of the valuable farm acreage and produced an equally small share of the important crops.[13]

Statistics on the value of real and personal property owned in Harrison County in 1850 and 1860 further indicate the importance of the slave to its economy. Slaveholding farmers, including those who owned farms and those who identified themselves as farmers but did not appear as landholders in the agricultural return, constituted 66 percent of the county's agricultural families in 1850. They owned 91 percent of all the real property listed as belonging to farmers. By 1860 this group had decreased to 63 percent of those who listed their occupation as farmer, but they still held 91 percent of the real property and 96 percent of the personal property claimed by the whole farming population.[14] Slaves themselves were the largest single item of personal property reported. These figures on agricultural production and property values indicate that slaveholders dominated the agricultural economy of antebellum Harrison County. The slave's productive capacity played a key part in creating this situation, although the causal connection between ownership of slaves and production is not proven here.

The black slave as agricultural laborer was cast primarily in the role of property. Typically his job was to work from daylight to dark at simple tasks that took advantage of his muscle power. His value generally depended on his capabilities as a field hand. A farm horse is valued on its working qualities and exploited in much the same fashion. Human qualities, however, contributed to the slave's value and potential in this role as laborer. The simplest task depended on the intelligence of the slave which permitted him to follow directions without constant supervision and guidance such as would have to be provided in working a horse. The use of one slave as a "driver" to keep the others working and enforce discipline with whippings was a common practice in Harrison County. Apparently some owners with large holdings avoided the expense of overseers by managing their own slaves with the aid of such "drivers." W. L. Sloan, according to one of his former slaves, demonstrated another more obvious way to use the slave's intelligence when he taught several bondsmen to read and write and used them to record work such as cotton picking in the field.[15] Thus even the role of agricultural laborer depended to some extent on the slave's human qualities, and some slaveholders found methods to allow fuller exploitation of the bondsman's potential in that area.

The African American slave's importance to the society of antebellum Harrison County did not end with his role as an agricultural laborer. Approximately 6 percent of the county's bondsmen in the 1850s apparently were not engaged in agriculture. Nonfarming slaveholders (109 in 1850 and 129 in 1860), who constituted slightly less than 20 percent of all slaveowners, held 364 bondsmen in 1850 and 584 in 1860. Living for the most part in the town of Marshall, these were generally small slaveholders (average of 3.34 slaves per owner in 1850 and 4.53 per owner in 1860) who pursued a wide variety of occupations. There were professional men including lawyers, doctors, ministers, and teachers;

tradesmen such as blacksmiths, tailors, printers, and carpenters; manufacturers including ginmakers and brickmakers; public officials such as judges and county clerks; and businessmen ranging from merchants and grocers to tavernkeepers and livery-stable operators. Certainly in some cases their slaves served only as household servants or personal servants for wives and children. Perhaps in a few cases the bondsmen were hired out or else used in agricultural pursuits in a fashion that did not show up in the federal census returns. It is difficult to imagine, for example, what other use W. J. Sorrelle, a Baptist minister, could have made of the seventeen slaves he owned in 1850. Apparently many of these nonfarming slaveholders employed their bondsmen in their occupations. Three examples from 1850 illustrate this possibility. G. B. Atkins, a brickmaker in Marshall, owned nine slaves, six of whom were males over eighteen years of age. J. P. Cooley, a tailor, owned one male slave over eighteen, and William P. Barrett, a grocer, held one adult male, one boy, and two girls.[16] No proof is available that these slaves and several hundred others like them assisted their owners in nonagricultural occupations, but very likely they did. Possibly some of these slaves possessed special skills. Clearly these occupations required intelligence and abilities not possessed by any other form of property.

Thus the slave provided agricultural and nonagricultural labor in antebellum Harrison County; beyond this he was thoroughly involved in the everyday social arrangements of the county's free population. The range of utility demonstrated by the slave is especially noteworthy when considering the nature of his role in society. In some cases his position was that of property pure and simple; in others, his humanity was plainly essential.

Tax records illustrate one way the slave figured heavily in his society albeit solely as a piece of property. The state of Texas and Harrison County naturally required sources of tax revenue to provide for public expenses, and slaves were by far the largest single item on the property tax rolls for the county in 1850 and 1860. For example, a sample of twelve of the largest slaveholders in the county in 1860 shows a total property valuation for tax purposes of $791,343 of which $557,360 or 71 percent was assessed on their slaves. Twelve small slaveholders (owning from one to nine slaves) were assessed $33,000 or 51 percent of their total property valuation of $64,359 on their slave property. State tax rates amounted to only one and one-quarter mills or .00125 cents on the dollar in 1860 so they do not seem burdensome by today's standards.[17] Nevertheless slaves were a major source of tax revenue.

Slaves were taxed as personal property; a riding horse would have been treated in precisely the same fashion. But it seems that the slave contributed to keeping tax rates low in a way possible only for a human. The Harrison County Commissioners Court Minutes for the 1850s indicate that while upkeep of the county's roads was a primary public concern, it cost local government little or nothing. The Commissioners Court simply appointed a citizen to be responsible for a particular section of road in his area and directed him to use his slaves and those of certain of his neighbors to do the work.[18] Individual responsibility and slave labor maintained most of the roads at no cost to the taxpayer. It was of course not unusual in free societies to have the citizens of an area "turn out" to maintain the roads, but the slave as human property provided a ready-made work force for the job in Harrison County.

The probate and estate records of Harrison County clearly demonstrate that the slave proved useful as a highly mobile means of conveying and distributing property in social arrangements such as marriage contracts, divorce decrees, and settlement of estates. The last will and testament of J. J. Webster, for example, probated in 1854, divided his estate into three shares of approximately $45,000 each in value for his son and the heirs of two daughters. To achieve an equitable distribution in this fashion, the son, J. B. Webster, received 29 slaves and 54 percent of the land while the two daughters' heirs received 37 and 34 slaves respectively and smaller shares of land. Stock and cash were then allocated to complete the distribution of property.[19] In this case the slave's humanity was largely unimportant, but, property in slaves was almost as handily divisible as stock or cash, and it was economically more feasible to divide it rather than land into small shares.

Slave property was usually distributed in some fashion in estate settlements, but in cases where a guardian or an administrator was appointed, the slave could be used over a period of time as an asset to the heirs. When Sheriff S. R. Perry was made administrator of the estate of S. J. Arnett in 1853, he apparently found it more profitable to hire out Arnett's slaves annually than to sell them. At the end of 1854, for example, he hired out seven slaves to the highest bidder for their services from January 2 to December 25, 1855, for a total of $431. The following year the same seven slaves hired for $549.20. Real property could have been rented in the same fashion, but there could not have been a comparable return from any other personal property left to a typical estate in the antebellum period.[20]

The Harrison County District Court Civil Minutes for January 17, 1851, show that when Mary Pridgen won a divorce from Wiley Pridgen the first step in their property settlement was the assignment of 29 slaves to her share. This case provides not only another example of slavery's usefulness in estate arrangements; it also suggests that the ownership of slave property could give women a degree of independence and security in Harrison County's agrarian society. The Texas Constitution of 1845 gave married females the right to hold real and personal property separate from the property of their husbands.[21] This meant that women could bring land and slaves to marriage and maintain separate ownership of them. In the event of divorce, they could take an important means of support with them from the marriage. Here the slave's human ability to work on his own was critical. The female left with hundreds of acres of land was none too secure unless adequate labor was available. When she had the land and the slaves to work it, she only needed to hire someone to direct them in producing a living.

Possession of slaves was, of course, similarly important to the security of the widowed female left with a family to support and no ability to work a farm herself. For example, John P. Thompson at his death in 1849 left his wife Elizabeth with eight children at home. He also left her a farm reported at 265 improved acres of land in the census of 1850 and a slave labor force that numbered 50 that same year. Although several of her children were grown, Elizabeth Thompson could not have produced her 1849 crops of 29 bales of cotton and 2,300 bushels of corn without slave labor. She might possibly have hired free labor, but probably the immediate expenses of operation would have been greater. Her slaves had the further advantage of being a readily negotiable, self reproducing capital investment.[22]

The case of Mrs. Nancy Beck provides an example of how the slave helped provide security for even a small farm operator. Isaac Beck died in 1850, leaving his wife and five children under twelve years of age with 70 acres of improved land and five young slaves. Ten years later Mrs. Beck still lived in Harrison County. From the census returns of 1860, it appears that she managed a farm of 100 improved acres worked by four slaves and produced 400 bushels of corn and five bales of cotton.[23] The slave's role in cases such as those of Elizabeth Thompson and Nancy Beck was the familiar one of agricultural worker, but no other type of property could supply intelligent labor with the same degree of utility for a female farm owner.

Women were only a small portion of Harrison County's slaveholders in 1850 and 1860. There were 48 female slaveholders in the county in 1850, and they owned 707 slaves. A decade later 52 women held 744 slaves. Females composed a very small percentage of all slaveholders in these years, but the security provided by slave property extended to many women who did not actually hold slaves in their names.[24]

The "Peculiar Institution" proved to be so flexible and adaptable to public and private needs that the black slave was thoroughly worked into the economic and social arrangements of Harrison County's society in the 1850s. Evidently, no form of nonhuman property could have proved equally useful in so many ways. Even the simple role of agricultural laborer depended to some extent on the slave's humanity. And slaveholders and slaveholding society at times employed arrangements that were based especially on his human qualities.

It is impossible to determine precisely how many slaveholders were bothered by the contradiction of holding people as things or how much tension was created by the institution. In the 1850s public statements casting unfavorable light on slavery were decidedly unpopular in Harrison County. The Marshall *Texas Republican*, edited by R. W. Loughery, was quick to label anyone who favored compromising in any way on the ultrasouthern position in the 1850s as a "submissionist." Editor Loughery was angrily surprised in 1856 to find the *Harrison Flag*, an American party paper, publishing a series of articles entitled "Texas— Dark and Bright Side" which included "domestic slavery" on the dark side. This betrayed, said the *Republican*, a "very decided squinting towards abolitionism."[25] Loughery had little to fear, however. In 1860, Editor John W. Barrett of the *Flag*, although he endorsed the moderate Constitutional Union party ticket of John Bell and Edward Everett, took great care to explain his support for the South and all southern institutions.[26]

Some slaveholders were well aware that their property was human and indicated their awareness in the special treatment of individual slaves in their wills. The County Commissioners Court demonstrated an interesting terminology in regularly referring to slaves as "hands." This may signify nothing, but it is clearly a reference to property with a word associated with humans. The constitution and laws of Texas demonstrated the free citizens' inability to think of the bondsman as property only, and the State Supreme Court regularly ruled in favor of protecting the slave from unreasonably harsh treatment in the antebellum period.[27] These recognitions of the slave's humanity, conscious or unconscious, would seem to indicate a problem of conscience for those who held men as things, but obviously the degree or effect of their sentiments cannot be positively established or measured.

The scarcity of records makes it difficult to say what recognition of the slave's humanity meant to the enslaved individual. Legally, it brought some degree of protection for his body and life although enforcement of the laws certainly was not perfect. Personally, it could mean special treatment for an old or especially favored bondsman or for a slave family. It might even mean that an owner would consider the psychological state of his workers and attempt to use good treatment as an inducement to good work. Dr. William Baldwin provided an unusual example of this approach. According to one of his former slaves, Baldwin kept a barrel of whiskey on his front porch and allowed slaves to get a drink on their way to the field. Still there was no guarantee that an individual owner would recognize his slaves' humanity. And the slave could hardly be secure in the knowledge that he was a human, let alone that he would be treated like one. Will Adams, born a slave in Harrison County in 1853, remembered years later that he had once remarked to his grandmother about how well their owners had treated them. He also remembered her answer: "Why shouldn't they—it was their money."[28]

The black slave was almost certainly a profit-producing part of Harrison County's antebellum society. This is not the place, however, to pursue the complicated and much-controverted question of the profitability of slavery. The matter of productivity and profitability is an important one, but it says little about the slave to differentiate him from any other piece of property. The African American was much more than a unit of capital investment and labor supply to Harrison County in the 1850s, and, although his humanity probably created tensions for many slaveholders, the African American's utility as a slave was frequently enhanced by his qualities as a human. Slavery might have disappeared had it been unprofitable, and its destruction would have been a simpler matter had the slave been white, but the institution's social utility extended beyond profitability and racial control. The Harrison County experience suggests that possibly Sellers and Morrow underestimated the complexity of the situation. The African American's humanity was the ultimate flaw of slavery, but, ironically, in some ways his capacities and contributions as a human only strengthened his bonds as property.

Notes

1. Statistics on slaveholders and slaves were compiled from microfilmed manuscript returns of the Seventh Census of the United States, 1850, Schedule 1, Free Inhabitants, and Schedule 2, Slave Inhabitants; and the Eighth Census of the United

States, 1860, Schedules 1 and 2. Hereinafter these manuscript returns on microfilm will be cited as Seventh Census, 1850, and Eighth Census, 1860, with appropriate schedule numbers. Total population figures are from United States Bureau of the Census, *Statistical View of the United States: A Compendium of the Seventh Census, 1850* (Washington, 1854), 314; U.S. Census Office, *Eighth Census of the United States: 1860. Population* (Washington, 1864), 485. My research relies primarily on the manuscript censuses, but in a few cases I used data from the published returns. Figures from these published returns often differ slightly from those I compiled from the manuscript censuses. For example, Bureau of the Census, *Statistical View of the United States, 1850*, p. 314, reports 6,213 slaves in Harrison County while I counted 6,190 from the manuscript returns. Minor discrepancies of this sort are to be expected when dealing with large amounts of quantitative historical data, and generally they are unimportant.

2. There were 76,781 families and 21,878 slaveholders in Texas in 1860. U.S. Census Office, *Eighth Census of the United States: 1860. Mortality and Miscellaneous Statistics* (Washington, 1866), 348–349; ibid., *Agriculture* (Washington, 1864), 247; ibid., *Population,* 486. Some families had more than one slaveholder, but the use of these figures to determine an approximate percentage of slaveholding families should be acceptable. The idea that only 25 percent of all southern families held slaves is generally accepted. See Kenneth Stampp, *The Peculiar Institution: Slavery in the Ante-Bellum South* (New York, 1956), 30–32.

3. Harrison County offers other advantages too. The size of slaveholdings ranged from the very small to the very large and slaves were used in a great variety of nonagricultural as well as agricultural pursuits. See notes 13 and 16.

4. This summary of the slave's legal position as property in Texas is drawn from Williamson S. Oldham and George W. White, *A Digest of the General Statute Laws of the State of Texas* (Austin, 1859). Sections pertinent to my paragraph are as follows: "Texas Constitution of 1895," 26; "Penal Code," 481, 521, 542–543, 559–562; "Code of Criminal Procedure," 640, 642, 670–673. Important statutes relative to slavery in Texas are found in H. P. N. Gammel (comp.), *The Laws of Texas, 1822–1897* (10 vols.; Austin, 1898), II, 345–346, 778–782, 1501–1504; III, 29, 911–912, 1502–1516; IV, 499–500, 947–949.

5. David Brion Davis, *The Problem of Slavery in Western Culture* (Ithaca, 1966), 60; Charles Grier Sellers Jr., "The Travail of Slavery," from Sellers (ed.), *The Southerner as American* (Chapel Hill, N.C., 1960), 40–71; Ralph E. Morrow, "The Proslavery Argument Revisited," *Mississippi Valley Historical Review,* XLVIII (June, 1961), 79–94.

6. Gammel (comp.), *Laws of Texas,* II, 345–346, 1296; III, 911–912; Oldham and White, *Digest of the Laws,* 561; A. E. Keir Nash, "The Texas Supreme Court and Trial Rights of Blacks, 1845–1860," *Journal of American History* LVIII (December,

1971), 622–642. Important legal cases rising from Harrison County, that are discussed in this article, included *Purvis* v. *Sherrod*, 12 Texas 140 and *Moore* v. *Minerva* 17 Texas 20. The quote from the constitution is found in Gammel (comp.), *Laws of Texas*, II, 345–346. Laws such as the "Act to Indemnify the Owners" were not unusual in the slave South.

7. Harrison County Estate Records (County Clerk's Office, Marshall), B, 266–267; E, 307–309; Harrison County Probate Minutes (*ibid.*), E, 353–354. Thompson's and Webster's wills are quoted from Estate Records B and E respectively. Saunders's will, made on January 2, 1861, is quoted from Probate Minutes.

8. *Purvis* v. *Sherrod*, 12 Texas 140. The slaves were freed, although they could not legally remain in Texas. Weathersby's will had provided funds to settle them outside the state.

9. My opinion that these wills were more typical than unusual is based on reading large numbers of such documents in the Harrison County courthouse.

10. Harrison County Estate Records, E, 333–334; Oldham and White, *Digest of the Laws*, 640.

11. The general idea is expressed in George R. Woolfolk, "Cotton Capitalism and Slave Labor in Texas," *Southwestern Social Science Quarterly*, XXXVII (June, 1956), 43–52. My research followed a number of ideas expressed in this article.

12. Seventh Census, 1850, Schedule 4, Agriculture; Eighth Census, 1860, Schedule 4, Agriculture. Comparisons with other counties are based on Bureau of the Census, *Statistical View of the United States, 1850*, 310–339, and Bureau of the Census, *Eighth Census: 1860, Agriculture*, 140–151. As in the case of slaves and slaveholders, my figures on agricultural production in Harrison County compiled from the manuscript census differ slightly from those in the published returns.

13. Seventh Census, 1850, Schedules 1, 2, and 4; Eighth Census, 1860, Schedules 1, 2, and 4. Harrison County farmers, regardless of the size of their slaveholdings, did not designate themselves as "planters" in the censuses of 1850 and 1860. The great majority (79 percent in 1850 and 70 percent in 1860) held fewer than 20 slaves. However, the mean slaveholding size was relatively large—12.9 slaves in 1850 and 16.2 in 1860—and there was a high degree of concentration of slave property in the hands of big slaveholders in both years. The nine men who owned more than 50 slaves in 1850 constituted only 2.3 percent of all slaveholders, and yet they held 9.7 percent of all slaves. In 1860 the 27 men who owned more than 50 slaves represented 5.7 percent of all slaveholders and owned 20.2 percent of the slaves. There was only one slaveholder, William T. Scott, who owned over 100 slaves in either census year. He held 103 in 1850 and 104 in 1860. The concentration of wealth and planter domination in Harrison County, especially as it related to agricultural production, is the subject of another study now in preparation.

14. Seventh Census, 1850, Schedules 1 and 4; Eighth Census, 1860, Schedules 1

and 4. Agricultural families include all those who were headed by a farmer whether they owned land or not. Personal property was not reported in the census of 1850.

15. Works Progress Administration, Federal Writers Project, *Texas Narratives, Slave Narratives: A Folk History of Slavery in the United States from Interviews with Former Slaves.* Vol. XVI in 3 parts (Washington, 1941), Part 1, pp. 191–192, 285; Part 2, pp. 195–197; Part 3, pp. 160–161.

16. Seventh Census, 1850, Schedules 1 and 2; Eighth Census, 1860, Schedules 1 and 2.

17. Records of the Comptroller of Public Accounts, Ad Valorem Tax Division: County Real and Personal Property Tax Rolls, 1836–1874, Harrison County, 1850, 1860. Microfilms of these manuscript tax records may he seen in the State Finance Building, Austin.

18. Harrison County Commissioners Court Minutes, 1850 (County Clerk's Office, Marshall), 205–207.

19. Harrison County Estate Records, E, 307–309.

20. Harrison County Probate Minutes, D, 348–349; Estate Record, F, 444; Estate Records, H, 540.

21. Harrison County District Court, Civil Minutes (District Clerk's Office, Marshall), 99–100, January 17, 1851; William M. McKinney, *Texas Jurisprudence* (45 vols.; San Francisco, 1929–1937), XXIII, 50.

22. Harrison County Estate Records, B, 266–267; Seventh Census, 1850, Schedules 1, 2, and 4. The importance of the slave as liquid capital is described in Woolfolk, "Cotton Capitalism," 43–44, 51–52.

23. Harrison County Probate Minutes, C, 30; Seventh Census, 1850, Schedules 1, 2, and 4; Eighth Census, 1860, Schedules 1, 2, and 4.

24. Seventh Census, 1850, Schedules 1 and 2; Eighth Census, 1860, Schedules 1 and 2. Slaveownership by females may have been underreported in the census due to combining by the enumerator of the slaves held by family members under the name of the head of the household.

25. *Texas Republican* (Marshall), July 19, 1856.

26. *Harrison Flag* (Marshall), August–December, 1860, passim.

27. Harrison County Commissioners Court Minutes, 1850, pp. 205–207, and throughout the 1850s; Nash, "Texas Supreme Court and Trial Rights of Blacks," 622, 630–631, 639.

28. *Texas Narratives*, Part 1, 1–3; Part 4, pp. 89–91. The quote is from Part 1, p. 1.

Emancipation and the Black Family
A Case Study in Texas

JAMES M. SMALLWOOD

Emancipation brought great changes in the family life of the ex-slaves; those changes included the legalization of black marriages by Congress in 1865. The Freedmen's Bureau applied the law in Texas when its agents entered the state later that same year. Bureau agents also acted as social workers for black families. They tried to help African Americans find lost family members; they encouraged couples to stay together and to remain in monogamous relationships, threatening fines and jail terms for violating marriage vows; they also forced men who left children destitute to pay child support; they punished fornicators, especially if both races were involved; and they tried to force white men to leave both freed women and girls alone and established heavy fines for white men who raped black women or girls. The black schools and churches also encouraged African American couples to stay together by stressing the virtues of monogamy, sobriety, and responsibility. The majority of families became more stable after a brief time of chaos wherein some slave-days mates dissolved their family ties, especially if one partner had been forced on the other.

James Smallwood uses material drawn from the 1870 census to demonstrate that in just the short span of five years living in freedom, most black families had become stable. Indeed, most indicators of that stability illustrated that black marriages and families compared favorably with those in the white community.

*

IN TRADITIONALIST historiography of the Reconstruction Era, myth and lore sometimes replaced the truth. This was often the case when scholars examined the evolution of the black community and, more specifically, the black family. Usually considered only in passing because both white and African American scholars had little interest in the black history *per se*, the black family remained a clouded enigma. Myths accepted as truth by Anglo historians abounded. Some scholars presented pictures of black marriages that became unstable because men neglected their responsibility to wives and children and left their homes. Thus, in this view, the matriarchy bred by slavery continued to develop. Many blacks, as the myth continued, would not work. Men left their families destitute, preferring to spend their time in idleness, in gaming, or in wandering over the countryside, presumably looking for handouts and new women. Some early scholars blamed the presumed condition of the black family on the inherent character of the freed-people. In the absence of a controlling institution such as slavery, disintegration of family and community represented a logical pattern. Others, to a degree more enlightened, held that the nature of antebellum slavery explained the weak structure of the black family.[1] Neither view is tenable, however, as this study, using data from select Texas counties, will demonstrate. We further hope here to be able to present a more accurate picture of the little understood black family as it emerged from bondage.

Emancipation after the Civil War brought changes in the family life of black Texans. One apparent trend, the rapid disintegration of some families because one of the mates desired a new partner, proved to be a temporary one.[2] Although some whites castigated freedpeople for weaknesses of character and morality, other factors, most of them rooted in slavery, explained the disruption of black families. Some form of family life always existed in slavery, but family structure remained weak. In Texas, as in all southern states, many slaveholders allowed the separation of families whenever it proved profitable. A few owners forced compulsory breeding upon slave women. Others forced blacks, men and women alike, to mate quickly and gave them little time to be selective. This practice increased the likelihood of unhappy unions. To produce more offspring, still other owners encouraged frequent mate changes. Moreover, slave marriages had no legal base, and owners recognized slave "marriages" only as long as it suited their whim. Miscegenation also strained family ties. It often left psychological if not physical scars on black women as well as the men who were powerless to protect their wives and daughters. Children suffered because their day care often evolved upon a "nanny" while the slaveholders sent their real mothers back to the fields. Only at night in the quarters could couples and parents adopt traditional roles that would have been expected of free people (Smallwood, 1974: 289–298; New Orleans Tribune, 1869; Barr, 1973: 13–38; Blassingame, 1972: 77–79).

In some cases the marital behavioral patterns and values forced upon bondsman by slaveholders extended into the post-war period. The white community's refusal to treat slave unions with the same reverence as Anglo marriages affected new freedmen. Some blacks who had more than one partner during slave times placed a premium on pleasure, not responsibility, and believed that frequent change was normal. Blocked from advancement and unable to express their worth in other ways, sexual prowess and conquests became "a highly respected avenue to status" (Blassingame, 1972: 85). Furthermore, black men and women developed fewer inhibiting sexual guilt complexes than whites because, unlike most Anglos, they had not been "enslaved" by a "puritanical [sexual] code" (Blassingame, 1972: 83).

References to illicit relations and "fornication" sometimes became a matter of semantics as freedmen applied the definition of "marriage" that they had learned in slave times. For some blacks, "marriage" still consisted of jumping over the broomstick and then living together. Equally, for some "divorce" consisted simply of leaving the old mate and choosing another. The breakup of many slave unions is explicable because, once emancipated, many people who had been forced to endure unhappy, perhaps forced, slave unions chose a new mate at the first opportunity (Slave Narratives, 1941; Hunter, 1922; Cotton, 1939: 5, 25; Smallwood, 1975: 44).

As had happened in the antebellum period, the actions of some whites undermined the stability of the black family. Many Anglo males still believed that they could take liberties with black women. Frequently, freedmen lodged rape charges against whites. In other instances whites used economic rather than physical pressure to force intimate relations with freedwomen. Threatening blacks with the loss of their jobs if they complained, some employers openly conducted affairs with the wives and daughters of black men.[3]

The Anglo practice of forcefully separating black children from their parents obviously sped the process of family disintegration. Possibilities of sexual exploitation and a cheap source of labor motivated whites to gain control of black minors by refusing to free them when their parents were freed, exploiting apprenticeship laws, or simply resorting to kidnapping. In many areas county judges allowed children to be apprenticed without consent of the individuals or their parents, even though the parents adequately provided for their children's welfare.[4]

Although these factors thus weakened black family ties, we find many countervailing forces working to strengthen the black family after emancipation—forces that finally dominated. Even in slave times black family life always existed, subject to the interests or whims of slaveholders. After emancipation, which imposed at least some limits to white control over black institutions, family ties became stronger. Important for the self-respect of freedmen, the United States Congress legalized slave marriages in March of 1865, and the Freedmen's Bureau applied this law to Texas one year later. Bureau policy recognized as married any blacks who previously had lived together. Others wishing to marry would, like whites, secure a license and take vows in either civil or religious ceremonies.[5]

In addition to enforcing congressional action that legalized black marriages, the bureau helped strengthen the black family in yet other ways. Most local agents worked tirelessly to secure the release of those adults and children whom whites held illegally. They also acted as marital counselors. With threats of fines and jail sentences, agents impressed upon freedmen the virtues of monogamous relationships. Local agents also ordered men who left children destitute to begin supporting them, made males responsible for breach of promise and children born out of wedlock, and punished fornicators, especially if both races were involved. In many instances when whites used economic pressure to sexually exploit black women, agents warned employers to stay away from freedwomen. When forceful rape occurred agents ordered Anglos to pay damages of up to $150 per offense when blacks could secure no redress in white courts. Such strong action regulating sexual indiscretions, duplicated by various agents throughout the state, helped reduce incidents of adultery and miscegenation and thus strengthened black family ties.[6]

Black schools and the newly emerging black churches also helped strengthen family structure. School teachers included morality lessons in their day, night, and Sabbath classes and left African Americans with definite impressions of how free people "should" behave. Likewise, both black and white preachers stressed sobriety, monogamy, and responsibility, while condemning vices that might disrupt families. Although they risked retribution that included assassination, some teachers and preachers used their community positions to investigate conditions of apprenticeships. In the uncovered evidence of illegal apprenticeship or mistreatment of children, official investigations followed that sometimes resulted in returning black children to their parents.[7]

Usually blacks needed instruction in morality less than Anglos supposed. After a brief period of flux during which ex-slaves left partners with whom they had been united in unhappy, forced "marriages," black families grew more stable. Most African Americans strongly desired to "do the right thing" and thereby to prove that they were worthy of freedom (*New Orleans Tribune*, 1869). Certainly sample census statistics suggest that the black family in Texas had achieved a remarkable degree of stability by 1870, and comparisons of data on black families and white families reveal far more similarities than differences.

Census data taken in 1870 from three Texas counties provide a profile of the black family as it emerged from slavery. Rural areas were chosen for this study because most blacks were, and would for decades continue to be, tied to the land. Moreover, samples were taken that represent different racial balances and different geographical regions of the state: Matagorda County in the southern part of the state, Smith County in the eastern, and Grayson County in the northeastern give a cross section of the population. The data used in this report were gathered by sampling every other white household and every third black household in Matagorda County (population: 1,753 whites and 2,373 blacks), every fifth Anglo household and every third African American household in Smith County (population: 9,401 whites and 7,131 blacks), and every tenth white and every other black household in Grayson County (population: 14,387 Anglos and 1,906 freedmen). The survey includes at total of 1,194 households with a population of 6,306 people. All residents were classified as members of all-black, all-white, or mixed households.

In samples for all three counties the size of black households, which often included more than one family, remained slightly below the average size of the white households, which also usually included more than one family. Similarly, family units themselves remained somewhat smaller in the African American community (Tables 1 and 2).

The average number of people in mixed households proved to be higher than the averages in either all-black or all-white households, a statistic explained by the fact that in most cases black servants joined already sizeable white families to work for them as domestics or, in fewer cases, as farm laborers (Table 3).

The data in Table 4 indirectly contradict theories proposing the historical instability of black families: A higher percentage of blacks than Anglos were married (as of the census year 1870), as indicated by the finding that a smaller percentage of unmarried adults lived in black families than in white families.

Table 1*

**Comparison of All-White and All-Black Households,
with Sample Statistics from Three Texas Counties (Mixed Households Excluded)**

	Matagorda County		Smith County		Grayson County		Totals and averages for all three counties	
	White	*Black*	*White*	*Black*	*White*	*Black*	*White*	*Black*
Households surveyed	147	149	203	230	207	196	557	575
Population surveyed	813	698	1148	1109	1161	890	3122	2787
Average number of people per household	5.53	4.69	5.65	4.82	5.61	5.00	5.61	4.85

*The data in all the tables were drawn from the Manuscript Census Returns, 1870,
Population Schedules, Matagorda County, Smith County, Grayson County, Texas.

Table 2

Comparison of Individual Family Units and Children per Couple,
with Sample Statistics from Three Texas Counties

	Matagorda County		Smith County		Grayson County		Totals and averages for all three counties	
	White	Black	White	Black	White	Black	White	Black
Couples surveyed	141	131	179	179	162	170	482	480
Children enumerated	374	237	535	471	445	522	1354	1230
Average number of children per couple	2.65	1.81	2.99	2.63	2.75	3.07	2.81	2.56

Table 3

Men, Women, and Children in Mixed Households

	Matagorda County		Smith County		Grayson County		Totals and averages for all three counties	
	White	*Black*	*White*	*Black*	*White*	*Black*	*White*	*Black*
Total mixed households	37		9		16		62	
Persons in mixed households	147	90	43	16	72	29	262	135
Average number of people in mixed households	6.40		6.55		6.31		6.40	
Percent of blacks in mixed households	37.97		27.12		28.71		34.01	
Percent of whites in mixed households	62.03		72.88		71.29		65.99	

Table 4

Comparison of Married and Unmarried 18-Year-Olds and Older
in White and Black Households, with Sample Statistics from Three Texas Counties

	Matagorda County		Smith County		Grayson County		Totals and averages for all three counties	
	White	*Black*	*White*	*Black*	*White*	*Black*	*White*	*Black*
Married 18-year-olds or older	250	264	374	374	369	384	993	1022
Unmarried 18-year-olds or older	113	86	192	192	195	156	500	434
Percent of unmarried 18-year-olds and older	31.73	24.57	33.92	33.92	34.57	28.89	33.49	29.81

A look at another group of data goes far in dispelling the myth, still persistent in some circles, that females headed many more black households than Anglo households. In all three sample counties percentages of black households headed by women remained relatively close to that of whites, with the average for all three counties running only slightly higher in the black community, 16.87 percent, than in the Anglo community, 15.80 percent (Table 5).

Similarities between the white and black family structure thus dominates the sample statistics, but differences are also found. Although regional variations proved to be great, economic considerations forced far more black women and children to work. Whereas approximately 1 percent of the white women worked outside the home, black women working ranged from a high of 58.20 percent in Smith County to a low of 16.26 percent in Grayson County. Likewise, many more black children worked than their Anglo counterparts (Table 6).

The superior economic position of the Anglo community is confirmed by inspecting the 1870 Manuscript Census Returns. A majority of whites in Smith and Grayson counties owned their own farms. In Matagorda County property-owning farmers and stock raisers dominated the economic life of their community. In the black community, however, most heads of households—88 percent in the three sample counties—labored as farm hands. Freedmen owned less than $4,500 in real property, and the estate of a black lawyer in Grayson County accounted for $2,000 of that total. Overall, less than 31 percent of the black heads had personal property worthy of census notation whereas almost 85 percent of the Anglo heads of households held some personal property.

This survey would suggest that by 1870 the black family in Texas had acquired a remarkable degree of stability. Excepting the difference noted about such as the high percentage of black women and children working and varied occupational patterns based largely along racial lines, the black family closely resembled the white. Households and individual families were approximately the same size, with about the same percentage headed by males. While Blassingame (1972: 77–79; 1973: 79–105) has already noted that the tendency toward matriarchy in slave households was not as strong as some scholars had previously supposed, this study confirms that the trend toward patriarchy evolved into the norm in the African American community in Reconstruction Texas, as men headed most black households. Legalization of marriages along with the actions of well-intentioned bureau agents, preachers,

Table 5

**Female-Headed Households and Number of Children in Each
(Mixed Households Excluded), with Sample Statistics from Three Texas Counties**

	Matagorda County		Smith County		Grayson County		Totals and averages for all three counties	
	White	*Black*	*White*	*Black*	*White*	*Black*	*White*	*Black*
Total number of households surveyed	147	149	203	230	207	196	557	575
Percentage of households that were female-headed	4.29	14.76	17.73	16.60	14.98	18.36	15.80	16.87
Average number of children in female-headed households	2.90	2.55	3.58	3.38	3.19	3.50	3.40	3.24

Table 6

Women and Children Working in All-White and All-Black Households

	Matagorda County		Smith County		Grayson County		Totals for all three counties	
	White	*Black*	*White*	*Black*	*White*	*Black*	*White*	*Black*
Women 18 years old and older not working	194	110	262	107	267	206	723	423
Women 18 years old and older working at jobs other than in their homes	2	85	3	149	3	40	8	274
Percent of women working	1.02	43.59	1.13	58.20	1.11	16.26	1.09	39.31
Female children 10 to 17 years old not working	92	42	130	15	136	122	358	179
Female children 10 to 17 years old working	3	43	1	92	2	10	6	145
Percent of female children working	3.16	50.59	.80	85.98	1.45	8.20	1.65	44.75
Male children 10 to 17 years old not working	64	27	53	3	138	101	255	131
Male children 10 to 17 years old working	42	38	103	99	14	24	159	161
Percent of male children working	39.62	58.46	66.03	97.59	9.21	19.20	38.40	55.13

and teachers, both black and white, helped stabilize the black family. In addition, most freedmen apparently had strong familial instincts—at least as strong as their white counterparts.

The question of black family stability and its similarity to the white family is not only important in itself but is also important to the interpretations of twentieth-century American history as well. As scholars such as Peter Kolchin (1972) point out, a generation of historians and sociologists have in part blamed "slave patterns" for the breakdown of the modern, urban, ghetto-dwelling black family. Yet as Kolchin suggests—and this study supports—blacks overcame many of the obstacles to stable family development as early as 1870 (see also Billingsley, 1968: 48–71). Twentieth-century ghetto disorientation probably should be explained less in terms of slave heritage and more in terms of the particular and total ghetto environment.

Notes

1. See Coulter (1947: 47–69) and Frazier (1939: 62–267). The recent study by Fogel and Engerman (1974, Vol. I: 5, 84–85, 127–128, 142–143) goes far in revising the traditional view of the slave family, which was found to be much more stable than previously supposed. Yet it is too early to accept uncritically the findings of Fogel and Engerman. Theirs was a path-breaking, significant study, but their methodology and hence their conclusions have been widely challenged. See, for example, Gutman (1975: 53–227). This book-length review article examines *Time on the Cross* in an almost microscopic way; Gutman takes issue with most of the book's conclusions and urges Fogel and Engerman to refine their methods.

2. For examples of the disintegration of some black families see Complaint, August 20, 1867, Austin Complaint Book, Vol. 52; Sub-Assistant Commissioner, Austin, Texas, Byron Porter to William Sinclair, July 11, 1866, *Letters Sent*, Vol. 100; W. B. Pease to E. Miller, February 18, 1867, *Letters Sent*, Vol. 102; Complaint, July 26, 1866, Houston Complaint Book, Vol. 109; Sub-Assistant Commissioner, Houston, Texas, John George to Texas Assistant Commissioner, May 8, 1867; Assistant Commissioner, Texas, Bureau of Refugees, Freedmen, and Abandoned Lands, Record Group 105, National Archives, Washington, D.C. (hereafter abbreviated BRFAL, RG 105, NA).

3. Complaints, December 25, 30, 1865, Houston Complaint Book, Vol. 109; W. Pease to [?] Shanks, Pease to [?] Beasley, May 16, 1867, *Letters Sent*, Vol. 102; Sub-Assistant Commissioner, Houston, Texas, Complaints, August 24, 28, 1867, Austin Complaint Book, Vol. 52; Sub-Assistant Commissioner, Austin, Texas, A. G. Malloy

to J. P. Richardson, Monthly Report, October 31, 1867, *Letters Sent,* Vol. 134; Sub-Assistant Commissioner, Marshall, Texas, BRFAL, RG 105, NA.

4. On family separation and illegal apprenticeships after emancipation, see, for example, James Oakes to James Kirkman, Monthly Report, July 31, 1867; Richardson to A. M. Bryant, September 27, 1867, Clarence Mauck to S. Starr, April 24, 1868, *Letters Sent,* Vol. 49; Sub-Assistant Commissioner, Austin, Texas, Charles E. Culver to J. Kirkman, August 15, 1867, *Letters Sent,* Vol. 78; Sub-Assistant Commissioner, Cotton Gin, Texas, BRFAL, RG 105, NA.

5. Circular no. 9, March 23, 1866, Special and General Orders, 1865–1869, Vol. 9, Assistant Commissioner, Texas, BRFAL, RG 105, NA.

6. Instances of the attempts of bureau agents to help stabilize the black family are plentiful, but see especially James Hutchinson to J. Kirkman, Monthly Report, April 30, 1867, *Letters Sent,* Vol. 78; Sub-Assistant Commissioner, Columbia, Texas, W. Pease to E. Miller, February 18, March 28, 1867, *Letters Sent,* Vol. 102; Porter to William Sinclair, July 11, 1866, *Letters Sent,* Vol. 100; Sub-Assistant Commissioner, Houston, Texas, BRFAL, RG 105, NA.

7. See Complaint, September 29, 1869, Post of Austin, "Report of Scouts, Indian Depredations, and Crimes," Fifth Military District, 1867–1870, RG 393, NA.

References

Barr, Alwyn. 1973. *Black Texans: A History of Negroes in Texas, 1528–1971* (Austin: Jenkins Publishing Company).

Blassingame, John W. 1972. *The Slave Community: Plantation Life in the Antebellum South* (New York: Oxford University Press).

———. 1973. *Black New Orleans, 1860–1880* (Chicago: University of Chicago Press).

Billingsley, Andrew. 1968. *Black Families in White America* (Englewood Cliffs, N.J.: Prentice-Hall).

Cotton, Walter F. 1939. *History of the Negroes of Limestone County from 1860 to 1939* (Mexia, Texas: News Print Company).

Coulter, E. Merton. 1947. *The South During Reconstruction, 1865–1877* (Baton Rouge: Louisiana State University Press).

Fogel, Robert W., and S. L. Engerman. 1974. *Time on the Cross: The Economics of American Negro Slavery,* 2 vols. (Boston: Little, Brown and Company).

Frazier, E. Franklin. 1939. *The Negro Family in the United States* (Chicago: University of Chicago Press).

Gutman, Herbert. 1975. "The World Two Cliometricians Made," *Journal of Negro History* 60 (June): 53–227.

Hunter, Francis L. 1922. "Slave Society on the Southern Plantation," *Journal of*

Negro History 7 (January): 1–10.

New Orleans Tribune. 1869. (February 26).

Slave Narratives. 1941. Statements of Sam Jones Washington and Fannie Brown, "The Slave Narratives: A Folk History of Slavery in the United States from Interviews with Former Slaves," Texas Narratives, 16 (Washington, D.C.: Works Progress Administration): 138, 155.

Smallwood, James M. 1974. "Black Texans During Reconstruction," (unpublished Ph.D. dissertation, Texas Tech University): 289–298.

———. 1975. *Century of Achievement: Blacks in Cooke County, Texas* (Gainesville: American Revolution Bicentennial Committee).

In Search of the Black Cowboy in Texas

MICHAEL N. SEARLES

In the next selection, Michael N. Searles presents an original essay that traces the genesis of black cowboys back to Africa. Particularly in West Africa, black people learned to handle both horses and cattle. In the New World, they worked cattle in South America, in the West Indies, and in Mexico. Some Africans who were brought to America in chains were put to work as cowboys during the colonial era, especially in the South. Slave cowboys associated their work with freedom, for they usually had more independence than other chattels in whatever setting, urban-rural or plantation-farm. Searles goes on to chronicle the evolution of the African American cowboy. Despite the association of black cowboys with freedom, discrimination did exist. Cattlemen usually gave their dark-skinned cowboys the dirtiest, most menial work. Despite such handicaps, African Americans who knew cattle and horses abounded in western Texas and western Oklahoma, and they participated in many of the "long drives" to faraway railheads. Searles chronicles the lives of several of them.

*

THE WORDS "black cowboys" are an oxymoron for much of the general public even with their inclusion in scholarly books, bibliographies, anthologies, and popular accounts generated over the past years.[1] The limited circulation of books on black cowboys may be one reason that a knowledgeable audience is so small. There are a great many Americans who have never seen a black man in the role of a cowboy in life or in literature. It has been only recently that western fiction has recognized black cowboys, and it was not until the 1950s that they were portrayed as legitimate characters on the silver screen.[2]

Selective black audiences were presented with a touch of the Old West in the late 1930s and early 1940s when Herb Jeffries blazed the trail in *Harlem on the Prairie, Harlem Rides the Range,* and *The*

Bronze Buckaroo. These movies were big hits with African Americans; however, they had a surreal quality since all the characters were black. A West peopled with all black folk may have given credence to a West peopled with no black folk, since an all-black West was not credible, even to a black audience.

The connection among black men, horses, and cattle began in Africa and spread to the Americas during the colonial period. Africans and Indians were often selected as cowboys in North and South America.[3] Peter H. Wood, who chronicled the history of blacks in South Carolina from 1670 to 1739, argues that African expertise developed the cattle industry in that state.[4] In South Carolina and Georgia, it became common practice to advertise and sell land, cattle, and a Negro with knowledge of tending cattle in a single package.

The history of black cattle tending in South America, the West Indies, and Mexico has been explored and presented by Richard W. Slatta and Terry G. Jordan. Both scholars supported the idea of active African involvement in cattle raising in the West Indies, South America, and Mexico. Concurrent with African participation in tending cattle was an expertise with horses. The ability with horses demonstrated by blacks caused some to believe that it was instinctual. Frederick Remington was neither the first nor the last to express this sentiment. In a turn-of-the-century magazine article, he stated that black cavalrymen carried on conversations with their horses and that it was perfectly apparent that the horses understood what they said.[5]

Black cowboys were found in states east and west of the Mississippi River; however, Texas claimed the largest concentration. In 1860, slaves and free blacks exceeded 30 percent of the Texas population with more than 183,000 people. Following the end of slavery, the numbers of African Americans in Texas continued to grow while steadily declining as a percentage of the total population. The large number of cattle in Texas offered opportunities for enterprising men to turn a profit. In selected Texas counties, the cattle to population ratio was higher than 40 to 1.[6] In those counties, especially in the southeast, black cowboys were the cowboys of choice for some ranchers.

A substantial number of slaves crossing the Red and Sabine Rivers was put into direct contact with cattle. In some cases, it was a first contact and for others it was a continuation of a tradition that extended back to Africa.[7] Sam Jones Washington, a slave of rancher Sam Young who lived along the Colorado River in Wharton County, Texas, spoke about cowboying as a slave and a freedman. Washington's words, a part

of the Slave Narratives of the Works Progress Administration (WPA),
suggest that some blacks associated the cowboy life with freedom.

> I first ran errands, and then massa larn me to ride, as soon as I could sit
> a horse. Then I stayed out with de cattle most of the time, and I was
> tickled. I sure liked to ride and rope those cattle, and massa always fixed
> me up with good clothes and a good horse and a good saddle. I stayed
> there till long after surrender.[8]

Like Sam Jones Washington, a number of other freedmen stayed on
their former masters' ranches and farms after surrender and throughout
the nineteenth century. Many of them did cattle work as long as it provided them with a living, but as the cattle business waned, they turned
to farming, sheep raising, service jobs, factory work, railroad work, and
the military. Sam Jones Washington typifies those men who turned
their hands to farming.

It is in the life of Washington that we confront the difficulty of finding the black cowboy. Many men labored for as many as twenty or
more years as cowboys, and then as a result of the economy, ill health,
or age left cowboy work with little evidence of their involvement.
While these cowboys had local notoriety, they were often ignored or
forgotten when town, county, and regional histories were written.

Much of what we know about these nearly anonymous black cowboys comes from the biographical sketches collected by the WPA. Tom
Mills spoke of his lifelong commitment to the cowboy life as follows:

> When I got to workin' for myself, it was cow work. I done horse back
> work for fifty years. Many a year passed that I never missed a day bein'
> in the saddle. I stayed thirteen years on one ranch. The first place was
> right below Hondo City.[9]

In his years as a cowboy, he saw the trails and recounted many of the
experiences reported by other black cowboys. He was expected to do
his job well and when white cowboys fouled up to keep it to himself.
Mills worked on other ranches delivering cattle down to the Rio
Grande until he finally quit ranching and became a stock farmer.

Black cowboys were expected to do the roughest, most dangerous
work and to do it without complaint. They often competed directly
with white southerners who had little love for black men. Some whites
had lost their land and possessions as a result of the Civil War, while

others remembered that slavery had excluded them from all but the meanest work. The decision to make slavery the centerpiece of southern economy and life was not a choice made by the slave population, but the freedman was a visible reminder of white degradation.

There are a number of instances where black cowboys were run off by white southerners whose hatred for blacks was palpable. While black cowboys were given opportunities to work, it was often provided by cattlemen who once owned slaves. Former slave owners continued the patterns of paternalism that existed during the antebellum period. Owners, foremen, and trail bosses sometimes forced white cowboys to accept the presence of black cowboys and while white cowboys were not generally free to shoot blacks, they made sure they did the meanest work.

In recollecting about black cowboys, John M. Hendricks, a well established cattleman made the following statement:

> They [black cowboys] did as much as possible to place themselves in the good graces of the [white] hands. This most often took the form of "topping," or taking the first pitch out of the rough horses of the outfit as they stood saddled, with backs humped, in the chill of the morning, while the [white] boys ate their breakfast. It was not unusual for one young negro to "top" a half a dozen hard-pitching horses before breakfast. . . . It was the negro hand who usually tried out the swimming water when a trailing herd came to a swollen stream, or if a fighting bull or steer was to be handled, he knew without being told it was his job.[10]

While more was expected of black cowboys, not every experience was a negative one. Some white cowboys formed friendships with black cowboys and, at least on the trail, worked and lived in relative equality.

Black cowboys seemed to enjoy life on the range, but it required a toughness of mind and spirit. One of the ways black cowboys tried to ensure themselves a job was to prove daily their worth to the boss and their fellow cowboys. In town after town in all regions of the West, black cowboys, broncobusters, and horse handlers gained reputations for being "the best cowboys to ever straddle a horse." Such stories were repeated in cowboy memoirs and by professional writers and prominent cattlemen of the West.

Upon hearing about the death of Bose Ikard, Charles Goodnight, whose name was synonymous with the cattle business in West Texas, had a monument erected with the following marker:

> Served me four years on the Goodnight-Loving Trail, never shirked duty
> or disobeyed an order, rode with me in many stampedes, participated in
> three engagements with Comanches, splendid behavior.[11]

Ikard was more than an average cowboy and was given many important
responsibilities. According to J. Evetts Haley, Goodnight's biographer,
Ikard served as Goodnight's detective, banker on the trail, and an all-
around cowboy. Haley further states that Goodnight extolled Ikard's
character with the extraordinary statement: "I have trusted him farther
than any living man."

Colonel Zack Miller lionized Bill Pickett, the man who invented
the rodeo sport of bulldogging and brought fame and fortune to the
Miller Brothers 101 Ranch Real Wild West Show. Colonel Miller wrote
a poem eulogizing Pickett's virtues shortly after his death. The poem
entitled "Old Bill is Dead" paid Bill *the supreme compliment of negat-
ing his color* [writer's emphasis] with the line "Bill's hide was black but
his heart was white." Colonel Miller expressed his sentiment with
great feeling and sincerity with no thought that his expression de-
meaned the man honored.[12]

George W. Littlefield, a prominent Texas cattleman, banker, and
philanthropist maintained a life-long relationship with black cowboy
Addison Jones. Old Add, or "Nigger Add" as he was generally known,
cowboyed for the Littlefield Ranch most of his life and broke in many
of the white and black cowboys who worked there. His ability handling
horses, counting cattle, and identifying ear marks and brands prompted
N. Howard (Jack) Throp, a cowboy and writer/songwriter to memorialize Add with a poem entitled "Whose Old Cow?"[13]

The list of notable black cowboys does not end with Bose Ikard, Bill
Pickett, and Addison Jones. Many white cattlemen and cowboys
praised black cowboys like Matthew "Bones" Hooks, Robert Lem-
mons, James Kelly, Jim Perry, Louis Powers, and Richard "Bubba"
Walker.[14] In small towns and on ranches throughout the West, white
cowboys recognized the skill and ability of black cowboys. Even today
in small hamlets and towns far off the interstates, old men sit outside
cafes and stores and talk about a particular black cowboy who could
ride anything he could throw his legs over.

Joseph H. Proctor, Ol' Proc, was such a man. He began his life on a
plantation in Burnett, Texas. He later trailed cattle from Texas to
Wyoming and Montana. He decided, after several trips, to stay in Montana, where he worked for a number of ranches. His abilities with a lar-

iat and with horses brought him great respect and admiration. When he died on July 29, 1938, the *Forsyth Time-Journal* wrote his memorial on its front page. The *Time-Journal* celebrated Proctor's life and made numerous references to his skills as a cowboy and his sterling character. It ended the lengthy tribute with words appropriate for any cattle baron or leading town citizen.[15]

Montana cowboy poet Wallace McRae wrote the poem "Ol' Proc" as a tribute to Joe Proctor, whose exploits were sung by McRae's grandfather and neighbors when Wallace was just a boy. The last stanza of his tribute poem indicates the presence and anonymity of black cowboys.

> *I couldn't wait to meet Mr. Proc,*
> *Whose peers all praised his ways with stock.*
> *But when his calloused hand gripped mine, surprise hit me in waves.*
> *Those old cowboys who cut no slack*
> *Deemed it unimportant Proc was black,*
> *And wasn't worth a mention that Joe Proctor's folks were slaves.*[16]

It was this anonymity, sometimes a result of courtesy and sometimes for other reasons, that kept black cowboys in the shadows. As the American West became symbolic of all that was good in the nation, there was a tendency to see a monochromatic landscape. The important figures who shaped the West were not red, brown, yellow, or black. In the history and literature of scholars and writers alike, the only color that mattered was white.[17] It was this lack of recognition that produced the popular notion that black cowboys did not exist.

Most black and white cowboys remained working men living from payday to payday throughout their lives. This was the case whether they continued to work as cowboys or made the transition to factory or other kinds of work. The rough and somewhat independent life on the range did not usually produce provident men with long-term goals of owning a spread of their own. There were some exceptions to this rule among white as well as black cowboys, but the transition was not an easy one. Sometimes, even when boys were of the same race and class, and were born in the same region, their accomplishments varied a great deal.

The coastal bend of Texas was the starting and sometimes the finishing place for a number of black cowboys. For some, however, the grass looked a great deal greener in West Texas. Jack Bess was born on Steve Bess's ranch near Goliad, Texas, in 1854. He lived his first eleven years as a slave and learned to like working horses and cattle. As was the case with other slaves, he continued in this pursuit throughout the Civil War and into freedom. Bess's recollections were preserved in the WPA Slave Narratives.

> Our beds was pretty good when uses dem. . . . Our log huts was comfortable as we had some kind of floors in all of dem. . . . De eats we know was jes' good eats, lots of meat and vegetables and de like; 'possum and coon and beef and pork all cooked good. Our clothes was jes' home spun liked all de others.[18]

Some of the slave narratives were as short as a page, while others extended for five or six pages. Bess's eighty-plus years were described in just one-and-a-half typed pages. He spoke of hearing the news of freedom and going to work on a ranch in the old Ben Ficklin community in what became Tom Green County. Ben Ficklin is remembered in Texas history as a rival settlement to San Angelo and the county seat until 1882, when it was washed away by a flood.[19] Bess spoke of his working one ranch and then another in Ben Ficklin before the creation of San Angelo, Texas.

Daniel Webster Wallace was born September 15, 1860, in Victoria County, Texas. Webster lived with his mother, Mary Wallace, in what might be described as commodious quarters by slave standards. His mother was a house servant and wet nurse for Mrs. Mary O'Daniel. Mary Wallace received her freedom and decided to stay with the O'Daniels as Webster began his early life chopping weeds and plowing for about thirty cents a day. As many other young boys of his day, the call of the trail and the cowboy life fueled his imagination.[20]

Neither Webster nor Jack Bess had much schooling, but they both treasured their dreams of becoming cowboys. The record does not indicate how Jack traveled from Goliad to Tom Green County, but Daniel Webster Wallace slipped away from his mother and joined a cattle drive heading for Coleman County. When Webster arrived in Coleman County, he was in the adjoining county where Jack Bess lived. Two black boys, formerly slaves, started new chapters in their otherwise fragmented lives as cowboys. It is not known whether the two boys knew each other, but that was unlikely. Yet they had begun their cowboy careers in close proximity and now once again were geographically connected in juxtaposed counties.

At this point, we can only speculate about the exploits and activities of Jack Bess. Daniel Wallace on the other hand would become the subject of a book, a master's thesis, an article in a West Texas yearbook, and a chapter in *Black Cowboys of Texas*.[21] Webster perfected his skills as a cowboy working for Sam Gholson, a buffalo hunter and Indian fighter, and the Nunn and Clay Mann outfits.[22] It was to be the Clay Mann brand, the numeral "80" that would forever be attached to his name: "80 John."

Daniel Webster Wallace was to shed Webster, his boyhood name, for "80 John," as he was to be known throughout Texas cattle country for the rest of his life. There was a certain irony in the fact that neither Webster nor "80 John" was a name of his choosing. "80 John" rode into Colorado City behind a dusty herd of Clay Mann's cattle but did more than "eat trail dust." He watched and listened to the actions and words of Mann as he learned the lessons that would later shape his life and career. "80 John" came to know the value of keeping his word and the value of a dollar. He acquired good business sense and came to appreciate the value of education in a world of business and finance.

While most other cowboys spent and drank up their money as fast as they got it, "80 John" had a portion of his salary withheld to acquire a nest egg for buying cattle and owning his own ranch. The element of trust that developed between Mann and Wallace was much like that of Bose Ikard and Charles Goodnight. In the days when transactions were often conducted with cash, cattlemen like Mann had large amounts of money that needed to be deposited in banks or transferred to a given rancher. Since cattle transactions were common knowledge, outlaws had a keen interest in large sums of money changing hands.

Mann's trust and faith in Wallace was demonstrated in his willingness to allow him to carry substantial cattle payments often many miles away. Wallace's experiences became a part of family conversations and may have been used by him to instill the same values in his children. The following story indicated the deep respect and friendship that existed between Mann and Wallace.

> In those days, when banks were hundreds of miles away and cash was paid in all transactions, Mann sent thirty thousand dollars with 80 John in a wagon to the Cross Tie Ranch near Midland. This was a trip that required three days travel. 80 John delivered the money which he had carefully guarded, sleeping with it under his head at night.[23]

Evidence that Wallace was taking to heart the lessons he learned about saving money was seen in 1885, when he bought two sections of land in Mitchell County and started homesteading while still working for Mann.

Wallace, who decided at the age of twenty-five that he needed an education, traveled back to Navarro County in East Texas and enrolled in an elementary school. While studying his ABCs, he wooed and married Laura Dee Owens, a recent high school graduate who planned to become a teacher. Wallace and his new bride returned to Mitchell County and established a life for themselves on one of the Mann ranches.

It was shortly after Wallace's return that Clay Mann died in 1889. Wallace stayed on with the Mann outfit and extended his loyalty to Mrs. Mann, who died two years later. He now could become an independent rancher and develop a life out of the shadow of his employer of fourteen years. His standing in the community and his business acumen allowed him to secure a bank loan, purchase cows, and lease pasture land. He joined the Texas and Southwestern Cattle Raisers Association and acquired access to its brand records and new methods of ranching.

Like other ranchers, Wallace had to endure the vagaries of nature and business cycles. He weathered droughts, "die-ups" [massive death of cattle], and poor market conditions with an ability that often exceeded that of his white neighbors. His keen insight and, at times, loans from "banker-friends" allowed him to continue or sometimes start again when others were forced out of the cattle business. Wallace's good judgment was clearly demonstrated when his financial holdings were assessed at the end of his life. He had acquired fourteen and one half sections of land and six hundred head of cattle that he owned unencumbered by mortgage, loan, or taxes.

Wallace supported churches in his community as well as numerous charitable causes. He had a special interest in the education of young people and assisted some in meeting their college expenses. Most likely, it was the lack of opportunity to gain an education that sparked his interest in seeing others acquire what was denied him. Wallace's generosity and support of education encouraged the officials of Colorado City, Texas, to name a school for black children in his honor.

When Wallace died on March 28, 1939, many of his friends and fellow cattlemen brought or sent condolences to his family. He was recognized as a pioneer, a leading citizen of Mitchell County, and a man worthy of respect.

In most respects, the lives of the two black cowboys Jack Bess and Daniel Webster "80 John" Wallace were quite different in what they were able to accumulate and their positions in society. Yet, until recently, a search of the public written record revealed very little about either Bess or Wallace. This lack of recognition began to change as Daniel Webster Wallace, the man known as "the most respected Negro ranchman in the Old West," received individual notation in the *Online Handbook of Texas*.

Bill Pickett, the most famous black cowboy of the old West, only recently regained some of the fame he had achieved in the halcyon days of the Miller Brothers' 101 Ranch Real Wild West Show. In 1977, Colonel Bailey C. Hanes wrote a well researched biography of Bill Pickett that introduced him to a general audience. In the foreword to *Bill Pickett, Bulldogger*, Bill Burchardt stated that Pickett's long and celebrated years as a rodeo star did not make him immune to obscurity:

> It seems incredible that the story of a man of Bill Pickett's stature could virtually sink from sight in a single generation, yet it has. We are emerging from an era which has buried the stories of many Americans of minority races: Negro, Indian, and others. The Bill Pickett story easily could have been lost completely. It has been badly warped in a good many magazine articles written by pseudohistorians and bigots intent on propaganda.[24]

Pickett's life began, like that of many other black cowboys, as a child of slaves. According to his family, Willie Pickett was born on December 5, 1870, in Travis County, Texas. The Pickett family, like many other South Carolina and Georgia slaves, were experienced in the handling of cattle. In 1854, they left South Carolina with their slave masters, Dr. Welborn Barton and Colonel Alexander Barton, and moved to the Lone Star State. When the Picketts arrived in central Texas, they continued to work as cowboys and wranglers for their owners.[25]

Bill was the second of thirteen children born to Thomas Jefferson and Mary Virginia Elizabeth (Gilbert) Pickett. Bill received little formal education and very early in his life devoted his time and energy to cow work. His cousins, Anderson Pickett and Jerry Barton, drove cattle up the Chisholm Trail when Bill was a young boy. Their stories of life on the trail provided Bill vicariously the hazards and excitement of encountering Indians, swollen rivers, and towns like Abilene, Kansas. Living around the cattle town of Austin also provided Bill ample opportunity to see cowboy life firsthand.[26]

At a young age, Bill observed a technique that would bring him fame and fortune. The practice of using dogs to search out and catch cattle was popular with some ranchers. Bill observed a bulldog holding a cow by its upper lip. Once the bulldog had a firm grip on the cow's lip, the cow would stand perfectly still. This chance observation stuck in Bill's mind and later was used by him to thrill and amaze audiences.

Pickett perfected the "bite 'em down style" of bulldogging and began to exhibit his talent at county fairs and less formal gatherings. He passed his hat at these events and received whatever the audience was willing to give. Bill's "bite 'em down style" of catching and holding cattle also proved valuable in the mesquite brush of central Texas. Cowboys were expected to locate and bring half-wild cows out of the thickets where they would hide. In the heavy brush country where it was very difficult to use a lariat, Bill would jump off his horse, and by grabbing and twisting the cow's horns, bring the cow to a stop. He would then bite into its lip until the animal offered no resistance. This practice allowed a cow to be roped and dragged into a clear area and constrained until it was tame enough to stay with the herd.[27]

By 1888, Thomas Pickett had moved his family to Taylor, Texas, where Bill and his brothers established a horse-breaking business. In December 1890, Bill married Maggie Turner and started his own family. With this new responsibility, Bill settled into the role of a responsible and respected member of the community. He worked on several ranches in the area, hunted, and picked cotton to make ends meet.

While Bill did exhibitions, his connection with promoters Lee Monroe and Dave McClure spread his fame across the state and the nation. Monroe, a rancher from Rockdale, Texas, arranged for Bill to perform in Houston, Dublin, and San Angelo as well as Forth Worth and Taylor. In 1903, McClure promoted Bill as the "Dusky Demon," a name that forever would be attached to him. Two of Pickett's biographers believed that McClure chose the "Dusky Demon" sobriquet to mask Bill's racial identity since a variety of nationalities could presumably be dusky. The Demon reference may have been added to suggest that his talents had a supernatural origin.

While black cowboys had long established themselves as expert horse handlers and riders, during the first half of the twentieth century, they generally were not permitted to compete in rodeo events with whites. In a segregated America, "the mixing of the races" was considered demeaning and against the law. The effort to introduce a less than candid portrait of Bill may have been an effort to shield his race until he gained enough fame to overcome it.[28]

In 1904, Pickett achieved national recognition when he performed at the Cheyenne Frontier Days. Cheyenne Frontier Days began in 1897 as a fair for excursion passengers on the Union Pacific Railroad and continued to attract visitors from throughout the United States and abroad. President Theodore Roosevelt and George Eastman of Kodak were two of the notables who visited Cheyenne Frontier Days during the early part of the twentieth century. While it was reported that Buffalo Bill's Wild West Show performed for a cheering crowd of six thousand in 1898, newspapers reported that over twenty thousand spectators watched and admired Bill Pickett in 1904.[29] The presence of the *Wyoming Times*, the *Denver Post*, and New York's *Harper's Weekly* also guaranteed perhaps millions of people not in attendance would learn about the fearless colored man from Taylor, Texas.

While each newspaper celebrated the courage and daring of Pickett, each in its own way wanted the reading public to know that bulldogging a steer had been performed by a black man. Each newspaper not only stated that Pickett was a Negro or a colored man, but the *Wyoming Times* thought it was important that its readers know that he had "strong ivory teeth." The *Denver Post* devoted two sections essentially written in dialect apparently to authenticate that Bill was a real Negro. The *Post* also thought that it should mention the connection between Bill's teeth and the tusks of an African elephant:

> The ivory adornments of that spacious opening in the colored man's face attest to the truthfulness of every word he uttered, for the teeth that remain are big and sharp and strong, but several are gone in part as the result of encounters with especially muscular steers, which refused to be humbled without a struggle.[30]

The *Harper's Weekly* article made no reference to Bill's teeth and refrained from the use of dialect in describing his accomplishments. John Dicks Howe, *Harper's* special reporter, wrote a descriptive article without offensive appellations until the last sentence of his story. He then stated: "So great was the applause that the *darkey* [writer's emphasis] again attacked the steer, which had staggered to its feet, and again threw it after a desperate struggle."[31]

In 1905, Pickett's career would make another leap forward when he performed at the National Editorial Association's convention in Oklahoma. The Miller Brothers, Zack, George, and Joe, who were responsible for his coming to the convention a few years later, made him the premier act in their Ranch Wild West Show. The 101 Wild West Show toured the United States, Canada, Mexico, South America, and England, entertaining millions of adoring fans. With the trip to England in

1914, Bill had the opportunity to meet British royalty and perform before the royal family.[32]

Pickett originated the rodeo sport of steer wrestling and established himself as the most famous black cowboy of the American West. In 1971, he was the first black cowboy to be inducted into the National Cowboy Hall of Fame in Oklahoma City, and in 1989 he was inducted into the Pro Rodeo Hall of Fame in Colorado Springs, Colorado. His name was resurrected in 1984 when a black rodeo company adopted it in forming the Bill Pickett Invitational Rodeo. In 1987, the North Fort Worth Historical Society commissioned a bronze statue showing Pickett bulldogging a one-thousand-pound longhorn. The life-like sculpture was unveiled on the grounds of the Cowtown Coliseum where Pickett had performed during its grand opening in 1908. Pickett received many other honors, including being selected for the 1994 stamp panel entitled Legends of the West.

Few cowboys, black or white, gained the renown of Bill Pickett, but black cowboys played their parts in transforming the West. They rode the lonely trails, branded and herded cattle, and continued to work cattle long after the long drives up the Shawnee, Chisholm, Western, and Goodnight-Loving Trails ended. They found work on ranches, in feedlots, at horse auction barns, on the rodeo circuit, and as horse traders and trainers. When new opportunity arose, some left their cowboy past and worked for the railroads or found jobs in cities. Some bought small ranches where they cowboyed on the weekend. Many left cowboy life and seemingly forgot that they once had worked on horseback.

The fragmented remembrance of black cowboy life and the scant written record would seem to evince the insignificance of the experience. Yet the lack of archival records and the relatively small numbers of black cowboys in some areas of the West do not tell the whole story. The black cowboy population had a dynamic impact on American life in several important areas. One of those areas was the music sung by cowboys as they sat around campfires and as they did night herding. Many of those songs were remembered and documented by working cowboys, song collectors, and folklorists. In the introduction of *Cowboy Songs and Other Frontier Ballads*, collected by J. A. and Alan Lomax, the following statement is found:

> Often the best of the singers were black cowboys, who brought their African and Afro-American heritage of hollers and herding songs to the Texas cattle country. Both Charles Siringo and Teddy Blue, two noted

cowboy historians, said that the best singers and musical cattle handlers were black cowboys from whom they learned their trade in the early days. John Lomax took down many of his finest songs, including "Home on the Range" and "Sam Bass" from black trail hands. Truly this western tradition linked many trails.[33]

In a conversation with a friend some years ago, the writer was told a story of her experience in Montana. She and a friend, both of whom were white school teachers in Chicago, stopped in a small café and received some ribbing by local cowboys. The cowboys could not understand how they could stand to be around *niggers*. When a black cowboy entered the café, the cowboys went over and greeted him with what appeared to be genuine affection and respect. Once the black cowboy left, my friend asked why they had been so antagonistic to them while they related so well to the black cowboy. Their response was that he was not black, he was a *cowboy*.

There are still black cowboys who earn their living in places as widely separated as Florida and California. A comprehensive account of those twentieth-century experiences has yet to be written. Although black men remain a minority among cowboys, their stories are worth collecting, assessing, and integrating into the broader fabric of the western region. How did the West change those black men who became cowboys? How did black cowboys change the West? Did the experience of the black cowboys have an impact of the way we see the West? There is much to be researched about the black cowboy's quality of life, his working relations with other cowboys, and the manner in which he negotiated the uncertain racial terrain in the West.

Notes

1. See Philip Durham and Everett L. Jones, *The Negro Cowboy*. New York: Mead, and Co., 1965. William Loren Katz, *The Black West*. Seattle: Open Hand Publishing, Inc. 1987. Kenneth Wiggins Porter, *The Negro on the American Frontier*. New York: Arno Press, 1971. W. Sherman Savage, *Blacks in the West*. Westport, Conn.: Greenwood Press, 1976. More recently a number of books and bibliographies have been added, including: Bruce A. Glasrud, ed., *African Americans in the West: A Bibliography of Secondary Sources*. Alpine, Texas: Sul Ross State University Center for Big Bend Studies, 1998. Art Burton, *Black, Red, and Deadly: Black and Indian Gunfighters of the Indian Territories, 1870–1907*. Austin: Eakin Press, 1991.

Cecil Johnson, *Guts: Legendary Black Rodeo Cowboy Bill Pickett.* Ft. Worth: The Summit Group, 1994. Glenn Shirley, *Marauders of the Indian Nations: The Bill Cook Gang and Cherokee Bill.* Stillwater, Oklahoma: Barbed Wire Press, 1994. Alwyn Barr, *Black Texans: A History of African Americans in Texas, 1528–1995, 2nd edition.* Norman: University of Oklahoma Press, 1996. Quintard Taylor, *In Search of the Racial Frontier: African Americans in the American West, 1528–1990.* New York: W. W. Norton and Company, 1998. Monroe Lee Billington and Roger D. Hardaway, eds. *African Americans on the Western Frontier.* Niwot: University Press of Colorado, 1998. Sara R. Massey, ed. *Black Cowboys of Texas.* College Station: Texas A&M University Press, 2000.

2. Robert G. Athearn, *The Mythic West in the Twentieth Century.* Lawrence: University Press of Kansas, 1986.

3. Richard W. Slatta, *Cowboys of the Americas.* New Haven: Yale University Press, 1990. See chapter 10, "Cowboy and Indians: Frontier Race Relations," pp. 159–173. Peter Iverson, *When Indians Became Cowboys: Native Peoples and Cattle Ranching in the American West.* Norman: University of Oklahoma Press, 1994.

4. Peter H. Wood, *Black Majority: Negroes in Colonial South Carolina from 1670 through the Stono Rebellion.* New York: Knopf, 1972.

5. Frederick Remington, "Vagabonding with the Tenth Horse," *The Cosmopolitan* 22 (February 1897): 352.

6. Terry G. Jordan, *Trails to Texas: Southern Roots of Western Cattle Ranching.* Lincoln: University of Nebraska Press, 1981, p. 127.

7. Wood.

8. Ron Tyler and Lawrence Murphy, eds. *The Slave Narratives of Texas.* Austin: State House Press, 1974, p. 56–57.

9. George P. Rawick, ed. *Texas Narratives,* Vol. 5, Part 4 of *The American Slave: A Composite Autobiography.* Westport, Conn.: Greenwood Publishing Company, pp. 102–103.

10. John Hendricks, "Tribute Paid to Negro Cowmen," *Cattlemen* 22 (Feb., 1936): 24.

11. J. Evetts Haley, *Charles Goodnight: Cowman and Plainsman.* Norman: University of Oklahoma Press, 1936, p. 243.

12. Cecil Johnson, *Guts: Legendary Black Rodeo Cowboy Bill Pickett.* Fort Worth: The Summit Group, 1994, pp. xvii–xix.

13. Michael N. Searles, "Addison Jones: 'The Most Noted Negro Cowboy That Ever "Topped Off" a Horse,'" in *Black Cowboys of Texas,* ed. Sara R. Massey. College Station: Texas A&M University Press, 2000, pp. 193–205.

14. Sara R. Massey, ed. *Black Cowboys of Texas.* College Station: Texas A&M University Press, 2000.

15. *Forsyth Time-Journal* (Forsyth, Montana), 4 August 1938.

16. Wallace McRae, *Cowboy Curmudgeon and Other Poems.* Salt Lake City: Gibbs Smith Books, 1992, pp. 44–45.

17. Kenneth Wiggins Porter, *The Negro on the American Frontier.* New York: Arno Press, 1971. Jack Weston, *The Real American Cowboy.* New York: Amsterdam Books, 1985. Lawrence B. de Graff, "Recognition, Racism, and Reflections on the Writing of Western Black History," *Pacific Historical Review* 44: 1 (February 1975) 22–51. Patricia Nelson Limerick, *The Legacy of Conquest: The Unbroken Past of the American West.* New York: W. W. Norton, 1987.

18. Rawick, *Texas Narratives,* Vol. 4, Part 1, pp. 72–73.

19. Walter Prescott Webb, ed. *The Handbook of Texas.* Vol 2. Austin: The State Historical Association, 1952, p. 539.

20. Joyce Gibson Roach, "Daniel Webster Wallace: A West Texas Cattleman," in *Black Cowboys of Texas,* ed. Sara R. Massey. College Station: Texas A&M University Press, 2000, pp. 181–191.

21. Hettye Wallace Branch, *The Story of "80 John:" A Biography of One of the Most Respected Negro Ranchmen in the Old West.* New York: Greenwich Book Publishing, 1960. Hertha Auburn Webb, "D. W. '80 John' Wallace—Black Cattleman, 1875–1939" Master thesis, Prairie View A&M College, 1957. R. C. Crane, "D. W. ('80 John') Wallace, A Negro Cattleman on the Texas Frontier," *West Texas Historical Association Yearbook,* 28 (Oct., 1952): 113–118.

22. Roach, "Daniel Webster Wallace," *Black Cowboys of Texas,* pp. 183–184.

23. Branch, *The Story of "80 John,"* p. 30.

24. Colonel Bailey C. Hanes, *Bill Pickett, Bulldogger: The Biography of a Black Cowboy.* Norman: University of Oklahoma Press, 1977, p. xi.

25. Hanes, *Bill Pickett, Bulldogger,* pp. 15–20.

26. Mary Lou LeCompte, "Pickett, William," *The Handbook of Texas Online,* 1999, www.tsha.utexas.edu/handbook/online/articles/view/PP/fpi4.html (24 November 2000). Hanes, *Bill Pickett, Bulldogger,* p. 24.

27. Le Compte, "Pickett, William," *The Handbook of Texas Online.* Hanes, *Bill Pickett, Bulldogger,* pp. 25–26.

28. Hanes, *Bill Pickett, Bulldogger,* p. 40. Cecil Johnson, *Guts: Legendary Black Rodeo Cowboy Bill Pickett,* p. 10.

29. Hanes, *Bill Pickett, Bulldogger,* pp. 45–46

30. Hanes, *Bill Pickett, Bulldogger,* pp. 41–42.

31. Hanes, *Bill Pickett, Bulldogger,* pp. 46.

32. Johnson, *Guts: Legendary Black Rodeo Cowboy Bill Pickett,* pp. 113–121.

33. J. A. Lomax and Alan Lomax, *Cowboy Songs and Other Frontier Ballads.* New York: Colliers Books, 1938, p. xviii–xix.

Black Urban Churches
on the Southern Frontier, 1865–1900

ALWYN BARR

Alwyn Barr's article underscores the importance of the black church in the lives of African Americans. Even during slave days, many chattels refused to allow whites to control their religious expressions. In their "invisible" church, they met together in the evenings, conducting their fellowship and worship away from the prying eyes of owners and overseers. In white services, if they were allowed to attend, slaves learned about obedience and about various sins such as stealing from their masters. In their own services, they learned about promises of God's blessing, about freedom, and about brotherly love.

Barr focuses on the urban black church and sees it as the primary institution in the lives of African Americans. His findings include widespread community involvement, with women often taking the lead socially. They formed women's groups, organized social outings, and did benevolent work such as caring for the elderly and the infirm. Black churches usually had strong ministers who tried to compel obedience to religious teachings. As time passed, the profile of ministers evolved thus: most were young and had at least some college credits, and they strongly supported education. As well, they stressed temperance and provided other moral direction for their flocks.

*

RELIGION BECAME an even more important source of strength in the lives of former slaves as they made the transition to free people after the Civil War and exercised greater control over their worship experiences. Furthermore, churches related to a variety of other activities pursued by African Americans after emancipation. Religion in the cities of the South differed from that of rural areas because of the greater concentration of potential church members, the increased opportunities for education of clergy, and the more diverse activities that competed with religion for the time and interests of individuals. Existing studies focus primarily on black churches in the Southeast, from the Atlantic coast to the Mississippi River. Thus it becomes important to explore African American religious activity in the smaller but more rapidly growing urban areas on the southern frontier, west of the Mississippi, in the period after emancipation. Those churches in Arkansas, Louisiana, and Texas might vary from the patterns of congregations in larger towns east of the Mississippi, especially since fewer free blacks or urban slaves lived west of the Mississippi before the Civil War. Four communities have been selected for the purpose of exploring church development in that region: Little Rock, the largest town in Arkansas; Shreveport, the major urban area in western Louisiana; and Houston and San Antonio, two of the three largest towns in Texas.[1]

Some patterns of post–Civil War black religious activity had antebellum origins. Occasional African influences still appeared in the late nineteenth century. In Little Rock an African American woodcutter, Jerry Vaughn, explained that he murdered a black carpenter named John Francis in 1872 "because he poisoned my hand; it is always cold, and . . . he was often throwing Lucy Scott into spasms." As late as 1884 a voodoo healer in Houston employed "a concoction out of herbs and the entrails of various reptiles gathered in the dark of the moon" that he placed on the skin of another man to repel the effects of a curse. Probably other instances went unreported. Yet African ideas did not dominate black religion in the postwar towns.[2]

Denominations led locally by white southerners often tried to keep their former slave members as a means of control or influence. Efforts to retain black members persisted the longest in Congregational, Episcopal, and Presbyterian churches. In Houston, Congregationalists offered Sunday School classes for African Americans as late as 1870, although the Presbyterian efforts lasted only into 1866. Whites and blacks conducted services at different times on Sunday in one Presbyterian church at Shreveport. The Episcopal church in San Antonio still maintained a "colored Sunday school" that met during the afternoon in 1872. White goals in these efforts reflected diverse views. Some acted out of evangelical commitment. The Houston *Telegraph* spoke for others who hoped to encourage "mutual dependence" and limit the impact of northern ideas. Although these practices disappeared in the 1870s, Anglo evangelists held special services for blacks or allowed segregated participation in their revivals even in the 1890s. In Little Rock during the summer of 1891, black church leaders helped conduct a revival in which 1,500 African Americans filled the back seats in a huge tent.[3]

Despite those efforts, most freed people moved quickly after emancipation to form their own evangelical Protestant congregations. In Houston and Little Rock the first groups evolved from separate slave churches that existed before the Civil War. William Wallace Andrews, whose master allowed him to live with his family in a house at the edge of town, gathered other slaves there for religious services beginning about 1848. On land provided by his owners, the Ashleys, Andrews and his slave congregation constructed their first Methodist church building during 1853 and 1854. Other bondsmen met occasionally as Baptists and apparently formed a congregation in 1858 under the leadership of Wilson Brown. When the Union army captured Little Rock in 1863, both congregations became churches for freed people. The Methodists joined the Methodist Episcopal Church and adopted the name Wesley Chapel, "amid shouts of thanksgiving and songs of praise to the Father in Heaven."[4]

Before the war Houston slaves had been allowed to construct a small church in the rear of the Methodist Episcopal Church, South. Upon emancipation, the members, led by former slave preacher Elias Dibble, transferred to the Methodist Episcopal Church and in 1866 erected on their own land Trinity M. E. Church. Blacks also met with the help of white missionaries at Anglo and German Baptist Churches as well as an arbor in 1865 to plan for the creation of Antioch Baptist Church in January 1866, under the direction of ex-slave preacher Sandy Parker. A newspaper reported "a deadly feud exists between several members of the African Methodist and Baptist churches," which may have reflected early competition for members as well as theological differences.[5] Whether slave congregations existed in Shreveport and San Antonio is unclear, but freedmen's churches formed quickly in both towns. In Shreveport, a Freedmen's Bureau officer spoke before black congregations in August 1865. Early buildings reflected hurried construction, for the floor in the Methodist church gave way under a large gathering. This congregation probably became St. James Methodist Church. By early 1866 the Baptists sought funds to construct a new building that would house Antioch Baptist Church.[6]

Religious organizations in San Antonio moved more slowly, probably because of a smaller black population. Local African American ministers, led by Nace Duval, a former slave preacher, established the first Methodist congregation by the fall of 1867. When ministers Richard Haywood of the African Methodist Episcopal Church and Joseph Welch of the Methodist Episcopal Church arrived in 1868 intense competition followed for support of the black Methodists and control of the existing church house. St. Paul Methodist Church held the original building, while the African Methodist congregation moved to the "old soap factory," a stone structure that became St. James A. M. E. Church. Four years later the African Methodists won a court suit over the initial building. A few blacks sought to attend a white Baptist revival in San Antonio during 1868. Yet the actual organization of a congregation did not occur until 1870 and 1871 when Nathan Shelton and white missionary J. F. Hines helped create Mount Zion First Baptist Church. They conducted early services beneath an arbor and at the houses of some members until the city made available a small building that could be placed on church land.[7]

In the years following the founding of congregations, black religious activities experienced three types of development in several growing frontier communities. The original congregations expanded in size and erected new buildings. New denominations appeared to provide more diverse opportunities for worship. As the cities grew in population the older denominations founded new congregations to serve new neighborhoods.

Fund raising for new buildings to house larger congregations included appeals to both black church members and to white friends of the congregations. To pay for a new church in 1866, black Baptists in Shreveport held a fair at a local theatre, with the opening night restricted to whites and a second day for African Americans. A supper in October 1867, followed in December by "a Fair to be given by the young ladies of the African Methodist Church" in San Antonio, gathered $300 from both blacks and whites for a new house of worship. In Little Rock, Wesley Chapel Methodists Episcopal Church held special meetings in July 1871 that promoted $3,020 in subscriptions for a new building. While the four $200 pledges came from whites, some blacks joined whites in promising $50 to $100 contributions. Bethel African Methodist Episcopal Church organized the same type of gathering a month later with even greater success, for subscriptions amounted to $4,370. A similar pattern of giving emerged, with some white Republican leaders contributing to both churches. Houston churches also held fairs to finance constructions.[8]

Disputes arose occasionally from fund raising activities. Reverend John T. Jenifer claimed in November 1871 that $300 gathered for construction of Bethel A. M. E. Church in Little Rock had been transferred to Campbell Chapel, "a branch church," by Elder Hagan Green. When Bethel church disapproved his action, Green left the congregation and, by February 1872, became a promoter of the new Colored Methodist Episcopal church in the city. Jerome Lewis, a Bethel church trustee for thirteen years, successfully sued in December 1883 for payment of a $300 loan to the church. Court proceedings revealed a complicated series of loans from congregation leaders who also donated various amounts of money or services to the church.[9]

Efforts to finance new facilities or improvements on older ones continued throughout the late nineteenth century. A descriptive volume on San Antonio in the 1880s noted several black churches "to which the white citizens are almost continually invited to contribute." Even at the end of the century, the black Presbyterians of Little Rock expressed appreciation for white assistance in building a new church. Yet black congregations raised increasing amounts within their own membership during the period. Bethel A. M. E. Church of Little Rock received contributions from women's groups, Sunday School classes and individual members in addition to public donations in the 1870s. A new African Methodist Episcopal Church Zion organized a Sunday excursion out of Little Rock to raise money in the summer of 1883. The Missionary Baptist Church of that city sold tickets to the opening of its "magnificent brick edifice" that fall. The following spring the Baptist congregation began renting pews at an annual rate of $20, which quickly raised over $500. Shiloh Baptist Church of Little Rock arranged a candy pull and a concert to pay for repairs in 1892. In Shreveport the women of St. Paul's M. E. Church helped pay for an organ with the proceeds of a concert in 1895. The Home Missionary Society of St. James A. M. E. Church in that city contributed to a building program through a similar entertainment that year. Antioch Baptist Church in Houston reduced its debts with a special Sunday meeting which generated over $100 in 1896.[10]

While most congregations remained small and conducted services in modest buildings, others achieved a degree of financial success. D. B. Gaines spoke of "the many well constructed and handsomely furnished churches" of Little Rock by the 1890s. First Baptist Church in the Arkansas city claimed buildings worth $25,000, in the 1890s. Watts Chapel Baptist Church of Houston was valued at $5,000 by that same decade. In the 1890 census the property of black Methodist congregations was worth $10,500 in San Antonio, $13,800 in Houston, and $36,000 in Little Rock.[11]

While the earliest congregations expanded their facilities, new churches began to appear, some representing new denominations. Following the original Baptist and Methodist Episcopal groups in each city came the African Methodist Episcopal Church, a black denomination based in the North, seeking to establish congregations in Little Rock, San Antonio, and Houston during the late 1860s and in Shreveport in the 1870s. White southern Methodists helped organize the Colored Methodist Episcopal Church in 1870 to limit northern influence. A C. M. E. congregation formed in Little Rock during 1871, but those in Shreveport and Houston did not appear until the 1880s.[12]

The appearance of missionaries of new denominations in the late 1860s generated lively and sometimes tense competition for the support of members and at times for control of buildings, or funds, as in the M. E.-A. M. E. conflicts at Little Rock. When a bishop founded the first Colored Methodist Episcopal church at Little Rock in 1871 it brought stinging criticism from the Methodist Episcopal minister, A. G. Gratton. He argued that southern white Methodist support for the new denomination meant it "is a shrewd dodge to get rid of the negro." Furthermore, he quoted the *Arkansas Gazette* as saying of the C. M. E. "the greatest feature about it is, no politics whatever has anything to do with the church." A C. M. E. spokesman responded that his church held the greater claim to legality and was not dominated by white Methodists.[13]

During the late 1880s and 1890s black congregations developed in Little Rock with ties to the Lutheran, Congregational, Christian, Episcopal, and Presbyterian denominations. The society of the Holy Ghost, a Catholic order, began activities for African Americans and immigrants of the community during 1878, though it seems to have been only temporary. St. Paul Lutheran Church organized in the city during 1886, followed the next year by a Congregational chapel. In 1887 the African Methodist Episcopal Church Zion also organized a St. Paul's congregation in Little Rock. Allison Presbyterian church formed in the Arkansas city in 1889 but refused to accept a black ministerial appointment. When St. Phillips' developed that same year as a black Episcopal mission in Little Rock, white Christ Episcopal Church refused to participate in the diocese council rather than work with black delegates. The congregation did not have a permanent pastor until the beginning of the twentieth century. In 1893 a Christian Church joined the diverse congregations of Little Rock.[14]

Catholic, Episcopal, and Church of God congregations also formed in San Antonio, Houston, and Shreveport. St. Mary's Church of San Antonio had followed the practice of seating blacks in the back pews. But

Father Richard Maloney and Margaret Murphy cooperated to establish St. Peter Claver church for African Americans in 1888. A black Catholic parish, St. Nicholas, was formed in Houston during 1887 but did not receive a priest or full recognition until the 1890s because of limited membership. An effort to form a Christian church in Houston during 1897 apparently failed. In 1900 the Episcopal Church organized Mission of Our Savior for African Americans in Houston. The same year Prophet R. K. Smith founded a Church of God in the bayou city but led his followers to Shreveport in 1901.[15]

As new denominations appeared, the Baptist churches and, to a lesser extent, the Methodist Episcopal churches expanded the number of their congregations. By the early 1880s Little Rock and Houston each contained four black Baptist churches, while San Antonio and Shreveport each had two. Methodist Episcopal congregations numbered two in each of the towns by the mid-1880s. As the nineteenth century ended Baptist churches had increased to twenty-five in Houston, eighteen in Little Rock, six in Shreveport, and three in San Antonio. By contrast Houston had the largest group of M. E. congregations with seven, followed by Little Rock with three.[16]

The apparently rapid growth of Baptist churches reflected in part the autonomy of congregations; that led to more frequent divisions. Members might break away to form new churches as a result of differences within an existing congregation, or simply to worship nearer their homes. Thus the Reverend Robert Woods led sixty people from First Missionary Baptist Church in Little Rock to create Mount Pleasant Baptist Church during 1875 following internal disagreements. Similar patterns seem to have existed in other towns. The Methodist denominations with their hierarchy of bishops produced a more orderly pattern. Yet divisions stirred some members of Wesley Chapel M. E. Church in Little Rock to depart and establish A. M. E. and Congregational churches in 1879 and 1880. Trinity M. E. church of Houston described itself as the "mother" to the younger M. E. congregations of the community. The holiness ideas split some churches, including the Baptists of Little Rock, in the 1890s.[17]

Congregations grew, not only in numbers, but some also expanded in size of membership. By 1892, First Baptist Church of Little Rock had an estimated 2,500 members. The continued division of that congregation into new churches apparently reduced that figure in the late 1890s to about 1,000—still an impressive size. By the 1890s Antioch Baptist of Houston claimed 850 members. Among the larger Methodist congregations of Little Rock in the 1890s were Bethel A. M. E. with 600 members, Wesley Chapel M. E. that counted 400 members, and Miles Chapel C. M. E. with 500 members. Watts Chapel Baptist Church of Houston claimed over 400 members by the 1890s. St. James M. E. Church in Shreveport attracted over 500 people on Easter Sunday in 1895. Early in the twentieth century black Baptists in Houston claimed 10,000 members in their churches, while the three Methodist denominations estimated 3,500 members in their congregations.[18]

Ministers provided leadership in the growth of churches but also reflected the status of their congregations as well as their personal backgrounds, both of which changed from the 1860s to later decades. Immediately after emancipation, former slave preachers led their congregations to reorganize as freedmen's churches. In Houston, Baptist Sandy Parker and Methodist Elias Dibble reflected that background as they urged their followers to "seek the friendship and good will of their white neighbors." Dibble, "long known in the city," received the "respect and confidence" of the white and black population. Nace Duval had led a slave congregation in Austin, but freedom brought him to San Antonio where he helped form a Methodist church. When he died in 1869, the newspaper noted that a "large number attended" the service for "this good old colored man and minister." Baptist Thomas Luke, a former slave preacher in Shreveport, had memorized numerous Biblical passages for use in his sermons. In Little Rock, Methodist minister William Wallace Andrews and Baptist preacher Wilson Brown led their congregations from slavery to the greater autonomy of freedom. Nathan Warren, who left Little Rock in the 1850s because of a new law against free blacks residing in Arkansas, returned to be an early minister of Bethel A. M. E. Church. To blacks he was "Father Warren," while whites called him "Uncle Nace."[19] These ministers provided continuity and stability amid extensive changes in the lives of urban freed people.

Some former slave preachers proved more confrontive in style. An A. M. E. minister believed the most successful postwar pastors to be "of orthodox blackness, to have a lusty voice," and "to have contempt for 'white folks' religion." R. Haywood, a former slave "exhorter" in his late forties, became an A. M. E. preacher and carried on a running struggle with a white M. E. minister in Houston and later in San Antonio during the late 1860s.[20]

For a brief period after the war, white ministers led Methodist Episcopal congregations until black pastors could be provided. Thus Joseph Welch conducted services in San Antonio during the late 1860s. When the new C. M. E. church raised that issue against the M. E. church, A. G. Gratton of Little Rock replied, in an argument that emphasized education: "Now we believe as much as . . . anybody in manning our colored work with colored men as far as we can for our good; but we believe the cause of religion and the cause of the colored people demand that we have intelligent men to expound the word of God to us. Colored men as soon as we can get them; white men till we can. . . ."[21]

A new generation from different backgrounds followed the slave preachers to the pulpits of urban churches in the Southwest. Almost without exception they accepted appointments to the city churches while still young men in their late twenties or early thirties. The great majority had been born in the South, but few in the states west of the Mississippi River. Two-thirds had attended colleges, with the Baptist and Methodist Episcopal ministers most likely to have had some higher education. Half had been teachers or professors at some time— again primarily Baptists or Methodist Episcopal preachers. Among the one-third who engaged in politics, the African Methodist Episcopal ministers appeared most active, although some Baptists became involved in government.[22]

Among these ministers some accomplished much while remaining representative in many ways. J. T. White served the black community through religion and politics. He was born on August 25, 1837, in Indiana, where he acquired a basic education. After arriving in Arkansas as a Baptist minister in the summer of 1865, he helped organize new churches in Helena and Little Rock. In 1867 he joined in the creation of the Arkansas Missionary Baptist Convention in the capital city. He won election as a delegate to the state constitutional conventions in 1868 and 1874. For two terms he served in the lower house of the state legislature before winning a seat in the state senate. He also received the appointive office of commissioner of public works. Following his political career he returned to full-time church work with the Benevolent and Church Aid Society and a church paper, the *Arkansas Review*.[23]

Another active minister, John T. Jenifer, advanced the cause of religion and education. He was born on March 10, 1835, in Maryland to slave parents. While still a bondsman he began to acquire an education and escaped to Massachusetts in the 1850s. He started to preach during the Civil War as an A. M. E. minister in the western states. While attending Wilberforce University he became the first black postmaster in the nation. From Ohio he came to Little Rock in 1870 and, despite some opposition, led the early growth of Bethel church. In Little Rock he received appointment to the committee of examiners for the public schools. Later he served churches in New England and Washington, D.C., while writing a history of the A. M. E. Church.[24]

Among influential ministers, J. P. Robinson made his greatest contributions within his denomination and in community economic development. He was born a slave in Mississippi. After the Civil War he worked in the fields and acquired an education at night or in the winter when cotton picking had ended. He became a teacher and preacher in Arkansas during the 1880s. As the minister of First Missionary Baptist Church in Little Rock he guided the payment of church debts and through his eloquent sermons attracted a large congregation. He attended Arkansas Baptist College, participated in the organization of the Capital City Savings Bank, and served as an officer of the state and national Baptist conventions.[25]

The appearance of a few women ministers in frontier South urban churches suggests some openness to greater participation. In August 1890 the Shreveport *Times* announced: "Rev. Mrs. Brantley will preach her farewell sermon at St. Matthew A. M. E. church Sunday night." Rachel Graham presented an evangelical sermon at Bethel A. M. E. Church in San Antonio during 1896. Yet the appearance of women in the pulpit remained an unusual occasion.[26]

The transition to new ministers sometimes stirred conflicts within the churches. When John T. Jenifer received the appointment to Bethel A. M. E. Church in Little Rock, he met opposition as a result of his northern background and the fears of others that "their removal would interfere with their political aspirations."[27]

In addition to problems within their churches, ministers occasionally had difficulties maintaining their image as moral leaders of the community. Marsh Hunsicker received a fine in Shreveport as a result of an altercation with a policeman in 1866. A Baptist preacher, Reuben Williams, died after being shot by young men who opposed his marriage to a woman in Little Rock during 1872. Dan Lee of Shreveport denied charges of verbal abuse in 1877 from a woman who claimed he tried to force his attentions toward her. A Little Rock minister faced trial for bigamy during 1890.[28]

Rumors of scandal or authoritarian leadership led to internal disputes within some congregations. The A. M. E. members in San Antonio gave a vote of confidence to Johnson Reed and declared him not guilty of reported improprieties in 1878. Yet a court settlement proved necessary the following year. A conflict at Mt. Zion Baptist Church in the Alamo city led to charges against laymen for disturbing worship. They retaliated in 1879 by seeking to dismiss Charles Augustus as minister although he denied any wrongdoing. The most explosive case occurred in Shreveport where turmoil existed for several months in Antioch Baptist Church between the minister, Luke Allen, and some members who resented his efforts to correct them. A Baptist council in Shreveport listened to charges that Allen made improper decisions about congregation members and money and, despite his defense, ordered him removed as pastor in March 1889. Lay leaders of the church replied that the council represented his enemies who had opposed Allen in association meetings for years and that it acted on false information. Opponents came to blows on at least one occasion. In June the Baptist district association supported the removal order but agreed to some remuneration for Allen.[29]

Such incidents attracted public attention and led to diverse judgments about black ministers. One white observer, perhaps influenced too much by colorful clashes, concluded that among African American ministers there were "many good ones; but as a class (they) are of questionable repute." D. B. Gaines of Little Rock with greater insight provided a middle-class view of the "status of the ministry" in the same period. He believed: "The Negro ministry compares most favorably with the ministry of any other race in shaping the destiny and uplifting the masses of its people. This is largely due to the fact that the Negro minister is almost the absolute leader of his people, while such is not true of other races." He divided black preachers into three groups: those who had acquired an education, those who had read privately to advance their knowledge and labored industriously—the largest group; and "a crowd of preachers who claim to be called of God to preach, but who seem to be left without a job." He suggested that because they "have simply chased around the country bellowing and hallooing, . . . it is this class that brought reproach upon the ministry."[30]

As ministers changed over time so did membership in the churches, which apparently ranged across the spectrum of social classes within the black community. Wesley Chapel M. E. Church at Little Rock in 1871 included among a group of its leaders a politician, a policeman, six skilled craftsmen—two blacksmiths, a brickmason, a carpenter, a painter, and a shoemaker—as well as a drayman and two unskilled laborers. Thus it contained strong representation from the developing black middle class. In the same year Bethel A. M. E. Church in the

Arkansas capital counted among a list of its supporters an attorney, a grocer, three law enforcement officers, two skilled craftsmen—a blacksmith and a plasterer—in addition to a drayman, two porters, and five laborers. Its leaders thus appear to represent both the middle class and the working class. The founders of Mount Zion First Baptist Church of San Antonio in 1871 seem to have been primarily working class, including a porter and several laborers. Miles Chapel C. M. E. Church of Little Rock also appears to have had a largely working class membership.[31] While one may discern a possible pattern for denominations, information is not available on most congregations that may have differed from one community to another.

While the composition of congregations remained diverse through the late nineteenth century, advances in education and economic status caused subtle changes in style. Of Bethel A. M. E. Church in Little Rock a member could say in 1883 "now we have a good people and a variety of colors, from the silky, glossy black, to those that it would take Gabriel with his telescope to tell the difference between them and the white race." By 1897 the Wesley Chapel M. E. Church in the Arkansas city could be described as "refined and dignified. There are quite a number of wealthy members connected with it." Another observer noted "The faculty and the majority of the students at Philander Smith College worship with this highly cultured congregation." The same writer, in discussing the Congregational Church of Little Rock, declared: "The membership is reasonably large and consists of many of the best people of the city."[32] These comments probably reflect the development of older congregations and some less evangelical churches into predominantly middle-class congregations.

Within the membership of these churches women assumed important roles from the beginning. The charter members of Mount Zion First Baptist Church of San Antonio in 1871 included thirteen women and only eight men. Female members frequently raised funds for the construction or improvement of the churches. "A Fair . . . given by the young ladies of the African Methodist Church for the benefit of the church" produced roughly $100 in December 1867. Among the 150 early contributors for the construction of Bethel A. M. E. Church in Little Rock were 43 women, including some who gave $50 to $75.[33]

The range of female church activities may be seen in the lives of two women. Darthula Wade Thompson, the wife of a Little Rock political leader, pursued religious work in First Baptist Church and later at Mount Pleasant Baptist Church. She served in the local women's group, became president of the board of directors that supervised a home for elderly women, presided over the Women's Baptist Missionary Association of Arkansas, and was present at national meetings of black Baptists. A church paper declared her "the best known woman in Arkansas" when she died in May 1896. Susie P. Legadry, a young woman in Shreveport, had been active as a leader in Sunday School and in weeknight church classes. She served the Epworth League at St. James M. E. Church as secretary. In the church she played the organ and participated in temperance meetings. She also had literary aspirations in poetry. The press described her as "a loving sister and an attentive daughter."[34]

Throughout the post–Civil War period male and female members of black churches focused upon certain basic religious activities and social goals. Evangelical efforts to bring Christianity into the lives of people and those people into the life of the church remained a central purpose of most congregations. Enthusiastic participatory A. M. E. church services in the evening at San Antonio attracted some unfavorable attention from neighbors kept awake in 1867. A congregational minister believed a black Houston congregation seemed devout—the preaching rather evangelical than instructive." R. B. White of Little Rock held services on the bank of the Arkansas River to baptize converts during 1872. Stephen Powers visited "a negro revival meeting" in Shreveport during the same period.[35]

Revivals, some with guest evangelists, continued through the 1890s. William Still of Little Rock described "a basket meeting on Sunday" where the church members "sang Spirituals and shouted." William Pickens, who also grew up in the Arkansas capital, recalled: "without dreams and visions no one was allowed to join the average Negro church of the past . . . a candidate was required to bring and sing a 'new song' to prove that he was really converted by God, for the doctrine was that 'the devil can convert you, but he can't give you a new song.'"[36]

Education joined evangelism as an early and continuing goal of the urban churches. The M. E. church in Little Rock presented a concert to aid black schools in 1868. Some Sunday schools taught religious thought through basic education in the years soon after emancipation. A new minister at the A. M. E. church of Little Rock in 1883 created a "moral and mental improvement society" that presented "readings, essays, solos, recitations, declamations, debating and speeches." The Catholic church organized schools for black students in Houston and San Antonio in the 1880s. In that decade interest also shifted to support for church-related colleges, such as Bethel Institute, an A. M. E. school in Little Rock, Philander Smith College, a Methodist Episcopal institution in the Arkansas city, and Baptist colleges in Texas.[37]

The black urban church went beyond efforts at conversion and education through contributions to community social life during the late nineteenth century. At an A. M. E. church fair in San Antonio during 1869 students sang while bakery goods were sold. Despite some controversy over the practice, black churches often organized excursions out of town for picnics. Shreveport congregations left by riverboat for Bayou Pierre in May 1877. Baptist and Methodist Sunday schools in Little Rock paraded within the city for recreation, music, and picnic speeches during the 1870s. Houston Sunday schools followed a similar practice in the 1880s. St. Paul's M. E. church of San Antonio offered piano and vocal music at a fund raising social in the fall of 1896.[38]

The social life of black church members usually remained within the bounds of efforts at moral development and concerns about family life. Bethel A. M. E. Church leaders, while seeking support for a new building in Little Rock, assured the public "we have struggled to rise to the higher paths of Christian morality and citizenship." Marriage ranked as an important topic in discussions among young adults at Wesley Chapel M. E. Church in the Arkansas city during the 1870s. It stood as one of the original goals to be promoted by Mount Zion First Baptist Church of San Antonio after its organization in 1871. Morality remained one of the focal points for discussion at a Methodist district conference in Shreveport during the 1880s. Collin Street Baptist Church investigated the personal conduct of a member, while other Little Rock congregations expelled members who had been seen dancing in 1892. The black Ministers Union of Houston took a stand against Sunday business activities in 1897.[39]

To promote and protect the citizenship of their members in the early years after emancipation, ministers spoke about political and civil rights during church services. Preachers in Shreveport presented to their congregations the Reconstruction Act that granted voting rights in April 1867. Little Rock churches held special Thanksgiving services in 1870. J. T. Jenifer at Bethel A. M. E. Church expressed appreciation for black economic and educational opportunities as well as "the prospects before them as a race." R. B. White of First Baptist Church offered thanks for constitutional rights, economic advances, good health, and spiritual salvation. At the M. E. church two addresses emphasized freedom, the rights of citizenship, education, and the opportunity to worship freely. At ceremonies to lay the cornerstone for a new First Baptist Church in Little Rock during 1882, the address by Julia E. Brown on "The Progress of the Africans in America" emphasized emancipation and voting rights as well as a growing economic base to support religion, education, and families. J. H. Iford, an A. M. E. minister of Shreveport, wrote to the church newspaper describing constraints on the movement and communications of new agricultural workers brought to the area from North Carolina in 1890. A local paper, the *Caucasian*, denied the report and urged that whites refuse assistance to black congregations as a result.[40]

Interest in political and social issues by black church members came to include concern about excessive use of alcohol in the 1870s, a view that increased in the decades to follow. When the Colored Baptist Convention of Arkansas met in little Rock during July 1871, temperance provided one topic for discussion. An A. M. E. church conference later that year also adopted a statement supporting temperance. Wesley Chapel M. E. Church in the Arkansas capital included drinking among its concerns at a gathering in 1874. A district conference of the M. E. chapel at Shreveport in 1883 placed the topic on its list of major issues. The state conference of the A. M. E. church at Little Rock in 1887 included a committee on temperance. St. Paul M. E. Church in the Louisiana city held a debate on the need for prohibition of alcoholic beverages in 1892. B. W. Roberts, the minister of St. James A.M.E. Church in San Antonio, spoke out in favor of temperance during 1896. A Women's Temperance Union formed at Antioch Baptist Church of Houston in 1897 to stimulate interest in the issue.[41]

Another growing interest for church members, along with temperance, became foreign missions, with Africa as a focal point for activity. Black Baptists in their state convention at Little Rock as early as 1871 counted missions among their goals to be pursued. Yet the issue became a major theme only in the 1880s. The A. M. E. annual conference for the state, held in Little Rock in 1887, included a committee on missions. A Baptist convention at Mount Zion Baptist Church in Houston emphasized African missions as well as education. Missions received discussions along with several other topics when the executive board of the Women's Baptist State Convention held sessions in Little Rock during April 1894. One speaker focused on missions during a celebration conducted at Bethel A. M. E. Church in the Arkansas city in 1896. At a Baptist Sunday school convention in San Antonio during 1897 mission activity in Africa received attention. The following year black Baptists of Texas held a convention at St. Emanuel Church in Houston specifically to consider international missions. At the C. M. E. conference held at Little Rock during 1898, the Women's Missionary Society presented speakers in favor of increased emphasis on missions.[42]

Occasionally the black urban congregations turned from the dominant religious and social issues to economic concerns. Elias Dibble and other Houston church leaders in the late 1860s helped form a "Mutual Benevolent Society" to assist the unfortunate in the community. At the A. M. E. state conference in Little Rock during the fall of 1887, one committee considered the question of homesteads for blacks. When the black Baptists in Arkansas convened at Little Rock in 1896, industrial training provided one focal point for their discussions. The A. M. E. church conference at Little Rock in 1897, at the end of a depression period, called for support of black businesses that in turn could hire more black employees.[43]

Concern for the elderly joined missionary efforts as an area of activity in the 1880s. At Bethel A. M. E. Church in Little Rock the Daughters of Zion presented an "Old Folks Concert and Tableaux" in 1884. An Old Ladies Home was organized in 1894 at Little Rock with a board of guardians that included women active in local churches. The "Sunshine Band," a children's musical group, performed for the women in the home soon after its creation. Congregations continued to support the home in the years to follow.[44] To achieve such a range of goals the churches held Sunday services that usually involved music, prayers, Bible readings, collection of funds to support the church, sermons, "shouting praise to God" especially by older members, and baptism of new converts. At Wesley Chapel M. E. Church in Little Rock services in the years immediately after the Civil War continued the pattern from slave days in which "the men went in one door and the women the other. They sat on opposite sides of the aisle." The practice changed in 1877 when John and Charlotte Stephens, a newly married couple, broke with tradition and began sitting together.[45]

Sunday schools supplemented the Sunday services by educating young people about religion in urban churches throughout the period, beginning certainly by the early 1870s. A visiting bishop provided special instruction for Sunday School teachers at Wesley Chapel M. E. Church in Little Rock during 1885 and at a Baptist church in Shreveport in 1897. The A. M. E. church in Shreveport conducted a Sunday school convention in the summer of 1886.[46]

In addition to Sunday Schools, special youth organizations met, sometimes in the evening on other weekdays, to expand the influence of the churches. Charlotte Stephen brought together an informal group to exchange ideas about religion at Wesley Chapel M. E. Church in Little Rock. More formal organization came in the 1890s. In Houston the Epworth League appeared in the M. E. churches during 1892, and in Little Rock by 1896. Christian Endeavor Societies formed in the A. M. E. churches of Houston in 1893 and in San Antonio during 1896. Baptist congregations created the Young People's Union at Little Rock in 1893, at Houston in 1895, and in Shreveport by 1900. These groups enjoyed debates, readings, essays, and singing, with the goals of advancing Christian education and moral living.[47]

Cooperative meetings among urban churches, beginning in the 1880s, reflected some effort to overcome early competitive conflicts. In Little Rock an Evangelical Alliance, representing four Methodist denominations and the Congregational church, held union services that moved from church to church during the first week of January 1886. St. Paul M. E. Church of Shreveport held a Sunday School picnic and invited the church schools of the other black congregations in 1887. A Ministerial Alliance met in Little Rock during 1894 to hear papers to discuss various aspects of religion. By 1896 it included preachers from the Methodists denomination, Baptist churches, and the Congregational church. A Ministers Union including both Methodists and Baptists also formed in San Antonio during 1897.[48]

Black religion, partially secret under slavery, emerged into an important role in the lives of city dwellers in the frontier South after the Civil War. Although a few African influences lingered and whites initially sought to retain some control over black religion, African American congregations quickly organized in each town. Most of the early churches evolved from slave congregations and joined the Baptist or Methodist Episcopal denominations.

Growth of black churches followed three patterns. The original congregations grew in size and built larger, more impressive structures, sometimes with assistance from sympathetic whites. New denominations also appeared—first the African Methodist Episcopal and Colored Methodist Episcopal churches in the late 1860s and 1870s, followed by Catholic congregations in the Texas cities and other Protestant groups in Little Rock. As the towns grew new congregations of the older denominations appeared, with Baptists apparently stronger west of the Mississippi than farther east.

Former slave preachers and a few white ministers provided leadership in the 1860s, a different pattern from many congregations east of the Mississippi River with larger free black populations before the Civil War. But the early preachers soon gave way to a younger generation of black clergy, some from east of the Mississippi, most of whom could claim some college education. This background probably also separated the urban congregations from rural churches. Occasionally a female minister joined their ranks for a brief period. Disputes over personal life or church leadership caused some abrupt changes of ministers, but an image of stable, committed clergy became dominant. Membership in the congregations reflected the spectrum of social classes, with the Methodist Episcopal and African Methodist Episcopal churches probably containing more middle-class participants. Women, who seem to have formed a majority of the members, played active roles in fund raising, Sunday schools, and missionary efforts.

From their founding the black congregations emphasized evangelism, education, and morality. They also contributed social events for the community and at times spoke out on political issues important to African Americans. Prohibition, missionary activities, concern for the elderly, and economic problems also attracted church attention on occasion. Sunday School and cooperative efforts among different denominations became additional avenues for the pursuit of these goals in the 1880s and 1890s.

Thus black churches became important institutions in the smaller cities of the frontier South, where one might have expected rural traditions and limitations to be stronger. Instead, African American religious efforts in the rapidly growing towns west of the Mississippi developed quickly into the full range of activities conducted in older cities to the east. That modernizing trend seemed to reflect the interaction of new denominational connections with the needs and concerns of an expanding urban population.[49]

Notes

1. For the growth of these urban areas see Alwyn Barr, "Black Migration into Southwestern Cities, 1865–1900," in Gary W. Gallagher, ed. *Essays on Southern History: Written in Honor of Barnes F. Lathrop* (Austin, 1980), 17–38.

2. Little Rock *Morning Republican*, January 30, 31, 1872; Houston *Post*, June 8, 1894.

3. James Burke to George Whipple, November 12, 1869, Burke to O. O. Howard, December 14, 1870, American Missionary Association Archives, microfilm, Texas Tech University; San Antonio *Express*, January 7, 1872; Joe Gray Taylor, *Louisiana Reconstructed* (Baton Rouge, 1974), 446; Little Rock *Arkansas Gazette*, June 6, 7, 1891; Mary Alice Lavender, "Social Conditions in Houston and Hanks County, 1869–1872" (M.A. thesis: Rice University, 1950), 178.

4. Adolphine Fletcher Terry, *Charlotte Stephens: Little Rock's First Black Teacher* (Little Rock: Academic Press, 1973), 23, 42, 48, 51; *Directory and Program of the Fifty-eighth Session of the Southwest Conference which will be held in Wesley Chapel Methodist Episcopal Church October 10, 1935*, p. 9; Paul D. Lack, "An Urban Slave Community: Little Rock, 1831–1862," *Arkansas Historical Quarterly*, 41 (Autumn, 1982), 269–270; Little Rock *Morning Republican*, July 24, 1871.

5. W. A. Leonard, *Houston City Directory for 1866* (Houston, 1867), 112; *The Red Book; A Compendium of Social, Professional, Religious, Educational and Industrial Interests of Houston's Colored Population* (Houston, 1915), 21–24, 72; *Antioch Baptist Church Centennial, Houston—1866–1966*, (p. 2); Houston *Tri Weekly Telegraph*, January 31, February 14, 1866.

6. Shreveport *Southwestern*, August 9, 16, 1865, March 21, 1866; Cornerstones of Antioch Baptist Church and of St. James Methodist Church, Shreveport.

7. San Antonio *Express*, October 7, 1867, April 6, 1868, March 17, 1870; Walter N. Vernon and others, *The Methodist Excitement in Texas: A History* (Dallas: Texas United Methodist Historical Society, 1984), 84; H. T. Kealing, *History of African Methodism in Texas* (Waco, Texas, 1885), 117–130; "History of St. James A. M. E. Church" (typescript); *History Highlights St. Paul Methodist Church: Mount Zion First Baptist Church, 1871–1971, San Antonio, Texas* (Waco; United Church Directories, 1971); San Antonio Baptist Association, *A Baptist Century Around the Alamo, 1858–1958* (San Antonio, Texas, 1958), 29.

8. Shreveport *Southwestern*, March 21, 1866; Little Rock *Morning Republican*, July 8, 10, August 8, 1871; Galveston *News*, October 30, 1874; San Antonio *Express*, October 12, December 9, 12, 16, 1867.

9. Little Rock *Morning Republican*, November 13, 16, 17, 1871, February 9, 1872; Little Rock *Arkansas Mansion*, December 1, 1883. See also John T. Jenifer, *Centennial Retrospect History of the African Methodist Episcopal Church* (Nashville, Tennessee, 1915), 100.

10. Stephen Gould, *The Alamo City Guide, San Antonio Texas* (New York, 1882), 49; Little Rock *Arkansas Gazette*, April 13, 1902, January 12, 1878; Little Rock *Daily Republican*, July 30, 1873; Little Rock *Arkansas Mansion*, July 28, November 10, 1883, February 9, 1884; Indianapolis *Freeman*, April 23, July 30, 1892, June 1, November 30, 1895; Houston *Post*, February 11, 1896.

11. David Blueford Gaines, *Racial Possibilities as Indicated by the Negroes of*

Arkansas (Little Rock: Philander Smith College, 1898), 120; Little Rock *Baptist Vanguard*, January 14, 1897; Indianapolis *Freeman*, September 16, 1893; U.S. Census Office, *Report on Statistics of Churches in the United States at the Eleventh Census: 1890* (Washington: Government Printing Office, 1894), 108–111.

12. For the pattern of denominational evolution see the city directories for Houston, Little Rock, San Antonio, and Shreveport; Pulaski County Marriage Records, Courthouse, Little Rock, Book, 13–2.

13. Little Rock *Arkansas Gazette*, August 12, 1871; Little Rock *Morning Republican*, August 10, 11, 14, 16, 18, 26, 1871; *Miles Chapel Christian Methodist Church* (Little Rock, 1970).

14. John T. Gillard, *The Catholic Church and the American Negro* (1929; reprinted New York: Johnson Reprint Corp., 1968), 41; Little Rock city directories, 1886, 1887, 1893–4, 1900–1901; Indianapolis *Freeman*, July 27, 1889; William P. Witsell, *A History of Christ Episcopal Church Little Rock, Arkansas, 1839–1947* (Little Rock, 1949), 72–74; David E. Finch, "Little Rock's Red Bishop Brown and His Separate Black Church," *Pulaski County Historical Review*, 20 (September, 1972), 27–34; Little Rock *Arkansas Gazette*, October 5, 1902.

15. M. J. Gilbert, ed., *Diamond Jubilee 1874–1949 Archdiocese of San Antonio* (San Antonio: Archdiocese of San Antonio, 1949), 137–138; Mary Immaculata Turkey, *Mother Margaret Mary Healy–Murphy* (San Antonio, 1968), 56–63; Carlos Castaneda, *Our Catholic Heritage in Texas, 1519–1936* (7 vols., Austin: Van Boechmann-Jones, 1936–1958), VII, 231; Indianapolis *Freeman*, April 29, 1893, March 6, 1897, March 16, 1901; Houston city directory, 1900–1901.

16. City directories for Houston, Little Rock, San Antonio, and Shreveport from the 1860s to 1900.

17. Little Rock *Daily Republican*, January 12, 1875; *History of First Baptist Church (Colored) San Antonio, Texas 1871–1944*, p. 9; *Directory and Program of the Fifty-eighth Session of the Southwest Conference . . . in Wesley Chapel Methodist Episcopal Church October, 30, 1935*, p. 9–10; *The Red Book*, 22; Little Rock *Arkansas Gazette*, September 22, 1898.

18. Indianapolis *Freeman*, December 31, 1892, September 16, 1893, April 27, 1895; Little Rock *Baptist Vanguard*, January 14, 1897; Gaines, *Racial Possibilities*, 121–124; Little Rock *Arkansas Gazette*, November 15, 1887; April 18, 1899; *Antioch Baptist Church Centennial, Houston, 1866–1966*, p. 2; *Red Book*, 21.

19. Leonard, *Houston City Directory*, 112; *Red Book*, 21; Vernon, *Methodist Excitement*, 84; San Antonio *Express*, March 1, 1869; interview with the Reverend B. Edward Jones, Shreveport, July 22, 1971; Clara B. Kennan, "First Negro Teacher in Little Rock," *Arkansas Historical Quarterly*, 9 (Autumn, 1950), 196–198; Margaret Smith Ross, "Nathan Warren, A Free Negro for the Old South," Ibid., 15 (Spring, 1956), 59.

20. Kealing, *African American Methodism in Texas*, 10–11, 117–121, 130.

21. Ibid., 129–130; Little Rock *Morning Republican*, August 14, 1871.

22. William J. Simmons, *Men of Mark* (Cleveland, 1887), 590–593; James T. Haley, *Afro-American Encyclopedia* (Nashville, 1896), 562–563; Indianapolis *Freeman*, January 24, October 10, 1891; I. Garland Penn, *Afro-American Press and Its Editors* (1891; reprinted New York, 1969), 258–261; E. M. Woods, *Blue Book of Little Rock* (Little Rock, 1907), 49–78; Kealing, *African Methodism in Texas*, 69–174, 181–185, 194–195, 199–202, 219–221; Houston *Post*, June 21, 1893; C. H. Phillips, *The History of the Colored Methodist Episcopal Church in America* (1898; reprinted New York, 1972), 222–227. This analysis is based on nineteen biographical sketches of ministers, eleven from Little Rock, four from Houston, three from San Antonio, and one from Shreveport.

23. Simmons, *Men of Mark*, 590–593.

24. Haley, *Afro-American Encyclopedia*, 562–563; Jenifer, *History of the African Methodist Episcopal Church*; Little Rock *Arkansas Mansion*, July 7, 1883.

25. Woods, *Blue Book of Little Rock*, 63–65; Gaines, *Racial Possibilities*, 42.

26. Shreveport *Times*, August 23, 1890; Indianapolis *Freeman*, July 18, 1896.

27. Jenifer, *History of the African Methodist Episcopal Church*, 99–100; Little Rock *Arkansas Mansion*, July 7, 1883.

28. Shreveport *Southwestern*, August 29, 1866; Little Rock *Morning Republican*, July 11, 1868; Little Rock *Daily Republican*, May 1, 3, 1872; Shreveport *Times*, May 25, 1877; Indianapolis *Freeman*, July 12, 1890.

29. San Antonio *Express*, December 8, 13, 17, 1878, July 20, 22, 26, 1879; Shreveport *Times*, March 17, 26, April 5, 7, May 10, June 23, 1889.

30. W. E. B. DuBois, *The Negro Church* (Atlanta: Atlanta University Publications No. 8, 1903), 165; Woods, *Blue Book of Little Rock*, 142–143.

31. List of church members from the Little Rock *Morning Republican*, July 10, August 8, 11, 1871, and *Mount Zion First Baptist Church, 1871–1971, San Antonio, Texas* were compared to occupations listed in the Little Rock city directory for 1971 and the San Antonio city directories for 1877–1882, the earliest ones available. These patterns continued for many black churches. Compare Indianapolis *Freeman*, December 2, 1893, to Little Rock city directory.

32. Little Rock *Arkansas Mansion*, July 7, 1883; Indianapolis *Freeman*, March 13, 1897; Gaines, *Racial Possibilities*, 124–125.

33. *Mount Zion First Baptist Church, 1871–1971, San Antonio, Texas*; San Antonio *Express*, December 9, 16, 1867; Little Rock *Morning Republican*, August 8, 1871.

34. Little Rock *Baptist Vanguard*, May 28, 1896; Indianapolis *Freeman*, November 2, 1895.

35. San Antonio *Express*, February 17, 20, 1867; James Burke, "A Texas Christ-

ian Among the Lowly," January 12, 1869, American Missionary Association Archives; Stephen Powers, *Afoot and Alone; A Walk From Sea to Sea by the Southern Route* (Hartford, Connecticut, 1872), 104; Little Rock *Daily Republican,* March 19, 1972.

36. Little Rock *Arkansas Gazette,* April 24, August 5, 1894; William Grant Still, "My Arkansas Boyhood," *Arkansas Historical Quarterly,* 26 (Autumn, 1967), 289; William Pickens, *Bursting Bonds* (Boston, 1923), 99.

37. Little Rock *Morning Republican,* May 28, 1868; Burke, "A Texas Christian Among the Lowly," January 12, 1869, American Missionary Association Archives; Little Rock *Arkansas Mansion,* November 10, 1883; Little Rock *Arkansas Gazette,* November 12, 1887, May 15, 1890; Houston *Post,* June 11, 12, 1892; Castaneda, *Our Catholic Heritage in Texas,* VII, 342.

38. San Antonio *Express,* June 6, 1869, September 3, 1896; Little Rock *Morning Republican,* May 17, 1870; Little Rock *Daily Republican,* May 21, 1872; Shreveport *Times,* May 20, 1877; Houston *Post,* May 15, 1887; Indianapolis *Freeman,* December 28, 1895.

39. Little Rock *Daily Republican,* December 9, 1874; Julia White Interview, in George Rawick, ed., *The American Slave: A Composite Autobiography* (Westport: Greenwood Press, 1972), XI, 130; *Mount Zion First Baptist Church, 1871–1971, San Antonio, Texas;* Shreveport *Times,* August 12, 1883; Indianapolis *Freeman,* May 14, July 23, 1892, April 17, 1897.

40. Shreveport *Southwestern,* April 3, 1867; Little Rock *Morning Republican,* November 26, 1870; Little Rock *Arkansas Gazette,* May 30, 1882; Shreveport *Weekly Caucasian,* February 27, March 6, 1890.

41. Little Rock *Morning Republican,* July 22, November 14, 1871; Julia White interview, in Rawick, *American Slave,* XI, 130; Shreveport *Times,* August 12, 1883, December 9, 1892; Little Rock *Arkansas Gazette,* November 10, 1887; Indianapolis *Freeman,* May 23, 1896, June 19, 1897.

42. Little Rock *Morning Republican,* July 22, 1871; Little Rock *Arkansas Gazette,* November 10, 1887, December 3, 1898; Houston *Post,* June 9, 1892, April 17, 1898; Little Rock *Baptist Vanguard,* April 27, 1894; Indianapolis *Freeman,* March 7, 1896; San Antonio *Express,* August 21, 1897. For a general study see Walter L. Williams, *Black Americans and the Evangelization of Africa, 1877–1900* (Madison, Wisconsin, 1982).

43. *Red Book,* 22; Little Rock *Arkansas Gazette,* November 10, 1887, August 20, 1896, November 12, 1897.

44. Little Rock *Arkansas Mansion,* February 6, 1884; Little Rock *Baptist Vanguard,* February 16, March 2, 1894; Indianapolis *Freeman,* November 16, 1895.

45. Little Rock *Arkansas Gazette,* November 3, 1899; Terry, *Charlotte Stephens,* 98.

46. Little Rock *Morning Republican*, July 22, 1871; Houston *Daily Telegraph*, May 12, 1872; Shreveport *Times*, July 18, 1880, August 28, 1886, April 11, 1897; Little Rock *Arkansas Gazette*, April 26, 1885.

47. Terry, *Charlotte Stephen*, 84–85; Indianapolis *Freeman*, September 17, 1892, October 7, 1893, November 23, 1895, March 14, 23, April 18, September 12, 1896, August 11, 1900; Little Rock *Baptist Vanguard*, September 29, 1893.

48. Little Rock *Arkansas Gazette*, January 3, 1886; Shreveport *Times*, May 15, 1887; Little Rock Baptist Vanguard, March 2, 1894, July 9, August 6, October 29, 1896; Indianapolis *Freeman*, April 17, 1897.

49. For comparative discussion of black churches in older southern cities see Howard N. Rabinowitz, *Race Relations in the Urban South, 1865–1890* (New York, 1978), 198–225; Clarence E. Walker, *A Rock in a Weary Land: The African Methodist Episcopal Church During the Civil War and Reconstruction* (Baton Rouge, 1982); David M. Tucker, *Black Pastors and Leaders: Memphis, 1819–1972* (Memphis, 1975); William E. Montgomery, *Under Their Own Vine and Fig Tree: The African American Church in the South, 1865–1900* (Baton Rouge, 1993).

William R. Shafter

Commanding Black Troops in West Texas

PAUL H. CARLSON

Black buffalo soldiers played a major role in conquering the great West. Discriminated against in pay, they often had inferior mounts and inferior weapons. They were usually assigned the toughest duty and did the most menial jobs. Yet, in the face of discrimination, they won the respect of their commanders and their enemies. Although Paul H. Carlson focuses on the career of William R. Shafter, a white officer commanding black troops, the heartiness and hard work of the troopers is demonstrated on every page of his narrative. In just one campaign in 1875, for example, Shafter's troopers traveled a total of 2,500 miles on the Llano Estacado and in the doing proved that the Great Plains were not the "Sahara of North America and paved the way for settlement."

Carlson also mentions Shafter's strong support for his African American charges. On one occasion he refused to allow civil authorities to arrest a man because he believed the arrest was nothing but legal hazing. Although his action likely cost him a promotion, he demonstrated that he would put the welfare of his men first. When campaigning, Shafter drove his men hard, sometimes expecting superhuman efforts. Yet, he was with them, standing up to every hardship that he put them through. At the same time, however, it should be noted that this was the same commander who vociferously pressed the charges that lead to the dismissal of black officer Henry O. Flipper. In the end, men like Shafter and his black soldiers helped open the vast western land to white (and black) settlement.

★

FROM THE West Texas Plains in the mid-1870s Captain Theodore Baldwin complained to his wife, "I do not think you would like to scout with Colonel Shafter."[1] The note was understated indeed. A martinet of force and persistence, Lieutenant Colonel William R. Shafter of the Twenty-Fourth United States Infantry Regiment always drove vigorously the black troops of his command. Many young officers, such as Captain Baldwin, grumbled about his dogged determination.

Typical of Shafter's drive was an episode in 1875. Upon leaving Casas Amarillas Lake, near present Littlefield on the Llano Estacado, in a southwesterly direction, Shafter had hoped to find sufficient water for his men and horses in the large circular depressions characteristic of the High Plains. During the first two days he was successful, but having found no water by the expiration of the third day, he concluded that he must either strike for the Pecos or turn back. Characteristically, the resolute officer ordered his African American command to make for the Pecos some eighty miles distant. During the following two days and one night of marching, the troops suffered desperately from heat, dust, and thirst. On the last night out, many of the officers, having lost all hope of reaching the river, wrote messages to be taken home by those fortunate enough to survive.[2] Worn men were tied in their saddles; others at gun point were forced to keep up. Shafter cajoled, wheedled, and drove his men. After great hardship and privation, everyone safely, but exhaustively, reached the river.[3] In such aggressive style, for more than a decade, Shafter directed black troops.

His black infantry in West Texas, however, was not the first that Shafter had led. During the Civil War he had enjoyed command of a volunteer unit and afterward in Louisiana with the colorful Ranald Mackenzie had organized and trained one of the regular army's first all-black regiments.[4] In 1867 with his troops he had been ordered to the lower Rio Grande and the following year moved to West Texas at Fort Clark.

As a subaltern to Ranald Mackenzie, Shafter at first had few field assignments. But with each opportunity to command he relentlessly pursued horse thieves, cattle rustlers, desperadoes, or Indian raiders who were ravaging the West Texas frontier. As one result he quickly became recognized as the most energetic man of his rank in the Department of Texas. As another he was soon considered a rough, insensitive commander of black troops who, to achieve a sense of discipline, did not hesitate to exert extraordinary and ruthless power.[5] In 1870 his reputation followed him to Fort Concho, at present San Angelo.

Here, the post surgeon was amazed at the energy and restlessness with which Shafter attacked his garrison chores. In his report for January 1870, the surgeon wrote that Shafter "has displayed an abundance of energy, devoting the first days of arrival to thoroughly policing the post . . . [and] seeing a large corral . . . in the process of construction."[6] In the weeks that followed Shafter continued to push his African American command in construction activities. The next month, the surgeon reported that "work upon the guard house and corral is progressing with unprecedented rapidity."[7]

Vigorous and efficient in his post command, Shafter likewise was energetic in the field. In mid-August, after being ordered to Fort Mc-Kavett, he planned to scour thoroughly the lower Pecos River. Taking 6 officers and 128 enlisted men of the Ninth Cavalry and Twenty-Fourth Infantry, he marched southwestward to the river, reaching it at a point about twenty miles below present Sheffield.

Here, Shafter temporarily divided his command. Leaving most of it in camp at the Pecos, he and Captain Edward M. Heyl, Ninth Cavalry, with fifteen men crossed to the west bank of the river, climbed up onto the table lands, and marched due south for twenty miles, keeping all the time within four miles of the river. Using his field glasses to examine each ravine, Shafter discovered no indications of Indians. There, he left the river and rode southwestward for six or seven miles to Painted Rock Arroyo, only ten miles from the Rio Grande. Again finding no signs of Indians, with his patrol he returned to the rendezvous camp.

For nearly a month afterward the command scouted in the vicinity of the lower Pecos. The hard-driving Shafter ordered his men to check every ravine. It was monotonous, exhausting work. No Indians were seen, neither were there trails nor other indications of Indians having passed through the country recently. Nevertheless, Shafter doggedly pushed his men to the task. The persistence brought some luck: eight Indian ponies, which Shafter estimated had been near the Pecos for six months, were caught.

In mid-September, unable to locate either Indians or recent signs of them, Shafter finally directed his tired troops back toward Fort Mc-Kavett. While returning, his scouts located several abandoned Indian villages, about thirty-five miles west of the headwaters of the North and South Llano rivers. One had contained possibly as many as 150 Indians. Nearby they discovered a large, permanent body of water about two hundred yards long and deep enough to swim horses. For years the army had heard reports of the water pond, but its location had been known only to the red men. Consequently the pond was a favorite and secure place for Indians who committed depredations in the country near the headwaters of the Nueces.[8]

The Pecos River campaign proved significant. Having marched nearly five hundred miles, the scout showed that no Indians were lurking in the vicinity of the Pecos and the headwaters of the Llano rivers. Eight horses had been captured. A strategic and favorite Indian camping place had been located, and no longer would the Indians be able to use the water hole as a safe rendezvous. Moreover, in the psychological warfare that figured vitally in Indian fighting, the expedition demonstrated to the Plains warriors that bluecoat troopers could campaign successfully in an area that Indians previously had thought inaccessible to the army.

Twice the following year Shafter led black soldiers into such supposedly impenetrable lands. In June 1871 with a command totaling eighty-six officers and enlisted men, he turned a routine pursuit of Comanche horse thieves into a major exploration of the Monahans Sand Hills and across the Llano Estacado.[9] He destroyed an abandoned Indian village, two dozen buffalo robes, skins, and a large supply of provisions. He captured twenty horses and mules. He discovered that Comanches and Lipan and Mescalero Apaches, longtime enemies, had concluded a peace in the Sand Hills and that Comancheros used the area as a place of barter.[10]

A month later Shafter penetrated another Indian sanctuary. This time he drove his black command from Fort Davis on an exhausting five-hundred-mile scout into the torrid Big Bend region of the Rio Grande. Here with his troops he explored the country, crossing and recrossing trails, noting important water holes, and marking the sites of old Indian camps. At San Vincente he discovered an important Apache crossing on the river. He reported abandoned Indian encampments twenty-five miles southwest of Pena Blanca. The grass along his line of march was excellent, but the only wood he found was very large cottonwood trees along the streams. Where he struck the Rio Grande, there was no timber.[11]

Although it had killed no Indians, the expedition had found abundant evidence that Apaches used the Big Bend as a sanctuary. Perhaps more important, Shafter added considerably to the geographical knowledge of the Chihuahuan deserts and Big Bend mountains. Indeed, the information he gained about their nature and resources enabled the army later to maneuver more confidently in the region. In addition, it smoothed the way for later settlement.[12]

No sooner had Shafter returned to Fort Davis than an Apache chief, who frequented the Big Bend and who had gone to Presidio to negotiate with the Mexican authorities for release of some children captives of his band, sent word from Presidio del Norte that he wished to surrender. Shafter sent Lieutenant Isaiah H. McDonald to receive the surrender. But perhaps because the Mexican residents there, who gained their living largely by supplying United States Army posts, did not welcome complete harmony between Indians and Americans, the *alcalde* of Presidio warned the chief that his departure would prejudice release of the children. Whatever the reason, McDonald returned to Fort Davis empty-handed. Shafter agreed with his lieutenant that "the local authorities at Del Norte do not want [the Apache] to make or keep peace with the United States."[13]

Meanwhile, at Fort Davis Shafter was active. He supervised the repair of buildings, the construction of corrals, and the remodeling of the hospital. In addition, whenever necessary, he protected his black troops against racial injustice and discrimination. In one incident he took the stage coach lines to task. The infantry in the West was often assigned to guard stage lines. At the end of such a tour of duty men usually returned to the post on an inbound stage. Unfortunately, Shafter's black troops at least once were kept off the stage and forced to walk back to the barracks. Indeed, the El Paso Mail Lines station keeper at Leon Hole refused to provide food and shelter for the station guards. The tempestuous Shafter became incensed and immediately warned the stage company officers against further discrimination toward his men. When the black guards were put off the stage, he wrote, they were obliged to walk to Fort Stockton and along the way to obtain their rations "by their wits." He demanded that his troops should "be fed by the company or allowed facilities at the stations for cooking their own rations."[14] He would "be glad to furnish mail escorts as long as they are wanted," he concluded, "but they must be properly treated."[15] Apparently his letter got results for the records show no further complaint against the stage company.

In another incident Shafter challenged civilian authorities. When the volatile sheriff of Presidio County injudiciously entered Fort Davis to arrest a black soldier for public drunkenness, Shafter, aware that the bluecoat would be summarily prosecuted, would not allow the officer to remove the trooper. Although such belligerency represented a serious breach of military discipline, Shafter refused to subject his troops to what he regarded as legal hazing.[16]

The consequences proved critical. Although the trooper was never arrested, Shafter was immediately removed from Fort Davis. Later, the incident may have been included as evidence to deny him an early graduation to the rank of colonel. Much later, in 1887, after he had obtained the colonelcy, the incident apparently was offered as one excuse to block his promotion to the rank of brigadier general.[17]

Although temporarily rebuked, Shafter was not forgotten. Since the Department of Texas needed durable, effective officers, in the summer and fall of 1872 with his crack command of black troops he teamed for three months with Ranald Mackenzie on the Llano Estacado. While Mackenzie with one force scouted the Palo Duro and crossed the High Plains to Fort Sumner and beyond, Shafter with another examined the Caprock escarpment along the Salt Fork (Main Fork) of the Brazos. His black command made certain that there were no Indians lurking at the foot of the Staked Plains, although it found abundant evidence of old Indian camps near all the springs it visited. In addition, the command located water and fuel supplies and for future operations in the vicinity of present-day Slaton and Lubbock made a map of the country scouted.[18]

The following year Shafter with his black troops aided Mackenzie again. This time he helped during preparations for the celebrated raid into Mexico against the Kickapoos. Although he did not cross into Mexico with Mackenzie, Shafter performed valuable service for the expedition. He provided important information on the Mexican population, the location of villages, and the whereabouts of Mexican troops. Mackenzie stated that he was under great obligation to Shafter for his cordial cooperation and active support throughout the 1873 expedition.[19]

In 1875, after a lengthy stint in New York to study infantry equipment, Shafter led a huge command of African American troops for six months on the Staked Plains of West Texas and Eastern New Mexico. The Llano Estacado campaign, as it was called, proved grueling. At one stretch during the wearisome expedition Shafter in ten days marched his men nearly three hundred miles. Since they were seldom in camp for more than one night, the men, in addition to marching thirty miles a day, had to pack their tents and other field equipment each morning and unpack it again each night. The subsequent wear and tear on both men and animals prompted one officer to complain that "our horses will go to the devil very fast at the rate Col. Shafter charges the whole command."[20]

The comment could not have been more pointed. In the field Shafter demonstrated an unsurpassed ability to get the utmost out of his soldiers. During the agonizing 1875 expedition, in which his command covered over 2,500 miles of the High Plains, many of Shafter's men returned from the first crossing of the Plains without shirts or shoes, most were missing some article of clothing, and all were exhausted. Nevertheless, only two weeks later, Shafter started back across the Plains again, and hardly had he completed the second crossing when a third was commenced. The Llano Estacado campaign was as successful as it was difficult. It swept the Plains clear of Indians, destroyed completely the dreary myth of the Plains as the dreaded Sahara of North America, and paved the way for settlement, which quickly followed.[21]

Even more arduous and successful was Shafter's 1876 expedition to the mouth of the Pecos River. Three times during the strenuous, five-months-long campaign, Shafter marched his well-disciplined black troops across the rugged Coahuila deserts of Mexico. In each instance the troops rode in over 100 degree heat, and on one occasion they went sixty-five miles through the parching desert without water. During the summer his men twice engaged and defeated Indians. Two large camps of hostiles were completely destroyed, another in the Carmen Mountains was discovered and its location noted, 137 horses and mules and much stolen stock was recovered, and an estimated eighteen Indians were killed or captured.[22]

Shortly after the close of the Pecos River expedition, Shafter became commander of the District of the Nueces. Embracing the upper Rio Grande border area from Laredo to old Fort Leaton, the region was a natural haunt and even a highway for roving bands of Lipan and Mescalero Apaches who slipped across the Rio Grande to prey upon the abundant cattle and horse herds along the upper reaches of the Nueces. Any luckless cowboy or traveler who got in their way, the Indians killed. One raid in 1878 resulted in the death of eighteen citizens, including some women and children.[23]

Protecting the Rio Grande frontier was no easy task. Not only was the topography of the territory on both sides of the river barren and waterless, but Mexican troops resented the presence of American soldiers south of the border. As a result, relations between the United States and Mexico were strained, and Mexican leaders protested each American violation of their country's soil. Moreover, by criticizing the border crossings, Democratic leaders in Washington hoped to embarrass the Rutherford B. Hayes administration. Consequently, Lieutenant Colonel Shafter needed to act with astute diplomatic good will and with the consummate skill demanded of desert campaigning.

Shafter was not timid in his new task. The audacious commander kept his bluecoats in the field. Small patrols suffered through December's cold, scouting relentlessly each trail and vigilantly watching for evidence of raiding parties from Mexico. The perseverance paid dividends. In January 1877, after some marauders were seen, Shafter from his headquarters at Fort Clark quickly dispatched Lieutenant John L. Bullis of his regiment and Captain Alexander B. Keyes, Tenth Cavalry, and over one hundred officers and men some 125 miles deep into the Santa Rosa Mountains of Mexico. The Bullis-Keyes raid recovered much stolen stock and led to the return of several horses and mules.[24]

Additional border crossings followed. In March Shafter waded the Rio Grande with a large detachment of black troops, but too late to rescue from jail two men, who had guided his troops the year previous, sentenced to die as traitors. In July Bullis splashed across the river but with little luck in striking Indians or recovering stolen stock. In the fall, as raiding increased, Shafter twice directed well-armed expeditions to pursue hostile Indians to their sanctuaries in Mexico.[25]

Indeed, Shafter took personal command of the first expedition. The raid into Mexico began near the end of September after black scouts reported to Bullis, scouting along the Rio Grande near the mouth of Las Moras Creek, that marauders had entered Texas. Bullis immediately sent word by courier to Shafter at Fort Clark. In turn the district commander ordered the scrappy lieutenant with his force of ninety men to cross the river on the twenty-eighth and wait for Shafter who, with about three hundred troops of the Eighth and Tenth cavalries, was on his way to join him. When he rode into camp about 2:00 p.m. the same day, Shafter ordered Bullis to start after dark for the Indian village near Saragosa. He promised to protect Bullis's rear in the event that there were wounded soldiers who might slow the retreating command. Both officers were well aware that a Mexican force of some two hundred soldiers, as well as dozens of thieves and desperadoes in the vicinity, would be watching for a favorable opportunity to strike the exhausted invaders.

About 11:00 p.m. Bullis started. Alternating his pace between a trot and a gallop during the long night ride, he reached Saragosa, about forty miles distant, at sunrise. Marching up Perdido Creek, he caught by surprise at about 8:00 a.m. the Lipans and Mescaleros who fled for safety upon sighting the charging American troops. Bullis's scouts and troops chased the terrified Indians for four or five miles, capturing before reining to a halt four women, one boy, twelve horses, and two mules. After burning the small village and destroying the camp equipage, Bullis, turning his troops due north toward the head of the San Diego River where he was to meet Shafter, marched at a fast walk or trot until he reached the appointed rendezvous about 9:00 p.m. His troops, who had been in their saddles continuously for twenty-two hours, rolled from the horses in exhaustion. The support troops were nowhere in sight.

Meanwhile, Shafter had waited until morning before starting for the rendezvous. After moving slowly up the San Diego River, he encamped a few miles from its head. On the following morning, September 30, a little after sunrise, he spied Bullis, who had had an apprehensive, but undisturbed, night's rest, moving northeastward toward the Rio Grande and not far behind a column of approximately ninety Mexican troops from Saragosa under Colonel Innocente Rodriguez. Immediately, he broke camp and joined his trusty subordinate.[26]

The combined command, nearly four hundred troops, continued toward the river at a brisk walk all day and late into the night. Colonel Rodriguez cautiously followed about a mile behind for a distance of ten miles, but then suddenly disappeared when Shafter began to maneuver his troops in preparation for battle.[27] No engagement took place, nor were any shots fired, and, when Shafter again headed for the Rio Grande, some of the officers grumbled about running from "a handful of Mexicans."[28] After wading the river at Lasora Crossing near San Felipe about midnight, Shafter rested his command for two days before returning to Fort Clark, where he arrived on October 4.[29]

The raid brought unfavorable reaction in the capitals of both countries. In Mexico City, the newspapers, exaggerating its significance, indicated that the American troops had flagrantly violated international law. They also boasted of how a small Mexican force of only ninety troops had easily repelled an American force four times its number. In Washington, the raid became an important factor that influenced the decision of Congress to investigate the Texas border troubles.[30]

The Congressional investigations revealed the need for additional troops in the District of the Nueces. Accordingly, in February 1878, when Colonel Ranald Mackenzie arrived with his Fourth Cavalry, Shafter was relieved of his command. Still assigned to the district, however, he once again found himself closely teamed with his former colonel.

With adequate troops to end the depredations, Shafter and Mackenzie wasted little time in bringing peace to the border. In April and May they planned and organized a major raid to destroy in Mexico hostile Indian lairs, and in June, with the army's approval, they carried it out. Twice during the bold assault there were confrontations, but not clashes, with Mexican troops who turned away after first challenging the Americans. Perhaps embarrassed that his troops had backed down in the face of the hated gringos, Porfirio Díaz, President of Mexico, took steps to cooperate with the United States in haulting depredations north of the Rio Grande. Consequently, no further border crossings were necessary and by the end of 1878 tension along the river had relaxed demonstrably.[31]

Early the following year Shafter left Texas. In March his long-awaited promotion to colonel came through, and he was transferred to the First Infantry Regiment stationed in Dakota. He returned to Texas in late 1880 to pursue followers of Victorio, the marauding Apache. Later he moved to Arizona to help pacify Apache renegades. In 1891, following the Wounded Knee incident, he participated in the Siouan Campaign, and in 1898, during the Spanish-American War, he led the American Expeditionary force to Cuba.

The techniques of command vary, of course, with the personality of the commander. While some men prefer to lead by suggestion or example or other methods, Shafter chose to drive his subordinates by bombast and by threats, and he believed that profanity was the most convincing medium of communication. Although his mannerisms achieved spectacular results, they did not win affection among his men. Good-humored, even jolly, in his intimate personal relationships, he was likely to give short, blunt answers to his subalterns, he would never allow his orders to be challenged, and he always demanded the same dogged determination from his men that he himself gave to field maneuvers.

Clearly, as a commander of black troops in West Texas, the volatile Shafter was tough and aggressive. Energetic, resourceful, and courageous, he possessed initiative, looked out for the welfare of his men and animals, and was utterly unafraid of responsibility. When he thought that they were not being treated properly, he vociferously defended his African American soldiers, and he always spoke highly of their ability. Most officers learned to like him and his men, although he rarely enjoyed their affection, and always remembered him as a zealous and forceful commander.

Notes

1. Captain Theodore A. Baldwin, Tenth Cavalry, to his wife, August 1875, in L. F. Sheffy, ed., "Letters and Reminiscences of Gen. Theodore A. Baldwin: Scouting

after Indians on the Plains of Texas," *Panhandle Plains Historical Review*, XI (1938), 7–30 (hereafter cited as Baldwin, "Letters and Reminiscences").

2. William G. Muller, *The Twenty-Fourth Infantry, Past and Present* (n. p., 1928), 1–8.

3. *Ibid.*; and Baldwin, "Letters and Reminiscences," 7–30.

4. Returns from Regular Army Infantry Regiments June 1821–December 1961 (Regimental Returns), Forty-First Infantry, February 1867, Microcopy No. 665, Roll 296, National Archives (NA).

5. James Parker, *The Old Army: Memories, 1872–1918* (Philadelphia: Dorrence & Co., 1929), 100.

6. Post Medical Reports, Fort Concho, January 1870, Book No. 401-3-7, December 1867–June 1889, Old Records Division (ORD), Adjutant General's Office (AGO), NA.

7. *Ibid.*, February 1870.

8. William R. Shafter to H. Clay Wood, Assistant Adjutant General, Department of Texas, October 10, 1870, Post Records, Fort McKavett, Record Group (RG), 191, NA, in Jerry Sullivan, ed., "Lieutenant Colonel W. R. Shafter's Pecos River Expedition of 1870," *West Texas Historical Association Yearbook*, XLVII (1971), 149–152.

9. Shafter to Wood, July 15, 1871, Letters Sent, Fort Davis, United States Army Command (USAC), RG 98, NA; Post Medical Reports, Fort Davis, June–July 1871, Book No. 7, 9–12, ORD, AGO, NA; Returns from U.S. Military Posts, 1800–1916 (Post Returns), Fort Davis, June–July 1871, Microcopy No. 617, Roll 297, NA; J. Evetts Haley, *Fort Concho and the Texas Frontier* (San Angelo, Texas: San Angelo Standard Times, 1952), 163–167.

10. Shafter to Wood, July 15, 1871, LS, Fort Davis, USAC, RG 98, NA.

11. Shafter to Wood, January 4, 1872, and February 1, 1872, LS, Fort Davis, USAC, RG 98, NA; Post Returns, Fort Davis, October 1871, Microcopy No. 617, Roll 297, NA.

12. Shafter to Wood, January 4, 1872, and February 1, 1872, LS, Fort Davis, USAC, RG 98, NA; Post Returns, Fort Davis, October 1871, Microcopy No. 617, Roll 297, NA; Post Medical Reports, Fort Davis, October–November 1871, Book No. 7-9-12, ORD, AGO, NA.

13. Shafter to Lieutenant Isaiah H. McDonald, Ninth Cavalry, December 8, 1871, in Shafter to Wood, January 4, 1872, LS, Fort Davis, USAC, RG 98, NA.

14. Shafter to F. C. Taylor, Agent, El Paso Mail Lines, ca. January 4, 1872, LS, Fort Davis, USAC, RG 98, NA.

15. *Ibid.*; Arlen Fowler, *The Black Infantry in the West* (Westport, Connecticut: Greenwood Publishing Corporation, 1971), 25–26.

16. Shafter to S. R. Miller, Justice of the Peace, Presidio County, November 6, 1871, LS, Fort Davis, USAC, RG 98, NA.

17. A. J. Evans, Brief for the Appellees, Presidio Mining Co. *v.* Alice Bullis, Supreme Court of Texas, Austin Term, 1887 (filed with 2220 Appointments, Commissions, and Personal (ACP) 1879, Letters Received (LR), AGO, RG 94, NA; David S. Stanley, Commanding the Department of Texas, to Adjutant General, United States Army, July 2, 1887 (filed with 2220 ACP 1879), LR, AGO, RG 94, NA.

18. Shafter, "Report of Scout," July 22, 1872, and Wentz C. Miller, "Report of Scout," September 2, 1872, in Ernest Wallace, *Ranald S. Mackenzie's Official Correspondence Relating to Texas, 1871–1873* (Lubbock: West Texas Museum Association, 1967), 101.

19. General Orders No. 6, Department of Texas, June 2, 1873, in Shafter Papers, Stanford University Library, Stanford, California (photocopies in Southwest Collection, Texas Tech University, Lubbock); Ernest Wallace, *Ranald S. Mackenzie on the Texas Frontier* (Lubbock: West Texas Museum Association, 1964), 92–114.

20. Baldwin, "Letters and Reminiscences," 7–10.

21. Shafter to J. H. Taylor, Assistant Adjutant General, Department of Texas, January 4, 1876, 4688 AGO 1876, LR, RG 94, NA. In 1876 Charles Goodnight trailed a large cattle herd from Colorado southeastward into Palo Duro Canyon.

22. Shafter to Taylor, June 20, 1876, in Shafter Papers; Shafter and Lieutenant John L. Bullis, Twenty-Fourth Infantry, Testimony before House Committee on Military Affairs, January 6–8, 1878, "Texas Border Troubles," 45 Cong., 2 Sess., *House Misc. Doc. 64*, 154–190; Paul H. Carlson," William R. Shafter: Military Commander in the American West" (unpublished Ph.D. dissertation, Texas Tech University, Lubbock, 1973), 180–219.

23. Captain John O. Elmore, Twenty-Fourth Infantry, to Acting Assistant Adjutant General, District of the Rio Grande, Fort Brown, May 23, 1878, 4584 AGO 1878 (filed with 1653 AGO 1875), Affairs on the Rio Grande and Texas, LR 1805,-89, NA.

24. Bullis, Testimony before House Committee on Military Affairs, January 8, 1878, as cited, 188–190; Post Returns, Fort Clark, January 1877, Microcopy No. 617, Roll 214, NA.

25. Taylor to Shafter, April 1, 1877, Taylor to Brigadier General Edward O. C. Ord, Commanding Department of Texas, April 5, 1877, Shafter to Taylor, October 1, 1877, and Shafter to Ord, December 24, 1877, in Shafter Papers; Fowler, *The Black Infantry in the West*, 14–35; Shafter and Bullis, Testimony before House Committee on Military Affairs, January 6–8, 1878, as cited, 154–190.

26. Bullis, Testimony before the House Committee on Military Affairs, January 8, 1878, as cited, 191–193; Shafter to Taylor, October 1, 1877, in Shafter Papers; Bullis to Helenus Dodt, Twenty-Fourth Infantry, Post Adjutant at Fort Clark, October 12, 1877, in Shafter Papers.

27. Bullis, Testimony before the House Committee on Military Affairs, January 8, 1878, as cited, 191–193; Shafter to Taylor, October 1, 1877, Shafter to Ord, De-

cember 24, 1877, and Bullis to Dodt, October 12, 1877, in Shafter Papers; also see J. Fred Rippy, *The United States and Mexico* (rev. ed. New York: F. S. Crofts and Company, 1931), 294–295.

28. Second Lieutenant Edward P. Turner, Tenth Cavalry, Testimony before the House Committee on Military Affairs, March 2, 1878, as cited, 269.

29. Post Returns, Fort Clark, October 1877, Microcopy No. 617, Roll 214, NA.

30. "Report and Accompanying Documents of the Committee on Relations of the United States with Mexico," 45 Cong., 2 Sess., *House Report* 701, 21–30; J. M. Callahan, *American Foreign Policy in Mexican Relations* (New York: The Macmillan Company, 1932), 190–193; Rippy, *The United States and Mexico*, 285–300; Chester L. Barrows, *William M. Evarts, Lawyer, Diplomat, Statesman* (Chapel Hill: University of North Carolina Press, 1941), 351–361.

31. General Orders No. 7 District of the Nueces, June 11, 1878, in Shafter Papers; Mackenzie to Assistant Adjutant General, Department of Texas, June 21, 1878, in Ernest Wallace, *Ranald S. Mackenzie's Official Correspondence Relating to Texas, 1873–1879* (Lubbock: West Texas Museum Association, 1968), 204–209; Wallace, *Ranald Mackenzie on the Texas Frontier*, 176–179.

John B. Rayner

A Study in Black Populist Leadership

GREGG CANTRELL

In Texas blacks were effectively disfranchised in the 1870s. Further, whites reduced them to serfdom economically. Segregation was widespread, but in Texas, as in some other parts of the South, the rise of populism gave blacks hope. They had become disenchanted with the Republican party after its white leaders rejected their party's African American constituency. In the 1880s and 1890s, blacks by the score flocked to the populist banner, promising as it did a wide spate of political and economic reforms. Thus began a new experiment in biracial political cooperation.

In his examination of black populism in Texas, Gregg Cantrell focuses on the public life of John B. Rayner, whose populist career lasted from 1892 to 1898. From his base in Robertson County, Rayner extolled the virtues of the movement as he traveled far and wide in eastern Texas, spreading word of the populist reform demands and trying to recruit party members. In the spring of 1896, for example, he spoke in seventeen towns in just a twenty-four-day, six-hundred-mile tour. Rayner was one of the few black populists who appeared before white audiences. Perhaps his light complexion and good stage presence helped account for his ability to communicate with whites.

Rayner was a most effective recruiter. In the climatic elections of 1896, he may have delivered as many as 25,000 votes to the Populist party. But in the end, the biracial political experiment failed. Nationally, populists fused with the Democrats in 1896 in an attempt to win the presidency for William Jennings Bryan. In Texas, white Democrats used intimidation and violence to stop blacks from voting, just as whites had done during Reconstruction.

*

IN THE LAST YEARS of the nineteenth century, before the wholesale disfranchisement of African Americans in the South, black voters in Texas faced difficult political choices. Since the end of Reconstruction the national Republican leadership had done little for blacks. Many southern white Republicans had abandoned the party's black core constituency to establish a segregated, "lily-white" faction. As southern

Republicanism fractured along racial lines, the postwar optimism of former slaves was replaced by bitter disillusionment. Certainly there were political issues of interest to black voters. Increasing numbers of blacks found themselves in the relentless grip of the crop lien and the ubiquitous furnishing merchants. Many black farmers, reduced to debt peonage, lived circumscribed lives uncomfortably resembling slavery. Yet if casting a Republican ballot seemed to offer no relief, moving into the ranks of the Democrats was even more unpalatable for black Texans. The party of "Redemption" was the party of the landlords and the furnishing merchants, and in Texas, as elsewhere in the South, it postured as the party of the Lost Cause and the white man. The situation was right for the emergence of a third party, a party for black voters who could find no better home and for poorer white agriculturists who shared a common economic fate. In the South, this was the setting for Populism.[1]

Many historians have emphasized the biracial nature of southern Populism. "While the movement was at the peak of zeal," wrote C. Vann Woodward, "the two races had surprised each other and astonished their opponents by the harmony they achieved and the good will with which they co-operated."[2] That African Americans constituted an important segment of the Populist electorate in Texas in particular cannot be denied. But on what terms did black Texans participate in Populism and with what results? Some scholars have cited racist remarks by prominent white Populists or documented cases of voter-buying as proof that Populists pursued the black vote out of sheer expedience, as Democrats sometimes did.[3]

Such arguments are built generally upon the study of two types of primary sources: white Populist newspaper editorials and voting records. Historians have consistently based their discussions of the racial aspects of southern Populism on "white" sources—sources that cannot provide a complete understanding of why significant numbers of blacks in the South were attracted to Populism. An obvious alternative is to view the third party's appeal from the perspective of black Populists, especially of articulate black political leaders. Black ideologues carried the message of the People's Party to the African American voters in ways no white politicos could duplicate.

John B. Rayner was Texas Populism's foremost black spokesman. He sat on the executive committee of the state Populist party and served as a full-time traveling lecturer and organizer. Despite Rayner's important position in the party, the scholar investigating his life confronts severely limited source materials, for two facts virtually assured Rayner's obscurity in turn-of-the-century Texas: he was a Populist and he was black. Neither are qualities that would endear him to white Texans in the first half of the twentieth century. By the time modern scholars began to reevaluate the multiracial character of Populism, only a fraction of the primary materials on black Populists such as Rayner had survived. From the relatively few extant sources, we can piece together enough of Rayner's career in the People's Party to offer an intriguing glimpse into one black Populist's mind and to shed light on the forces that drew blacks into the movement. "There is still not sufficient evidence," wrote Norman Pollack, "to indicate whether Populists enlisted the support of Negroes in order to use them to get elected, or whether such support was founded on a genuine desire to extend a hand of friendship and justice for its own sake."[4]

Rayner's career provides evidence that blacks cannot be written off as mere pawns in the Populist revolt. Instead, Rayner and thousands of African Americans in Texas saw in Populism an opportunity to gain a real voice in the democratic process, and they seized that opportunity.

John B. Rayner was born in North Carolina, the son of Kenneth Rayner, a white planter and three-term Whig congressman, and a slave mother, Mary Ricks. He was raised by his maternal grandparents, who were servants in the Rayner mansion in downtown Raleigh, a stone's throw from the state capitol. John Rayner received special attention from his white father, who provided him a college education after the Civil War. After finishing his education, he moved to the heavily black town of Tarboro in Edgecombe County, where he held the offices of constable, magistrate, and deputy sheriff during North Carolina's Reconstruction era. By any standard, he was an ex-slave of unusual achievement by the time he moved to Texas in 1880 or 1881.[5]

Rayner came to Texas as the leader of a sizeable migration of black farmworkers. More than likely he had been employed as a labor recruiter by Brazos Valley planters who were expanding their cotton-growing operations. African Americans were fleeing North Carolina by the thousands in the early 1880s, in search of better jobs and a less repressive racial climate. Although Rayner's destination—Robertson County—was still a very southern place, it apparently seemed like a distinct improvement to the families that Rayner led to Texas. Rayner bought a comfortable frame house in the black section of Calvert and spent the next few years teaching, perhaps occasionally preaching, and undoubtedly following the political situation closely. The 1882 tax records of Robertson County indicate that the Rayners owned one city lot and two cows valued at a total of $110.[6]

During Rayner's first ten years in Texas, the state's African Americans became increasingly dissatisfied with their political role. When he came to Texas, Rayner, like practically all black southerners, was a Republican. Although he never ran for office in the state, he was what a friend of his called "a public man."[7] Rayner's shift in political allegiance from the Republican to the People's Party corresponds closely to the changes taking place in black politics during the 1880s.

These changes had their roots in the southern strategy of Republican president Chester Arthur in the 1884 election. Arthur's political adviser on southern matters, Navy Secretary William E. Chandler, abandoned the Grant/Hayes/Garfield reliance on the votes of blacks and transplanted northerners ("carpetbaggers") in an attempt to lure the South's white businessmen into the Republican fold. To accomplish this meant reading blacks out of the local Republican organizations. White Republicans already had begun to chafe under the leadership of black political bosses such as Galveston's Norris Wright Cuney; hence in 1884 two developments took place. First, white Republicans bolted the party to choose "lily-white" slates of candidates. Second, the white faction began to advocate "fusion" (political alliances) with southern independents of one type or another whenever the defeat of Democratic candidates seemed possible. African Americans were left out of this political calculus and their interests left unattended. The split in the party and the policy of fusion led Rayner and thousands of other blacks to leave the Party of Lincoln by the early 1890s.[8]

The immediate cause of John Rayner's disillusionment seems to have been the 1892 gubernatorial race.[9] Two years earlier the progressive Democrat James Hogg had won the governor's office on his promise to regulate the railroads, creating a rift between the conservative Democrats (variously called "Bourbons," "Redeemers," or "Gold Democrats"), under the leadership of George Clark, and the Hogg progressives. With hopes of unseating Hogg, the Clark Democrats joined forces with the Cuney-led black Republicans on an independent ticket. Black Republican leaders openly endorsing a conservative Democrat for governor of Texas created among blacks widespread discontent with the treatment they were receiving at the hands of the Republican Party.[10]

The 1892 election returns reveal exactly how confused the state's black voters had become. Hogg had expressed concern over black education and lynching and thus carried about half the black vote. Clark, supposedly in coalition with the black faction of the Republican Party, won only about 30 percent. The Texas People's Party, which had been founded in 1891, polled about 20 percent of the black vote.[11] The Republican organization had gone too far in endorsing one white-supremacist Democrat in hopes of defeating another. Tired of seeing his people used as pawns of white politicians, Rayner turned his attention to the Populist cause.

Texas Populism traced its roots to the agrarian discontent of farmers caught in the crunch of a deflationary economy tied to the gold standard and constantly falling crop prices. Populists were seeking political solutions to the same problems that had earlier spawned the short-lived Greenback Party, the Grange, and the Farmers' Alliance. At the center of the Populist demands was a proposed program called the Subtreasury Plan, an innovative system of U.S. government-sponsored agricultural credit to help stabilize crop prices and provide low-interest farm loans. Populist platforms also called for government ownership of communication and transportation networks, focusing particularly on the railroads. Fair elections, protection of debtors, and a flexible paper currency were other important Populist demands. The entire Populist program was aimed at helping farmers escape the cycle of debt and dependency that characterized southern agricultural life. Since the majority of African Americans in Texas were poor farmers, Populist reformers such as John Rayner had every reason to expect a receptive audience in the black community.

Sometime between 1892 and 1894 Rayner became known as a "public man" at the state level. The lessons of ten years had taught him a number of important facts about black politics in Texas. For example, Rayner undoubtedly knew the demographics of the state, at least in general terms: 22 percent of the state's total population was black, and 15 percent was foreign-born (or of foreign-born parentage). The implications for politicians were clear: as long as whites remained united under the Democratic banner, black votes were of little consequence, but when the Populist party began attracting large numbers of white farmers, blacks suddenly became the swing element.[12]

This realignment of Texas politics presented blacks with unprecedented opportunities. Rayner realized that if blacks would vote as a bloc, they could exercise a degree of power unknown to them since Reconstruction. And if they could create an alliance with one of the white parties, blacks could extract a larger measure of political and economic justice. Rayner decided relatively early that, of the white parties, Pop-

ulism was the place for blacks to cast their lot. How the Populists convinced Rayner of this, and how Rayner convinced black voters, remains
one of the unique stories in southern race relations and politics.

If Populists were to succeed in building a biracial agrarian coalition,
they had to make inroads into the so-called Black Belt—those counties
having a black majority. In 1890 there were sixteen such counties in
Texas, and the African Americans living in them voted in large numbers.[13]

Unfortunately for Rayner and the Populists, it was in the Black Belt
counties (such as Rayner's home county, Robertson) that white Democrats normally held the firmest control over black voters. The Democrats' standard procedure in such counties called for economic intimidation and mass bribery with liquor or money to keep blacks in line.[14]
In the Black Belt counties, the one thing essential for black political
power—a divided white community—was missing. Whites subordi-
nated factional bickerings to the consuming issue of racial solidarity.[15]

How, then, would the Populist party approach black voters? Could
Texas Populists compete with the wealthier, entrenched Democrats for
the apparently manipulable black vote? The Democratic Party traditionally had courted the black electorate, but only to perpetuate white
supremacy. Might the Populists appeal to blacks on a higher plane,
rather than resorting to bribes or threats? In 1891, at the first convention of the Texas People's Party in Dallas, party leaders answered in the
affirmative. "I am in favor of giving the colored men full representation," announced convention president H. S. P. "Stump" Ashby in a
speech before the assembled delegates. When the applause subsided, he
continued: "We want to do good to every citizen of the country, and he
is a citizen just as much as we are, and the party that acts on that fact
will gain the colored vote of the south." The convention then backed
up its rhetoric by appointing two African Americans to the party's state
executive committee.[16] Never before in the history of the South had a
party composed of white southerners, meeting in convention, formally
extended the offer of political equality to blacks. The logic of this position seemed irrefutable to an anonymous delegate who described the
plight of blacks plainly but eloquently: "They are in the ditch just like
we are."[17]

This is not to say that the Populists stood for social intimacy between the races. The fact is that white southerners (not to mention
northerners) in positions of power never seriously advocated complete
equality for African Americans until the second half of the twentieth

century. Populists, like other white southerners, criticized Grover Cleveland for inviting a famed black activist and his white wife to Washington receptions; the doctrine of white supremacy and the miscegenation taboo were ingrained too deeply in virtually every white southern mind, Populist or Democratic.[18]

Rayner was a realist, and he could not have been blind to the fact that white Populists stopped far short of advocating full equality. A white in the late nineteenth-century South speaking of the social mixing of the races was likely to be ostracized by polite society; a black doing the same was inviting the lynch mob. In this environment, political and economic justice were lofty goals for a black leader to strive for; hence Rayner kept his personal thoughts on racial equality to himself as he set out to stump the state on behalf of the People's Party. Later in life, he would write privately about the white man's "hallucinated idea of his race superiority."[19]

Rayner's career as a Populist spanned six years, from 1892 to 1898. He apparently became involved in the local Robertson County Populist organization, which sent him as a delegate to the 1894 state convention in Waco. At that meeting Rayner played a major role in the public proceedings and was elected to the state executive committee and the platform committee, where he exercised his influence in securing planks promising reforms in the brutal convict lease system and increased black control over African American schools. He then commenced a wide-ranging speaking tour that threatened both his health and personal safety, traversing the state from the Red River to the Gulf Coast. "I am hard at work day and night for our party," he explained without exaggeration.[20] The tireless committeeman soon became a full-fledged Populist traveling lecturer and organizer, and notices of his speaking engagements began to appear regularly in the party's official organ, the Dallas-based *Southern Mercury*. He maintained exhausting travel schedules throughout much of 1895 and the election year of 1896.[21] On one speaking tour in the spring of 1896, Rayner delivered speeches in seventeen towns over a twenty-four-day period, traveling over six hundred miles.[22] Party officials realized the value of their black committeeman's services. "The work I want Rayner to do," wrote Stump Ashby, "no white man can do."[23] Another important organizer of Texas Populists, Harry Tracy, described Rayner as "the ablest colored speaker in the state" and recommended him "to the officials of the peoples party as the most useful speaker they can employ to plant our principles among the colored voters."[24]

Rayner's fervent belief in the Populist cause motivated him to labor for the party despite the lack of any salary. He was certainly no ordinary African American "'fluence man,'" paid by whites to round up black votes at election time.[25] Notices of Rayner's speaking engagements in the *Southern Mercury* often were accompanied by pleas for donations to help defray his travel expenses.[26] At one point he announced that Populist groups requesting his services should "please enclose stamps if they wish an answer," because "to answer them all would starve my family to buy postage and stationery."[27] Robertson County tax records reveal that by 1896 Rayner's property in Calvert was valued at $550, making him a modest member of the black middle class.[28] He probably continued to teach school when time off from his politicking allowed it.

Time off, however, was rare for Rayner during these years, for he performed the duties of Populist organizer as well as those of lecturer and party official. Rayner was said to have trained scores of lieutenants to assist him in spreading the Populist gospel among the black community.[29]

He attended countless picnics and barbecues for the purpose of organizing black Populist clubs. In the summer of 1895, the following notice appeared in the *Southern Mercury:*

A great many counties will have barbecues and speakings next month. All that may need my services will please notify me immediately so I can be with you. Let us make next month an educational month, and I hope the white people will assist my people (the negroes) in working up barbecues and speakings, so I may have an opportunity of speaking to my people on the issues of the day.

J. B. Rayner
Calvert, Texas[30]

Rayner's physical attributes made him particularly well-suited for the task at hand. He was stoutly built with rugged features and a good voice for public speaking. A light complexion, which "revealed his negro blood only to those familiar with his origin," gave him a decided advantage in his dealings with white people. Rayner held the unusual distinction (for blacks) of having frequently addressed white audiences.[31] On one occasion he "came in like a storm" to deliver his standard stump-speech at Market Square in Houston, and white hecklers tried to disrupt his talk. Undaunted, he "aroused the crowd to numerous applauses by his quick-witted thrusts," telling the hecklers that they were "unmanly" in trying to keep him from exercising the privilege of free speech. That Rayner dared to castigate white hecklers in public bears witness to his courage, and the fact that he could get away with it suggests that white Populists were willing to stand by their black ally. After his appearance a spectator told a reporter, "Houston has felt the storm and may take gracious comfort that a single house is left standing or that one lone official is left to tell the tale of political devastation."[32]

The huge Populist encampments provided opportunities for the party's great speakers to showcase their oratorical talents. Resembling the religious camp meetings on which they were modeled, the encampments attracted thousands of men, women, and children who "sang of Populism, . . . prayed for Populism, . . . read Populist literature and discussed Populist principles with their brethren in the faith, and . . . heard Populist orators loose their destructive thunderbolts in the name of the People's Party."[33] John B. Rayner's name can be found among the list of speakers at the Waco encampment held in July 1895. Others on the three-day program included "General" Jacob S. Coxey, Stump Ashby, Charles W. Macune, Cyclone Davis, and—for the sake of debate—Democrats Richard Coke and George Clark. Rayner's speech opened the encampment's "Colored People's Day," and although there is no record of his having addressed white audiences at this meeting, his appearance among the biggest celebrities of Populism no doubt enhanced his standing among Populists of both races.[34]

While few of Rayner's spoken words were recorded, those that do survive explain why he achieved such success as an orator and help to illuminate his character.[35] The black Populist possessed a sharp tongue and a keen sense of humor, qualities that enabled him to silence an opponent in debate or make light of the potential dangers he often faced on the lecture circuit. In the spring of 1896 he spoke in Austin and then dropped in on the state Republican convention, which was in an uproar over the withdrawal of the so-called "lily-white" faction from the convention. A reporter for the *Southern Mercury* recorded the scene as Rayner entered the hall:

> The colored populist, J. B. Rayner of Calvert, came into the convention while pandemonium was in its fiercest rage. He said he had never yet gotten over his boyish craze for "goin' to the circus." . . . An old darkey

with deep wrinkles of republican prejudice along the sides of his neck and up the back of his head said to Rayner: "I don't feel a bit proud of this thing." "Why don't you come to the people's party," asked the colored apostle. "Never!" said old prejudice, with his wrinkles swelling; "I'd mos' as soon think o' jinin' de dimekrats." "Then whenever you decide to quit the republican party go and join the democrats," said Rayner, "we don't want any such niggers as you; a nigger has to have some sense before he can become a populist."

When he was finished excoriating the old Republican, Rayner turned his attention back to the reporter who had inquired about the Populist's upcoming lecture agenda. With what must have been a sly but self-effacing grin, Rayner explained that he was going down into the Black Belt "to investigate the impression that has gotten out that no other than a republican speaker can get a respectful hearing in that region."[36] He knew only too well that the "respectful hearing" awaiting a black Populist organizer in those regions might likely consist of physical assaults or gun-play, for partisans from either major party might view Populist power as a potential threat. Historians have acknowledged that Rayner "took his life in his hands when he went into certain counties of East Texas."[37]

Rayner claimed to have delivered 25,000 African American voters into the Populists' hands by 1896.[38] While this figure is impossible to verify, one need only study the goings-on at the 1896 state convention to gauge Rayner's stature among both the whites and the blacks of his party. The annual meeting convened in Galveston on the 9th of August. By this time, Rayner had served in the party's upper echelon for two years. When the chair declared the floor open for nominations for executive committeeman-at-large, a black delegate renominated the incumbent Rayner. For reasons unclear, Rayner indicated a desire not to seek another term, but the chair refused to recognize him. Rayner finally gained the floor on a point of personal privilege and stated his intention to withdraw, whereupon his supporters raised such objections that the roll call proceeded. "Votes came to Rayner right and left," wrote a reporter for the *Galveston News*. A white nominee withdrew his own name from consideration, and Rayner was re-elected by acclamation. A black delegate later told a newsman covering the event that he wished "to thank the convention for recognition of his race by the election of Rayner."[39]

In 1896, fusion at the national level with the Democrats dealt a mortal blow to Populism. Texas Populists managed to survive to the end of the century in a handful of local third-party strongholds, but state leaders were demoralized by the national party's decision to nominate Democrat William Jennings Bryan. The movement had lost its vitality.[40]

Events in Rayner's home county in 1896 dramatically illustrate the lengths to which Democrats would go to end the Populist experiment in biracial democracy at the local level. On the fateful election day of that year, Robertson County Democrats "quietly deposed" the black town marshal in the county seat, Franklin, before the polls opened. Forty men with Winchester rifles stationed themselves at the courthouse to turn away all but Democratic voters. In the lower end of the county, a large company of black voters was marching from their homes in the Brazos bottoms, accompanied by a brass band, to cast their votes in Hearne. An armed delegation of Democratic horsemen accosted them on the Little Brazos River bridge, throwing the band instruments into the river and dispersing the crowd. At Hearne, "a great number of pistol shots were fired in front of the polls when the negroes from the bottom came in to vote," and subsequently the box polled six hundred fewer votes than in the previous election. In one rural precinct, the presiding officer reported that "a masked man took the box and returns away from him." In another the Democratic candidates for sheriff and tax collector stood at the door of the polling place, one with a gun and the other with a club, and held off black voters. About mid-afternoon word reached the Democratic county judge that in spite of these efforts the election might hinge upon his home precinct. "I went down to the polls and took my six-shooter," he recalled. "I stayed there until the polls closed. Not a negro voted. After that they didn't any more in Robertson County." The judge boasted that he personally stood off one thousand African Americans that day. When asked many years later about his violent role in bringing white rule back to the county, he explained that "I only shot when I thought I had to. I know God pulled me through."[41]

It is not known whether John B. Rayner personally witnessed the violent end of Populism in his home county; he left no personal account of his years as Texas's leading black Populist. Amazingly, though, he returned to the campaign trail in the autumn of 1898, speaking on "The Negro's Place in Southern Politics."[42] But by then he must have known that the African American would have no place in the new political order of the twentieth century. His own people had been terrorized, and

the state and national organizations lay in shambles. Rayner soon retired to his home and family and spent his last twenty years raising
funds for black vocational education.[43]

The old Populist's private papers reveal the totality of the third
party's defeat and the depths of Rayner's disillusionment. What is remarkable about the Rayner Papers is not what they contain, but what
they omit: beginning shortly after the turn of the century and ending
with his obituary, all references to the People's Party, Populism, or
Rayner's political career in the 1890s are conspicuously absent. The
black leader most likely destroyed all evidence that would connect him
with the Populist revolt, perhaps fearing for the safety of himself and
his family. Rayner did return to politics—primarily as a newspaper es-
sayist—after the turn of the century, but he never mentioned Populism
in those writings, either. Indeed, most of his published political writings urge blacks to leave all political matters in the hands of whites.
The price exacted by broken dreams of black equality had brought
Rayner to the point where he avoided any reference to Populism, even
in his later years when it would have been safe for him to reminisce.
He died a bitter man.[44]

How, then, are we to evaluate the meaning of Rayner's experience?
Rayner's pieces in the *Southern Mercury* demonstrate his capacity for
shrewd political reasoning. In one such article, he listed the options
available to his people in the upcoming election. One by one, he eliminated the choices that he considered untenable and then arrived at
his conclusion: "The next is the people's party, God's viceregent in
politics, and this party is made up of the middle class or yeomanry of
the country. . . . Vote the people's party ticket; we will get better
wages for our work and we will have better times in the south."[45]
Rayner was voicing a pragmatic argument to black Texans by
appealing to their economic self-interest. He realized the Populist victories would not mean full participation for his people in American
society, but he saw in Populism the chance for meaningful progress.
The concepts of economic cooperation and extensive government
intervention would have benefited black and white alike. As one of
the most educated blacks in Texas, Rayner had critically evaluated
the Populist economic alternative and wholeheartedly accepted it. As
a member of the party's platform committee, he had helped incorpo-
rate planks calling for political and economic equality for both races.
As a respected member of the state executive committee, he had
worked closely with white party leaders and had found most of them

to be sincere. The Texas People's Party's record on civil rights will never be considered sterling by twentieth-century standards, but for every vote bought by a Populist, or every racist remark uttered by a party official, there was a farmer like the one who wrote:

> I am a gray-headed ex-slave and thank God that the great common people who gave me my freedom are moving to free all mankind under the stars and stripes. Chatel [sic] slavery has been destroyed. Now let us all white and black strike till the last foe expires for industrial freedom. We have just organized a pop[ulist] club among my people here and intend to make ourselves felt at the next election.[46]

Clearly, many black Populists believed that the party had more to offer them than patronage, whiskey, or protection—the traditional sops of white politicians to blacks.

When John B. Rayner joined the People's Party in 1892, white Populist leader Stump Ashby remarked that there were only a "comparatively small number of colored men, who with rare courage stood with us in the fight for principle."[47] Rayner was in the vanguard of that fight, and by the end of the era he and his lieutenants had converted thousands of blacks to the Populist cause and given them the dream of someday achieving a measure of equality. The Democratic majority moved to crush Populism only when these dreams appeared to be coming true.

Notes

1. See Gerald H. Gaither, *Blacks and the Populist Revolt: Ballots and Bigotry in the "New South"* (University, Alabama, 1977); Lawrence Goodwyn, *Democratic Promise: The Populist Moment in America* (New York, 1976); Norman Pollack, ed., *The Populist Mind* (Indianapolis, 1967); C. Vann Woodward, *Origins of the New South, 1877–1913* (Baton Rouge, 1951); Woodward, *The Strange Career of Jim Crow* (New York, 1957).

2. Woodward, *Strange Career,* 63.

3. See John D. Hicks, *The Populist Revolt: A History of the Farmers' Alliance and the People's Party* (1931; repr. Lincoln, Nebraska, 1961); Richard Hofstadter, *The Age of Reform: From Bryan to F. D. R.* (New York, 1955); Roscoe C. Martin, *The People's Party in Texas: A Study in Third Party Politics* (1933; repr. Austin, 1970).

4. Pollack, *Populist Mind*, 359.

5. Early research into Rayner's parentage and childhood was done by Jack Abramowitz, "John B. Rayner—A Grass-Roots Leader," *Journal of Negro History* 36 (April 1951): 160–93. Since the original publication of the present article in 1985, a book-length study of Rayner and his father has been published, expanding our knowledge of Rayner's early life; see Gregg Cantrell, *Kenneth and John B. Rayner and the Limits of Southern Dissent* (Urbana and Chicago, 1993).

6. Robertson County Tax Rolls, 1882.

7. Martin, *People's Party in Texas*, 126.

8. Lawrence D. Rice, *The Negro in Texas, 1874–1900* (Baton Rouge, 1971), 35–42.

9. For discussions of this race, see Alwyn Barr, *Reconstruction to Reform: Texas Politics, 1876–1906* (Austin, 1971); Harrell Budd, "The Negro in Politics in Texas, 1867–1898" (Master's thesis, University of Texas, 1925); Rice, *Negro in Texas*, 70–78.

10. Rice, *Negro in Texas*, 67.

11. Alwyn Barr, *Black Texans: A History of Negroes in Texas, 1528–1971* (Austin, 1973), 75.

12. Martin, *People's Party in Texas*, 87.

13. Ibid.

14. Ibid., 93.

15. Hicks, *Populist Revolt*, 253; Martin, *People's Party in Texas*, 97; Woodward, *Origins of the New South*, 326–27.

16. *Dallas Morning News*, 18 August 1891.

17. Ibid.

18. Jack Abramowitz, "The Negro in the Populist Movement," *Journal of Negro History* 38 (July 1953), 279; Goodwyn, *Democratic Promise*, 299.

19. Undated manuscript in Rayner Papers, Center for American History, University of Texas, Austin.

20. *Southern Mercury*, 4 October 1894.

21. *Southern Mercury*, 13 June, 25 July, 15 August 1895; 23 January, 16 April 1896.

22. Ibid., 16 April 1896.

23. Ibid., 13 June 1895.

24. Tracy, quoted in Abramowitz, "John B. Rayner," 165.

25. For a description of the "'fluence man" in Texas politics, see Martin, *People's Party in Texas*, 179–80.

26. *Southern Mercury*, 13 June 1895, 23 January 1896.

27. Rayner, quoted in Girard T. Bryant, "J. B. Rayner, A Negro Populist," *Negro History Bulletin* 3 (May 1940), 125.

28. Robertson County Tax Rolls, 1896.

29. Goodwyn, *Democratic Promise*, 331. See also Martin, *People's Party in Texas*, 126–27.

30. *Southern Mercury*, 25 July 1895.

31. Martin, *People's Party in Texas*, 127.

32. *Houston Post*, 22 October 1896.

33. Martin, *People's Party in Texas*, 127.

34. *Southern Mercury*, 9 April 1896.

35. The *Southern Mercury* published several Rayner essays describing the political situation and African Americans' place in Texas. See "The Colored Brother: A Spicy Letter From J. B. Rayner," 12 December 1895; and "Political Imbroglio in Texas," 9 April 1896. A reporter for the *Houston Post* also quoted some extended passages from a Rayner stump speech in 1896; see *Houston Post*, 22 October 1896.

36. Southern Mercury, 9 April 1896.

37. Goodwyn, *Democratic Promise*, 302; Martin, *People's Party in Texas*, 133.

38. *Galveston Daily News*, 9 August 1896.

39. Ibid.

40. For an account of Populism's demise in one Texas county, see Lawrence Goodwyn, "Populist Dreams and Negro Rights: East Texas as a Case Study," *American Historical Review* 76 (December 1971), 1435–56.

41. Norman L. McCarver and Norman L. McCarver Jr., *Hearne on the Brazos* (San Antonio, 1956), 27 (first quotation); *Galveston Daily News*, November 7, 1896 (second quotation); *Bryan Eagle*, November 12, 1896 (third quotation); *Houston Press*, February 18, 1931 (fourth, fifth, and sixth quotations).

42. *Southern Mercury*, 8 September 1898.

43. See Cantrell, *Kenneth and John B. Rayner*, chaps. 14–15.

44. Goodwyn, *Democratic Promise*, 302–303; Rayner Papers. Rayner's post–1900 political and social writings were published frequently in the *Houston Chronicle* and *Houston Post*.

45. *Southern Mercury*, 12 December 1995.

46. Ibid., 2 April 1896.

47. *Lampasas People's Journal*, 9 December 1892, as quoted in Bruce Palmer, *"Man Over Money": The Populist Critique of American Capitalism* (Chapel Hill, 1980), 186.

The El Paso Racial Crisis of 1900

GARNA L. CHRISTIAN

In this article, Garna L. Christian explores the causes and consequences of the 1900 El Paso crisis that pitted black soldiers at Fort Bliss against civilians. The blow-up occurred soon after the veteran Twenty-Fifth Infantry arrived. The unit had fought in Cuba during the Spanish-American war, and many of its members were determined to no longer accept racial discrimination and second-class citizenship. If they had to, some were willing to fight rather than return to a system, a society, that degraded African Americans. But the situation was complex, for some men in the regiment stirred white anger by getting drunk in public, by committing minor robberies, and by causing other mayhem, including altercations in the red light district of the city. On one occasion, forty soldiers at the fort refused to allow civilian authorities to arrest one of their cohorts until a military officer appeared and brought the men under control. Then, early on February 17, 1900, a tragedy occurred when some soldiers tried to storm the city jail and secure the release of one of their number whom authorities had arrested on a charge of drunkenness. In the melee a soldier and a lawman were killed.

Christian goes on to chronicle the trials, in all their complexity, that followed. In a sense, justice was finally rendered, and most of the black soldiers tried went free. But in a sense, the racial violence in El Paso in 1900 foreshadowed similar outbreaks that would occur in the coming years as African Americans, both civilian and military, continued to fight for their rights.

*

WITH THE ARRIVAL of Company A of the Twenty-Fifth Infantry in late April of 1899, El Paso and the military renewed a racial relationship that had existed for more than a dozen years after the end of the Civil War. Among the first troops stationed at Fort Bliss after the conflagration were two companies of the 125th United States Colored Troops. Company A of the Twenty-Fourth Infantry occupied Camp Concordia outside El Paso in 1870, within four years of the organization of the regiment, and black units of the Twenty-Fifth Infantry and Ninth Cavalry continued to occupy the site until the garrison moved to Hart's Mill in late 1881. During these years, as elsewhere in the West, African American soldiers pursued marauding Indians and banditos, strung hundreds of miles of telegraph wire, and maintained roads in serviceable condition, while boasting one of the lowest alcoholism and desertion rates in the military.[1]

Various factors encouraged the renewal of harmonious race relations in 1899. Black soldiers customarily faced less discrimination in isolated and vulnerable communities that harbored other, larger minority populations, such as Mexican Americans, than in the more populated and safer garrison towns farther east. In the fifteen years of African American occupation at Fort Bliss not only had there been no confrontations between civilians and soldiers, as at Jacksboro and San Angelo, but whites of the Fifteenth Infantry amicably shared the post with blacks for a period of sixteen tranquil months. Civic leaders, distressed by the recent depletion of Fort Bliss during the Spanish-American War, appreciated the necessity of welcoming the soldiers if the city was to continue maintaining a garrison. Accordingly, the local press reported the presence of black troops courteously, even enthusiastically.[2]

Another favorable factor resided in the unusually high status enjoyed by El Paso blacks in comparison to blacks elsewhere in the state. Comprising less than three percent of the city's population, African Americans provided an unusual share of El Paso's business and professional men, leaving many of the menial jobs and the attendant ones to the more numerous Mexicans and Chinese. The press favorably, if infrequently, reported the activities of "The Four Hundred" in social and cultural spheres. Politically, the collective astuteness of local blacks kept them active long after Bourbon Democrats had diminished the black influence in other Southern cities.[3]

Still, the Confederate orientation of El Paso posed a potential obstruction to the further assimilation of both African American civilians and soldiers. Much of the white population, including the Democratic establishment, shared the racial perspectives of the majority of Southern whites in a period of deteriorating race relations. The old biases strongly surfaced when their preeminent position in society appeared threatened by blacks. The Republican preference of the African Americans often drew criticism and ridicule from Democrats in election years. As elsewhere, insecure El Paso whites viewed the black in uni-

form as a symbol of authority and a challenge to white supremacy.
Conversely, the battle-hardened black heroes of Cuban campaigns were
determined not to accept meekly further manifestations of racism. The
ingredients for racial strife existed at the time of the arrival of the
Twenty-Fifth Infantry at Fort Bliss that spring day in 1899.[4]

The insidious tentacles of Jim Crowism, fashioning de facto and de
jure segregation northward and southward and racial lynchings across
the land, edged ever closer to the mountain pass. Newspaper dis-
claimers of military misconduct, in themselves a reflection of the deepening apprehension, soon gave way to items cataloging disorders.
Minor robberies and instances of drunkenness on the part of soldiers
expectedly took place. The commander of Fort Bliss declared a postside
saloon off limits to his men after a series of disturbances and shootings
at the establishment. Such incidents had been common occurrences
when white troops garrisoned the mesa, and the local press continued
to treat them as such, but each transgression appeared to many whites
a certification of racial instability.[5]

Against this backdrop of increasing antagonism toward the dusky
inhabitants of the fort, comparatively minor offenses ballooned to
alarming proportions. After a soldier carried a bicycle to an El Paso repairman, a local resident charged him with theft of the wheel. Army
authorities incarcerated the soldier in the post guardhouse to await
transfer to the city jail. When the deputy sheriff and the repairman
drove to the reservation, however, a group of at least forty soldiers
blocked their departure with the prisoner. Only the appearance of an
armed army officer dispersed the surly crowd, producing ugly murmur-
ings on the streets of El Paso the following Saturday evening. Captain
Robert H. R. Loughborough, post commander, telephoned an apology
to the sheriff's office, promising to punish the culpable.[6]

Such incidents served merely as prelude for the pre-dawn violence
of February 17, 1900, which resulted in controversy that rocked the
city for more than a year and sparked the first black-white racial crisis
at El Paso. In the early morning hours a band of soldiers assaulted the
city jail in an apparent effort to release one of their comrades held on a
drunkenness charge, resulting in the shooting deaths of one soldier and
a popular lawman, Newton Stewart. A jailer, Dick Blacker, escaped
possible death by leaping to safety through an open window after
briefly exchanging gunfire with the attackers.[7]

Relying on circumstantial evidence and a partial account by
Blacker, the police and press pieced together a narrative. The previous

day local authorities had arrested a member of Company A on charges of drunkenness and disorderliness in the red light district of the city. An employee of a meat market stated that he saw a dozen or more soldiers in canvas clothing carrying rifles and at least one axe into town around five o'clock on the morning of the shootings. He was unable to identify any of the figures. The men apparently entered the police station, at which Stewart was on duty, in an attempt to free the prisoner.[8]

Blacker, the jailer, was asleep in an adjoining room. One news report stated that a scuffle awakened him, while another quoted Blacker as saying that he was unsure as to what caused him to awaken at that moment. He maintained that he awoke to see a black soldier pointing a rifle at his breast. Blacker managed to leap from the bed, seize his sixshooter, and shoot the hulking soldier dead center as the latter fired erratically. The jailer and the soldiers momentarily exchanged shots; then Blacker leaped to safety through an open window. When Blacker returned minutes later, the station was empty, save for Stewart, laying unconscious on the floor from two rifle wounds. The officer died several hours later without regaining consciousness.[9]

Investigators found grim evidence of the violence. Bullet marks pocked the walls in both rooms of the police station. An examination showed that Stewart had been struck in the shoulder, apparently from a shot fired from an open window, and in the face at close range, indicating an exchange of rounds in the interim. A trail of blood extended a hundred yards from the station to the lifeless body of Corporal James H. Hull, in death clutching a rifle. A second rifle lay on a nearby street, as if dropped by someone in flight. But the assailants had disappeared into the night, and Blacker was no more able than the meat market employee to identify them.[10]

The trail pointed to the fort on the mesa. Soon after the shootings, several townspeople joined a police officer in circling the post as a security measure but found no trace of the fugitives. Several hours after that, a peace officer and a member of the fire department rode to the base to apprise the startled post commander of the tragedy. Captain Loughborough appeared incredulous until informed by the corporal in charge of arms that the keys to the arms racks were missing from beneath the pillow where the non-commissioned officer had hidden them the previous night. Loughborough now termed the murder of Stewart "a disgrace on Fort Bliss and a discredit to the army," promising to cooperate fully with civil authorities.[11]

The pledge failed, however, to appease the more hot tempered

among the citizenry. Mayor Joseph Magoffin defended the post commander as "a West Pointer and a strict disciplinarian who will not let
any guilty man escape" in the face of criticism from irate residents.
The police chief dispersed a mob outside the city jail that demanded
the soldier, Corporal Samuel E. Dyson, whose arrest evidently had trig-
gered the violence. A number of distraught persons expressed desires to
transfer Company A from their midst, while scattered exhortations of
marching on the fort and "exterminating the negro soldiers" chilled
the air.[12]

More ominous yet were the mouthings of some civil officials. "I
have been opposed," declared the county attorney, "to the policy of
being lenient with soldiers who get into trouble in town." The city attorney blamed the deaths on "the inherent meanness" of the black.
"He is not fit to be a soldier," he reproached, "and should never be allowed to have a gun in his hands." The collector of customs termed the
soldiers "breeders of trouble" and urged their removal from El Paso.
"The negro is the same wherever you find him," asserted the federal official, whose superiors subsequently reprimanded him for the statement: "Put him into a uniform and he thinks he can run things to suit
himself."[13]

Cooler heads prevailed. Community leaders, mellowed by years of
active cooperation with the military and desirous of maintaining a garrison, sought to smother the flames of indignation. The *Times*, partisan
to the white supremist policy of the Democratic Party, ran a series of
editorials calling for conciliation. "Let no guilty negro escape," urged
one, "but don't blame another soldier simply because he is black." The
pleas for patience had their effect, but more important in pacifying the
townfolk was the electrifying statement of Loughborough, released
within a day of the shootings, that he had placed in custody the perpe-
trators of the foul deed.[14]

A few days later three peace officers rode to Fort Bliss to receive
three soldiers whom Captain Loughborough had apprehended at the
base. The wanted men were Sergeant John Kipper, age twenty-five, Corporal William Powell, age twenty-seven, and Private Leroy Roberts,
twenty-seven. Powell, earlier detained on suspicion, had implicated the
others when promised "protection" by Loughborough and Sheriff James
Boone and promptly named Kipper as the instigator. The prisoners expressed alarm at the prospect of a white lynch mob, but the mayor
sought to allay their fears by suggesting that the city would be satisfied
merely to know of their capture. The three soldiers were joined shortly

by Corporal Gardner Davis, who had been entrusted with the arms keys, and Privates William H. Davis, Boyer Wright, and Elmore Sears as a result of Powell's confession and eyewitness reports which placed them in suspicious circumstances.[15]

The news reports of the arrests did produce a calming effect on the population. An editorial praised Loughborough "for his prompt apprehension of the guilty men" well in advance of any court decision. But news bulletins from other locations kept alive in the public mind the spectre of a black uprising. In Montgomery, Alabama, a thousand blacks gathered ominously at the site of a black family sprayed with bullets. In Taswell, West Virginia, a mob lynched an African American who allegedly had assaulted a white teenager, while a Pueblo, Colorado, black suffered the same fate after reportedly killing two young white girls. By comparison El Paso's racial news items contained little emotional impact.[16]

Still, the trial of Sergeant Kipper loomed in the foreground and none could predict its impact on race relations in the West Texas city. Of the several forthcoming trials, Kipper's stood above the others in public interest for several reasons. In addition to being the alleged leader of the assault on the jail, Kipper was a personable and educated man who possessed a splendid military record that included heroism in Cuba. A reporter later described him as "something of a hero in the eyes of the colored people" of El Paso.[17]

The Kipper trial began in the state district court at El Paso on May 1, 1900, attracting a large gathering of spectators. The prominence of the court officials enhanced public interest in the trial. Judge Anderson M. Whitehall had earned the respect of the legal community and the citizenry at large while presiding over the 34th Judicial District Court for the past two years. District Attorney John M. Dean, first elected to his position sixteen years earlier, had since served a term as state senator and was becoming recognized as a Bible scholar. Defense attorney Marvin W. Stanton had been a pioneer lawyer at El Paso in the early 1880s and a city alderman subsequently.[18]

Stanton entered the courtroom armed with motions for continuance and change of venue. Maintaining that his client had been allowed insufficient time to obtain witnesses in his behalf, the defense attorney turned his fire on Powell, the state's witness, charging him to be antagonistic and unreliable. The change of venue motion he based on racial grounds. Contending that African Americans were systematically excluded from serving on El Paso grand juries, Stanton paraded twenty-five leading black citizens before the court who swore they had never been impaneled. The defense argued further that racial animosity in the city precluded a fair trial for Kipper. Witnesses for the two sides disagreed as to whether public feeling warranted a removal of the trial, though they agreed that sentiments had run strongly against the black soldiers at the time of the crime.[19]

Although the court denied the defense motions, impaneling the petit jury indeed proved an arduous task. At the end of a full day of juror selection, attorneys agreed on only nine members. None was black and only one bore a Spanish surname. The defense dismissed several venire men who admitted bias against Kipper, though it seated several who expressed prejudice against the black race but not against the defendant specifically. Stanton subsequently exhausted his peremptory challenges before the final jurors were selected. Three more white men were added to the panel. The defense then objected to the absence of blacks on the jury, but the court denied that the jury selection constituted racial discrimination. Reporters described Kipper as appearing anxious and worried for the first time.[20]

The prosecution's star witness, Powell, did not testify the first day, but other soldiers submitted damaging circumstantial evidence against Kipper. One witness claimed that the defendant had obtained ten cartridges from him the night before the attack on the jail. Another testified seeing Kipper pull off a pair of fatigues on the morning of the assault, though admittedly from a poor vantage point. A third witness saw Kipper originally return to the post at two o'clock on the morning of the assault, bolstering the prosecution's contention that the sergeant went back to Fort Bliss after failing to release Dyson and then organized an attack force.[21]

The eagerly awaited Corporal Powell appeared before a packed gallery on the fourth day of the trial. Powell stated that Kipper had awakened him and others on the morning of February 17 and told them "to come downtown to get Corporal Dyson out of jail." The eight men, Powell among them, dressed in fatigues, carried rifles and axes, and kept to the shadows. At the jail, Powell said, Kipper told three men to enter the station by knocking down the door with an axe and when inside to demand the cell keys. Kipper then handed the keys to the post arms racks to one of the three. Powell, on the outside, heard three shots and saw the soldiers scatter. He and Carroll then returned to the barracks together.[22]

The defense failed to shake Powell's testimony in any significant respect. While admitting that he had confessed in order to escape punishment for his part in the raid, Powell denied that he was promised anything other than protection for telling the truth. Although some of his statements appeared vague, the witness did not contradict himself in the course of the cross examination. Powell also denied the defense's charge of soliciting money from various soldiers in return for not implicating them in his testimony.[23]

Blacker, the jailer, detailed essentially a story consistent with his previous statement which had been published in the press at the time of the crime. He testified that Kipper had "kicked pretty loud" on the jail door after midnight when he attempted to bail out Dyson. Blacker told him to return later to speak with the police captain, but Dyson called out to Kipper, who then tried to enter the cell. At that point Blacker said that he had commanded the defendant "to get out," whereupon Kipper answered "all right" and left. The jailer added little to his earlier account of the attack on the jail, in which he stated that he had fired at an armed soldier and leaped through an open window in a volley of bullets.[24]

The defendant, John Kipper, took the stand on the fifth day of the trial, as public excitement mounted. Nattily attired and well composed throughout the proceeding, he testified that he had been born in Galesburg, Illinois, twenty-six years earlier and had served four years of military duty in Montana, Florida, Cuba, and Texas. Kipper stated that while on pass on February 16, he had spent much of the afternoon in Dunn's Road House, where Dyson later joined him. The two then passed some time in an El Paso saloon. After the men parted, Kipper was dining in a restaurant in the early hours of the seventeenth when two soldiers brought him the news of Dyson's arrest. Kipper denied that the men formulated any definite plans for their comrade's release, though he admitted attempting to bail out Dyson.[25]

Kipper denied any complicity in the assault on the jail. He stated that he returned to the barracks when rebuffed by Blacker and fell asleep, only learning of the attack the next morning. He pointedly repudiated the testimony of five soldiers whose circumstantial evidence suggested his guilt and the statements of Powell that placed him at the eye of the conspiracy. Under questioning Kipper acknowledged that authorities had found a set of his fatigues inside a tile pipe on the reservation and that his story had failed to convince the post commander. He further told of the difficulties encountered in obtaining counsel because the federal government had refused to release his pay when he needed money to enlist attorneys.[26]

The defense then called a series of witnesses in an effort to weaken the state's charges. A corporal testified that Captain Loughborough had offered him "protection" in return for a confession until the soldier managed to convince his commanding officer of his innocence. Another soldier contradicted the statement of a hospital corpsman that the latter had arisen early enough on the morning of the crime to have witnessed Kipper's return.[27]

Such efforts proved unavailing. After several hours of deliberation, the jury found Kipper guilty of murder in the first degree and sentenced him to life in the state penitentiary. "When he had learned of his fate" a reporter observed, "Kipper manifested no joy or disappointment. He remained in his chair as calm and unconcerned as though he had no vital interest in the case." So confident had been the spectators of the verdict that they remained in the courtroom for an hour after the jury retired, anticipating an early decision. Many of them expected the death penalty; a few thought he would be acquitted. Reportedly the sentence, which surprised many in the gallery, constituted a compromise. On the first ballot ten jurors voted the death penalty and two believed the defendant not guilty.[28]

The prosecution subsequently brought other alleged participants in the assault before the court. Private Joel Elazer escaped conviction when Powell, the state's key witness, failed to place him at the scene of the crime. Private Benjamin F. Carroll, allegedly the man who shot Stewart, initially drew a deadlocked jury, with two jurors favoring execution and ten supporting life imprisonment. Eventually the majority ruled, and Carroll received the same sentence as Kipper.[29]

Although other soldiers remained under indictment, the legal machinery appeared to be grinding to a conclusion in the matter. The white population of El Paso seemed satisfied with the verdicts, while the local African Americans manifested no outward displeasure at the decisions. Captain Loughborough received a promotion to the rank of major and prepared to join the Sixth Infantry in the Philippines. The Twenty-Fifth Infantry also made ready to confront their "little brown brothers" in the islands. While the El Paso press cautioned that the latter rotation need not be regarded as having "anything to do with the recent troubles between the negro troops and the citizenry," a San Antonio news release was less gracious. "The welcome news comes from Washington," it trumpeted, "that the negro soldiers will leave this city . . . on their way to the Philippines."[30]

But the issue would not die down. The Kipper defense, already planning an appeal, was heartened by a decision of the United States

Supreme Court that overruled a conviction of a Texas black, Seth
Carter, on the basis that the grand and petit juries that determined his
fate had excluded blacks. A local editor conceded the importance of the
decision to the Kipper case. When Kipper appealed his conviction on
the points raised in the Carter decision, the prosecution assumed that
Carroll would do the same. On April 10, 1901, the State Court of Criminal Appeals confirmed the speculation by ordering a new trial for Kipper and one month later for Carroll.[31]

The legal delays frustrated those El Paso whites who restlessly
awaited the departure of the Twenty-Fifth Infantry. Their distaste even
carried over to black civilians. "Negroes are becoming more numerous
in El Paso every day," brooded a newsman, despite the census report
that showed only a slight increase. When sixty-nine members of the
Twelfth Cavalry appeared at the depot to replace the evacuating residents of Fort Bliss in mid-May, townspeople were agog at the troopers'
pigmentation. "The Twelfth Cavalry is white," exulted a reporter.
"That is better luck than El Paso expected. . . ."[32]

Meanwhile, military and civil authorities strained to accommodate
the demands of justice. The two sectors stood in conflict over the dispo-
sition of key witnesses in the forthcoming retrials of Kipper and Carroll.
Whereas the army desired to dispatch Company A against the Filipino
insurrectionists as quickly as possible, the prosecution sought to retain
the witnesses within the court's jurisdiction until the legal process had
run its course. The question of rendering unto Ceasar produced a statement from the judge advocate of the Department of Texas that even
though the state could not compel the retention of the witnesses, the
army would cooperate as long as possible to see justice done.[33]

The issue of retaining witnesses divided the prosecution and defense also, as each accused the other of deliberately prolonging the judicial process. District attorney Dean charged that defense attorney Stanton sought to discourage cooperation from the army by summoning an
excessive number of witnesses and publicly predicting that the trials
would consume two years. Stanton's objective, according to Dean, was
to place the witnesses beyond the reach of the courts and thereby free
his clients. Stanton, for his part, asserted that Dean stood to gain mon-
etarily by prosecuting the cases one at a time rather than collectively.
They likewise differed on the necessity of the physical presence of the
witnesses in court. Stanton offered to waive his clients' constitutional
right to face their accusers by accepting written testimony from the
witnesses. Dean countered that the recent decision of *Marshall Cline*

vs. *Texas* explicitly disallowed the presentation of depositions by prosecution witnesses.[34]

A crisis occurred on May 11, 1901, when the adjutant general's office, pressed by the exigencies of the Filipino revolt, notified Dean of the imminent embarkation of Loughborough and his men for the Philippines. The prosecuting attorney appealed to Governor Joseph D. Sayers for intercession. The Texas chief executive promptly wired Washington that the removal of the witnesses would "cause miscarriage of justice" and asked revocation of the orders. The adjutant general suspended the order "for the purpose of affording time for correspondence with Governor Sayers." After an exchange of notes between Sayers and William Cary Sanger, acting Secretary of War, Dean assured Washington of his intention to dispose of the cases between June and "December next."[35]

Events now fell quickly into place. The jury commission created a grand jury for the June term of the district court that featured one black, George B. Duvall, among a sea of whites. Since another African American sat on the jury commission, a newsman asserted "that little technicality" that had reversed Kipper's conviction would now be eliminated. In a matter of days the grand jury returned indictments against Kipper, Carroll, Davis, and Roberts. Each pleaded not guilty, and Stanton moved for a continuance until October. Failing this, the defense attorney asked a change of venue on two grounds. First, he charged, the defendants could not receive a fair and impartial trial in El Paso because of prejudice against them; secondly, the lengthy proceedings, he said, virtually had depleted the reservoir of potential jurors. The court heard testimony on the venue motion and moved the trial to Dallas County, noting that the criminal district court in that city was nearly always in session.[36]

Accordingly, the Fort Bliss contingent of the Twenty-Fifth Infantry moved eastward to Dallas, rather than westward to Manila. A number of El Pasoans accompanied the troops; thirty-five military and twenty-five civilian witnesses, the county sheriff and his aides, and defense attorneys. The state shackled the prisoners and kept them under strict surveillance. With the Davis trial scheduled first, the cases opened in July, 1901, earlier than anticipated. Public interest in the prosecutions also moved eastward; curious Dallasites packed the galleries for the duration of the trials.[37]

Though the times scarcely appeared propitious for black defendants in an East Texas courtroom, no racial incidents ensued in the Jim Crow city of Dallas during the proceedings. Fort Bliss blacks demonstrated drill and sham battle maneuvers for the benefit of Saint James Church and smartly marched at the Colored Fair. The prosecution, moreover, was hanging fire. The Dallas County district attorney dismissed the case against William H. Davis for insufficient evidence, a jury acquitted Leroy Roberts, and the court released Benjamin F. Carroll on motion of the state. Apprehensive relatives of the slain Stewart employed a private prosecutor to assist the state as the Kipper trial approached.[38]

Charges of perjury against witnesses rebounded through the hall of justice. Following the conviction of Boyer Wright for inducing Private Arthur B. Taylor to perjure himself during the previous trials, an exasperated Judge Charles Clint exclaimed: "The action of witnesses in these El Paso cases is unprecedented and unheard of and . . . must stop." A few days later Private William J. Hunter joined his comrades in jail on a charge of perjury. The most sensational perjury charge involved "Black Fannie" and Corporal Samuel F. Dyson, whose arrest the previous year led to the slaying of Stewart. Judge Clint ruled Dyson guilty of contempt for having wired the woman to leave El Paso in order to avoid testifying against Kipper. El Paso police apprehended Fannie as she prepared to escape to Mexico and transported her and two other women to Dallas.[39]

The Kipper trial, roundly considered the headliner of the series, bedeviled the jury. The prosecution's singular reliance on Powell's testimony, charges of perjury, and a parade of conflicting witnesses augmented the confusion. After extensive deliberation, the jury reportedly locked at eight-to-four for acquittal, leading Judge Clint to discharge the panel and reset the trial. A second jury deliberated but a short time before finding Kipper guilty of murder in the first degree and sentencing him to life at hard labor in the state penitentiary. Only two votes were taken, the first resulting in nine for hanging and three favoring a life sentence. "Black Fannie," subsequently charged with perjury, admitted under oath that Kipper told her on the night of Dyson's arrest that he intended to obtain a gun and "kill the white _____."[40]

Defense attorney Stanton made out eighty bills of exceptions, but to no avail. The State Court of Criminal Appeals reviewed the Kipper conviction in December of 1903, sixteen months after the transfer of the remainder of the Twenty-Fifth Infantry from El Paso to the Philippines, and struck down every basis for appeal. John Kipper ultimately served ten years of his sentence. On June 20, 1913, Governor O. B. Colquitt granted him a conditional pardon and relieved the state of the customary expense of purchasing railway transportation. The pardon described Kipper as a model prisoner, sufficiently punished.[41]

The murder trials of the soldiers of the Twenty-Fifth Infantry were enacted at El Paso in the setting of a race-conscious frontier community during a period of deteriorating race relations throughout the nation. The events surrounding the death of lawman Newton Stewart produced the first significant clash between the civilian population of El Paso and the military establishment at Fort Bliss. Yet El Paso avoided the racial bitterness and recriminations that engulfed other communities in comparable situations.

After an initial emotional flurry, the citizenry bridled its wrath and awaited the outcome of lengthy legal proceedings against the accused. The defendants received due process, although Major Loughborough sought the guilty with such vengeance that defense attorney Stanton considered him "an assistant to the prosecution." The volume of motions raised by Stanton verified the diligence of the soldiers' counsel. The State Court of Criminal Appeals scrutinized both district trials of Kipper, ultimately upholding his conviction as justifed.[42]

Against the destructive impulses in El Paso pressed a set of stabilizing influences. Among these were the sobriety of the civic and military leaders, the restraint of local newspapers, the tradition of cooperation between the civilian and military sectors, the uninterrupted efforts of the city fathers to expand Fort Bliss for security and economic reasons, the absence of previous conflicts between whites and blacks, and the distance of El Paso from other sites of racial violence. Such influences diminished the likelihood of public outbursts such as those that accompanied the Brownsville Raid of 1906 and the Houston riot of 1917.

El Paso and Brownsville offer certain similarities in time and circumstance. Both were frontier garrison communities from their inception with small black populations and large Hispanic majorities. While the West Texas city was rapidly diversifying its economy and expanding in size, however, the South Texas community remained a relatively stagnant backwater. Its minute African American population lacked the status and cohesion of El Paso's and the press was openly hostile to the black troops, denigrating their presence and ignoring blatant inequities practiced against them. In sum Brownsville lacked countervailing influences against covert and overt racism.[43]

Houston in certain ways suggests a closer parallel to El Paso. More expansive and cosmopolitan than the latter city, Houston also sought troops to bolster a vibrant economy and soothed the apprehensions of its citizenry by positive statements from the press and business community. But Houston was also more steeped in Southern mores than El Paso and less endowed with strong civic leadership at the time of crisis. The press threw off its restraint after the riot, spreading seeds of additional racial discord by calling for reprisals and printing explosive rumors. Significantly, Texas and the nation were more formally white supremist by 1917 than at the turn of the century. Just as the Houston tragedy anticipated the urban riots of 1919, it may be said that the garrison town clashes of the early 1900s still earlier reflected the lengthening shadows of racial strife engendered by hardening racial patterns and the new self awareness of the African American forged in Cuban and Philippine campaigns.[44]

The Kipper affair of 1900 ended in less bitterness and division than its later counterparts at Brownsville and Houston, but like them it deepened racial tensions. When black troops returned to Fort Bliss five years after the departure of Company A, they found that they had to account for more than their own actions. The ghost of slain Newton Stewart hovered over their presence.[45]

Notes

1. John N. Nankivell, *History of the Twenty-Fifth Regiment, United States Infantry, 1869–1926* (New York, 1969), pp. 18, 35; Jack D. Foner, *Blacks and the Military in American History* (New York, 1974), pp. 52, 53, 56, 60–61; John M. Carroll, ed., *The Black Military Experience in the American West* (New York, 1971), pp. 65, 78, 92, 96–98, 349; Arlen L. Fowler, *The Black Infantry in the West, 1869–1891* (Westport, 1971), pp. 16–17, 24; William H. Leckie, *The Buffalo Soldiers: A Narrative of the Negro Cavalry in the West* (Norman, 1967), pp. 6, 98, 238, 259; Marvin Fletcher, *The Black Soldier and Officer in the United States Army, 1891–1917* (Columbia, 1974), p. 22; Alwyn Barr, *Black Texans: A History of Negroes in Texas, 1528–1971* (Austin, 1973), pp. 86–88; Allan W. Sandstrum, "Fort Bliss: The Frontier Years" (M.A. thesis, Texas Western College of the University of Texas, El Paso, Texas, 1962), pp. 175–176.

2. Foner, *Blacks and the Military,* p. 57; Fletcher, *The Black Soldier,* p. 25; Frank N. Schubert, "Black Soldiers on the White Frontier: Some Factors Influencing Race Relations," *Phylon,* XXXII, no. 4 (Winter, 1971), pp. 411–415; Sandstrom, "Fort Bliss," pp. 175–176; *El Paso Times,* April 30, 1899, p. 2.

3. Marilyn T. Bryan, "The Economic, Political and Social Status of the Negro in El Paso," *Password of the El Paso Historical Society,* XIII, no. 3 (Fall, 1968), pp. 73–75, 79–83.

4. *Ibid.,* p. 75; Lieutenant Colonel Cyrus S. Roberts to the Adjutant General, Department of Texas, San Antonio, Texas, February 28, 1900, Adjutant General's Office Central File, 1890–1917, file no. 325267, RG 94, National Archives and Records Service, Washington; Foner, *Blacks and the Military,* pp. 74–78.

5. *El Paso Times,* December 12, 1899, p. 7; December 24, 1899, p. 6; January 5, 1900, p. 5.

6. *Ibid.,* October 29, 1899, p. 8.

7. *El Paso Herald,* February 17, 1900, p. 1.

8. *Ibid.*

9. *Ibid.*

10. *Ibid.*

11. *Ibid.; El Paso Times,* February 18, 1900, p. 7.

12. *El Paso Times,* February 18, 1900, p. 7.

13. *El Paso Herald,* February 17, 1900, p. 1.

14. Colonel Chambers McKibben to the Adjutant General of the Army, San Antonio, Texas, February 20, 1900, AGO file 325267, RG 94, National Archives; *El Paso Times,* February 18, 1900, p. 4.

15. *El Paso Times,* February 23, 1900, p. 6; Roberts to the Adjutant General, Department of Texas, San Antonio, Texas, February 28, 1900, AGO file 325267, RG 94, National Archives.

16. *El Paso Times,* March 3, 1900, p. 6; March 4, 1900, p. 2; April 21, 1900, p. 1; May 23, 1900, p. 2.

17. *El Paso Herald,* August 21, 1901, p. 5.

18. *El Paso Times,* August 6, 1890, p. 7; April 22, 1923, p. 16; *El Paso Herald,* March 28, 1893, p. 1; October 25, 1902, p. 8; June 10, 1904, p. 1; July 28, 1904, p. 4; August 20, 1909, p. 1.; October 8, 1914, p. 2; April 21, 1923, p. 19; August 23, 1932, p. 5.

19. *El Paso Times,* May 1, 1900, p. 5.

20. *Ibid.,* May 2, 1900, p. 6; May 3, 1900, p. 6.

21. *Ibid.,* May 3, 1900, p. 6.

22. *Ibid.,* May 4, 1900, p. 6.

23. *Ibid.*

24. *Ibid.*

25. *Ibid.,* May 5, 1900, p. 7.

26. *Ibid.*

27. *Ibid.*

28. *Ibid.*, May 6, 1900, p. 7.

29. *El Paso Herald*, November 14, 1900, p. 4; November 16, 1900, p. 5; November 20, 1900, p. 4.

30. *Ibid.*, August 9, 1900, p. 1; September 7, 1900, p. 1.

31. *Ibid.*, July 2, 1900; November 20, 1900, p. 4; Texas provided more test cases on the right of blacks to serve as jurors than any other Southern state. Still, by the turn of the century, relatively few blacks sat on grand or petit juries. See Lawrence D. Rice, *The Negro in Texas, 1874–1900* (Baton Rouge, 1971), p. 256. *Kipper* vs. *State*, Court of Criminal Appeals of Texas, April 10, 1901, *Southwestern Reporter*, LXII, pp. 421–422.

32. *El Paso Herald*, March 27, 1901, p. 8; May 16, 1901, p. 8; July 15, 1901, p. 2; 1910 Federal Population Census, Supplement for Texas, Federal Archives and Records Center, Fort Worth, Texas, p. 650.

33. J. M. Dean to Elihu Root, El Paso, Texas, June 21, 1900, AGO file 330323, RG 94, National Archives; Assistant Adjutant General to J. M. Dean, Washington, June 29, 1900, *ibid.*, Adjutant General to Commanding Officer, Department of Texas, August 23, 1900, *ibid.*; Captain R. H. R. Loughborough to Adjutant General, Department of Texas, Fort Bliss, Texas, August 20, 1900, *ibid.*; G. H. Liebe to Adjutant General, San Antonio, Texas, March 27, 1901, *ibid.*

34. Memorandum for Carter, Miscellaneous Division, Adjutant General's Office, March 22, 1901, *ibid.*; Roberts to Adjutant General, Department of Texas, San Antonio, Texas, March 13, 1901, *ibid.*; Roberts to Adjutant General, Department of War, San Antonio, Texas, April 22, 1901, *ibid;* Dean to Roberts, El Paso, Texas, April 23, 1901, *ibid.*; M. W. Stanton to Roberts, El Paso, Texas, April 22, 1901, *ibid.*; Dean to William Cary Sanger, El Paso, Texas, May 29, 1901, *ibid.*

35. George Andrews to Dean, Washington, May 11, 1901, *ibid.*; Joseph D. Sayers to Adjutant General, Austin, Texas. May 16, 1901, *ibid.*; Andrews to Commanding Officer, Department of Texas, Washington, May 17, 1901, *ibid.*; Sanger to Sayers, Washington, May 20, 1901, *ibid.*; Dean to Sanger, El Paso, Texas, May 29, 1901, *ibid.*

36. Stanton to Roberts, El Paso, Texas, June 14, 1901, *ibid.*; *El Paso Herald*, June 3, 1901, p. 4; June 14, 1901, p. 1.

37. *El Paso Herald*, June 29, 1901, p. 5.

38. *Ibid.*, July 23, 1901, p. 1; July 29, 1901, p. 1; August 2, 1901, p. 1.

39. *Ibid.*, August 5, 1901, p. 1; August 15, 1901, p. 1; August 17, 1901, p. 1.

40. *Ibid.*, August 6, 1901, p. 1.; August 21, 1901, p. 1; August 23, 1901.

41. *Ibid.*, August 24, 1901, p. 1; *Kipper* vs. *State*, Court of Criminal Appeals of Texas, December 9, 1903, *Southwestern Reporter*, LXXVII, pp. 612, 617–618; conditional pardon by the Governor of the State of Texas, no. 11566, Texas Department of Corrections, Huntsville, Texas, June 20, 1913.

42. Roberts to Adjutant General, Department of Texas, San Antonio, Texas, March 13, 1901, AGO file 330323, RG 94, National Archives.

43. John D. Weaver, *The Brownsville Raid* (New York, 1970), pp. 20–28, 75; Ann J. Lane, *The Brownsville Affair: National Crisis and Black Reaction* (Port Washington, 1971), pp. 5, 8–9, 14–15; James A. Tinsley, "Roosevelt, Foraker, and the Brownsville Affray," *Journal of Negro History*, XLI, no. 1 (January, 1956), pp. 43–44; Fletcher, *The Black Soldier*, p. 120.

44. Robert V. Haynes, *A Night of Violence: The Houston Riot of 1917* (Baton Rouge, 1976), pp. 16, 23–24, 51–53, 201–202, 205–206; Edgar A. Schuler, "Houston Race Riot of 1917," *Journal of Negro History*, XXX, no. 3 (July, 1944), pp. 304, 309, 333. Hardening racial patterns stemming from economic, political, and social frustrations of whites is discussed in C. Vann Woodward, *The Strange Career of Jim Crow* (New York, 1966), p. 81. For effects in Texas see Barr, *Black Texans*, p. 88.

45. The Brownsville Raid prompted fiery Congressional oratory and bills to eliminate black military units. See Fletcher, *The Black Soldier*, p. 158; the Kipper issue was revived by the El Paso press after a series of distant racial conflicts. See *El Paso Times*, August 25, 1906, p. 3; *El Paso Herald*, December 6, 1906, p. 6.

PART TWO

The Twentieth Century Experience

★

The Twentieth Century Experience
An Introduction

IN TEXAS the nadir of the African American experience extended into the twentieth century. However, blacks increasingly protested their "second class" citizenship. For example, discriminatory laws and customs provoked reactions in the black community such as the one in Houston in 1904. There, people of color boycotted the city's street cars to register their complaint against segregation. A far more serious protest occurred in Brownsville in 1906. There, a local merchant insulted a black soldier who retaliated with several blows. Because of the altercation, Brownsville was put off-limits to soldiers from the nearby fort. At least twelve African American troopers defied the order and went to town, where a mini-war ensued—a mini-war that left one white man dead and two others wounded. Although only a few African Americans were involved in the fray, an investigative report prompted President Theodore Roosevelt to discharge dishonorably three entire companies of black soldiers.

Despite such unfair treatment, black Texans coped as best they could. They also continued to build their social lives, lives that in part mirrored those of whites. They married. They tried to be good parents to their children. They worked hard. Their churches flourished, as did their underfunded educational institutions. Fraternal self-help organizations grew in size and number as did all manner of social clubs for women. Top entertainers emerged from the black community in a steady stream throughout the years. Those who became well known included jazz and ragtime musicians such as Huddie "Leadbelly" Ledbetter, Scott Joplin, and Blind Lemon Jefferson. Writers included Maud Cuney Hare, Theodore Sylvester Boone, and Bernice Love Wiggins.

In addition to their cultural efforts, black Texans also proved to be patriotic. Both soldiers and civilians ardently supported the United

States in the Spanish-American War, while some troopers were with General "Black Jack" Pershing's expedition to Mexico in 1916. But, perhaps more important, the African American community rallied to the cause during World War I. They participated in rationing programs, worked for the Red Cross (on a segregated basis), bought war bonds, and engaged in other positive war-related civilian efforts. In addition, the black community furnished the military with approximately 25 percent (about 31,000 men) of the Texans called to serve, even though African Americans made up only about 16 percent of the total population. The black men who fought were so lethal that the Germans called them "Hell Fighters."

Despite the firm black effort, occasionally trouble flared on the home front, especially wherever the segregated camps for the African American men were located. Incidents occurred in such places as San Antonio, Del Rio, and Waco, but Houston was the scene of the worst trouble. There, whites daily insulted the African American soldiers. Segregation and discrimination followed them everywhere. Then, on August 23, 1917, the police harassed a black soldier along with his woman friend and next arrested a black military policeman who tried to intervene. Following these actions, 150 African American service men poured into the city like an avalanche. The result left seventeen people dead and sixteen others wounded. Although whites had created the conditions for violence to flourish, the military command dealt most harshly with the blacks involved: nineteen were executed and ninety were imprisoned for varying terms.

Although black Texans who served in Europe, especially in France, experienced greater freedom, once they returned home it was "business as usual." Violence abounded in the form of lynching and white-instigated race riots. Worse, the Georgia reincarnation of the Ku Klux Klan in 1915 led to even more trouble once the Klan spread to Texas. White members of the Klan attacked blacks, Jews, Catholics, labor organizers, socialists, communists, and other "undesirable" groups. One notable atrocity occurred in little Kirvin, Texas. On May 6, 1922, whites there burned three African Americans at the stake in the middle of the town square. The three victims had previously been in police custody and therefore should have been protected.

Responding to the increased violence, thousands of African Americans voted with their feet. They left the Lone Star State and headed north or west; others moved from small rural communities to larger towns and cities within the state, and others migrated to Texas cities from states such as Arkansas and Louisiana. The overall result was that the aggregate number of black Texans rose from 600,000 in 1900 to 900,000 by 1940. Given the plight of those who remained in Texas, the state chapter of the National Association for the Advancement of Colored People (NAACP) stepped up its activities of active protest and legal challenges to discrimination. The Texas attorney general tried in 1917 to suppress the organization by claiming it was not chartered to do business in the state. Then, when NAACP Executive Secretary John R. Shilladay, a white, went to Austin to protest and to defend against the attorney general's charges, a local constable and a county judge joined the white mob that gleefully beat Shilladay unconscious, left him in a gutter, and permanently ruined his health. Meanwhile, Governor H. P. Hobby publicly supported the mob, not a one of whom faced arrest.

Continuing to struggle economically through the 1920s, most black Texans still worked as farmers, but only about one in five owned their own land. Fully 80 percent of those in agriculture remained sharecroppers and tenants, and most were poverty-stricken. Conditions worsened when the Great Depression began in 1929. Even more so than before, blacks were the last hired and the first fired. When the Depression began, black Texans suffered more than whites. Indeed, whites began taking over jobs that had traditionally been performed by black people. That practice simply worsened the already terrible job market for the people of color. Thus, unemployment in the black community was higher than in the white.

Beginning in 1933 the New Deal brought some relief, but discrimination within the programs was often a problem. For example, the Civilian Conservation Corps set up numerous camps throughout the Lone Star State but did so on a segregated basis; white and black people were not mixed together in the camps. The Agricultural Adjustment Administration had an especially negative impact on black tenants and sharecroppers. Nevertheless, New Deal programs helped all the poor—white and black—cope with the Depression as the economic disaster ran its course. Also significant, the Depression continued the rural-to-urban shift, as poor blacks and whites left their broken-down rented farms when they sought jobs with New Deal agencies or other urban jobs. Over time, the population shift became a blessing: by the 1940s the old pattern of sharecropping that had impoverished thousands of blacks and whites was fading away. The invention of the mechanical cotton picker in 1944 sped the end of the old farming system and helped end the South's age of feudalism.

Even in the depths of the Depression, observers noted positive changes. Out of the Texas Centennial, for example, came the Negro Day at the State Fair in Dallas in 1936. Led by A. Maceo Smith, Afro-Texans showed their wares during the celebration. Laborers built the Hall of Negro Life during that year, and the work of artists like Aaron Douglass—who rose to fame during the Harlem Renaissance—and Houston's Samuel Countee were prominently featured along with the work of Galveston's Frank Sheinall. Perhaps even more important, the 1936 Centennial spawned two new organizations for black uplift: the Texas State Conference on Branches of the NAACP and the Texas State Negro Chamber of Commerce. Blacks in Texas looked ahead to the new decade of the 1940s with a measure of hope.

Franklin D. Roosevelt's massive war preparedness campaign of 1940 and 1941 and then America's entry into World War II helped lift the nation out of the Depression. Black Texans, like their counterparts across the country, saw better times economically. Roosevelt's Executive Order 8802 forbade discrimination in defense industries holding government contracts. African American men and women took advantage of Roosevelt's policies. Whites had "Rosie the Riveter," who was "makin' history workin' for victory," but so, too, did the black community. In addition, African Americans participated in bond drives, planted "victory gardens" to ease food rationing, skimped on various consumer goods, and cooperated with drives to conserve fuel, rubber, and other items. Then, too, military men acquitted themselves well, both stateside and in the two war theaters—despite the fact that most were relegated to service units.

The need for massive industrial output for the war effort encouraged the continuing rural-to-urban population shift, which boded well for the black community. Yet as more whites and blacks congregated in urban areas, racial troubles sometimes flared as the groups competed for jobs and housing. In Dallas, for example, a rash of bombings shook and destroyed some black homes in South Oak Cliff. Worse was the Beaumont race riot of 1943 when an unidentified assailant was accused of raping a young white woman. Assuming that a black had committed the crime, a white mob declared war on the local African American community, resulting in a fifteen-hour riot.

After the war, many African Americans took advantage of the GI Bill, which offered them a subsidy to attend college and/or a discounted interest rate if they wished to finance a home. In addition, many also benefited from the generally prosperous economy from 1945 through the 1960s. For example, between 1940 and 1960 the median income for African Americans increased from 37 percent to 50 percent of the median for whites, but, ultimately, the blacks' concern for economic uplift had to share time with their concern for civil rights. This movement had the potential to effect the black community politically, socially, and economically.

The Supreme Court's decision in *Smith vs. Allwright* affected not only Texas but had a region-wide impact throughout the "lily white" South. The court ruled that primaries in one-party states were tantamount to election, and that no voter could be denied the right to vote in those primaries because of skin color. The results were almost immediate. For instance, in the 1946 Democratic primary, approximately 75,000 blacks voted in Texas. Subsequently, the African American communities' new political clout was demonstrated when white politicians began speaking to black audiences and started advertising in black-owned newspapers. Increasingly, more African Americans registered and voted in Texas elections. By 1958, the number of blacks registered to vote had risen to 226,495. As the voting bloc continued to increase, racist white politicians had to continue to modify their political positions to win those votes.

Black Texans were also involved in other Supreme Court decisions that advanced the cause of civil rights. In 1946 Heman M. Sweatt, a war veteran and a graduate of Wiley College, tried to register to attend the University of Texas Law School but was refused; whereupon, the NAACP (led by Thurgood Marshall, chief legal counsel of the NAACP, and William J. Durham of Dallas) went to court arguing that the old *Plessy vs. Ferguson* "separate but equal" ruling was not being obeyed, for Texas had no public law school for people of color. The Houston chapter of the NAACP, led by Lulu White, and Carter Wesley, found the plaintiff as well as being major players in the case. The Texas legislature tried to make the separate-but-equal point moot by creating a sham school in Houston and later expanded it into Texas Southern University. Yet the new law school was not equal to the one in Austin. In *Sweatt vs. Painter* in 1950, the Supreme Court ruled that Sweatt must be admitted to the University of Texas Law School. Soon, other African Americans followed Sweatt's example and forced universities' dental, medical, and graduate schools to integrate.

African Americans in Texas also sought entrance into undergraduate schools. In an admirable development, Del Mar Junior College in Corpus Christi voluntarily integrated in 1952, and in 1954 both the

University of Texas and Southern Methodist University accepted black undergraduates. Those actions were soon followed by many other schools. Later in 1954, the black community had even more to celebrate when the Supreme Court ordered public schools to integrate in the famous *Brown vs. Topeka* decision.

In Texas the historic Supreme Court decision spawned mixed reactions. In 1954 Governor Allan Shivers won reelection while promising to use all legal means to resist integration of schools; yet in 1955 and 1956 sixty-six school districts in the state integrated, including districts in Austin, San Antonio, and El Paso. But negative reactions to such racial progress mounted. As they did all across the South, White Citizens Councils coalesced. Called an "uptown Ku Klux Klan" by one Southern editor, the councils claimed 20,000 Texas members by 1955. On the 1957 election ballot, the councils supported three referendums that passed by a four-to-one margin—one against interracial marriage, one against mandatory attendance in integrated schools, and a third favoring interposition by the states against federal laws and their enforcement. At Mansfield, near Fort Worth, more than 250 angry whites stormed their local school to prevent any people of color from enrolling. To his discredit, Governor Shivers called out the Texas Rangers—not to control the mob but to help remove the black students.

As late as 1964, when President Lyndon B. Johnson persuaded Congress to pass the Civil Rights Act, only 373 Texas school districts had integrated. The students involved numbered only 18,000 out of 325,000 African American students. Thus, only about 5 percent of the African American students attended integrated schools. Shocking though it was, the statistics gave Texas first place in school integration compared to the other ex-Confederate states. Further, no governor after Shivers ever again considered legal maneuvers to interfere with integration. Even earlier, the Texas delegation to Congress gained national note. When Dixiecrats in Congress issued their Southern Manifesto in the mid-1950s, pledging never to support *Brown vs. Topeka*, Senators Lyndon B. Johnson and Price Daniel bravely refused to sign the tract as did most of the House members from the Lone Star State.

Meanwhile, black Texans and their white supporters continued the civil rights struggle. They redoubled their pressure on the courts. They also took the movement into the streets with direct, non-violent protest. Black-owned newspapers kept the fires alive by reporting continued violence aimed at the NAACP, by lambasting hospitals that refused to admit African Americans, by condemning "Negro day" at the

State Fair, and by continuing complaints about segregation and the in-equalities of job opportunities and pay. At the local level, activists con-tinued to work through the NAACP, the Southern Christian Leader-ship Conference (SCLC), and local churches. In Dallas, for example, leaders like Juanita Craft worked with local youth councils to organize peaceful protests.

Positive results of black activism came haltingly. Victories included winning the right to serve on juries, securing equal pay for African American teachers, eliminating residential segregation in most major Texas cities, and gaining jobs on the police forces of urban areas. Sit-ins in Houston and Marshall led to an end to segregation in places of public accommodations. In 1958, African American Hattie White won elec-tion to the Houston School Board, the first such win since Reconstruc-tion.

After Congress passed the historic Civil Rights Act, integration of schools moved forward because districts did not want to lose federal funds. By 1965 all but 66 of Texas's 772 biracial districts had started in-tegration or had filed plans to do so. By the academic year of 1966–1967, approximately 47 percent of African American students at-tended integrated schools. Further, the act of 1964 forbade segregation of public accommodations. Soon, all the dual facilities for the races began to disappear. Gone were the two water fountains—one each for whites and blacks. Gone were four bathrooms, since the two genders needed only one each. Gone were segregated movie theaters, segregated train stations, segregated taxi companies, and segregated telephone booths. African Americans in Texas and the nation finally had legal equality.

The act of 1964 also called for an end to job discrimination and dis-crimination in the voting process. Continuing Southern resistance to the latter forced President Johnson—who became known as the "Civil Rights President"—to pressure Congress until it passed the Voter Regis-tration Act of 1965, which, over time, ensured that African Americans would fully enjoy their right to vote. In allowing the black voter bloc to grow, the act forced many more Texas politicians to moderate their views on racial issues. It also opened political doors for black leaders like Dallas's Joe Lockridge, who won election to the Texas House of Representatives in 1966. Other blacks were elected to various local offices around the state. In Houston, Judson Robinson, who won elec-tion to the city council in 1971, became the first African American to sit on that local body since Reconstruction. Another pioneer was Barbara

Jordan, who became the first black woman to serve in the Texas Senate before becoming the state's first black congresswoman in 1972. Her political rise became a symbol of the progress that the black community was making. Nationally recognized, she gave the keynote speech at the 1976 Democratic National Convention. As if to honor civil rights pioneers like Jordan, Texas's pledge to end Jim Crow was reaffirmed in 1969 when the legislature passed a law expressly forbidding segregation.

As the 1960s gave way to the 1970s, integration of schools remained one focus of civil rights leaders. After a successful California experiment (voluntary) to use busing to achieve racial balance, more school districts across the nation tried the tactic which, for a time, was mandated by the federal courts. However, President Nixon adamantly opposed busing as did new Texas Republican Senator John Tower. The struggle over busing continued into the mid- and late-1970s as the white community in Texas and the nation became increasingly opposed to the plan. Ronald Reagan's triumph in 1980 signaled the end of the controversy: the new administration killed the tactic as a way to achieve racial balance.

By the 1970s the black plight appeared to worsen, in part because of the lack of concern from the majority of Americans and in part because of the general downturn in the economy, which affected Texas just as it did the larger nation. The decade saw both recession and inflation. Unemployment, the prime interest rate, and inflation (called the "misery index" when added together) all hit double-digits. Grossly underrepresented in the higher paying and higher status jobs, about one-third of all black Texans were employed as unskilled laborers. The unemployment rate for African Americans was about twice as high as the rate for the state as a whole.

Conditions improved but little for Texas's black citizens in the 1980s. More black workers moved into the middle class, and more black professionals could be counted across the state, but a two-tiered African American community was in the making. Part of what W. E. B. Du Bois once described as the "talented tenth," some blacks secured educations, worked hard, began to prosper, and even gained more political input in the Democratic party. But such progress occurred while African Americans trapped in the inner cities of Houston, Dallas, Fort Worth, and San Antonio remained mired in poverty. They were people of little hope who saw illegal drugs run rampant. Gang violence flourished, and the crime rates went off the chart. The phenomena of "resegregation" made the problems even worse.

In the face of the mounting problems of the inner cities, everyone who could get out did so. "White flight," from the cities to the suburbs, ongoing since the 1950s, was expanded by the flight of black professionals who also began to leave the cities. Business tended to follow the flight, while thousands of minorities poured into the now-inexpensive vacated space in the inner cities. The results were predictable and catastrophic. The tax base of the central cities was lowered at just the time that the poor were crowding in. Reduced city services were inevitable despite the fact that the lower classes needed them so much. Further, even as whites and black professionals lived in suburbia, they commuted back into the cities to monopolize the best jobs, but then took their money away and spent it elsewhere. The inner cities subsidized suburbia while receiving little in return—for example, as the inner cities' tax base eroded, schools suffered from declining budgets.

Riding Ronald Reagan's coattails, the Republican party grew stronger in Texas as affluent whites and a handful of successful blacks flocked to its banner. They pushed for continued retrenchment in social programs, while increasing the nation's deficit. Meanwhile, by 1989, when Reagan left the presidency, 3.1 million Texans (or almost 20 percent of the state's population) still lived below the poverty line. Thus, the gains made in Johnson's "War on Poverty" were reversed. Among the poverty-stricken, African Americans, Hispanics, and the elderly made up the bulk of the total.

Texas may well be headed toward a reckoning with its past. Today, the black and Hispanic populations are growing tremendously. Some statisticians predict, for example, that by 2010 white children will comprise a minority of students in the state's public schools. The sheer numbers may force the white community to become more inclusive and to develop more tolerance for other groups. Such numbers are already having a political effect, for more African Americans and Hispanics are winning elective office every year. While discrimination against minorities stands as a failure of American democracy, the minorities are fighting their way in. They are challenging white supremacy and may one day become victorious. As the new political clout of minorities grows, great economic and social changes will come, and will, no doubt, surprise many whites who choose to ignore the demographic trends.

In the 1990s the general Texas economy improved, especially during the administration of President Bill Clinton. The state continued to diversify its production and to lessen dependence on extractive industries such as petroleum and lumber, while the service sector expanded. More high-tech companies moved to Texas and finance and trade also prospered. The state benefited from the North American Free Trade Agreement (NAFTA)—the agreement led to expansion in trade-related jobs. Yet even as the state economy improved, blacks saw but few of the benefits, especially those who were undereducated and still trapped in the cycle of poverty in the inner cities. Considered together, blacks and Hispanics still formed too much of the underclass while tremendous social and economic problems continued to fester.

Yet even as many problems remained unsolved, there were bright spots and some progress. In 1983, for example, Dallas was named as one of the ten best cities nationwide for people of color because of increased opportunities for African Americans. In 1992 Amarillo's Morris Overstreet won a seat on the Texas Court of Criminal Appeals, a first for a black Texan. As well, employment opportunities for African Americans increased in most of the state's major cities. In 2001 Houston was named the best city for African Americans. Continuing cultural strides were evident in the work of intellectuals such as Ntozake Shange, playwright and novelist, whose 1982 effort, *Sassafras, Cypress, and Indigo,* became a best-seller as did her *Betsey Brown* in 1985. Short story writer J. California Cooper of East Texas also gained national note for award-winning stories like *A Place of Mine* (1984) and *Family* (1991).

Clearly, progress, on one hand, and continuing racial inequities, on the other hand, coexist in Texas. But those who remember the old days of rigid segregation, widespread white violence against blacks, and the "second-class" citizenship grudgingly meted out to African Americans, the future does not look all that bleak. Overall, there has certainly been much progress in the last two generations. The future holds the prospect of even more progress as blacks continue their struggle to be included into the Republican ideal of America.

If only Estevan were here to tell us the outcome of the saga that he began in 1527 when he waded ashore on the coast of Texas.

The "Waco Horror"
The Lynching of Jesse Washington

JAMES M. SORELLE

As valiantly as black leaders, organizations, and race activists strove to improve their position in Texas, whites did their utmost to prevent black equality by responding viciously. Using violence and intimidation, whites maintained themselves as the dominant race in Texas society while at the same time keeping blacks subordinate and in their "place." In one particularly virulent example of the extent to which whites would punish alleged violators of their racial code—while at the same time reminding other blacks of the punishment for misbehaving—whites in Waco, Texas, exhibited more than usual outrageous behavior. They brutally lynched an illiterate, probably mentally retarded, black man who was found guilty by a jury (after only four minutes of deliberation) of the rape and murder of a white woman. White townspeople burned Jesse Washington's body, mutilated it, and hauled it off in a sack before dragging it behind a car. Youths even broke out his teeth and sold them for souvenirs. No one, James SoRelle reminds us, was arrested even though photographs and common knowledge pointed to the guilty culprits. Even the Christian ministers of Waco did not denounce the atrocity. The NAACP used the episode to work for a federal antilynching law, but American involvement in World War I derailed that effort.

*

DURING THE YEARS from 1889 to 1918, the United States experienced 3,224 lynchings within its borders, or roughly one every three days. Nearly 80 percent of the victims were African Americans, and the vast majority of the incidents occurred in the South. Georgia, for example, held the dubious distinction of leading all states with a total of 386 lynchings, while Mississippi and Texas followed closely with 373 and 335, respectively. These statistics furnish an irrefutable record of mob violence and seem to corroborate Mr. Dooley's characterization of the racial climate confronting black Americans in the early twentieth century: "Th' black has manny fine qualities," the bartender-sage told his friend, Hennessey. "He is joyous, light-hearted, an' aisily lynched."[1]

For some white Americans, lynching apparently represented a justifiable means of punishing alleged black criminals and of providing a vivid reminder that white supremacy still reigned in the land. "The white man in lynching a Negro does it as an indirect act of self-defense against the Negro criminal as a race," one apologist argued. "When the abnormally criminal Negro race . . . puts himself [sic] in harmony with our civilization, if ever, through assimilating our culture and making our ideals its own, then may it be hoped that his [sic] crimes will be reduced to normal and lynching will cease, the cause being removed." Such a statement reveals the climate of opinion that no doubt led J. W. Bailey, editor of the *Biblical Recorder*, to observe: "Lynching, mobspirit, lawlessness, are in the blood of our people." Many other whites, simply preferring to ignore the problem, would have agreed with the reader of the *Crisis*, the official organ of the National Association for the Advancement of Colored People, who expressed his dissatisfaction with "so much talk about the lynching of Negroes" in the pages of that journal.[2]

On the other hand, a vocal minority of Americans, by publicly denouncing the trend toward mob violence in the country, refused to support a conspiracy of silence with respect to lynching. Bishop Charles B. Galloway of the Methodist Episcopal Church, South, proclaimed that "Every Christian patriot in America needs to lift up his voice in loud and eternal protest against the mob-spirit that is threatening the integrity of this Republic." Similarly, the NAACP from its inception considered lynching (which the *Crisis* identified as "the standard American industry") one of the most important problems in the country, and the eradication of lynching one of the most important planks in its program for racial advancement. Of particular concern to individuals and organizations determined to halt episodes of mob-inflicted violence was the fact that, while the frequency of lynchings began to decline after 1900, those incidents that did occur were often characterized by extreme barbarity. Few examples of lynch law in twentieth-century America demonstrate this more graphically than the mutilation and burning of Jesse Washington at the hands of a white mob in Waco, Texas, on May 15, 1916—an episode dubbed the "Waco Horror."[3]

Located on the banks of the Brazos River in the fertile blackland region of Central Texas, Waco was a thriving community in 1916. Local boosters described the Lone Star state's eighth largest urban area (estimated population 33,670)[4] as "The Wonder City" and emphasized the "progressiveness" of the town. Economic opportunities reportedly abounded, particularly in businesses associated with the cotton culture of the surrounding agricultural districts. In addition, city fathers depicted Waco as a center for wholesale dealers and for the rapidly expanding insurance business. One publication of the Young Men's Business League described Waco in 1912 as "a true Southern city which is possessed of all the business possibilities of the metropolitan cities of the nation. . . ." Wacoans also expressed pride in their religious and educational institutions, which included sixty-three churches of various denominations and Baptist-affiliated Baylor University, the state's oldest college. The influence exerted by these institutions probably explains the message on a large electric sign that spanned one of the principal street intersections, proclaiming Waco to be "The City With a Soul."[5]

Despite Waco's aura of middle-class respectability in 1916, the city's history had been interspersed with episodes of violence, thus earning the town the sobriquet "Six Shooter Junction." This frontier tradition of lawlessness, though less evident after the turn of the century, surfaced on numerous occasions and shattered the idyllic image so carefully crafted and defended by Waco's community leaders. The lynching of Jesse Washington for the murder of a white woman was one of those occasions.

Early in the evening on May 8, 1916, Chris Simons was walking toward his home on the outskirts of Robinson, a small farming community seven miles south of Waco, when he heard screams coming from the direction of George Fryer's place, some five hundred to six hundred yards down the road. Simons ran to the Fryer home, where he encountered the hysterical twenty-two-year-old Ruby Fryer and her fourteen-year-old brother, George Jr., who were staring at the lifeless form of their mother, fifty-three-year-old Lucy Fryer, sprawled across the doorway of the seed shed. Upon learning from the children that their father was working in the fields, Simons hurried to find the elder Fryer. Informed of the tragic news delivered by his neighbor, Fryer drove to Waco, the county seat of McLennan County, where he reported the crime to Sheriff Samuel S. Fleming. Fleming swiftly assembled an investigative team, composed of his deputies, local constables, and a number of Waco policemen, and departed for Robinson.[6]

The report of Lucy Fryer's murder spread rapidly through the Robinson community, and several local men banded together to offer their assistance to Sheriff Fleming and his contingent of law enforcement officials. Meanwhile, Dr. J. H. Maynard, a physician from nearby Rosenthal, arrived to examine the dead woman's body. Maynard discovered several deep gashes in Lucy Fryer's head, including two massive wounds penetrating the brain cavity. These blows, the doctor determined, had been delivered by an assailant who used a heavy, blunt instrument.[7]

Suspicion fell almost immediately upon Jesse Washington, an illiterate seventeen-year-old African American who, with his brother, William, had worked as a hired hand on the Fryer farm since January. Shortly after 9:00 p.m., an entourage of peace officers drove to the Washington place, where they discovered the young suspect (wearing a blood-stained pair of overalls and undershirt) sitting outside whittling on a piece of wood. Following a few routine questions, Deputy Sheriffs Lee Jenkins and Barney Goldberg took the Washington family into custody and escorted them to Waco for further interrogation, after which William and his parents were released. During this questioning in Waco, Jesse Washington offered several conflicting statements but consistently denied any knowledge of the circumstances surrounding Lucy Fryer's death.[8]

The arrest of Jesse Washington produced a volatile climate in Robinson. One Waco paper reported that local law enforcement officials quickly "realized that the enormity of the crime would cause the hot blood of the Robinson countrymen to flame and cry for protection of their women and homes against the lust of the brute." Aware of the potential for mob violence, Sheriff Fleming decided to remove the black suspect beyond the reach of a lynching party. During the predawn hours on Tuesday, May 9, Fleming transferred his prisoner to Hillsboro, a small town thirty-five miles north of Waco. Once in Hillsboro, Fleming resumed his questioning of the accused in the presence of Hill County Sheriff Fred Long, an interrogation that climaxed with Jesse Washington's confession that he indeed had killed Lucy Fryer. Washington identified the murder weapon as a medium-sized blacksmith's hammer and told his interrogators that he had hidden the hammer in a field on the Fryer place. With this information in hand, Sheriff Fleming returned to Waco, while Sheriff Long escorted the confessed killer to Dallas, where Washington dictated a confession to Dallas County Attorney Mike T. Lively in which he admitted to raping and murdering the wife of his employer. The black youth signed this confession with an X in lieu of his name, which he was incapable of writing. Lively then had Washington locked in the Dallas County jail to await trial and, presumably, to protect him from possible mob assault.[9]

Meanwhile, Sheriff Fleming arrived back in Waco and, accompanied by deputies Lee Jenkins and Joe Roberts and County Prosecutor John B. McNamara, drove to the Fryer farm. There the search party discovered a blood-caked blacksmith's hammer under a pile of hackberry brush adjacent to the field in which Jesse Washington had been working the previous day, and precisely in the location the black youth had described as the hiding place for the murder weapon.[10]

The discovery of the hammer allegedly used to kill Lucy Fryer, coinciding with the publication of the black suspect's confession in the Waco newspapers, inflamed passions among Robinson's citizenry still further and led some to insist upon drastic action. Shortly after 10:00 p.m. that evening, Sheriff Fleming encountered a procession of some 500 citizens from Robinson, Rosenthal, and several smaller communities in southern McLennan County headed toward Waco along the Lorena road. The ringleaders of the group demanded that Fleming release Jesse Washington to them so that swift "justice" might be carried out, and one of the men reportedly declared: "When we left home tonight our wives, daughters and sisters kissed us goodbye and told us to do our duty, and we're trying to do it as citizens." When Fleming informed them that the suspect had been removed from the city for safekeeping pending his trial, several of the men refused to believe him and requested to search the jail. Fleming acquiesced, and the caravan of automobiles, buggies, and horses carrying the vigilantes proceeded toward Waco. Upon their arrival at the county jail, the men conducted a meticulous search of the cells, including close scrutiny of every black prisoner. Having satisfied themselves that Washington was not there, the men left quietly and returned to their homes. Following this initial attempt to circumvent the judicial process, community leaders in Robinson assured Waco law enforcement authorities that no further mob action would be planned as long as the legal system operated swiftly in convicting and punishing the confessed rapist and murderer.[11]

Officials in Waco needed little encouragement to resolve the case quickly. On Thursday, May 11, a McLennan County grand jury convened and required only thirty minutes to return a murder indictment against Jesse Washington. District Judge Richard I. Munroe appointed six young Waco attorneys to defend the accused and set the trial date for the following Monday. The Morning News, noting these preliminary maneuvers, predicted that "justice will move on swift feet in the case."[12]

The trial of Jesse Washington commenced at 10:00 a.m. Monday, May 15, in the Fifty-Fourth District Court of McLennan County, with

Judge Munroe presiding over a courtroom filled to capacity. Spectators packed the balcony, and some stood on railings and benches to obtain a better view. On several occasions prospective jurors had to be lifted over the crowd to reach the front of the courtroom. Judge Munroe periodically sought to preserve decorum by gavelling for silence and reminding several of the male onlookers to remove their hats. Those who could not get inside congregated around the courthouse, lining the sidewalks on all sides. Among this crowd of bystanders (described as the largest ever seen in the city) were several African Americans whom one Waco paper characterized as "quiet and seemingly not much excited."[13]

Among some of the white spectators, however, the mood was ugly. Trouble was narrowly averted before the trial when Jesse Washington, whom Sheriff Fleming had brought back to Waco the previous evening, was escorted into the courtroom by sheriff's deputies. At the sight of the defendant, an unidentified white man pulled a revolver and declared, "Might as well get him now." Violence was prevented by another white spectator, who overpowered and disarmed the gunman and proclaimed, "Let them have the trial. We'll get him before sundown, and you might hurt some innocent man." At another point early in the proceedings an anonymous voice called out, "Don't need no court."[14]

The trial proceeded rapidly. Jury selection required a mere thirty-five minutes, as the defense counsel, headed by Joseph W. Taylor Jr. offered no peremptory challenges to prospective jurors. Once the jury was empanelled, Judge Munroe read the indictment and asked the defendant to state his plea. When Washington seemed puzzled by the request, the judge asked the black youth whether or not he had committed the crime for which he was being prosecuted. Munroe explained that a guilty plea would result in hanging or a sentence of from five years to life in the state penitentiary. The defendant's response consisted of a muttered, "Yeah," which the court translated as "Guilty."[15]

Upon the completion of these preliminary matters, the prosecuting attorney, John B. McNamara, opened the case for the state. Dr. Maynard took the witness stand to describe the wounds inflicted upon Lucy Fryer but, curiously, made no mention of evidence of a sexual assault. Following this medical testimony, Mike Lively, Fred Long, and W. J. Davis, a legal investigator and former Dallas policeman, related the details of Jesse Washington's confession in Dallas and identified the defendant as the person who, in their presence, had admitted raping and murdering Mrs. Fryer. Sheriff Fleming and his deputy, Lee Jenkins, described to the court their roles in the arrest of the defendant and the successful search for the murder weapon. Finally, Chris Simons and Constable Leslie Stegall offered testimony pertaining to their discovery of the dead woman's body on the evening of May 8. Attorney McNamara then read Washington's confession into the court record and rested his case.[16]

The counsel for the defense, which chose to ask only one question during cross-examination of the state's witnesses, opened and closed its case by calling a single witness—Jesse Washington. Joe Taylor asked his client if he had anything to say to the jury in his own behalf. The black man replied, "I ain't going to tell them nothing more than what I said— that's what I done. . . ." Washington's subsequent remark was unintelligible to the courtroom. Taylor told the jury, "He says he is sorry he did it." The young counselor then asked the defendant if he had something more to add. Washington remained silent, at which point the defense rested.[17]

In his summation, Prosecutor McNamara praised Joe Taylor and the other young Waco attorneys for complying with their legal duty to defend their client. Furthermore, he lauded the fairness of the trial, proclaiming: "The prisoner has been given a fair trial, as fair as any ever given in this court room." This statement produced a round of applause culminating in "a mighty yell" among courtroom spectators, after which the jury retired to consider the fate of the accused.[18]

The deliberations did not take long. The jury returned after only four minutes, and Foreman William B. Brazleton, a prominent Waco businessman, read the verdict: "We, the jury, find the defendant guilty of murder as charged in the indictment and assess his penalty at death." Following a second reading of the jury's decision, Judge Munroe began writing the verdict into the docket book, and law officers were preparing to remove Jesse Washington from the courtroom, when pandemonium erupted. An unidentified white spectator yelled, "Get the nigger," and a group of men surged forward, seized the convicted youth, and hustled him down the stairs at the rear of the courthouse where a crowd of about four hundred persons waited in the alley. A chain was thrown around Washington's neck, and he was dragged in the direction of the river, where, someone suggested, he could be hanged from the city's historic suspension bridge, the site of the lynching of another African American, Sank Majors, in 1905. Instead of continuing to the bridge, however, the mob turned on Second Street and marched toward city hall, where another group of vigilantes had gathered to build a bonfire. As the crowd pushed forward to this destination, several individuals attacked the struggling Washington, tearing the clothes from his body, stabbing him with knives, and battering him with bricks, clubs, and shovels.[19]

By the time the procession reached the city hall grounds, Jesse Washington was semiconscious and bleeding profusely. The leaders of the mob picked up their victim, tossed him onto a pile of dry-goods boxes that had been gathered under a tree, and doused his body with coal oil. The chain wrapped around Washington's neck was thrown over a sturdy limb of the tree, and several men united to jerk their victim into the air for all to see. "When the negro was first hoisted into the air," the Waco *Times-Herald* reported, "his tongue protruded from his mouth and his face was besmeared with blood." Then Washington's body was lowered onto the pile of combustibles, and several whites advanced to cut off the African American's fingers, ears, and toes. One eyewitness reported that the mob also emasculated the black youth. Many spectators of this grim affair also seemed anxious to assist in burning the convicted slayer. According to the *Times-Herald*, "[P]eople pressed forward, each eager to be the first to light the fire, matches were touched to the inflammable material and as smoke rapidly rose in the air, such a demonstration as of people gone mad was never heard before." The flames swiftly engulfed Jesse Washington.[20]

As news of the lynching spread through the city a large crowd consisting of men, women, and children assembled to watch the grisly spectacle. Many Waco businessmen left their places of employment downtown to witness the events on the city hall lawn. Mayor John R. Dollins and Chief of Police Guy McNamara viewed the event from the mayor's office in city hall, while local photographer Fred A. Gildersleeve, forewarned that Washington would be lynched at the conclusion of the trial, had set up his camera to take pictures of the incident. Of the female bystanders, one local paper reported: "[A]s matters progressed . . . they seemed to get accustomed to what was taking place, and some of them were soon laughing, and chatting, albeit their faces were in some cases still blanched." One well-dressed woman applauded gleefully "when a way was cleared so that she could see the writhing, naked form of the fast dying black." A large number of children, including students from nearby Waco High School who had rushed to the scene during their lunch hour, also witnessed this exhibition of horror. Other spectators leaned out of the windows of nearby buildings to get a better look.[21]

As the body continued to burn, some onlookers searched the ground for bits of bone, broken links of the chain noose, and pieces of the hanging tree—items that presumably could be kept or sold as souvenirs. Within two hours the smouldering remains of Jesse Washington consisted of little more than a charred skull and torso. In midafternoon a horseman approached, lassoed the burned corpse, and dragged it through the main streets of downtown Waco. At one point during this macabre procession, the skull bounced off and was retrieved by a group of young boys who extracted the teeth and sold them for five dollars apiece. Finally, several men placed the victim's remains in a cloth bag and pulled the bundle behind an automobile to Robinson where they hung the sack from a pole in front of a blacksmith's shop for the community's residents to see. Later that afternoon Constable Les Stegall retrieved the body and turned it over to a Waco undertaker for burial.[22]

Thus ended an episode that most Wacoans probably preferred to forget. Repercussions on the state and national level, however, kept the lynching in the public eye for several months and brought condemnation upon Waco, the state of Texas, and the nation as a whole for permitting a climate of race relations to exist that tolerated such an atrocity.

In the wake of the events of May 15, the response by local whites to the lynching of Jesse Washington varied from vigorous approval to public condemnation of the mob's actions. Glenn Brick, whose brother Earle had served on the jury that had convicted Washington, proclaimed that his only regret was not having been present to assist the vigilantes. The typical white Wacoan, according to the *Morning News*, either seemed satisfied with what had transpired or refused to comment on the incident. For its own part, the *Morning News* expressed regret over the mob's actions but also voiced resentment over the "wholesale denunciation of the south and of the people of Waco" that followed. The *Times-Herald* refrained from editorial comment entirely, noting on the day following the lynching: "Yesterday's exciting occurrence is a closed incident." NAACP investigator Elizabeth Freeman reported to Royal Nash, the executive secretary of the association: "I find very few who really condone all that was done—but when they make it personal they feel that they would have done likewise." On a later occasion, she informed Nash: "The feeling amongst the best people is one of shame for the whole happening. They realize it could have been stopped if they had had a leader—now they think they are right in trying to forget it & fancy the world will do so too." When Freeman questioned Judge Munroe about his failure to halt the mob by using the pistol he kept hidden in a drawer at the bench, the judge responded, "Do you want to spill innocent blood for a nigger?" The apparent failure of Waco's religious leaders to condemn publicly the affair particularly distressed the NAACP investigator. "Cannot get the ministers to aid," she told her superiors in New York. "They simply say it is deplorable." On May 21 she reported: "So far I have not found a Christian (?) minister who has protested against the action of the Waco folk."[23]

Some whites in McLennan County seemed disturbed not so much by the lynching per se but rather by the mob's treatment of Jesse Washington's burned corpse. John Strauss, one of Robinson's educational leaders, claimed that the people in his community unanimously condemned the dragging of the black victim's body through the streets of Waco. "If only they had just hung [sic] him," wrote Elizabeth Freeman in attempting to characterize local white opinion, "they felt that would have been all right, but the burning—the dragging of the charred torso through the streets is so much worse than his crime."[24]

Not all local whites, however, shared the opinion that silence and inaction were the most appropriate responses to the lynching. Several leading Wacoans, including jury foreman William Brazleton and local newspaperman Edward M. Ainsworth, argued that some public protest should be made. Moreover, they were especially critical of the city's law enforcement officials for not intervening to prevent mob violence. In addition to the opposition voiced by a few individual citizens, a special committee of the faculty at Baylor University issued a series of resolutions condemning the mob's actions and expressing concern that the incident "will evoke from the outside world reproaches unmerited by the majority of the people of our fair city and county. . . ." These attempts to challenge the legitimacy of the mob in taking Jesse Washington's life, however, clearly represented a minority course of action among white residents of Waco and McLennan County.[25]

Blacks living in Robinson and Waco generally reacted to the events surrounding the murders of Lucy Fryer and Jesse Washington either by keeping their thoughts to themselves or by taking a conciliatory course. One of the few blacks to offer his opinions publicly was C. H. Dorsey, a Robinson school teacher, who characterized Mrs. Fryer's murder as a "most horrible outrage." Dorsey gave assurances that all respectable black Robinsonians deplored Washington's crime and proclaimed that the incident had produced no pernicious repercussions in community. "[T]he white people of Robinson," he wrote prior to Washington's trial, "have shown the negroes here the same sympathetic helpful spirit that they had always shown before. . . ." In Waco, the Reverend John W. Strong, dean of the all-black Central Texas College, and the Reverend I. Newton Jenkins, pastor of the New Hope Baptist Church, expressed their regret with respect to the crime that had taken Lucy Fryer's life, but in a confidential statement to Elizabeth Freeman, they noted their disappointment that Waco's white clergymen had not been more outspoken in denouncing the brutal and extralegal execution of Jesse Washington. After interviewing several local blacks concerning their views of the events that had transpired between May 8 and May 15, Freeman concluded: "The feeling of the colored people is that while they had one rotten member of their race the whites had 15,000."[26]

While most local blacks were reluctant to condemn the lynching, at least one black in Waco refused to curb his outrage. A. T. Smith, managing editor of the *Paul Quinn Weekly*, the school paper at all-black Paul Quinn College, published several articles denouncing the incident. Richard D. Evans, a black attorney in Waco, commented that the Smith articles "took this city to task harder than any I have read on the lynching." In fact, one of the editorials included an unfounded charge (reprinted from the Chicago *Defender*, one of the nation's leading black weeklies) that George Fryer Sr., not Jesse Washington, had murdered Lucy Fryer. This charge led to Smith's arrest and conviction on charges of criminal libel. Attorney Evans informed the NAACP that the Smith case had produced additional racial tensions in Waco and that, despite Evans's decision to defend the embattled editor, "The colored people here were afraid to help him [Smith] and afraid for me to do so. . . ."[27]

Elsewhere in Texas, newspapers published a report of the lynching distributed by the Associated Press wire service. A few white dailies in the larger cities offered editorials condemning the brutality of the incident and bemoaning the fact that public opinion everywhere would blame the entire state for the affair. The San Antonio *Express*, for example, called for a halt to lynching in the South, adding, "The Waco disgrace is the disgrace of Texas." The Austin *American* admitted that Jesse Washington deserved to die for his crime (a common sentiment in the state press) but not at the hands of a band of vigilantes. Particularly distressing to the *American* was the occurrence of such a barbaric event "in one of [the state's] great centers of learning, of boasted civilization. . . . A city of good people, of fine homes, of refinement. . . ." The two major white dailies in Houston published criticisms of the lynching that resembled each other in tone. "Not a word of defense is there to offer; not an extenuating circumstance to plead," the *Chronicle* proclaimed in its editorial. "Bestial cruelty, though seemingly sanctioned by religious indignation, never did, and never will, strengthen those customs, institutions and standards which make society respectable and the individual's life safe." The *Post* agreed that "From no angle viewed, can there be the least excuse, much less justification, offered for" the lynching and asked in a tone of rhetorical indignation, "Oh Shame! where is thy blush?" In Dallas the white dailies remained editorially silent. Nor was the Dallas *Express*, a black weekly, substantially more forceful. Usually known for its hard-hitting attacks against all forms of discrimination against blacks, the *Express* assumed a restrained position and maintained that no mob would have wreaked vengeance in Waco had Lucy Fryer not been murdered. "There is a time to talk and a time not to talk," the *Express* informed its readers. "To our mind, here is a time for thought."[28]

Outside the state, reaction to the lynching was generally harsh. "Waco did more than burn a Negro," one California newspaper explained. "[S]he burned her own courage, decency and character, outraged the imaginations of her young people, and smeared a foul disgrace across her civic life." The New York *Times* objected to the mob's refusal to permit the law to take its full course in punishing Jesse Washington and emphasized the boldness of the vigilantes in acting in broad daylight. Waxing hyperbolic, the *Times* concluded that the lynching had been carried out "apparently by the whole population of the place."[29]

Several progressive journals added their voices to the wave of indignation produced by the Waco affair. The *Independent* characterized the lynching as "an orgy of mob brutality and savage lust" and, in a subsequent issue, proclaimed: "Waco is indelibly disgraced. Texas is indelibly disgraced. The United States is indelibly disgraced. . . . Nothing in the reports of the atrocities in Belgium, East Prussia, Serbia or Armenia shows a more hideous state of public opinion than that manifested by the people of Waco in participating in such a degrading display of wanton savagery." The *New Republic* called the lynching in Waco "a filthy crime" and expressed dismay that Fred Gildersleeve's photographs of the incident "showed a typical straw-hatted summer crowd gazing gleefully at the hideous crisp of what was once a Negro youth." Oswald Garrison Villard's *Nation* castigated the faculty of Baylor University for failing to condemn publicly the episode. This uninformed assertion elicited a prompt response from Dean John L. Kesler, the university's acting president, who apprised Villard of the faculty resolutions deploring the action of the mob. Kesler further reported hat he had "condemned [mob law] in as strong words as the English language would permit without violating the ten commandments" in the presence of eight hundred students assembled for chapel services. Initially, Dean Kesler claimed that the lynching had been denounced from the city's leading pulpits in sermons delivered by the Reverends Frank P. Culver of Austin Avenue Methodist Church, Charles T. Caldwell of the First Presbyterian Church, Frank S. Groner of Columbus Street Baptist Church, and Joseph Martin Dawson of First Baptist Church. Villard noted the correction to his earlier charge but maintained that "Waco cannot hold up its head until the criminals are punished."[30]

At the same time that the editors of several major newspapers and journals condemned the Waco lynching, their comments produced rebuttals from a number of whites who attempted to justify the mob's action or, at least, to place the blame elsewhere. One northern-born Texas resident complained that the *Nation* should direct its editorial venom against the crime of rape rather than lynching. "It may be bad to lynch," he admitted, "but is it not far worse for a dehumanized fiend, swelling with bestial lust, to lay his cursed hands on a pure, defenceless woman to satisfy his animal nature?" A white Floridian added the oft-repeated reminder that northerners could not possibly understand race relations in the South and, therefore, could not react objectively to the lynching of blacks. The only preventive for black crime, he concluded, lay in "a sure, swift punishment as was meted out by the Ku Klux Clansmen [sic] in the days of reconstruction." The editors of the *Outlook* condemned the failure of Waco officials to prevent the incident. "Political, moral, and physical cowardice are written all over the story," the journal charged. At the same time, the *Outlook* offered a unique (though highly questionable) interpretation to account, at least in part, for the recurrence of lynchings in the United States by blaming "a small group of Negro leaders who have been preaching covetousness and envy as virtues, and who have tended to dull the minds of some of their followers to a sense of duty and to the importance of self-control."[31]

The public response by blacks on the national level to the Waco lynching fell into two categories—either one of conciliation or one of condemnation. Even when not compelled to silence by geographical proximity to McLennan County, a few blacks took a conservative stance. For example, a black Georgian asked that the race as a whole not be judged by the acts of "troublesome and insolent" Negroes like Jesse Washington. "Our beloved neighbors will attest," he continued, "that the negro is the last one in general to harbor a desire to defend from just punishment any sort of criminal."[32]

In contrast, the black press outside Texas almost uniformly denounced the mob's actions in Waco. The Savannah *Tribune*, referring to lynching as the "popular life-taking game in the southland," characterized the Waco incident as "about as barbarous a deed as can be committed." In an editorial for the New York *Age*, James Weldon Johnson declared that the details of Jesse Washington's death were "enough to make the devil gasp in astonishment. . . ." Johnson called upon President Woodrow Wilson to condemn such lawless incidents in a public statement and asserted that nowhere else in the world "could be found a people so close to the brute but they would have done such a deed. In comparison with them [the Waco vigilantes], a crowd of Mexican bandits is a company of high-souled, chivalrous gentlemen." Perhaps the most outraged protest in the black press, however, emanated from the offices of the Chicago *Defender*. Edited by Robert S. Abbott, the *Defender* immediately announced its belief in Jesse Washington's innocence, arguing that the black youth had been railroaded by the Waco judicial system. Several of the *Defender*'s reports of the lynching were sensationalist in nature, including the previously cited publication of the unfounded rumor that George Fryer had been arrested and charged with murdering his wife.[33]

Of all the national attention devoted to the Waco lynching, however, the most far-reaching demonstration of outrage generated by the affair occurred within the ranks of the National Association for the Advancement of Colored People. Reports of the incident stirred the NAACP to launch a full-scale investigation of the lynching. The Association contacted Elizabeth Freeman, who was attending a women's suffrage convention in Dallas, and asked her to travel to Waco to collect data relating to Jesse Washington's death. Freeman's findings appeared (as previously noted) in a supplement to the July 1916 issue of the *Crisis*, entitled "The Waco Horror." The journal's editor, W. E. B. Du Bois, sermonized: "To other persons we say as we have said before: any talk of the triumph of Christianity, or the spread of human culture, is idle twaddle so long as the Waco lynching is possible in the United States of America."[34]

Several NAACP officials saw in the "Waco horror" a powerful cause celebre upon which the association might expand its antilynching crusade to include a federal law prohibiting the crime of lynching. In late July, Joel E. Spingarn, chairman of the NAACP's board of directors, and Oswald Garrison Villard, the organization's treasurer, issued a joint appeal for contributions to an antilynching fund to finance "the first nation-wide campaign against the ancient American institution of lynching that ever gave promise of wiping the blot once [and] for all from our escutcheon." The following month, Spingarn informed Philip G. Peabody, a prominent Boston attorney who had expressed interest in financing an antilynching campaign, that "The publicity we gave Waco has roused a fighting spirit we must not let die." Meanwhile, Villard, in an appeal for financial assistance for the NAACP's Anti-Lynching Fund, proclaimed: "The crime at Waco is a challenge to our American civilization, yes, to every American. . . ."[35]

Invigorated by the national attention devoted to the lynching of Jesse Washington, the NAACP's antilynching crusade proceeded at such a furious pace during the remainder of 1916 that Joel Spingarn optimistically declared the campaign "the most striking achievement" of the year. By early 1917, however, international events dominated the nation's attention to such an extent that little interest could be generated for reforms in the realm of race relations. With the entrance of the United States into World War I in April, NAACP leaders probably realized that they had little hope of winning support for such a politically divisive issue as a federal antilynching law. Consequently, while NAACP antilynching efforts continued on several fronts during the war, the "Waco Horror" was relegated to an anonymous position among thousands of instances of mob violence inflicted upon black Americans in the pre–World War I era.[36]

In many respects the events surrounding the lynching of Jesse Washington differed little from other episodes of mob violence in the United States. The incident occurred in the South, and the victim was a black male who had confessed to crimes that in the eyes of some white southerners made lynch law justifiable, even necessary. Nor was the barbarity of the mob particularly unusual for the time. Moreover, the refusal of Waco officials to seek indictments against the ringleaders, even though their identities were known throughout the city, indicates that this incident followed a pattern generally adopted by local officials dealing with similar acts of violence.[37]

Significantly, however, in lynching Jesse Washington, the mob in Waco unwittingly provided the NAACP with a cause celebre that the national association could utilize to invoke support for a systematic campaign to halt lynchings. To capitalize upon Philip Peabody's offer to fund an antilynching crusade, the NAACP needed a particularly sensational incident to demonstrate to the American people the urgency of a federal antilynching bill. The burning and mutilation of an illiterate black farm hand, graphically documented by Fred Gildersleeve's camera, packed the necessary emotional punch to dramatize the exigency of federal action. In addition, the fact that this incident occurred in a city reputed to be an enlightened, respectable, middle class community supplied the NAACP further evidence of the breadth of a lynching mentality in the United States. And yet, despite the seemingly advantageous timing of the "Waco Horror," the campaign fell victim to the inopportune entrance of the nation into the First World War, thereby forcing the NAACP to postpone its federal antilynching crusade until 1919.

"What's goin' to happen to th' naygur?" Hennessy asked Mr. Dooley in a conversation over the "Negro problem" in the United States. "Well," said Dooley, "he'll ayther have to go to th' north an' be a subjick race, or stay in th' south an' be an objick lesson."[38] While the NAACP had hoped to exploit the "Waco Horror" to further its antilynching program, Jesse Washington's death unfortunately became but another "objick lesson" reminding blacks of the dire consequences awaiting those who stepped outside their "place" in American society.

Notes

1. National Association for the Advancement of Colored People, *Thirty Years of Lynching in the United States, 1889–1918* (New York, 1919), 7; Finley Peter Dunne, "The Booker Washington Incident," *Mr. Dooley's Opinions* (New York, 1901), 210 (quotation).

2. Winfield H. Collins, *The Truth About Lynching and the Negro in the South* (New York, 1918), 70–71 (first quotation); "Some Thoughts on Lynching," *South Atlantic Quarterly*, V (Oct. 1906), 353 (second quotation); J. H. T. to the Editor, *Crisis*, VII (Nov., 1913), 348 (third quotation).

3. "Some Thoughts on Lynching," 353 (first quotation); James Weldon Johnson, *Along This Way: The Autobiography of James Weldon Johnson* (New York, 1933), 310; *Crisis*, IX (Mar., 1915), 196 (second quotation); Walter White, *Rope and Faggot: A Biography of Judge Lynch* (1929; reprint ed., New York, 1969), 19–20. The specific title "Waco horror" seems to have originated with the editors of the *Crisis*, who published an account of this incident as an eight-page supplement to their July

issue. Prior to the appearance of this report, however, the Houston *Chronicle* expressed its editorial opinion of "The Horror at Waco," and a New York *Times* editorial stated that the mob in Waco had "Punished a Horror Horribly." See "The Waco Horror," Supplement to the *Crisis*, XII (July, 1916), 1–8; Houston *Chronicle*, May 16, 1916; and New York *Times*, May 17, 1916. Previous discussions of this affair include brief accounts in Charles F. Kellogg, *NAACP: A History of the National Association for the Advancement of Colored People, 1909–1920* (Baltimore, 1967), 218; Robert L. Zangrando, *The NAACP Crusade Against Lynching, 1909–1950* (Philadelphia, 1980), 29–30; and a more thorough exploration in Rogers M. Smith, "The Waco Lynching of 1916: Perspective and Analysis" (M.A. thesis, Baylor University, 1971).

4. United States Department of Commerce, Bureau of the Census, *Fourteenth Census of the United States Taken in the Year 1920* (11 vols.; Washington. D.C., 1921–23), III, *Population, 1920, Composition and Characteristics*, 1,015. The Census Bureau set Waco's population in 1910 at 26,425; ten years later the figure stood at 38,500. The town's population in 1916 can be estimated by computing the percent of increase between 1910 and 1920 and assuming that the increase occurred evenly over the decade. Although no certain degree of accuracy can be claimed for this figure, it undoubtedly is more accurate than the Waco city directory's estimate of 45,237. See R. L. Polk & Co. (comps.), *Waco City Directory, 1916* (Houston, 1916), 21.

5. *Waco City Directory*, 1916, 21 (first quotation), 51–54; Charles E. Gilbert Jr. (comp.), *Waco* (Waco, 1912), [63] (second quotation); William H. Curry, *A History of Early Waco with Allusions to Six Shooter Junction* (Waco, 1968), front flyleaf (third quotation).

6. Testimony of Chris Simons in *State of Texas Versus Jesse Washington*, District Court of McLennan County, Texas, Fifty-Fourth Judicial District, March Term, 1916, Cause No. 4141, p. 6; Elizabeth Freeman, "The Waco Lynching," 8, National Association for the Advancement of Colored People Archives (Manuscript Division, Library of Congress, Washington, D.C.; hereafter cited as NAACP Archives).

7. Waco *Morning News*, May 9, 1916; Waco *Times-Herald*, May 9, 1916; testimony of Dr. J. H. Maynard in *Texas v. Washington*, 1–2.

8. Waco *Morning News*, May 9, 1916; Waco *Times-Herald*, May 9, 1916.

9. Waco *Morning News*, May 10, 1916 (quotation); testimony of Fred Long, Mike T. Lively, and W. J. Davis in *Texas v. Washington*, 2–4.

10. Testimony of S. S. Fleming in *Texas v. Washington*, 4–5.

11. Waco *Morning News*, May 10, 1916; Waco *Times-Herald*, May 10, 1916 (quotation).

12. Waco *Morning News*, May 11, 12, 14 (quotation), 1916. In Texas the common practice in cases involving murder and criminal assault, where the guilt of the

accused was beyond doubt, was to insure the defendant a speedy jury trial and, following a guilty verdict, to carry out the death sentence at the end of a thirty-day waiting period. "This has had the effect," the *Morning News* reported, "of stopping many of the lawless demonstrations which formerly characterized the commission of the diabolical crime of which Washington stands accused and to which he has confessed." Ibid., May 13, 1916.

13. Ibid., May 16, 1916 (quotation); Waco *Times-Herald*, May 15, 1916.

14. Waco *Morning News*, May 16, 1916.

15. Ibid.

16. *Texas v. Washington*, 1–9.

17. Ibid.

18. Waco *Morning News*, May 16, 1916.

19. Ibid. (quotations); Waco *Times-Herald*, May 15, 16, 1916.

20. Waco *Times-Herald*, May 15, 1916 (quotations); Waco *Morning News*, May 16, 1916; Freeman, "The Waco Lynching," 14.

21. Estimates of the size of the crowd varied widely. Waco's afternoon newspaper set the figure at 10,000 while the morning paper claimed that 15,000 persons had witnessed the burning. Elizabeth Freeman, an English suffragist who investigated the lynching for the NAACP, reported that during her early interviews concerning the incident most citizens admitted to the larger number, but as they became more suspicious of her motives, subsequent witnesses stated that only 500 bystanders had gathered on the city hall lawn. A popular account of the episode published a half century later claimed that 1,000 persons had watched the execution. Waco *Times-Herald*, May 15, 1916; Waco *Morning News*, May 16, 1916 (quotations); Freeman, "The Waco Lynching," 15, 20, 21; Curry, *A History of Early Waco*, 90.

22. Waco *Times-Herald*, May 15, 1916; Waco *Morning News*, May 16, 1916; Freeman, "The Waco Lynching," 15–16.

23. Waco *Morning News*, May 16, 19, 24 (first quotation), 1916; Waco *Times-Herald*, May 16, 1916 (second quotation); Elizabeth Freeman to Roy Nash, (May 20, 1916) (third and sixth quotations); Freeman to Nash, (May 24, 1916) (fourth quotation); Freeman to Nash, (May 21, 1916) (seventh quotation), NAACP Archives; Freeman, "The Waco Lynching," 11 (fifth quotation), 17.

24. Waco *Morning News*, May 16, 1916; Freeman to Nash, (May 20, 1916) (quotation), NAACP Archives.

25. Freeman, "The Waco Lynching," 18–19, 23; Waco *Morning News*, May 28, 1916 (quotation).

26. Waco *Morning News*, May 14, 1916 (first and second quotations); Freeman, "The Waco Lynching," 2 (third quotation), 3.

27. R. D. Evans to the Editor, *Crisis*, XIII (Jan., 1917), 122 (quotations), 123;

Memorandum from Roy Nash to Joel Spingarn, Aug. 11, 1916, NAACP Archives. After waiving his right to a jury trial, Smith was sentenced to one year of hard labor on a county convict labor gang.

28. San Antonio *Express*, May 17, 1916 (first quotation); Austin *American*, May 17, 1916 (second quotation); Houston *Chronicle*, May 16, 1916 (third quotation); Houston *Post*, May 17, 1916 (fourth and fifth quotations); Dallas *Express*, May 20, 1916 (sixth quotation).

29. San Francisco *Bulletin*, May 16, 1916, reprinted in *Crisis*, XII (Aug., 1916), 189 (first quotation); New York *Times*, May 17, 1916 (second quotation).

30. "A Terrible Crime in Texas," *Independent*, LXXXVI (May 29, 1916), 325 (first quotation); "An American Atrocity," ibid., LXXXVII (July 31, 1916), 146 (second quotation); Editorial, *New Republic*, VII (June 3, 1916), 102 (third quotation); "The Will-to-Lynch," ibid., VIII (Oct. 14, 1916), 261 (fourth quotation); "Moving Against Lynching," *Nation*, CIII (Aug. 3, 1916), 101; Editorial Comment, ibid., CIII (Oct. 5, 1916), 322; J. L. Kesler to the Editor, Oct. 15, 1916, ibid., CIII (Dec. 28, 1916), 609 (fifth quotation); Editorial Comment, ibid. (sixth quotation).

31. J. T. Winston to the Editor, May 26, 1916, *Nation*, CII (June 22, 1916), 671 (first quotation); Elliott G. Barrow to the Editor, June 22, 1916, ibid., CIII (July 6, 1916), 11 (second quotation); "To Lynch or Not to Lynch?" *Outlook*, CXV (Jan. 2, 4, 1917), 138 (third and fourth quotations).

32. Robert F. Gibson to the Editor, June 23, 1916, *Nation*, CIII (July 13, 1916), 35.

33. Savannah *Tribune*, July 8, 1916 (first and second quotations); New York *Age*, May 25, 1916 (third and fourth quotations); Chicago *Defender*, May 20, 27, June 3, 1916.

34. Roy Nash to Elizabeth Freeman, May 16, 1916, NAACP Archives: "The Waco Horror," 1–8; W. E. B. Du Bois, "Lynching," *Crisis*, XII (July, 1916), 135 (quotation).

35. Cleveland *Advocate*, July 22, 1916 (first quotation); Joel E. Spingarn to Philip G. Peabody, Aug. 4, 1916 (second quotation), NAACP Archives; *Crisis*, XII (Aug., 1916), 168 (third quotation).

36. *Crisis*, XIII (Feb., 1917), 166 (quotation); Kellogg, *NAACP*, 220, 227–231. The "Waco Horror," however, was not completely forgotten following America's entrance into World War I. Among the literature distributed for the NAACP-sponsored "Negro Silent Protest Parade" in New York City on July 28, 1917—a demonstration against mob violence held in the wake of the East St. Louis race riot—was the following statement: "We march because we want to make impossible a repetition of Waco, Memphis, and East St. Louis, by arousing the conscience of the country and bringing the murders of our brothers, sisters, and innocent children to justice." Zangrando, *The NAACP Crusade Against Lynching*, 37, 38 (quotation).

37. Freeman, "The Waco Lynching," 13. After several days of talking to local citizens about the lynching, Elizabeth Freeman had acquired the names of six men who represented "the disreputable bunch of Waco" and who had participated in the mob's activities. Ibid., 19. The pattern adopted by local officials in the United States of refusing to seek prosecution of known mob participants is noted in Arthur F. Raper, *The Tragedy of Lynching* (Chapel Hill, N.C., 1933), 2, 13–17, and Zangrando, *The NAACP Crusade Against Lynching*, 4, 8.

38. Finley Peter Dunne, "The Negro Problem," *Mr. Dooley's Philosophy* (New York, 1906), 217.

Black Labor, the Black Middle Class, and Organized Protest along the Upper Texas Gulf Coast, 1883–1945

ERNEST OBADELE-STARKS

Although most black Texans worked in agriculture, along the Texas gulf coast some found employment in industry. These African American laborers struggled to acquire meaningful advances in job opportunities and in wages vis-à-vis whites. In this struggle, as Ernest Obadele-Starks points out, they received help from middle class blacks, including leaders such as Norris Wright Cuney, Clifton F. Richardson, Carter Wesley, and C. W. Rice. However, the middle class activists did not always agree with each other, and certainly not with the laborers, and as Obadele-Starks noted, "by the thirties black unionists generally viewed the organizing efforts of black elites as self-serving formulas for personal and political gain." Because of earlier successes, the large number of black workers on the coast gave them strength through unity, and enabled them to distance themselves from the African American middle class. On the other hand, generally the black middle class continued to champion the cause of the black laborers.

*

FROM THE latter part of the nineteenth century through the first half of the twentieth century the black working and middle classes along the Upper Texas Gulf Coast, a region that served as the model of industrialization in the New South, developed a variety of strategies to combat racial inequities in several key industries.[1] The wide range of responses to racial biases in this region's workplaces indicated that African Americans shared distinct perspectives on organized protest against race and class domination. While the black working class struggled to establish itself as a vital force in the Texas labor movement, black politicians, community leaders, and newspaper editors presented themselves as allies of, and in some instances, the leaders and spokespersons of black workers and used a variety of tactics to combat oppression. Black elites used their education, community influence, and resources, and often resorted to controversial protest strategies to achieve their goal of a well-organized and racially unified black laboring class. Gradual changes in the labor movement, however, brought about new outlooks on the role of the black middle class, and over a period of time, their long-standing alliance with black workers diminished.[2]

One of the earliest and most significant collaborations between the black working and middle classes along the Upper Texas Gulf Coast following the Civil War and Reconstruction occurred when Norris Wright Cuney, a respected black labor leader and politician from Texas, organized the Galveston Colored Screwmen's Benevolent Association (CSBA) in 1883. Cuney defied white opposition to black unionization and established a precedent of organized protest among black workers. Cuney's clout and influence helped empower black dock workers and demonstrated the need for middle-class blacks to assist black laborers in their workplace struggles. Cuney's organizing successes reflected an important step toward improving work opportunities for black longshoremen who had been denied equal work opportunities and union representation by white longshoremen.[3]

Discrimination against black dock workers along the Texas Gulf Coast dates back to the evolution of the first longshoremen union in Texas. The all-white Galveston Screwmen's Benevolent Association (SBA), founded in 1866, denied black workers equal employment and refused them access to its union.[4] Cuney acted aggressively against these practices and encouraged black freight handlers to disrupt the strikes of white longshoremen and accept work from employers at wages less than those of white unionists. Cuney focused on finding as much employment for as many black longshoremen as he could. By the late 1880s many steamers along the Gulf Coast suspended their loyalties to white workers in exchange for greater profit and allowed "colored gangs on board to do work traditionally reserved for whites." When the Mallory Steamship Company of Galveston began using cheaper black labor in 1885, it angered some white longshoremen, who "walked off ships in protest."[5] The Mallory Company's decision to use less expensive black labor led to a city-wide strike of nearly two thousand members of the Knights of Labor. The strike stifled business in the city, increased antiblack sentiment, and fostered ugly rumors of race riots. It failed, however, to deter Cuney or his followers from agitating for workplace equality and organizing black longshoremen throughout the region.[6]

Cuney's ascendancy from a plantation near Hempstead, Texas, to an advocate for black labor was influenced by a wide range of circumstances. Following his early education in Pittsburgh, Cuney settled in Galveston around 1860 to study law. Opportunities presented by Reconstruction allowed Cuney to put his law school experiences to work. Cuney first connected with the Radical Republicans of Texas and in 1871 served as sergeant-at-arms of [the] Texas Twelfth Legislature. From 1872 to 1896 he worked as a Texas delegate to the national Republican convention and for several years was recognized as an important voice for the Texas Republican party.[7] When well-to-do blacks such as Cuney aided black workers in their day-to-day struggles it strengthened the relationship between the two groups and allowed black workers to exercise a measure of influence and leverage against white unions.[8]

Black workers grew to rely on black elites well into the twentieth century. Increased black migration to industrial centers during the racially combative Jim Crow years compelled African Americans to redouble their efforts to gain equal access to employment opportunities. Black unionists in particular looked toward political and social organizations to help galvanize the black working class. They struggled to blend facets of ideological, institutional, and political perspectives into a unified core of resistance against race and class domination. Organizations such as the National Urban League, the Universal Negro Improvement Association (UNIA), and the National Association for the Advancement of Colored People (NAACP) provided much of the leadership needed to improve working conditions.[9]

The NAACP, particularly, emerged as an antisegregation body and a link between the black working and middle classes. The NAACP worked closely with prominent community figures, black labor leaders, and the black proletariat to curtail workplace inequalities. Founded in 1909 in New York City, the NAACP expanded its influence during the war years. The number of branches grew from less than a hundred before World War I to more than four hundred in cities and towns by 1921.[10]

NAACP national membership soared from around ten thousand in 1917 to nearly eighty thousand in 1919. In 1918 four local branches of the NAACP in Texas joined the El Paso chapter, which was established in 1915 to expand the influence of the organization throughout the state. The NAACP recruited from within the middle- and working-class ranks. The organization also pursued janitors, laborers, letter carriers, housekeepers, laundresses, and seamstresses, and, as Steven Reich argues, the black working class likely constituted the core of the membership. Dr. C. B. Charlton initiated the establishment of the

Beaumont branch of the NAACP in 1917. After receiving correspondence from several Beaumont residents and following an organizing tour throughout Texas by Mary B. Talbert, president of the National Association of Colored Women's Clubs, the NAACP approved a charter for the Beaumont chapter in 1918. At Galveston, black unionists from ILA union Local 807 organized an NAACP branch of their own. When the Houston NAACP staged a public "ILA Day" in October 1937 at the Bethel Baptist Church to honor the community endeavors of black ILA unions, it reflected not only the civil rights organization's support for black longshoremen, but also the expanding support of the black bourgeoisie for black unionism.[11]

Despite these organizational attempts to overcome racial injustices, blacks, to a large degree, still depended on influential community leaders to spearhead their labor protest. One of the more notable persons to address the concerns of black workers during the 1920s was Clifton F. (C. F.) Richardson Sr. Born in Marshall, Texas, Richardson attended Bishop College and graduated with a journalism degree. When Richardson formed the National Negro Business League he provided a base for economic organization and an alternative for black workers alienated from better paying jobs. Richardson's affiliation with the NAACP, his ownership of weekly newspapers, and his community activism, served as a model of leadership for the black working class. He put his education and business expertise to work when he co-founded the Houston *Informer* newspaper in 1919 and later bought into the Houston *Defender* following a dispute with his friend and business partner Carter Wesley. Richardson was among the black leaders who, as the *Informer* reported, represented "the growing consciousness of colored Americans" as he commanded "the ear of the enemies of the race." Richardson encouraged "white people who wanted their Negroes to stay on the job . . . to give extra attention to them and help build them up." When Richardson addressed the black citizens of Port Arthur at the Sixth Street Baptist Church in June 1919, he spoke to the "rapid strides" black longshoremen and refinery workers had made in their struggles to confront the racial constraints and prodded other black workers to follow their example. By December 1922 Richardson and the *Informer* were printing weekly advertisements for the Colored Workingmen & Women's Association of Texas, an organization that met twice a month to promote black working class unity, provide sick pay for its members, and dispense unemployment benefits to working families.[12]

The animosity felt by many whites toward the expanding presence

of black labor and their community leaders such as Richardson was reflected in a 1921 Magnolia refinery monthly news magazine article.
White unionists at this Beaumont, Texas, refinery complained that
"mules, niggers, wheelbarrows, and a few white men, made up a large
part of the plant," which they relied on for their livelihood.[13] These
types of racial hostilities along the Upper Texas Gulf Coast surfaced
within the context of pervasive antiblack and antilabor union sentiment indicative of the 1920s. Management domination of the region's
workforces during this decade placed extreme pressure on both black
and white workers. Company unions circumvented labor discontent by
gaining the allegiance from the most influential employees. Limited alternatives to company unions discouraged worker resistance and drove
workers toward employer representation. Company-sponsored unions
permeated the Upper Texas Gulf Coast during the 1920s and black
workers, anxious to gain workplace security, divided their allegiances
between black elites and their employers.[14]

A segment of the black workforce at the Hughes Tool Company in
Houston devoted its loyalties to company management throughout
most of the 1920s despite the racially separate company-based union
and biased contracts it established for black workers. Although many
blacks supported the company union and worked in all major production departments of this oil drilling equipment plant, they held only 26
of the company's 270 skilled jobs. The company's contracts drew a clear
distinction between "white men's jobs" and "Negro jobs." They paid
blacks lower wages than whites, and assigned them to the most difficult
tasks.[15] The Hughes Tool Colored Club (HTCC) provided a "separate
but equal" welfare organization that offered comparable welfare benefits such as health care, life insurance, and burial services for its black
workers but failed to establish equal job opportunities.[16] "There was a
great wide gulf between what we were given and what a white person
was given" Columbus Henry, a union president of Hughes' black union,
insisted. "We did the dirty work. In other words, that broom, that Georgia boogie, that wheel barrel, the cleaning up was ours but anytime a
machine was used . . . that was the white man's job."[17]

Carter Wesley, a black businessman and editor of the Houston Informer newspaper, was the most effective voice among the black middle class to speak out against the conditions at Hughes Tool. Wesley
used the constraints of the HTCC as a springboard to stir up the company's black work force.[18] Although Wesley could boast of no prior
labor experience, he recognized that his resources offered black work-

ers a useful base to help advance equality, which he used during the 1930s and 1940s to combat racism. Personal experiences shaped Wesley's commitment to racial justice. After graduating from Houston's public schools, Wesley attended the predominately black Fisk University in Tennessee and later served in World War I as one of the first black officers in a segregated United States military. Following a short legal practice in Oklahoma, Wesley returned to Houston in 1927 and invested his time and earnings to fight racism along the Upper Texas Gulf Coast. After a bitter falling-out with C. F. Richardson, his partner and co-founder of the Houston *Informer*, Wesley gained control of the newspaper and used it as a platform to expand the voices of opposition to the racist practices of labor unions and employers. He preferred to fight the battle for racial equality through boycotts, public criticism, and fund raising. Wesley used his own judgment and experience to formulate and dictate his protest strategies. Thus, when he fought for separate but equal labor unions in Texas, he not only spoke to the issue of equality but also to the numerical strength of black workers. Wesley recognized black workers' strong commitment to organized labor, and he promoted dual unionism as a protest strategy. Although Wesley strongly urged black workers to maintain their association with organized labor his dual union approach met with resistance from blacks who refused to place race loyalties ahead of union allegiance.[19]

Black workers at Hughes remained reluctant to follow Wesley and believed that the only way to have a "real union . . . was to organize with the CIO." The changing nature of the labor movement during the 1930s allowed black workers to steer clear of black elites such as Wesley and look more toward the National Labor Relations Board (NLRB) and the Congress of Industrial Organization (CIO) as remedies to their workplace problems. The NLRB grew out of President Franklin Roosevelt's New Deal agenda. It compelled employers to recognize NLRB-sanctioned labor unions and outlawed company-controlled unions. The NLRB gave rise to the CIO, which served as an alternative to the more racist unions and federations that had hindered black working class progress before the 1930s.[20]

Although Wesley welcomed the CIO's claim to improve working conditions for blacks, he cared more about maintaining his control over Hughes' black unionists. The organizing efforts of the CIO jeopardized Wesley's ambitions and created much controversy. On more than one occasion near riots erupted between advocates of the CIO and Wesley's traveling entourage. In one instance, Wesley and George Duncan, a

black unionist from Hughes, exchanged "considerable abusive language" at a labor forum in Houston. Each charged that the other had
gotten personal in their criticism. "While no licks were passed . . .
Hughes Tool workers began to gather around" Wesley, forcing the editor to make a narrow escape from the angry mob. Hughes' black workers often resorted to "pistols, knives, and mudslinging" when it came
to their union loyalties.[21]

Black workers at Hughes Tool took special efforts to defy black
elites. Their agitation was not selective and periodically resulted in violence. For instance, when the Rev. L V. Bolton, pastor of the Mount
Corinth Baptist Church, barged into the office of C. W. Rice, editor of
the *Negro Labor News*, a weekly Gulf Coast labor newspaper, it demonstrated that Hughes' black workers would not hesitate to resort to violent tactics to protect their union interests. A "Texas Jack knife"–
wielding Bolton vented his anger following the publication of several
articles that accused the minister of issuing "hot checks" to area merchants. Rice, however, remained convinced that the confrontation was a
result of "a labor union controversy" involving the representation for
black workers at the Hughes plant.[22] It is not surprising that black
workers during the thirties, in contrast to the late nineteenth century,
rejected the less than appealing strategies of the black middle class. By
the thirties black unionists generally viewed the organizing efforts of
black elites as self-serving formulas for personal and political gain.
Moreover, by the 1930s the Upper Texas Gulf Coast comprised a large
concentration of Texas' black workforce and unlike the late 1800s,
when Cuney had organized black longshoremen, black labor could now
boast significant numerical clout and consequently rely less on the
black middle class and more on the efforts of their rank and file to
combat workplace inequities.[23] Although black workers grew less dependent on the black bourgeoisie during the 1930s, black elites remained a significant voice of protest for black labor. Typically, black busi-
nesspeople encouraged black workers to rethink their union loyalties
and place race advancement before class concerns. Speaking and acting
on behalf of the black working class, the views and actions of the black
middle class did not always mesh with or satisfy those they claimed to
represent. Instead, it fueled further tension between the two groups.

This growing strain between black labor and the black middle class
surfaced between Rice and black railroad workers. Despite a history of
workplace neglect, blacks in the railroad industry rejected overtures
from black elites who had offered to join them in their struggles. For

many years black railroad workers experienced circumstances similar to those of most black workers in the region. Railroad unions offered few skilled jobs for African Americans and instead assigned them to low-grade work. The highest upgrading opportunities for blacks were limited to the lowest classification for whites. Black trainmen were designated as car riders while whites doing the same work received better job titles, higher wages, and greater union representation. Black railroad workers exercised limited authority, were denied voting privileges in union elections, paid compulsory dues to the nearest white union locals, and were contractually forced to concede seniority rights to white workers.[24]

In the midst of these controversial issues Rice stepped forward and initiated his own attack on railroad unions. As president of the Texas Negro Business Association and an advocate of Booker T. Washington and the Tuskegee philosophy of self-help for the race, Rice, a prominent middle-class newspaper publisher from Houston and the self-appointed voice of Texas Gulf Coast black labor, stirred African American railroad workers although his life experiences reflected a sharp contrast from those he purportedly represented.[25]

Following his childhood education in rural Tennessee in the early 1900s, Rice moved to Texas where he attended college, worked for the Texas Department of Agriculture, and later started several businesses in Houston. Rice used his community status, financial clout, and *Negro Labor News* newspaper to draw attention to the plight of the region's black railroad workforce. He criticized the racist policies of railroad unions and encouraged African Americans to abandon their union loyalties and organize into a solid bloc to offset racial discrimination in the industry. Rice discouraged blacks from joining any railroad union that failed to establish racial equality. He insisted black workers "demand that organizers present a copy of the by-laws and constitution" of their unions so that African Americans "may read and understand that no Negro can become a bonafide member" of railroad unions along the Gulf Coast.[26]

During the 1930s and 1940s Rice embarked upon several strategies to combat workplace inequities. First, he attempted to organize black railroad carmen (coach cleaners) in the AFL-controlled Brotherhood of Railroad Carmen. Rice also convinced a district federal judge to grant a temporary restraining order against the Brotherhood of Railway Carmen's control over black carmen. Rice viewed the AFL's racial policies as unconstitutional because it allowed labor organizations to make contracts on behalf of workers who did not belong to the organization. He also complained that the AFL allowed election irregularities to persist. Election mediators, Rice charged, compromised their authority in a 1938 union election for the bargaining rights of black carmen. Election monitors, Rice charged, suggested "that it was best for Negro workers to go along with white organizations until they could learn more about the technique of the organized labor movement." The perception of black workers as incapable unionists motivated Rice to further his efforts to obtain racial equality.[27]

To a certain extent, Rice reformulated an older view that expected blacks to ally with white capital and reject overtures from discriminatory unions. He made several attempts to rally black railroad workers and he relentlessly pursued his goal of a racially unified black labor community.[28] Black railroad workers at various rail shops, however, rejected his efforts to do so. They refused to fully accept Rice's leadership and were particularly troubled by his ownership of an employment referral service that many blacks along the Upper Texas Gulf Coast relied on for jobs during the Depression. The workers who used the agency often complained of being overcharged for the service. They decried Rice's blacklisting practices and criticized his ties with white employers. In sum, most workers viewed Rice as an outside agitator and "renegade" with questionable motives.[29]

Rice's association with the white business community also helped splinter the black middle class. Although African American elites generally shared common financial interests as they struggled to maintain credibility with the black working class, their views on black labor often clashed. The limited authority they exercised over unions during the thirties and forties reinforced the need for them to maintain an amiable, active, and trusting relationship with black labor. Consequently, the black bourgeoisie faced two distinct obstacles. On the one hand, they competed among themselves for worker allegiance, while on the other hand, they advocated a unified black labor community.

As the relationship between black workers and the black bourgeoisie waned, animosity within the black middle class intensified. The criticism and infighting mounted as elites struggled for black working class loyalties. Although ideology played an important part in the efforts of black elites to garner a following among black workers, their personal ambitions were driven by political aspirations. When Rice, eager to protect his limited influence over the black working class, challenged his counterpart Carter Wesley to a labor debate he thought it would help him repair his tarnished image among the region's workforce and offer an opportunity to respond to Wesley's intense public criticism of his labor politics.[30]

According to Rice, Wesley failed to respond to his invitation for a debate even though he continued to hurl criticism about the *Negro Labor News* editor's labor policy. Wesley accused Rice of being the "spokesman of employers and the bigger white people in the community" rather than a genuine voice for black labor. Public outcries against Rice's movement convinced Wesley that the *Negro Labor News* editor and his followers did not "now and has not for years represented the thought of Negroes" along the Upper Texas Gulf Coast.[31]

The travails of black workers along the Upper Texas Gulf Coast lasted through the 1940s and offer a compelling example of the varied protest strategies of the black labor community as they grappled with workplace injustices. The multifaceted goals and visions of African Americans demonstrate the complexity of day-to-day decisions involving race and union loyalties and suggest that black labor reflected a dynamic community with diverse dialogue. Despite the differences in their protest strategies, most sought equal pay, racial access, and fair representation. Indeed, the Upper Texas Gulf Coast black labor community became an important vehicle in advancing these concerns.

Notes

1. The Upper Texas Gulf Coast includes Chambers, Galveston, Harris, and Jefferson counties. On the industrial growth of the Upper Texas Gulf Coast see Ray Marshall, "Some Reflections on Labor History," *Southwestern Historical Quarterly*, 75 (Oct., 1971), 137–85; Joe Feagin, *Free Enterprise City: Houston in Political-Economic Perspective* (New Brunswick, N.J.: Rutgers University Press, 1988); Joseph A. Pratt, *The Growth of a Refining Region* (Greenwich, Conn.: JAI Press, 1980). For general studies on the working class in Texas see Ruth Allen, *Chapters in the History of Organized Labor in Texas* (Austin: University of Texas Publication, 1941); Robert E. Zeigler, "The Workingman in Houston, Texas, 1865–1914" (Ph.D. diss., Texas Tech University, 1972); and James C. Maroney "Organized Labor in Texas, 1900–1929" (Ph.D. diss., University of Houston, 1975).

2. Recently, historians have begun to re-evaluate the role of the African American labor community in the American labor movement. These historians agree that black labor, particularly in the South, developed a tradition of activism that helped shape working class identity. For example, see Eric Arnesen, "It Aint Like They Do

In New Orleans: Race Relations, Labor Markets, and Waterfront Labor Movements in the American South, 1880–1923," in Marcel van der Linden and Jan Lucassen (eds.), *Racism and the Labour Market: Historical Studies* (New York: Peter Lang Publishers, 1995), 59; Eric Arnesen, "What's on the Black Worker's Mind?: African American Workers and the Union Tradition," *Gulf Coast Historical Review*, 10, no. 1 (1994), 5–18. Also, see Joe William Trotter Jr., *Coal, Class, and Color: Blacks in Southern West Virginia 1915–32* (Urbana: University of Illinois Press, 1990); Robin D. G. Kelley, *Hammer and Hoe: Alabama Communists during the Great Depression* (Chapel Hill: University of North Carolina Press, 1990); Michael Honey, *Southern Labor and Black Civil Rights: Organizing Memphis Workers* (Urbana: University of Illinois Press, 1993); Keith Griffler, *Black Radicals Confront White Labor, 1918–1938* (New York: Garland Press, 1995); William H. Harris, *The Harder We Run: Black Workers since the Civil War* (New York: Oxford University Press, 1982).

3. "Longshoremen Workers: Texas Labor Movement Collection, Box 2E304, folder 4, Center for American History, University of Texas at Austin (hereafter cited as TLMC). See Maude Cuney-Hare, *Norrris Wright Cuney: A Tribune of the Black People* (New York: Crisis, 1913), 42–63; Merline Pitre, *Through Many Dangers, Toils, and Snares: The Black Leadership of Texas, 1868–1900* (Austin: Eakin Press, 1985), 192–94; Marshall, "Some Reflections on Labor History, 142; James V. Reese, "The Evolution of an Early Texas Union: The Screwmen's Benevolent Association of Galveston, 1866–1891," *Southwestern Historical Quarterly*, 75 (Oct., 1971), 170, 180–81.

4. Reese, "The Evolution of an Early Texas Union," 144; Allen Clayton Taylor, "A History of the Screwmen's Benevolent Association from 1865 to 1924" (M.A. thesis, University of Texas, 1968), 71. Also, James C. Maroney "The International Longshoremen's Association in the Gulf States during the Progressive Era," *Southern Studies*, 16 (Summer, 1977), 225–32. For more on the evolution of longshoremen unions along the Gulf Coast consult Eric Arnesen, *Waterfront Workers of New Orleans: Race, Class, and Politics, 1863–1923* (New York: Oxford University Press, 1991).

5. "Negro Longshoremen 1898–," TLMC Box 2E304, folder 4; "History of Black Longshoremen," TLMC Box 2E304, folder 4; Also, see Pitre, *Through Many Dangers*, 188–97; Paul Douglas Casdorph, "Norris Wright Cuney and Texas Republican Politics, 1883–1896," *Southwestern Historical Quarterly*, 68 (Apr., 1965), 455–64; Virginia Neal Hinze, "Norris Wright Cuney" (M.A. thesis, Rice University, 1965), 23–34; Hare, *Norris Wright Cuney*, 42–49.

6. "Longshoremen Workers," Box 2E304, folder 4, TLMC; Kenneth Kann, "The Knights of Labor and the Southern Black Worker," *Labor History*, 18 (Winter, 1977), 56.

7. Hare, *Norris Wright Cuney*, 1–23; Pitre, *Through Many Dangers*, 188–97; Casdorph, "Norris Wright Cuney and Texas Republican Politics," 455; Hinze, "Norris Wright Cuney," 54–81.

8. Black and white longshoremen throughout the Texas Gulf Coast, for example, agreed to divide work equally. They adopted what became known as the ILA's fifty-fifty plan. The two races had debated the idea of dividing work equally along racial lines as early as the turn of the twentieth century. The ILA officially adopted the policy in 1924. Because the proposition drew so much resistance from union locals, the ILA did not enforce it and union locals refrained from implementing it. See International Longshoremen Association (ILA) 1936 District Proceedings, Galveston, Texas; "Gilbert Mers Report on Work Conditions in the Gulf Coast," Gilbert Mers Collection, MSS 63, folder 3, Houston Metropolitan Research Center, Houston, Texas (hereafter cited as HMRC); LeRoy Hoskins to Ernest Obadele-Starks, April 14, 1995, interview, East Texas Economy Oral History Collection, Public History Institute, University of Houston. Also, see Arnesen, *Waterfront Workers of New Orleans*, 95–98; Gilbert Mers, *Working the Waterfront: The Ups and Downs of a Rebel Longshoreman* (Austin: University of Texas Press, 1988).

9. Jim Crow here is defined as the racial discrimination that resulted from a system of laws that segregated the races and sanctioned the social, political, and economic domination of whites over blacks. For example, see James Martin SoRelle, "The Darker Side of Heaven: The Black Community in Houston, Texas, 1917–1945," (Ph.D. diss., Kent State University, 1980). For more on the origins and the nature of Jim Crow, see C. Vann Woodward, *Origins of the New South, 1877–1913* (Baton Rouge: Louisiana State University Press, 1951); George B. Tindall, *The Emergence of the New South, 1913–1945* (Baton Rouge: Louisiana State University Press, 1967); and Neil McMillen, *Dark Journey: Black Mississippians in the Age of Jim Crow* (Urbana: University of Illinois Press, 1989).

10. See Charles Flint Kellogg, *NAACP: A History of the National Association for the Advancement of Colored People, vol. I, 1909–1920* (Baltimore: Johns Hopkins University Press, 1967); John Hope Franklin and Alfred A. Moss Jr., *From Slavery to Freedom: A History of Negro Americans* (1947; reprint, New York: Alfred A. Knopf, 1988), 88–89; August Meier and Elliot Rudwick, *From Plantation to Ghetto* (1966; reprint, New York: Hill and Wang, 1976), 87–89; Alan H. Spear, *Black Chicago: The Making of a Negro Ghetto, 1890–1920* (Chicago: University of Chicago Press, 1967), 227–31.

11. *Negro Labor News*, Oct. 23, 1937; Nancy Dailey, "History of the Beaumont, Texas Chapter of the National Association for the Advancement of Colored People, 1918–1970" (M.A. thesis, Lamar University, 1971), 23–46; Michael L. Gillette, "The NAACP in Texas, 1937–1957" (Ph.D. diss., University of Texas, 1984), 1–5; Steven A. Reich, "Soldiers of Democracy: Black Texans and the Fight for Citizenship, 1917–1921," *Journal of American History*, 82 (Mar., 1996), 1490–91.

12. Houston *Informer*, June 28, 1919, Mar. 13, 1920, Dec. 23, 1922; Howard

Beeth and Cary D. Wintz (eds.), *Black Dixie: Afro-Texan History and Culture in Houston* (College Station: Texas A&M University Press, 1992), 128.

13. The *Magpetco* was a monthly plant magazine published during the 1920s at Magnolia's Beaumont refinery. Quote is found in the *Magpetco*, 1 (Apr., 1921), 13.

14. Harvey O'Connor, *History of Oil Workers International Union-CIO* (Denver: Oil Workers Intl. Union-CIO, 1950), 114–15, 118; Harris, *The Harder We Run*, 83–84; Robert H. Zieger, *American Workers, American Unions, 1920–1985* (Baltimore: Johns Hopkins University Press, 1986), 48–49.

15. Independent Metal Workers Union Collection, RG-1, box 1, file 1, HMRC (hereafter cited as IMWU); *Negro Labor News*, Mar. 30, 1940; Michael R. Botson Jr., "Organized Labor at the Hughes Tool Company, 1918–1942: From Welfare to the Steel Workers Organizing Committee," (M.A. thesis, University of Houston, 1994), 50–64; Michael R. Botson Jr., "Jim Crow Wearing Steel-Toed Shoes and Safety Glasses: Dual Unionism at the Hughes Tool Company, 1918–1942," *The Houston Review: History and Culture of the Gulf Coast*, 16, no. 2 (1994), 101–16.

16. Botson, "Organized Labor at the Hughes Tool Company," 50–51.

17. John S. Gray III, "Social Inequality of Hughes Tool Company Between 1928 and 1964," (unpublished term paper Rice University, 1981), RG-1, box 1, file 17, IMWU; Botson, "Organized Labor at the Hughes Tool Company," 50; Botson, "Jim Crow Wearing Steel-Toed Shoes," 101.

18. *Negro Labor News*, April 13, 1940; Botson, "Organized Labor at the Hughes Tool Company," 63.

19. Merline Pitre, "Black Houstonians and the Separate But Equal Doctrine: Carter W. Wesley Versus LuLu B. White," *The Houston Review: History and Culture of the Gulf Coast*, 12, no. 1 (1990), 23–36; also see Nancy Ruth Bessent, "The Publisher: A Biography of Carter W. Wesley," (Ph.D. diss., University of Texas, 1981).

20. For a perspective on blacks and the New Deal see Harvard Sitkoff, *A New Deal for Blacks: The Emergence of Civil Rights as a National Issue*, vol. I (New York: Oxford University Press, 1978); Raymond Wolters, *Negroes and the Great Depression: The Problem of Economic Recovery* (Westport: Greenwood Press, 1970); Leslie H. Fishel, "The Negro in the New Deal Era," *Wisconsin Magazine of History*, 48 (Winter, 1964–65), 111–26. For discussions on the formation of the NLRB see James A. Gross, *The Making of the National Labor Relations Board: A Study in Economics, Politics and the Law, 1933–1937* (Albany: State University of New York Press, 1974). The most thorough treatment of the CIO is Robert Zieger, *The CIO, 1935–1955* (Chapel Hill: University of North Carolina Press, 1995). On the CIO in the South, see Zieger, *The CIO*, 74–78, 227–36. Murray E. Polakoff, "The Development of the Texas State CIO Council," (Ph.D. diss., Columbia University, 1955) is the best source on the CIO in Texas. For discussions on the CIO's racial practices,

see Michael Goldfield, "Race and the CIO: The Possibilities for Racial Egalitarianism during the 1930s and 1940s," *International Labor and Working-Class History*,
44 (Fall, 1993), 1–32; Judith Stein, "The Ins and Outs of the CIO," *International
Labor and Working-Class History*, 44 (Fall, 1993), 53–63; Gary Gerstle, "Working-
Class Racism: Broaden the Focus," *International Labor and Working-Class History*,
44 (Fall, 1993), 33–40; Robert Korstad, "The Possibilities for Racial Egalitarianism:
Context Matters," *International Labor and Working-Class History*, 44 (Fall, 1993),
41–44.

21. Allison "Bud" Alton to Ernest Obadele-Starks, April 21, 1995, interview,
East Texas Economy Oral History Collection, Public History Institute, University of
Houston; *Negro Labor News*, Mar. 16, 20, May 18, 1940, Jan. 9, 1943.

22. *Negro Labor News*, Jan. 23, 1943.

23. From 1910 to 1940 the population of Houston, the economic center of the
Upper Texas Gulf Coast, nearly quintupled, a growth exceeded in this era by only
one major city, Los Angeles. By 1930, Texas led the South in the employment of
blacks in the industrial workforce and employed more blacks in manufacturing jobs
than its rival southern cities of Memphis, New Orleans, and Atlanta. Houston also
ranked as the largest city in Texas, the second largest in the South, and the twenty-
first largest in the nation. See U.S. Department of Commerce, Bureau of the Census,
the Labor Force: Parts I, II, III at the Fifteenth Census (Government Printing Office:
Washington, D.C., 1940).

24. "Resolution of Colored Trainmen of America," Feb. 13, 1938, Association of
Colored Trainmen Collection, HMRC, unprocessed. Florence Murray, *The Negro
Handbook*, 1942 (New York: Wendell Malliet and Company, 1942), 138–39; F. E.
Wolfe, *Admission to American Trade Unions* (Baltimore: Johns Hopkins University
Press, 1912), 119–20; W. E. B. DuBois (ed.), *The Negro Artisan* (Atlanta: Atlanta University Publications, 1902), 167–68; Herbert Roof Northrup, *Organized Labor and
the Negro* (New York: Harper & Brothers Publishers, 1944), 48–99. The Brotherhood
of Sleeping Car Porters formed the first nationally recognized black railroad union
with full bargaining rights. See William H. Harris, *Keeping the Faith: A. Philip Randolph, Milton P. Webster, and the Brotherhood of Sleeping Car Porters, 1925–37*
(Urbana: University of Illinois Press, 1977), 26–65.

25. C. W. Rice was the principal owner of the *Negro Labor News*. To a large extent, the labor assessments of Rice reflected the polemics that passed between political opponents. Thus, Rice's publications could be considered subjective and partisan. See Hobart T. Taylor, "C. W. Rice: Labor Leader" (B.A. thesis, Prairie View State
Normal and Industrial College, 1939); C. W. Rice Family and *Negro Labor News*
Collection, RG MSS 242, 1936–1954 correspondence folder, HMRC; Rice Collection; Botson "Organized Labor at the Hughes Tool Company," 57–58; *Negro Labor*

News, Apr. 9, Sept. 17, Oct. 29, 1938, June 24, Nov. 11, 13, 25, Dec. 9, Dec. 23, 1939. Apr. 22, 24, May 6, July 15, Aug. 19, Sept. 2, 17, Dec. 23, 1944.

26. *Negro Labor News*, Apr. 9, 1938, Nov. 13, Dec. 23, 1939.

27. *Negro Labor News*, Apr. 9, 1938.

28. *Negro Labor News*, June 24, 1939.

29. *Negro Labor News*, Apr. 9, 1938, May 27, Nov. 11, 1939, Jan. 23, 1943; O'Connor, *History of Oil Workers International* Union, 315; Maurice Easterwood to Ernest Obadele-Starks, April 21, 1995, interview, East Texas Economy Oral History Collection, Public History Institute, University of Houston.

30. *Negro Labor News*, Nov. 11, 1939.

31. *Negro Labor News*, Dec. 26, 1942.

Semi-Professional African American Baseball in Texas before the Great Depression

ROBERT C. FINK

As we all recognize, white southerners developed an effective (from their perspective) segregated, Jim Crow society to keep blacks separate and unequal as well as to harass the African American population. Prominent 1920s black Texas author William Pickens denounced Jim Crow as a contrivance to humiliate, harass, and torture them. In all walks of life, including recreation and athletics, black Texans lived separate lives. Despite this segregation, black Texans found a number of ways to provide themselves with athletic opportunities. As Robert Fink shows in the following article, black Texans were active participants in the national pastime: black baseballers played in everything from sandlot pick-up games to their own professional leagues. Fink examines semi-professional leagues in particular. These teams faced numerous obstacles including lack of attendance, financial difficulties, inadequate playing fields, and promotional failures. But they provided black Texans with entertaining, high quality performances. A number of the Texas performers continued their careers by joining black professional teams in cities such as New York, Philadelphia, and Kansas City.

*

FROM THE SPORTS beginning, baseball has played a significant role in the social lives of African Americans. Early accounts tell of slaves playing games in the American South before the Civil War. By 1867, games occurred in the North between organized black teams, such as the Excelsiors of Philadelphia and the Uniques of Brooklyn. Also, in 1884, Moses Fleetwood Walker became the first African American to play major league baseball, competing for Toledo of the American Association. Unfortunately, by 1887, the white major league managers and owners agreed as a group to prohibit blacks from participating on white teams.[1]

African Americans responded to their exclusion by creating their own leagues and teams. For the next sixty years, black baseball teams and players uplifted the spirits of African Americans. These teams and players eventually changed the way baseball was played.[2]

The experience of African American baseball in Texas offers a good example of the opportunity offered by all-black teams for athletic participation. The players became heroes in their respective towns. Also, the games served as a means to celebrate Texas's African American community.

The influence of African American baseball in Texas reached beyond the state's borders as players and teams from the state changed the broader picture of black baseball in the United States. No one person had a greater impact on African American baseball than Andrew "Rube" Foster, a native of Calvert, Texas. Through his roles as pitcher, manager, team owner, and later as the founder and president of the Negro National League, the country's first professional black league, Foster served as the most powerful man in black baseball.[3]

Other Texans left their mark on the game. "Smokey" Joe Williams, considered by some to be the greatest Negro League pitcher, at the age of forty-four struck out twenty-seven batters for the Homestead Grays in a twelve-inning shutout against the Kansas City Monarchs.[4] Over his twenty-year career in both the Negro Leagues and in Mexico, Willie Wells received recognition as the best defensive shortstop in black baseball.[5]

Within the state of Texas, professional African American baseball made an appearance in the form of the Texas-Oklahoma-Louisiana League. The T-O-L operated from 1929 to 1931. Its tenure marked a high point for professional black baseball in Texas.[6]

The majority of the African Americans in Texas who played baseball, though, never made it to the professional level. Only a small minority of black Texans played in the Texas-Oklahoma-Louisiana League during its three-year existence. While professional black baseball received most of the attention in the press, a vibrant black semi-professional scene existed in the state throughout the first half of the twentieth century. While the levels of organization and quality of talent varied greatly among the different teams, the one characteristic that united semi-professional black baseball, as well as distinguished it from professional African American baseball, was the fact that none of the semi-professional players made their living playing baseball. They all worked other jobs as their careers and played baseball only in their free time.

Semi-professional African American baseball formed the foundation of black baseball in Texas. Numerous semi-professional teams appeared, thrived, fell on hard times, and disappeared, mirroring the peaks and valleys that occurred in professional black baseball. Also, semi-professional black baseball evolved along with changes in America and showed how major events in American history, such as the Great Depression and World War II, affected the lives of African Americans. As a result, all of black baseball in Texas began at the semi-professional level.

The exact date when the first semi-professional African American baseball team actually played its first game in Texas, or even the name of the first team, remains unknown. By early 1900, the few existing black newspapers made only occasional references to teams in Texas. The acknowledgment of these teams usually came only as a reference point in articles on the beginnings of star players in professional African American baseball, such as Rube Foster, or as opponents of Texas's black college teams. To establish fan recognition, an African American team usually took its name from the local white team, just adding the word "black" to the title, such as the Abilene Black Eagles.[7]

Being semi-professional, the teams never played a set schedule. They picked up games wherever possible, taking on all challengers. When the Dallas Black Giants faced the San Antonio Black Bronchoes in a two-game series during June of 1919, it was the first time the two teams played each other in several years because of the previous inability to reach a mutually advantageous game date.[8]

The black teams also lacked permanent playing facilities. They performed in the local white stadiums at the discretion of the white teams. In the last week of August, 1919, the San Antonio Black Aces and Beaumont Black Oilers prepared to play a four-game series in Beaumont at the local white stadium, while the white Aces and Oilers faced each other in Galveston. The first game in Galveston received such a low attendance that the white teams moved the remainder of their games to Beaumont, forcing the black teams to cancel their series.[9] The only other playing facilities available for African American teams were substandard fields in black neighborhoods or rural areas. In Dallas, the Black Giants played at Garder Park, a baseball field that flooded so badly when it rained, the *Dallas Express* called it ". . . an ideal spot for fishing or yacht racing."[10] In Abilene, the Black Eagles played outside the city limits on pasture land that lacked fences, bleachers, and even a backstop.[11]

These black semi-professional teams appeared and disappeared quickly, regularly changing sponsors and players. What records happen to exist usually refer to players by their last name, or in many cases, by nicknames, such as "Tank" Stewart, a pitcher for the Austin Black Senators.[12] Teams also changed names regularly. At the start of the 1919 baseball season, the San Antonio team went by the name of the Black Bronchoes. By August, the team changed its name to the Black Aces.[13] Because of these factors, records are shoddy at best for the African American teams during the first few decades of the 1900s.

By 1920, black semi-professional baseball in Texas started to change. Black newspapers in the state began to offer more coverage of Texas teams. Also, with America experiencing a period of economic prosperity coming out of World War I, African Americans around the country, as well as in Texas, became more interested in baseball. In Chicago, Rube Foster's Negro National League attracted large numbers of black fans to its games.

In Texas, several businessmen who sponsored different African American baseball teams from around the state tried to create a semi-professional league of their own. Calling it the Texas Colored Baseball League, representatives for each team met in Fort Worth on Sunday, March 21, 1920, to organize the league's operating procedures. The men present at the meeting assigned franchises, set schedules, appointed umpires, and set roster limits. Also, they created a guarantee fund of one hundred dollars per team to ensure against game forfeitures.[14] Unfortunately, from the very beginning the Texas Colored League's publicity department failed to inform the public of the league's actions. This lapse caused uncertainty among baseball fans if the league really existed or not, if the meeting succeeded, and what took place. As a result, fan support for the T.C.L. was minuscule from the very beginning.[15]

On account of this failure to promote itself, the Texas Colored League suffered financially. It lost over five hundred dollars in its inaugural game between Dallas and Fort Worth because of low attendance stemming from the lack of publicity.[16] In an effort to cut down on expenses, the league hired schoolboys to work as official scorers, since they worked for less pay than did adults.[17]

Also, to attract fans to games, Dallas businesses gave out free prizes at the Black Giants' games. The prizes, though, went to the players for accomplishments on the field, such as a free shoeshine for the first player to hit a triple, and not to the fans. As a result, these promotions failed to bring fans to Dallas's games.[18] Even with all the problems, the league survived its first year, as Fort Worth won the pennant.

In 1921, the members of the Texas Colored League met again, this time in Beaumont, in an effort to keep the league alive. First, the team representatives cleared up obligations from the previous year to Waco and Austin who dropped out of the league. Next, they decided to adopt a traveling umpire system, while playing only one game a week. Also, they established a limit of sixteen players per team, as well as adopted a maximum salary cap. Finally, every team paid a two-hundred-dollar deposit to the league, guaranteeing the team's commitment to play the entire season.[19] With the Texas Colored League working to promote itself better, and Beaumont, Dallas, Fort Worth, Galveston, Houston, and Shreveport preparing to compete, excitement in the black press and across Texas for African American baseball ran high.

The *Houston Informer* detailed elaborate accounts of the Houston Black Buffaloes' accomplishments on the field. In March, the paper told of the team's spring training workouts under manager W. B. Patterson, as well as their pre-season exhibition games against local black colleges.[20] In East Texas, J. S. Payne, a black sports promoter from Shreveport, Louisiana, attempted to form the Tri-State Baseball League, consisting of teams from Texas, Louisiana, and Arkansas.[21] Further adding to the excitement, catcher Chris Spearman of the Dallas Black Giants signed to play for the Brooklyn Royal Giants, while Chaney White and Willis Rector, both also former Black Giants, joined the Philadelphia Hilldales.[22]

The Texas Colored League kicked off its season on April 16 with a game in Dallas between the Black Giants and the Fort Worth Black Panthers. Before the game, the league held a large parade through the city's streets, complete with a brass band, club officials, local businessmen, and amusement concerns. Also, the players for both teams rode in automobiles escorted by two mounted policemen.[23]

In reporting the happenings of the Texas Colored League, African American newspapers related the games in detail. For a three-game set between the Dallas Black Giants and the Houston Black Buffaloes in 1921, the *Houston Informer* referred to the series as ". . . the greatest games witnessed here in several years. . . ."[24] The article went on to give an inning by inning account of the games, detailing the exploits of such players as "Coon" Pryor and "Sweetheart" Lewis. As well as describing the black semi-professional games, the newspapers offered critiques of the teams' play. According to the *Informer*, the Houston Black Buffaloes' inability to execute the squeeze play "made our team look like a tore up cigar on Market Street in Philadelphia. . . ."[25]

During the early 1920s, through the efforts of organizations such as

the Texas Colored League, semi-professional African American baseball in Texas established itself with the fans as a dominant sport. Players, such as Fort Worth's ace pitcher, whom the fans knew only by his
nickname of "Black Tank," became local celebrities. The players'
names appeared as often in newspaper articles as the play by play and
box scores of the games.

Fan interest and black newspaper coverage skyrocketed in the late
1920s. One game between the Black Buffaloes and the Fort Worth Black
Panthers registered the largest crowd to witness a game in Houston up
to that point.[26] In 1922, Dallas drew an average of three thousand fans a
game.[27]

The semi-professional black teams also went on tours of the state,
further building up fan knowledge as well as excitement over African
American baseball. For a team such as Houston to play against teams
in Dallas, Fort Worth, and Shreveport, for example, allowed for the creation of rivalries based around city pride. As a result, non-baseball fans
became more interested in the achievements of their local black baseball team because of the opportunity for Houston to claim superiority
over San Antonio, for example. Also, playing black college teams, such
as Paul Quinn College in Waco, or teams from smaller towns such as
Corsicana or Mexia, allowed teams to pad their win-loss records, further attracting fans who wanted to watch a successful team.[28]

As semi-professional black baseball established itself and grew in
popularity in the early 1920s, the sport still experienced some problems.
One problem faced by these early semi-professional teams centered on
players. Team rosters changed frequently as players switched teams for
more money and a chance to play on a winning team. In May 1921, the
Houston Black Buffaloes demonstrated this trend when they signed a
new starting catcher, "Georgetown" Williams, as well as a utility player
named Burney, both from Prairie View University. At the same time,
the Black Buffaloes saw their first baseman, "Billy Bowlegs" Curtis,
leave Houston and sign with the Galveston Black Oilers.[29]

The main problem for black baseball centered on sporadic game attendance. One weekend series of games might draw several thousand
fans. But another series, such as the three games in Shreveport between
the Houston Black Buffaloes and the Shreveport Black Gassers, according to the *Houston Informer*, attracted barely "enough people at the
game to start a fuss with the peanut vender."[30] Homer E. McCoy, a
local black businessman who served as secretary of the Houston Black
Buffaloes, as well as formed the National Negro Business League in

Houston in 1927, expressed his disappointment over the small number of ticket receipts for the series.[31] While these fluctuating attendance numbers might not hurt the individual black semi-professional teams that much, they proved deadly to an ill-prepared league like the Texas Colored League.

As the black teams in Texas improved in playing ability, their national reputation grew. After the 1922 season, the Memphis Red Sox, Champions of the Negro Southern League, came to Dallas and faced the Black Giants in a seven-game series. The Dallas black press called the series the "Battle for the Championship of Dixie."[32] Even though Memphis defeated Dallas rather handily, the Black Giants still managed to win two of the seven games.

In April of the next year, both the Wichita Red Sox and the Kansas City Monarchs, two professional black teams, came to Texas for spring training and played the majority of the Texas teams. In Houston, the two teams faced the Black Buffaloes at Scott Street Park, a new stadium at the end of the Pierce Car Line, which allowed easier access to the games for Houston's African American population.[33] Houston got swept in both series by their professional opponents, but the *Houston Informer* tried to put a silver lining on the games, stating Houston "played a nice game in spots."[34]

An attempt to revive the Texas Colored League took place in March of 1923. Representatives from around the state met in Houston. At the meeting, the league elected officers, naming A. R. Pryor of Dallas as president and secretary-treasurer. The team representatives also adopted a schedule, and chose the cities to participate in the circuit. Dallas, Beaumont, Fort Worth, Galveston, Houston, Shreveport, and San Antonio all received franchises because of their existing African American teams and large populations.[35] Charles C. Caffey, owner of the Houston Black Buffaloes, stated he possessed "one of the best teams that ever represented Texas on the diamond . . ."[36]

The same problems the previous league experienced still existed: unequal and sporadic attendance. In Dallas, five thousand fans turned out for a game between the Black Giants and the Galveston Black Sand Crabs, the largest crowd in the history of Dallas's Riverside Park, the Black Giants' new home.[37] Other games saw only a few hundred spectators attend.

Dallas finished in first place when the season ended in August, earlier than planned. Again the Black Giants faced Memphis in the best of nine games "Dixie Championship." Dallas lost for the second straight year. The problems of money and attendance proved too much for the league to handle, and with the end of the 1923 season came the end of the Texas Colored League, but the teams that made up the league continued to play and to increase their fan base.[38]

Other African American semi-professional teams appeared across Texas during the 1920s, further promoting black baseball. Usually associated with some form of local business or organization, these teams rarely played outside their region. In Houston, the Houston Postoffice Carriers annually fielded a team, competing against other groups within the city, but occasionally against teams from around the state. The Houston Postoffice Carriers faced the Galveston Carriers at West End Park in Houston for the two teams' "Decoration Day" contest.[39] The annual contest created a strong rivalry, with Galveston swearing "eternal vengeance" after its defeat in 1922.[40] The Houston Carriers also participated in charity events, such as a benefit game against the city's Colored Commercial Club to raise money for Union Hospital in Houston.[41]

As the interest in African American baseball continued to grow, the number of fans who turned out for semi-professional games increased. For one game between Houston's Colored Commercial Club and the Prairie View University faculty team, a "large and noisy crowd who cheered misplays with as much gusto as good plays" witnessed the contest.[42] The C. C. C. proved victorious, winning nine to six, but after the game, every fan in attendance, along with the players for both teams, received a complimentary dinner courtesy of the university. Dean Rowe of Prairie View summed up the game and the excitement surrounding black baseball at the time, saying, "I have paid $1 to see many games that did not come up to the game this afternoon."[43]

The success of these local teams, like the Houston Postoffice Carriers, led to the creation of semi-professional black leagues situated entirely within Texas's larger cities. In Houston, local businesses created the City Colored League of Amateur Baseball Teams in 1924. The six-club league played games every Saturday from May until August. Each team also paid a ten-dollar membership fee to cover league costs.[44]

While the Texas Colored League had some success as described above, the leagues that incorporated teams from around the state experienced problems, Houston's city league, which changed its name to the Houston Colored Amateur Baseball League, lasted for several years. Teams represented a wide variety of local businesses from the Post Office and Lincoln Theater to the Climax Pharmacy and Orgen Barber

Shop. According to the *Houston Informer*, Houston became the first city in America, and particularly the South, to promote organized amateur baseball for African Americans.[45]

The last half of the 1920s proved the high-water mark for the popularity of African American baseball in Texas. Texas established a national reputation as a significant home of black baseball. In 1925, the Houston Black Buffaloes split a six-game series in Birmingham, Alabama, against the Birmingham Black Barons of the Negro Southern League. In the series, Houston's pitchers struck out Birmingham's star hitter, "Mule" Sutters, in all four of his at bats. According to the *Houston Informer*, the Birmingham white press called Houston "the hardest hitting team that has graced that field for some time."[46]

By the end of the 1920s, semi-professional African American baseball in Texas reached its peak in athlete participation and fan support. The Great Depression of the 1930s and World War II created hard times for black baseball all over the country as young men focused their attentions on work and the war effort instead of baseball. Because of the financial strain created by the United States' economic situation, coupled with wartime restrictions on travel and the loss of players, numerous semi-professional black baseball teams in Texas closed down.

After the war, though, enthusiasm ran high to rebuild black baseball in Texas, but in 1947, the baseball world turned upside down. On April 15, Jackie Robinson, former All-American athlete at the University of California Los Angeles and an African American, played first base for the Brooklyn Dodgers in a game against the Boston Braves.[47] Robinson became the first African American to play major league baseball since Moses Fleetwood Walker in 1885. Robinson's success in baseball (he won the Rookie of the Year Award in 1947, the National League MVP in 1951, and a World Series Title in 1955) solidified the fact that African Americans could compete in major league baseball.

Also, when Robinson broke the color barrier in major league baseball, he paved the way for every black player who followed him into integrated professional baseball. Larry Doby of the Newark Eagles joined the Cleveland Indians later in the 1947 season. The next year, more African Americans entered the major leagues. Not only did these players join former white teams, but they excelled at the game. After Robinson, Don Newcomb and Satchel Paige both won Rookie of the Year awards. Roy Campanella won two National League MVP awards for the Dodgers. Black fans turned out by the thousands to watch these African American players compete in major league baseball.

While the success of black players proved profitable for major league baseball, black baseball suffered severely. Fans now preferred to attend the games of the integrated professional teams, as opposed to those of the all-black teams. When the Brooklyn Dodgers played the Fort Worth Cats, a member of the white Texas League, in a spring training game, over eleven thousand fans, half of whom were black, came from all over the state to watch the games.[48] As fan support shifted away from African American baseball, so did press coverage. The black newspapers continued to write of the exploits of black major leaguers, while ignoring the all-black teams.

The loss of their best players and fans, as well as coverage by black newspapers, proved to be the death sentence for African American baseball teams. By 1949, the Negro National League no longer existed. Over the next decade, the majority of the once-great African American professional teams around the country closed down, as their best players joined integrated teams.

In 1949, the Newark Eagles, of the Negro American League, moved to Houston as a last gasp to survive. Despite the arrival of a professional black team, the interests of African American baseball fans in Texas turned to integrated major league teams. The black press in Texas also lost interest in African American baseball. Weekly, numerous articles appeared in Texas's black newspapers that covered every detail of the on and off field activities of African American stars in the major leagues. As a result, the Houston Eagles attracted small numbers of fans, failed to make any money in Houston, and left after the 1950 season.

Over the next several decades, Texans watched their best black players signing with major league teams, as in the case of Ernie Banks of Dallas. Banks, who became the first African American to play for the Chicago Cubs, won back to back National League Most Valuable Player Awards in 1958 and 1959.[49] His twenty-year professional baseball career culminated in induction into the Professional Baseball Hall of Fame in 1975.

Also in the early 1950s, the Texas minor leagues began to integrate. George Nicholson signed with Phoenix of the Arizona-Texas League in 1950. He struck out in five of his first six at bats and the team promptly cut him, but in 1951 La Mesa of the West Texas-New Mexico League signed shortstop J. W. Wingate. Wingate played well and soon became a fan favorite.[50] The Texas League followed, integrating in 1952 when Dick Burnett, president of the Dallas Eagles, signed pitcher Dave Hoskins. Hoskins, a former member of the Homestead Grays, finished the 1952 season with a record of twenty-two wins and eleven losses, while batting .328.[51] Smaller teams, such as the Abilene Blue Sox, followed suit, when they signed local star George Forkerway in the early 1950s.[52]

As black Texans rejoiced in the integrated local teams, no complaints appeared concerning baseball's integration. The new equal opportunity in the sport marked the end of an era, as African American baseball in Texas ceased to exist. When the all-black baseball teams closed and African American ball players integrated white teams, a piece of the state's history disappeared from the public's consciousness.

At the same time, the legacy of black baseball in Texas continued in the black Texans who excelled at the major league level. Frank Robinson, from Beaumont, became the first person to win the Most Valuable Player award in both the National and American League, winning with Cincinnati in 1961 and Baltimore in 1966. Robinson also became the first African American manager of a major league team when he managed for Cleveland from 1975 to 1977.[53] Joe Morgan of Bonham began his professional career with San Antonio of the Texas League and went on to play for the Houston Colt .45s, Texas's first major league team. He lead the Cincinnati Reds to victories in the World Series in 1975 and 1976, also earning the National League's Most Valuable Player Award both years.[54] Still others, such as Austin native Don Baylor, who won the Most Valuable Player award in 1978 with the California Angels and later became the first manager of the Colorado Rockies, achieved enormous success.[55]

The baseball legacy of Texas's black community continued with the arrival of the National League's Houston Colt 45s, who later became the Houston Astros, and the Texas Rangers of the American League. African American fans now followed the accomplishments of black players on Texas's professional teams. Men like J. R. Richard of the Astros and Ferguson Jenkins of the Rangers became heroes to a new generation for black Texans. While popular knowledge of semi-professional black baseball in Texas declined after the sport's peak before the Depression, the heritage of teams like the Houston Black Eagles still exist today as African Americans compete at every level of organized baseball from Little League up to the Major Leagues.

Notes

1. Mark Ribowsky, *A Complete History of the Negro Leagues: 1884 to 1955* (Secaucus, N. J.: Citadel Press, 1995), 10–11; Robert Peterson, *Only the Ball was White: A History of Legendary Black Players and All-Black Professional Teams* (New York: Oxford University Press, 1970), 17, 22; Sol White, *Sol White's History of Colored Base Ball, with other Documents on the Early Black Game: 1886–1936*, ed. Jerry Malloy (Lincoln: University of Nebraska Press, 1995), 76–77.

2. Donn Rogosin, *Invisible Men: Life in Baseball's Negro Leagues* (New York: Kodansha International, 1983), 5.

3. James A. Riley, *The Biographical Encyclopedia of the Negro Baseball Leagues* (New York: Carroll and Graf Publishers, 1994), 290–292.

4. Buck O'Neil, *I Was Right on Time: My Journey from the Negro Leagues to the Majors* (New York: Simon & Schuster, 1996), 140.

5. John Holway, *Black Diamonds: Life in the Negro Leagues from the Men who Lived It* (New York: Stadium Books, 1991), 123.

6. Rob Fink, "African American Baseball in Texas: 1900–1950" (Thesis: Texas Tech University, 1999), 104–130.

7. George Forkerway, Interviewed by Author, 19 August 1999.

8. *Dallas Express*, 7 June 1919.

9. Ibid., 30 August 1919.

10. Ibid., 17 May 1919.

11. Forkerway, 19 August 1999.

12. *Dallas Express*, 24 May 1919.

13. Ibid., 23 August 1919.

14. Ibid., 27 March 1920.

15. Ibid., 13 April 1920.

16. Ibid., 17 April 1920.

17. Ibid., 10 April 1920.

18. Ibid., 24 April 1920.

19. *Houston Informer*, 5 March 1921.

20. Ibid., 26 March 1921.

21. *Dallas Express*, 12 March 1921.

22. Ibid., 9 April 1921.

23. Ibid., 23 April 1921.

24. *Houston Informer*, 14 May 1921.

25. Ibid.

26. Ibid., 21 May 1921.

27. *Dallas Express*, 27 May 1922.

28. Ibid.

29. *Houston Informer,* 28 May 1921.

30. Ibid., 4 June 1921.

31. Ibid.

32. *Dallas Express,* 9 September 1922.

33. *Houston Informer,* 7 April 1923.

34. Ibid., 21 April 1923.

35. *Dallas Express,* 5 May 1923.

36. *Houston Informer,* 31 March 1923.

37. *Dallas Express,* 14 July 1923.

38. Ibid., 18 August 1923.

39. *Houston Informer,* 26 May 1923.

40. Ibid.

41. Ibid.

42. Ibid., 30 June 1923.

43. Ibid.

44. Ibid., 5 April 1924.

45. Ibid., 26 April 1924.

46. Ibid., 22 August 1925.

47. Peterson, *Only the Ball was White,* 198.

48. *Houston Informer,* 20 April 1948.

49. Alwyn Barr, *Black Texans: A History of African Americans in Texas, 1528–1995* (Norman: University of Oklahoma Press, 1996), 226.

50. Jules Tygiel, *Baseball's Great Experiment: Jackie Robinson and his Legacy* (New York: Vintage Books, 1983), 269.

51. Bill O'Neal, *The Texas League: 1888–1987, A Century of Baseball* (Austin: Eakin Press, 1987), 108–109.

52. Forkerway, 19 August 1999.

53. *The Baseball Encyclopedia: The Complete and Definitive Record of Major League Baseball,* 10th ed. (New York: Macmillan, 1996), 1524.

54. Ibid., 1386–7.

55. Ibid., 770.

Black Culture in Urban Texas

A Lone Star Renaissance

NEIL SAPPER

In the following thought-provoking article, Neil Sapper persuasively illustrates that "black culture in Texas was conceived by black artists within the black community for black audiences." Using a framework crafted by Louis Harlan, Sapper depicts the role of black Texans in the years between 1930 and 1954 by focusing on African American history, music, painting, literature, and theater. As Sapper points out, a flourishing black culture, especially in the urban centers, existed. Key examples of African American cultural efforts in Texas include celebration of Texas's black emancipation day, Juneteenth; the development of the Negro Hall of Life at the Centennial Exposition in 1936; the work of artists such as John Biggers; and the efforts of talented black writer J. Mason Brewer. But, as Sapper notes, African Americans faced many difficulties, including the fact that the color line existed at all cultural events. In fact, in one of the great ironies of Jim Crow behavior, too often when nationally prominent black artists performed in the Lone Star State, whites viewed them while blacks were relegated to dress rehearsals, were segregated in upper balconies, or were denied attendance altogether.

*

SOME OF THE GREATEST contributions to Afro-American culture appeared during the Harlem Renaissance of the 1920s, a period of considerable artistic activity.[1] Harlem, as the black community of New York City, benefited from the migration of large numbers of Afro-Americans, who streamed into the city from southern states to fill the labor needs of the war industries created by World War I.[2] The urbanization of black people resulted from a push-pull phenomenon: the poverty of southern agriculture pushed Afro-American migrants toward the magnetic attraction of northern industrial cities.

The movement of significant numbers of black Texans from the countryside came a decade later and brought growth to the cities of the

Lone Star state.[3] The rural-urban shift in Texas continued through the 1940s until the 1950 census revealed that more black Texans lived in the city than on the farm.[4] Just as Harlem became a mecca for black people in New York City, black communities within the cities of Texas became increasingly separate culturally.

Given the persistence of racial discrimination in Texas, as elsewhere in the nation, and the improbability of full integration of black people into the larger white society in the near future, the capacity of black people to create and preserve a separate culture within this segregated society should be studied. A framework for the analysis of black cultural history was suggested in 1969 by Louis R. Harlan, a perceptive student of black history.[5] To Harlan, the cultural history of black people was discernible through black artistic expression in the preservation of black history, in music, in painting, in literature, and in the theater. Within such a framework, the cultural history of the black people of Texas was more than a pale reflection of the cultural history of the larger community in the period of stress and upheaval between 1930 and 1954.

In 1954, the leading black newspaper in the state noted that the typical black Texan had become better clothed, better housed, and better educated than ever before in the previous two and one-half decades but decried the fact that the artistic expression of black people in Texas had not developed in a similar fashion. The dearth of such activities as amateur theatrical groups, choral clubs, community bands and orchestras, literary societies, and historical societies caused the newspaper to proclaim that cultural sterility had overtaken black Texans by 1954.[6] Although the jeremiad of *The Informer* sought to awaken greater artistic activity among the black people of Texas, the cultural history of black Texans was varied and full during the eras of the Great Depression, World War II, and Postwar Recovery.

The annual commemoration of the emancipation of the black people of Texas on June 19, 1865, has been one continuous expression of the history and folklore of a formerly captive people. Although "Juneteenth" has been held up to ridicule by white observers as a day of watermelon- and barbeque-eating, black Texans have dedicated themselves to the preservation of the memory of the heritage of emancipation.[7] For example, on the seventy-fourth anniversary of the order of emancipation in Texas, the black people of Houston dedicated a new clubhouse-auditorium in Emancipation Park in a two-day program on June 18 and 19, 1939.[8] Emancipation Park was the sole municipal park available to black Houstonians and had been purchased by the black community and deeded to the City of Houston. The dedication program opened with appropriate music provided by the Houston Military Band, and then J. Will Jones, the supervisor of music in the Houston Public Schools, led the audience in singing James W. Johnson's anthem "Lift Ev'ry Voice." Under Jones' direction, the Houston Municipal Massed Choir then sang "Down by the Waterside" and "In My Heart." After the dedicatory litany and prayer, the clubhouse and swimming pool personnel were introduced to the audience. The services concluded with the singing of "Lift Ev'ry Voice." On the second day of the celebration a barbeque was held on the picnic grounds of Emancipation Park. The honored guests, who included former slaves, older black people, and veterans of both the Spanish-American War and World War I, were given places on the program to provide reminiscences and an oral rendition of black history.

In Walker County, to the north of Houston, a group of seventeen black Huntsville citizens purchased more than nine acres of land in Huntsville and organized the Huntsville Band and Park Association to operate a park and sustain a brass band for the black people of Walker County.[9] The park, also called Emancipation Park, was dedicated on June 19, 1932. Thus the black people of Texas attempted to memorialize a day of great meaning through the preservation of local history and the creation of cultural activities.

In November 1934, during its nineteenth annual session in Houston, the National Association for the Study of Negro Life and History observed a more formal effort to preserve the history of black people.[10] The five-day meeting pointed up the low level of consciousness among black Texans concerning their common history. In an address delivered on November 10, 1934, L. Virgil Williams, the principal of all-black Booker T. Washington High School in Dallas, noted that only five black schools in Texas offered full and accredited courses on black history in 1934.[11] Each of the five schools used Carter G. Woodson's *Negro Makers of History*, and the five schools subscribed to *The Informer*, the *Houston Defender*, the *Dallas Express*, the *Journal of Negro History*, *Opportunity*, and *The Crisis*. In addition the schools supported literary societies, history clubs, Phillis Wheatley Clubs, and Paul Dunbar Clubs. Unfortunately, the recommendation of the Association that such courses be offered more widely in the Lone Star state was not implemented in any great measure.[12]

In 1935, a more concrete effort evolved to illustrate and preserve the history of black Texans. The occasion was provided by the Texas Centennial Exposition, which was to be held in Dallas in 1936. When the Texas Legislature determined that the Texas Centennial Exposition, commemorating the achievement of independence from Mexico, would be placed in Dallas, a group of black Dallasites led a movement to gain black participation in the celebration. A group of black leaders, with A. Maceo Smith as their spokesman, appeared before the Appropriation Committee of the House of Representatives in Austin in 1935.[13] State officials, however, refused the requests for state funds for a black exhibit. Requests to municipal officials in Dallas, the exposition-city, met a similar negative response.[14]

Only the federal government responded positively to the concept of a black exhibit in the Texas Centennial Exposition. In order to supervise federal assistance of the Texas celebration, Congress had created a United States Texas Centennial Commission to oversee the $3 million federal grant to the Centennial.[15] A member of the Commission, Daniel C. Roper, consulted with Eugene K. Jones, his black advisor in the Department of Commerce, about the request of the black Texans for federal assistance. Evidently the advice was persuasive to Secretary Roper because he recommended that the Commission allocate $100,000 to the black exhibit, and the Commission complied with his recommendation. To oversee the black exhibit, the Commission created an Advisory Committee for the Hall of Negro Life, under the chairmanship of Eugene K. Jones.[16] The Advisory Committee recommended the appointment of Jesse O. Thomas and A. Maceo Smith as General Manager and Assistant General Manager, respectively, of the Hall of Negro Life. Jesse O. Thomas was a former official in the National Urban League, and A. Maceo Smith had spearheaded the drive that resulted in an exhibit to illustrate the progress, achievements, and history of the black people of Texas and the United States.

The Commission allocated $50,000 for the construction and fitting of an exhibit building on the Exposition grounds in Dallas. Although the Advisory Committee originally planned to secure the services of a black architect, a black contractor, and a black builder, no black labor of any type was utilized in the construction of the Hall of Negro Life because the primary contractor who had supervisory control of the other Exposition buildings also held control of the black exhibit hall.[17] The effect of this form of discrimination was illustrated by the fact that the white contractor painted the black exhibit hall without prior consultation with the primary contractor. The interior of the building was painted deep green and red because the contractor "knew the Negroes could not assemble enough exhibits to fill the building," and he knew that "Negroes liked loud colors."[18]

Although the Hall of Negro Life was the first exhibit hall to be completed on the Exposition grounds, the building remained unoccupied on June 6, 1936, because white officials failed to expedite its opening.[19] Nearly two weeks after the Exposition began to admit patrons, the Hall of Negro Life, located on the southwest corner of the Exposition grounds, officially opened on June 19, 1936, with a dedicatory ceremony featuring the placing of the cornerstone.[20]

The 403,227 visitors who ultimately passed through the L-shaped building viewed exhibits in nine general exhibit areas. The first exhibit viewed, upon leaving the lobby, was the Education Exhibit, which featured visual materials contributed by eleven black colleges, including Prairie View, Bishop, and Wiley.[21] Upon leaving the first exhibit, the visitors viewed the Aesthetics Exhibit, which featured paintings supplied by the Harmon Foundation, which recognized outstanding achievements by black Americans. Among the works of the thirty-six exhibiting artists was an oil painting, "My Guitar," by Samuel A. Countee of Houston. Countee, one of the finest native black artists in Texas, had received a scholarship to the School of the Museum of Fine Arts in Boston following his graduation from Bishop College in 1934.[22] Other attractions in the Aesthetics Exhibit included recorded music furnished by RCA Victor and the broadcast of a Marian Anderson concert in Copenhagen via a national radio hookup.[23] Other exhibits included the areas of agriculture, business, social service, newspapers, mechanic arts, public health, and the legal profession.

Other events involving black participation in the Texas Centennial Exposition included an interracial track meet in the Cotton Bowl, a special day—Negro Education Day—for black school children to attend the Exposition, an all-black cast presenting Macbeth, a football game between Prairie View and Wiley College in the Cotton Bowl, and a concert by Duke Ellington and his orchestra.[24] In addition to the integrated track meet, the Harlem Unit of the WPA Theatre Project of New York City presented Macbeth in the open amphitheatre located in the square formed by the wings of the Hall of Negro Life; the capacity audience of 2,000 spectators was a mixture of blacks and whites.[25]

Despite such special events in addition to the attractiveness of the Hall of Negro Life, only one-half of the 66,000 black visitors to the Exposition on Negro Education Day toured the exhibits in the Hall of

Negro Life. The black exhibit, located outside the obvious traffic pattern in the Exposition grounds, was victimized by the discriminatory practices of the sight-seeing buses, as well as the "for colored only" signs above drinking fountains and entertainment entrances.[26] The lack of support among black Texans for the Exposition, other than the special events that were keyed specifically to black participation, prompted the Director General of the Texas Centennial, Harry Olmstead, to proclaim in the black weekly in Dallas that "Negroes are, of course, welcome to the Centennial each and every day."[27] The white leadership of the Exposition commissioned a poem by J. Mason Brewer, the native Texan folklorist and poet, to appeal for increased black attendance:

> There's plenty to see in Dallas at the
>   Exposition show,
> So everybody in Texas with good sense
>   ought to go
> Whether you are White or Indian, Mexican
>   or Negro.
> You've heard some propaganda about black
>   treatment there.
> About the way they bar Negroes and treat
>   them real unfair,
> But all of this is like a cloud; it's mostly
>   in the air.[28]

Despite the poetic blandishments, black attendance at the Exposition, exclusive of the special events for black patrons, averaged seventy persons per day.[29]

The Hall of Negro Life became the only building to be demolished after the Exposition closed in November, 1936. Despite the assumption among Black Texans that the Hall of Negro Life, like the other exhibit halls, would be a part of the Pan American Exposition of 1937, black participation was eliminated from the successor to the Centennial Exposition.[30] Although the second year of the Exposition in 1937 ostensibly was dedicated to Pan Americanism, the building erected to replace the Hall of Negro Life was an amusement hall. The Pan American Exposition of 1937 did not feature a single display of exhibits from the other Americas; the Hall of Negro Life obviously had been eliminated for reasons other than relevance.[31]

The effort to preserve the black cultural heritage in Texas was not limited to the construction of the Hall of Negro Life in 1936. Within five years after the Centennial, a professor of English at Samuel Huston College in Austin, J. Mason Brewer, directed a ten-week research study of the black people in Travis county. The study, which was undertaken by twenty-two students in Brewer's classes, utilized city and county records and the recollections of former slaves, in addition to the more traditional areas for research, such as libraries and archives.[32] The research project was culminated by a "Negro History Night" in the chapel of Samuel Huston College on August 2, 1940. In addition to a presentation of the status of black life in Travis County in the areas of health, education, religion, and economic sufficiency, the program included music by some old fiddlers in the black community, a string orchestra playing works by black composers, and the introduction of a few former slaves who still lived in the community.

Despite such efforts, a black observer noted in 1952 that the history teachers in the seventeen black high schools of Texas that were accredited by the Southern Association of Colleges and Secondary Schools were still having to teach children "that which life does not confirm."[33] Even more striking was the fact that the number of accredited high schools offering courses in black history in Texas had shrunk to three in the eighteen years between 1934 and 1952.[34] Whatever else, the preservation of the heritage of black people in Texas had not thrived in the twenty-five years since the advent of the Great Depression.

Another form of artistic expression—music—did thrive among black Texans. In fact, the musical abilities of Jules Bledsoe, a Waco native who was educated in Bishop College, were widely appreciated outside Texas, both in New York City and in Europe.[35] Although Bledsoe began his professional career in 1925 while studying at Columbia University, he did not achieve musical stardom until he sang "Old Man River" in the part of Joe in Florenz Ziegfeld's production of Showboat in 1930.[36] He left the musical in 1934 to star in Eugene O'Neill's The Emperor Jones on Broadway; Bledsoe later toured in Europe with a road company in the O'Neill drama. The renowned baritone remained in Europe and starred in a number of roles until the German invasion of France in 1940.[37]

While Jules Bledsoe, a native artist, gave only two performances in Texas after he achieved great fame as a singer, black Texans had opportunities to hear other black performers who toured in Texas.[38] One of the prominent black artists to tour in Texas during this period was the tenor, Roland Hayes. In March 1931, Hayes presented a concert in Houston to an integrated audience of more than 5,000 people.[39] In March 1935, Hayes returned to Houston and an audience of more than 2,000 attended the recital in the City Auditorium. Then years later, in March 1945, a sparse attendance figure for his third concert in Houston moved Hayes to observe that he did not believe "that Houston is a music center."[40]

Such declining interest was not the case for Marian Anderson, the great contralto, who visited Texas on numerous occasions. Marian Anderson performed in Houston for the first time in March 1931. In a benefit concert for the Bethlehem Settlement House for underprivileged black children in Houston, she provided a program that included classical music, German lieder, semi-classical love songs, and spirituals.[41] Marian Anderson returned to Houston in 1937 for a second concert; she already had been acclaimed by Arturo Toscanini and Jean Sibelius as one of the greatest singers in the world.[42] In 1939, prior to her Easter concert at the Lincoln Memorial in Washington, D.C., Miss Anderson appeared in Waco Hall on the Baylor campus and later performed before 5,000 people in her third Houston concert.[43] A fourth Houston concert followed in May 1940, and she captivated her audience with the concluding number, the spiritual "Sometimes I Feel Like a Motherless Child."[44] In 1941, slightly more than a month before the United States went to war, she returned for a fifth concert in Houston. The City Auditorium was filled to capacity to hear her program of works by Handel, Bach, Scarlatti, Brahms, Rachmaninoff, Boatner, Lawrence, Burleigh, and Brown. She concluded the performance with a group of traditional spirituals.[45] In 1948, Marian Anderson returned to Texas as the first black artist to appear with the Dallas Symphony Orchestra in a concert in the Fair Park Auditorium in Dallas.[46] Her final concert in Texas was a triumphant success as the integrated audience called forth ten encore performances although she sang none of the lieder, nor any of the spirituals, for which she was so famous.[47]

While Marian Anderson sang to integrated audiences in Houston, Waco, and Dallas, other performances by black artists were subjected to the customary segregation practices. In 1943, George Gershwin's *Porgy and Bess* was slated to play before an all-white audience in Houston until the Houston Chapter of the NAACP forced the City Council, under legal threat, to open the balcony of the Music Hall on the second night of the two-night performance.[48] The road-show featured a native

Texan, Etta Moten, in the title role of Bess. The mezzo-contralto had studied at Paul Quinn College in Waco and appeared in several films before assuming the lead in George Gershwin's opera from the original star, Ann Brown.[49]

The color line appeared in later performances involving black performers. In 1947, a road-show performance of the enormously popular *Carmen Jones* came to the Music Hall in Houston for six performances within a four-day period.[50] The libretto, which utilized the Bizet operatic score, was written by Oscar Hammerstein II and had achieved great success on Broadway. The Houston performances were graced by the original cast, including Muriel Rahn, Muriel Smith, John Bubbles, Ford Buck, and 125 other black performers.[51] Despite the portraying of black characters, only one of the six performances was totally opened to black Houstonians as a benefit performance for the Houston Branch of the NAACP.[52] Although black people were forced to sit in the highest balcony in the Music Hall at all five performances, the black patrons were accorded seats on all levels of the theater at a single performance on January 13, 1947.

A similarly ironic incident occurred in Dallas in November 1951, when Duke Ellington's orchestra was booked for two performances in the Fair Park Auditorium. The black bandleader was to perform for an all-white audience at 8:00 p.m.; the performance for black patrons was scheduled to begin at 11:00 p.m.[53] A campaign was mounted by the Dallas branch of the NAACP, however, and the threats of a boycott by the black community prompted the promoters of the concert to open the earlier performance to black patrons. The mutually contradictory implication of a black orchestra performing before racially segregated audiences carried far less weight with the promoters than the prospect of a black boycott.[54]

The color line, however, always existed at cultural events. In 1931 in Houston the Houston Symphony Orchestra concerts were available to black patrons in "special reserved seats."[55] In 1933, the Houston Civic Opera presented *Aida* with five guest operatic stars supported by a cast of 900. Not only did segregated seating prevail, but some black Houstonians accepted roles as either Ethiopian slaves or prisoners, while white people took the roles of the Ethiopian heroine, Aida, and her father. It was necessary to smear burnt cork on the faces of the two white people in the leading roles, but the slaves and prisoners required no such makeup.[56] The Majestic Theatre in Dallas, in 1936, conducted the same operation when the San Carlo Opera Company presented four operas in three days. The white theatrical management reserved "300 seats . . . in the colored balcony for all four performances" for the black patrons.[57] In 1944, the sole opportunity for black opera patrons in Houston to attend a local production of Puccini's *Tosca* was a dress rehearsal. Because the demand of white patrons pre-empted any seating for black patrons in a "colored balcony" in the City Auditorium, two dress rehearsal performances were opened to black patrons.[58] While the preservation of a semblance of separate but equal opportunity was preserved by admitting black patrons to dress rehearsals, the cultural inequity was pronounced nonetheless.

In March 1944, the Houston Symphony Orchestra performed in a Sunday afternoon concert for the black school children of the Houston Public Schools. Although the concerts for white school children had been a long-standing practice, the concert marked the first such performance for black school children in Houston.[59] The attendance at this event prompted continuance of the concerts; the Symphony conductor, Ernst Hoffman, explained the significance of each strain of music so that the children listened with understanding to music by such composers as Wagner and Rimsky-Korsakov.[60] By 1950 the Dallas Symphony Orchestra was participating in a similar program for black school children in Dallas.[61] The extension of such cultural opportunities to the black school children came as a result of the untiring efforts of the music education personnel in the public school systems of Houston and Dallas.[62]

Unlike white symphony concerts for black audiences, the music of black Texans was the blues. A spontaneously generated art form—folk art—the blues was basically a vocal music in its beginnings as it derived from worksongs, field hollers, and spirituals. By the beginning of the twentieth century, the blues had developed a strong instrumental tradition. In this sense, instrumental blues and jazz were inseparable. After World War I, black urbanization patterns gave opportunities to Afro-American musicians. Because of limited entertainment outlets for black people in Texas, the itinerant bluesmen were popular features in the nightclubs and bars of the new ghettos of the Lone Star state.[63]

Dallas was the most important Texas city for blues and jazz expression. In pre-jazz days, it had been a rendezvous point of Huddie Ledbetter (Leadbelly), Blind Lemon Jefferson, T-Bone Walker, and Sammy Price. During the 1920s, Dallas swarmed with blues singers, boogie woogie pianists, and small combos with constantly shifting personnel in the black establishments.[64] Of all of the bands, the most professional and warmly remembered was the Alphonso Trent Orchestra.

Alphonso Trent, a native of Fort Smith, Arkansas, was attracted to the musical opportunity that abounded in Dallas. The Trent Orchestra moved from all-black audiences to play a lengthy eighteen-month engagement at the Adolphus Hotel. Until the Trent Orchestra left Dallas in 1934, a victim of the Great Depression like other Texas bands, the best of Texas jazz groups broadcast a nightly performance on radio station WFAA.[65]

Radio stations in Texas provided additional cultural opportunities for black people to appreciate music. In addition to the standard offerings of the radio networks and local stations, black performers began to present their talents on the airwaves of Texas by the 1930s. Radio station WBAP in Fort Worth carried a program featuring the Prairie View Choral Club in April 1933. In commemoration of Negro Health Week, which had been inaugurated by Booker T. Washington, the program consisted largely of inspirational music.[66] Another black college musical group, the thirty-voice a capella choir of Samuel Huston College, performed in a series of weekly broadcasts in 1934 and 1935, on radio station KNOW in Austin. The broadcasts, which were made from the college chapel in Austin on Thursday evenings, were regularly carried by the member stations of the Southwest Network.[67] Another musical aggregation, Wings Over Jordan, a twenty-six-voice gospel-singing group, performed in Houston's City Auditorium in a concert that was broadcast over radio station KTRH during World War II.[68] The singing group, founded in Cleveland by the Reverend Glenn T. Settle, was the most popular gospel-singing aggregation in black America and appeared in Texas communities on numerous occasions during the 1930s and 1940s. Thus the medium of radio provided additional cultural opportunities for the black people of Texas.[69]

Despite the growing importance of radio as an organ of black culture, black radio personalities did not appear in Texas until 1947. The first regular black performer on a Texas radio station was Lavada Durst, who broadcast under the pseudonym "Dr. Hep Cat." Durst presented three daily programs on radio station KVET in Austin.[70] By 1951, KTXN in Austin had employed two black broadcasters, Tony Von Walls and Myrtle Royster, both of whom presented daily programs.[71] The potential market among black people prompted the two white partners operating radio station KWBC in Fort Worth to allocate a six-hour daily block of programming to the black communities of Fort Worth and Dallas.[72] In Houston, ethnic broadcasting became a reality in 1954 when radio station KYOK devoted its entire broadcasting ef-

forts to the black community in the Bayou City.[73] Although KYOK was
operated by white owners, the broadcast personnel were integrated
with the addition of three black personalities, who also worked on the
KYOK sales staff.[74]

The color line was not limited to the aural arts in Texas. It was observed during the first great display of the work of black artists in the
United States, which opened in Houston in September 1930. The exhibit, which consisted of seventy-three examples of painting and sculpture selected from the three hundred entries for the Harmon Awards,
was held for two days in the Houston Museum of Fine Arts.[75] Despite
the fact that the black school children of Houston contributed pennies
for the packing, repacking, and transportation of the artifacts to the
next exhibit, the Museum reserved only one day of each month for
"colored patrons"; black patrons were required to seek an appointment
for visits at other times.[76] Thus the paintings, etchings, prints, and
sculpture that had been created by black artists were not freely accessi-
ble to black Houstonians.

Such a restrictive policy at the Museum of Fine Arts discouraged
most black patronage. In fact, the liberalization of the admissions policy for black patrons in the midst of World War II nearly went un-
heeded. Ellie A. Walls, a columnist for *The Informer* and an instructor
in the Houston College for Negroes, reported in 1944 that she belatedly
had learned that the Museum had been opened to black patrons on Friday afternoons for two and one-half hours, beginning at 2:00 p.m.[77] As a
community leader and a supporter of cultural opportunities for black
Texans, Ellie Walls noted that, due to the previous restrictions upon
black attendance, she had not been to the Museum more than twice in
the fifteen years since the exhibit of black art in the museum in 1930.
The stifling restrictions were modified even more within one year as
the Museum was opened to black patrons for five and one-half hours on
Friday afternoons in 1945.[78] This restriction was not even relaxed in
1946, however, for an exhibit of 100 paintings and drawings by the
black school children of Houston.[79]

Despite the restrictive admission policies of the Museum of Fine
Arts, displays of the work of black artists appeared in the black communities of several Texas cities. In 1933, the opening of the renovated black
library branch in Houston featured an exhibit of the paintings of eight
black artists.[80] Three of the paintings on display in the exhibit were the
work of Samuel Countee, who had entered several paintings in the
Harmon Exhibit. The art exhibit in the Carnegie Colored Library in

Houston continued as an annual event in 1934.[81] The Fifth Annual Exhibit at the Negro Carnegie Branch Library in 1937 featured the work of a self-taught black artist from Galveston, Frank F. Sheinall.[82] In addition to the art display, the formal opening of the exhibit in June 1937 featured a program that included two vocal solos, an instrumental selection, a quartet, and three guest speakers.[83] In 1948 a group of black artists in San Antonio exhibited their work in the Pine Street Branch YWCA. Three women showed their paintings, another woman read her poetry, and a fifth black woman presented a piano recital.[84] A year later, in May 1949, the First Annual Festival of Fine Arts was held at the Texas State University for Negroes (TSUN) in Houston. The organization of the festival called for daily symposia on the phases of art and music and nightly recitals and productions.[85] Another display of artistic expression was exhibited in a collection of paintings and pottery shown in the Julia C. Hester Settlement House in Houston in June 1949. The fifty works of art, which were lent by the Museum of Fine Arts, were dominated by the work of an art instructor at TSUN, John T. Biggers.[86]

In March 1950, John Biggers achieved further recognition when his drawing, "The Cradle," received the $200 Purchase Prize in the Houston Museum of Fine Arts Annual Exhibit. The artist-instructor discussed his work at a forum held at the Museum and described his drawing as a result of a personal social problem that drove him to express himself and thus "bridge the gap to social normalcy again."[87] Biggers, a North Carolinian who came to the TSUN faculty in 1949, received the honor of an exhibit of his work in the Houston Museum of Fine Arts in 1954. Fifteen paintings were displayed in the Blaffer Room of the Museum: "The Cradle," "Quiltin'," "Women and Children," "Cotton Pickers, I and II," "Two Heads," "The Planters," "The Sleepers," "Coming Home From Work," "Diggers," "Sleeping Children," "Cotton Choppers," "Harvesters," "Sleeping Boy," and "News Boy."[88] Much of his work portrayed non-Texas themes, with West Africa exerting a great impact upon Biggers' choice of subjects for his paintings. But the greatest achievement of John Biggers, which was completed in April 1953, was his mural in the Blue Triangle Branch YWCA in Houston. Entitled "Negro Women's Contribution to American Culture," the mural embodied the artistic expression of a people and bridged the gap that John Biggers had described.[89] Of all of the painters and sculptors representing black Texas, John Biggers achieved the greatest national stature. Other black Texans, though, found creative inspiration in their state.

Another premier black artist, called "the State's only Negro writer of importance," was J. Mason Brewer, a poet and folklorist.[90] Brewer wrote with a dual purpose: he believed that black life in Texas deserved representation in literature, and he also hoped to arouse an interest among black people in their own artistic capacities.[91] In keeping with his first artistic purpose, Brewer published *Negrito*, a volume of dialect poetry, in which he attempted to include illustrations of the "embodiment of the Negro Soul . . . in the uneducated Negro's own speech."[92] In a series of epigrammatic poems, Brewer managed to frame some incisive portraits of black politicians and clergymen. In "Politician," Brewer wrote

> He struts befo' de brethren,
> An' make de sistren think
> Dat he am one big race man,
> Den sells 'em fuh uh drink.[93]

This cynical view was unrelieved by the black poet's portrayal of the "City Preacher" which claimed

> He preach de gospel once uh week
> Put Christians in de sky
> Drives 'is packard ebry day
> An' pass de needy by.[94]

Brewer attempted to fulfill his second artistic purpose in arousing "Texas Negroes . . . to accomplish greater things . . . in poetry" with the publication of an anthology of verse written by black Texans.[95] Brewer's anthology, *Heralding Dawn*, contained a poem by Malcolm C. Conley that Brewer claimed was the earliest work by a black Texan to be published in a national publication. Conley's poem, "American Ideals," which was previously published in the journal of the NAACP, *The Crisis*, captured the essence of white civilization:

> The red man looking upon rivers, plains,
>   and seas,
> Said, "Lord, let me hunt."
> The white man looking thereupon
> Said, "Lord, let me possess."
> The black man, thereupon gazing,

Grew strangely fond
Of something vaguely beyond.
He with an open chest
Gave his heart a throbbing fling
Unto the glimmering mountain crest;
The stars his supplication hastened
     to ring
When he shouted aloud, "Lord, let
     me sing!"[96]

In 1936, at the time of the Texas Centennial Exposition, Brewer encouraged the members of the Bellerophon Quill Club of Booker T. Washington High School of Dallas to publish an anthology of poems that were dedicated to the Centennial Exposition. Although the verse written by the thirteen contributors was somewhat immature in expression, nevertheless it was thoughtful and vibrant in tone. Thus, in the midst of the decade of the Great Depression, J. Mason Brewer edited two anthologies of verse written by black Texans, both young and old, which were dedicated to the arousal of poetic expression among black Texans.

In the deepening crisis that presaged the involvement of the United States in World War II, Brewer wrote a prophetic poem that reflected the spirit of black people during wartime. The poem, "Bewilderment," received third prize in the National Poetry Contest in *The Crisis* in 1941. Speaking for his fellow black Americans, Brewer captured the bitterness evoked by the disparity between creed and practice in the United States:

I do not know my way about yet in
     my native land;
Sometimes I sit among the crowd when
     often I should stand.
Ofttimes when I attend a show and
     "America" is played,
I sit there in the balcony, unmovable—
     afraid. . . .
And even though I stand erect when
     "Stars and Stripes" pass by,
I know deep down within my soul my
     standing is a lie. . . .[97]

Even more poignant was an autobiographical poem, "Too Far Trip," which Brewer wrote in 1947. The poet related the experience of taking his young son to see the Alamo in San Antonio and, after viewing the shrine, taking the boy to the municipal zoo. The boy was given five cents to ride a pony, but the keeper looked sharply at the boy and said, "This ain't for you." And Brewer wrote,

> He looked up at the keeper,
> And hung his proud head down
> And took a pocket mirror out
> And saw that he was brown.[98]

During the same postwar period, Brewer published another anthology of work by his students. The collection of short stories—*Silhouettes of Life*—was written by the students in Brewer's creative writing course in the Department of English in Samuel Huston College in 1946 and 1947.[99] All of the stories revolved around romantic themes, but the concluding poem by Donald S. Cameron sounded a more realistic tone because it called forth the experience of black students in the postwar era. In "A Seventeen-Year-Old College Freshman Comments on the College Vet," Cameron wrote,

> I wouldn't be a veteran in College;
> I'll tell you the reason why . . .
> You never have any money
> And there's nothing you can buy.[100]

Certainly J. Mason Brewer had succeeded, by 1948, in his dual purpose in bringing an effective portrayal of black life in Texas to literature and in arousing an interest among black people in their own artistic capabilities.

The black press in Texas made another effort to arouse black people to pursue their artistic talents. The black weeklies in Houston and Waco encouraged contributions from their readers in short sketches, essays, and verse. Throughout 1932, J. Walter Fridia, a black physician in Waco, contributed philosophical poems to *The Informer* that were placed on the Houston weekly's editorial page. The most evocative of the physician's poetic efforts came in the fifth verse of an eight-verse poem entitled "Much in a Name."

Ambition it will always check,
It's like a millstone 'round your neck;
You cannot rise, you cannot go,
As long as you are called "Negro."[101]

In September 1933, the black weekly in Waco solicited local contributions, and during that month it published a short story, "Doomed to Despair," by Jennie V. Mills, a Waco housewife.[102] Her story, a rather confused account of lost love, was not succeeded by any further contributions to the Waco weekly; the effect of the Great Depression may have precluded any such leisure-time activities as amateur literary enterprises.[103]

The Informer announced, in February 1935, the appearance of a new feature because the weekly received a substantial number of unsolicited poems, jokes, and essays. The new feature, "Dreamship," consisted of four or five poems that were published weekly and provided an outlet for poetic expression among black Texans. One of the first poems published in "Dreamship" reflected the effect of lynchings upon young black people in Texas; in "Query," Walter K. Waring was moved to ask

There had been a lynching
That day, somewhere.
A Negro had been burned
Alive, I think
Downtown white people
Stared at my dark skin,
Women, men all stared
Because I was a Negro, too,
And one had been lynched
That day somewhere.
I wonder if people think
Of Christ when they stare
At Jews?[104]

The black weekly continued to publish the contributions of black writers and poets in "Dreamship" until the outbreak of World War II. The wartime restrictions upon newsprint reduced the publication of contributions from readers to sporadic appearance.

During the postwar period the black weekly in Houston rekindled its efforts to promote cultural accomplishments among black Texans. In July 1949, *The Informer* announced a short story contest that closed on November 15, 1949.[105] A three-judge panel was to award four prizes for the best stories; although the stories were not to exceed 3,500 words, there was no restriction as to theme. On December 24, 1949, the black weekly announced that David Abner, an undergraduate student at TSUN, had received the $100 first prize for "Fourteen Guys," a story of a rifle squad in Italy during World War II.[106] One week later, it was announced that a second prize award of $75 had been made to Bettye D. Wilson for "When Blood Runs Black," a portrayal of a black victim of a white mob.[107] James A. Brooks, a theology student at Morehouse College, received the third prize of $50 for a story entitled "The Sable Night," which he had written in an English course in college.[108] A romantic story, "The Lady Wore Leopard," by Bill Smallwood received the fourth prize, $25.[109]

Another area of cultural activity, the amateur theatrical production, elicited the interest of black Texans. In March 1931, the Houston Negro Little Theatre organized to provide an important cultural outlet in the black community.[110] After its members participated in a drama workshop that was sponsored by Booker T. Washington High School in Houston, the first season of the Houston Negro Little Theatre was launched on May 8, 1931, at the Pilgrim Auditorium in the Bayou City. The program consisted of three short plays, two of which—*White Dresses* and *No 'Count Boy*—were written by Paul Green and the third, *The Slave*, was written by Elizabeth Yates.[111] In November 1932, the efforts of the Houston theatrical group were augmented by a road show performance of Paul Green's *In Abraham's Bosom* by the amateur black theatrical troupe from San Antonio.[112]

Despite the efforts of these amateur groups, the third season of the Houston Negro Little Theatre saw declining participation and limited interest in such activities among black Houstonians.[113] The Great Depression was reaching new depths of economic privation, yet in 1934 the theatrical group underwent a complete reorganization and the organizers made plans to continue the work of the Houston Negro Little Theatre. The instrumental leader of the reorganization movement was James A. Hulbert, the librarian in the Carnegie Colored Library.[114] The head librarian agreed to serve as business manager of the new organization and provided space for work and rehearsal in the basement of the library. The twofold objectives of the reorganized theatrical group to furnish a means of dramatic expression for black Houstonians and to create community interest in drama, were tested when the Houston Negro Little Theatre made its debut in 1935 with a one-act play entitled *No Sabe*.[115] The mystery melodrama, which was presented at no charge to the public, attracted 250 spectators and seemed to capture some interest among black Houstonians.[116]

With this auspicious second beginning, the black theatrical organization presented Oscar Wilde's comedy of manners, *Lady Windemere's Fan*, at the Pilgrim Auditorium in February, 1935. In addition to a large audience, the successful effort was supported by thirty-three patrons within the black community.[117] Within a month, the amateur drama group performed in a pair of one-act plays to capacity audiences.[118] Such activity in the black community of Houston resulted in a renewal of interest in theatrical activities; in 1940, the Department of Recreation sponsored a drama tournament at the Emancipation Park Clubhouse for the three black playgrounds in Houston.[119] The competition, which presented several one-act plays, was judged by representatives of the Houston Negro Little Theatre.

At the onset of World War II, the Houston Negro Little Theatre remained quite active, as the group presented Thornton Wilder's *Our Town* in November 1941, a locally written Christmas pageant by Robert T. Holland entitled *A Christmas Story*, and Orville Snapp's *Everybody Works but Father* in April 1942.[120] The exigencies of the war-crisis made demands upon the black people of Houston, however, and the amateur theatrical movement in Houston was interrupted for the duration of World War II. Black Houstonians turned their efforts to more immediate concerns in morale-building agencies such as the USO; in every war bond campaign, black people held rallies in schools, churches, and community centers to sell bonds. Thus the hiatus in amateur theatrical activity in Houston extended throughout the wartime crisis.

Not until 1947 did black dramatic enterprise revive in Houston. In October 1946, a black drama student, Vernon J. B. Chambers, was employed by the Department of Recreation. Chambers, who had studied at the Pasadena Playhouse under Gilmor Brown, dedicated himself toward reviving the Houston Negro Little Theatre.[121] This second reorganization of the group moved slowly at first, but within five years the black dramatic movement was thriving. In February 1953, the black community in Houston enthusiastically attended a performance of Tennessee Williams's *The Glass Menagerie*.[122] And this effort was complemented by the presentation of Sophocles's *Antigone* in May 1953. Utilizing contemporary costumes, the portrayal of *Antigone* received popular acclaim and was played again in June 1953 because of public demand.[123]

The renewed success of the amateur dramatic group in Houston prompted a similar movement in the black community of Dallas in 1953. An organizational meeting was held under the leadership of George V. Allen. Because of encouraging response, the group met for a second time and chose "Round Up Theatre" as a name for the organization; George V. Allen was the unanimous choice for chairman.[124] During the remainder of the year, the Round Up Theatre presented two plays for the black community in Dallas. Both plays, *Walls Rise Up* and *Our Town*, were performed in the auditorium of Booker T. Washington High School before enthusiastic audiences.[125] In January 1954, the Round Up Theatre undertook Tennessee Williams's *A Streetcar Named Desire* and again played a full house in the high school auditorium.[126]

Thus the Little Theatre movement, although confined to the largest black communities, provided an outlet for black cultural aspirations which had no other channel of expression. At the same time, the dramatic groups contributed to the existence of intelligent public opinion within the black community of Texas. If nothing else, the Little Theatres marked a period of self-expression and self-revelation among the black people of the state. They worked, in some small way, to fill an intellectual and emotional void in the lives of the black people of Texas during the Great Depression, the second World War, and the Postwar Recovery.

It has been argued that the Harlem Renaissance aimed at cultural equality and cultural legitimacy.[127] First-class citizenship was a goal of Afro-Americans at several levels: social, economic, political, legal, and cultural. Just as black people in New York City sought authenticity in their cultural claims, blacks in Texas cities sought the same things. The forces that created the Harlem Renaissance were not created in a vacuum. The same held true for the cultural accomplishments of the black people of Texas.

One of the most controversial aspects of the Harlem Renaissance was the role of white patrons and popularizers of black artists. Wealthy sponsors, like Mabel Dodge, and critics, like Carl Van Vechten, have been portrayed as both positive supporters and negative patronizers and exploiters of black artists. Whatever assets and debits in the historical record, no white Texans fulfilled analogous roles in the Lone Star Renaissance. The public attention and support obtained by black artists in the state was gained without concerted encouragement from white patrons and critics. If anything, the usual white response was to burlesque black efforts or to ignore them.[128]

Another controversial aspect of the Harlem Renaissance centered upon the function of black art. Critics of this cultural expression, like Harold Cruse and Nathan Huggins, have argued that the efforts of the Harlem Renaissance were not directed toward the edification of Afro-Americans. The outpouring of literary and musical expression in Harlem had more impact upon whites than blacks. This criticism, whether valid or not, did not hold true for the cultural accomplishments of black Texans in the midst of the twentieth century. Black culture in Texas was conceived by black artists within the black urban community for black audiences. Although some exceptional cases like that of J. Mason Brewer, the first black member of the Texas Folklore Society, could be cited, it should be recalled that Brewer also wrote racially conscious poetry that was not accommodationist in tone. Black culture in Texas was created, in the main, for black Texans and stands as their authentic expression in the arts.

Notes

1. Nathan I. Huggins, *Harlem Renaissance* (New York: Oxford University Press, 1971), p. 9.

2. Ibid., p. 14.

3. Neil Sapper, "A Survey of the History of the Black People of Texas, 1930–1954" (Ph.D. dissertation, Texas Tech University, 1972), pp. 184–189, passim.

4. Ibid., pp. 249–250.

5. Louis R. Harlan, "Tell It Like It Was: Suggestions on Black History," *Social Education*, XXXIII (April 1969), p. 393.

6. Editorial, *Informer* (Houston), March 13, 1954, p. 12.

7. Editorial, *Waco Messenger*, June 16, 1933, p. 2; Ibid., June 15, 1951, p. 4.

8. *Informer* (Houston), June 24, 1939, pp. 1, 8; Houston Park Department, *Program: Dedication Services and 74th Juneteenth Celebration* (Houston, Texas, 1939), pp. 2–4, passim.

9. Bettie Hayman, "A Short History of the Negro of Walker County, 1860–1942" (unpublished M.A. Thesis, Sam Houston State Teachers College, 1942), pp. 55–57, passim.

10. The National Association for the Study of Negro Life and History was founded in 1915 through the efforts of Carter G. Woodson and Charles Wesley. *Dallas Express,* October 27, 1934, p. 9.

11. Association for the Study of Negro Life and History, *Program for the Annual Meeting* (Houston, Texas, 1934), p. 2; L. Virgil Williams, "Teaching Negro Life and History in Texas High Schools," *Journal of Negro History,* XX (January 1935), p. 15. The five black high schools offering courses in black history in 1934 were located in Dallas, Cameron, Hawkins, Jacksonville, and Liberty.

12. In 1935, Herbert High School in Beaumont was permitted, by the Board of Education of Beaumont, to add a course in black history. *Informer* (Houston), February 9, 1935, p. 1.

13. A. Maceo Smith, private interview, Fort Worth, Texas, October 15, 1971; Jesse O. Thomas, *Negro Participation in the Texas Centennial Exposition* (Boston: Christopher Publishing House, 1938), p. 13. The state-wide organization for black participation in the Centennial included Willette R. Banks and Charles Bellinger.

14. At the time that A. Maceo Smith and the other black leaders were lobbying for state support for a black exhibit, Ammon S. Wells announced his candidacy for the seat in the House of Representatives that had been vacated by Sarah T. Hughes in 1935. A. Maceo Smith felt that the Wells candidacy had a deleterious effect upon the receptivity of the Texas Legislature to any requests from black Texans. Smith, private interview, October 15, 1971.

15. Thomas, *Negro Participation,* p. 19. The Commission was composed of Vice President John N. Garner, Secretary of State Cordell Hull, Secretary of Agriculture Henry A. Wallace, and Secretary of Commerce Daniel C. Roper.

16. The ten-member Advisory Committee included Frederick D. Patterson of Tuskegee Institute, Willette R. Banks of Prairie View, Robert L. Vann of the *Pittsburgh Courier,* and Robert C. Weaver. Thomas, *Negro Participation,* p. 19.

17. *Informer* (Houston), February 8, 1936, p. 8; Thomas, *Negro Participation,* p. 20.

18. Thomas, *Negro Participation,* p. 21.

19. *Dallas Express,* June 13, 1936, p. 1. Opening the Hall of Negro Life was not among the first priorities of the white officials who directed the Exposition.

20. Thomas, *Negro Participation,* p. 56. The cornerstone was emblazoned with the motto, "A Tribute to the Past, and a Challenge to the Future," which was furnished by Mrs. A. H. Dyson, the wife of a black dentist in Dallas. *Dallas Express,* June 13, 1936, p. 1.

21. Texas, Centennial Exposition, *Official Guide Book* (Dallas: Texas Centennial Central Exposition, 1936), p. 73; Thomas, *Negro Participation,* p. 30.

22. "Texas-Centennial Celebration, 1936," Texas Southern University Library, Heartman Collection, Vertical File.

23. Thomas, *Negro Participation*, p. 133.

24. Ibid.

25. Texas Centennial, *Guide Book*, p. 73; *Informer* (Houston), August 8, 1936, pp. 1, 3.

26. *Informer* (Houston), July 11, 1936, sec. 2, p. 4; *Dallas Express*, October 31, 1936, p. 1.

27. *Dallas Express*, August 29, 1936, p. 1.

28. J. Mason Brewer, "The Negro and the Texas Centennial Exposition," *Informer* (Houston), August 8, 1936, sec. 2, p. 4.

29. Charles H. Bynum, II, "The Centennial in Retrospect," *Dallas Express*, October 31, 1936, p. 2.

30. *Dallas Express*, November 28, 1936, p. 3; ibid., February 6, 1937, p. 8; *Informer* (Houston), January 30, 1937, p. 1.

31. Thomas, *Negro Participation*, p. 122.

32. Unidentified newsclipping, 1940, University of Texas, Archives, Negro scrapbooks; J. Mason Brewer, ed., *An Historical Outline of the Negro in Travis County* (Austin: Samuel Huston College, 1940), pp. 2–3.

33. Westerfield T. Kimble, "An Analysis of the Methods of Teaching History in the Seventeen High Schools for Negroes in Texas Accredited by the Southern Association of Colleges and Secondary Schools" (M.A. thesis, Prairie View, 1952), p. 129.

34. Ibid., p. 32.

35. Florence B. O'Brien, "Adequacy of Texas History Texts in Reporting Negro Achievements" (M.A. thesis, Stephen F. Austin State College, 1939), p. 45.

36. Ibid.; "Texas Negroes in the World of Music," University of Texas, Institute of Texan Cultures, Negro Collection.

37. *Waco Messenger*, July 23, 1943, p. 1. Bledsoe returned to the United States and died in California at the age of 44. He was buried in Waco, and his tombstone was inscribed with the last bar of "Old Man River" and carried the words, "He Just Keeps Rolling Along."

38. Bledsoe sang for the British War Relief in Fort Worth in 1941 and he delivered a concert at Waco Hall on the campus of Baylor University in March, 1941. *Waco Messenger*, March 21, 1941, p. 1.

39. *Informer* (Houston), February 14, 1931, p. 1; February 25, 1931, p.1; March 21, 1931, p. 1.

40. Ibid., March 10, 1945, p. 13.

41. Ibid., April 4, 1931, p. 1.

42. John Hope Franklin, *From Slavery to Freedom* (3d ed.; New York: Alfred A. Knopf, 1967), p. 520.

43. *Waco Messenger*, March 31, 1939, p. 1; *Informer* (Houston), April 1, 1939, p. 2. The famous Easter concert in 1939, before 75,000 people, was a resounding re-

buke to the refusal of the DAR to permit Marian Anderson to use Constitutional Hall in Washington.

44. *Informer* (Houston), May 18, 1940, p. 7.

45. Ibid., November 1, 1941, p. 1. The great contralto performed in a sixth concert in Houston in March 1943. Ibid., March 20, 1943, pp. 1, 8.

46. *Dallas Express*, February 7, 1948, pp. 1, 8. Marian Anderson had appeared in six previous concerts in Dallas, beginning in 1938. In 1950, Viola Dixon, a pianist, became the first black Texan to play with the Dallas Symphony. Ibid., April 1, 1950, p. 19.

47. Marian Anderson sang three solos prior to the demands for encores: Monteverdi's "Lamento di Ariana" and "O Don Fatale" and "Don Carlo" by Verdi.

48. *Informer* (Houston), January 22, 1944, pp. 1, 12.

49. "Negro Histowall," University of Texas, Institute of Texan Cultures, Negro Collection; *Waco Messenger*, January 8, 1954, p. 1.

50. *Informer* (Houston), December 21, 1946, p. 3; January 11, 1947, p. 13.

51. A native of Houston, Clarice Rhodes, was a singer-dancer in the chorus.

52. *Informer* (Houston), January 11, 1947, p. 13.

53. *Dallas Express*, November 3, 1951, pp. 1, 10.

54. Ibid.

55. *Informer* (Houston), October 31, 1931, p. 2.

56. Ibid., May 20, 1933, p. 2.

57. *Dallas Express*, January 4, 1936, pp. 1, 4. The program consisted of Pucini's *La Boheme*, Wagner's *Tannhauser*, and two Verdi operas, *La Traviata* and *Il Trovatore*.

58. *Informer* (Houston), April 8, 1944, p. 13.

59. Ibid., March 25, 1944, p. 2.

60. Ibid., November 22, 1946, p. 2.

61. *Dallas Express*, March 4, 1950, p. 1.

62. *Informer* (Houston), November 22, 1946, p. 2; *Dallas Express*, March 4, 1950, p. 1.

63. Ross Russell, *Jazz Style in Kansas City and the Southwest* (Berkeley: University of California Press, 1971), p. 38.

64. Ibid., p. 54.

65. Ibid., pp. 61–63, passim.

66. *Dallas Express*, April 22, 1933, p. 1.

67. *Dallas Express*, November 3, 1934, p. 1. The subscribing stations included WRR (Dallas), WBAP (Fort Worth), KTRH (Houston), KTSA (San Antonio), WACO (Waco), and stations in Oklahoma and Arkansas.

68. *Informer* (Houston), February 20, 1943, p. 13.

69. The Ebenezer Choir, of the Ebenezer Baptist Church in Austin, presented a

musical program which was carried over the Texas Quality Network each Sunday morning for a two-year period, 1938–1941. Brewer, ed., *An Historical Outline of the Negro in Travis County*, p. 37.

70. J. Mason Brewer, *A Pictorial and Historical Souvenir of Negro Life in Austin, Texas, 1950–1951* (Austin, 1951), p. 11.

71. Ibid. Myrtle Royster on October 1, 1951, became the first black woman radio personality in Texas. Her show featured household advice and provided biographical sketches of famous black people. A native of Minnesota and a graduate of the University of Minnesota, she also chaired the Department of Art in Tillotson College in Austin.

72. *Informer* (Houston), October 17, 1953, p. 9; *Dallas Express*, October 17, 1953, p. 1. The owner-operators of KWBC, Jack Flood and Joe Evans, promised to devote an additional segment to the Mexican-American communities of Fort Worth and Dallas; ethnic broadcasting had become, by 1953, a lucrative enterprise.

73. *Informer* (Houston), April 3, 1954, pp. 1, 10.

74. The black radio personalities in KYOK were Harrel Tillman, Lloyd Johnson, and Bruce Miller; the first black radio broadcaster in Houston was Lonnie Rochon, who presented a nightly program on KNUZ in February, 1948. Ibid., February 21, 1948, p. 1.

75. Ibid., September 27, 1930, p.1. The Harmon Awards had been made by the William E. Harmon Foundation to outstanding black Americans since 1926.

76. Ibid., October 4, 1940, p. 8; Ellie A. Walls, "Facts and Figures," ibid., January 8, 1944, p. 15.

77. Walls, "Facts and Figures," ibid., January 9, 1944, p. 15.

78. Ibid., April 14, 1945, p. 1.

79. Ibid., January 19, 1946, pp. 1, 8.

80. Unidentified newsclipping, July 1933, Houston Public Library, Texas Collection, Negro History Scrapbooks.

81. Editorial, *Informer* (Houston), October 17, 1934.

82. Ibid., July 3, 1937, p. 5. Frank Sheinall, an elevator operator, painted in oil as an avocation and first gained critical attention with a display of his work at the Texas Centennial's Hall of Negro Life in 1936.

83. Program, Fifth Annual Art Exhibit, June 27, 1937, Houston Public Library, Texas Collection, Negro History Scrapbooks.

84. *Informer* (Houston), February 14, 1948, p. 2.

85. Ibid., May 7, 1949, p. 1. The recitals and productions were performed by individual students at TSUN, by the University Chorale and Concert Band, and the University Players.

86. Ibid., June 11, 1949, pp. 1, 8.

87. Ibid., March 25, 1950, p. 1.

88. Ibid., January 23, 1954, p. 1.

89. Ibid., November 28, 1953, p. 10.

90. W. Eugene Hollon, *The Southwest: Old and New* (New York: A. A. Knopf, 1961), p. 424. Brewer became the first black writer elected to the Texas Institute of Letters on February 19, 1955. James W. Byrd., *J. Mason Brewer*, Southwest Writers Series, No. 12 (Austin: Steck-Vaughn Company, 1967), p. 5.

91. Kenneth W. Turner, "Negro Collectors of Negro Folklore: A Study of J. Mason Bewer and Zora Neale Hurston" (M.A. thesis, East Texas State College, 1964), p. 73.

92. J. Mason Brewer, *Negrito: Negro Dialect Poems of the Southwest* (San Antonio: Naylor Printing Co., 1933), p. 14. Brewer dedicated his work to his colleague and patron, J. Frank Dobie.

93. Brewer, *Negrito*, p. 22.

94. Ibid., p. 24.

95. J. Mason Brewer, ed., *Heralding Dawn* (Dallas: June Thomason Printing, 1936), p. x.

96. Ibid., p. 13; Malcolm C. Conley, "American Ideals," *Crisis*, April 1930, p. 28. Conley, who was educated in the black schools in Tyler, graduated from Tuskegee Institute, where he was Class Poet.

97. J. Mason Brewer, "Bewilderment," *Crisis*, May 1941, p. 162.

98. J. Mason Brewer, *More Truth Than Poetry* (Austin: n.p., 1947), p. 17.

99. J. Mason Brewer, ed., *Silhouettes of Life* (Austin: Samuel Huston College, 1948), p. 2. The collection included six short stories and one poem. One of the contributors, a business instructor named John T. King, later became president of Huston-Tillotson College.

100. Ibid., p. 61.

101. *Informer* (Houston), October 8, 1932, p. 2. J. Walter Fridia's contributions ended with his death in February 1933. Ibid., February 11, 1933, p. 1.

102. *Waco Messenger*, September 29, 1933, p. 5.

103. At no time did J. Walter Fridia publish any poetry in the *Waco Messenger*.

104. *Informer* (Houston), March 2, 1935, p. 8.

105. Ibid., July 23, 1949, p. 1.

106. Ibid., December 24, 1949, p. 2.

107. Ibid., December 31, 1949, p. 2.

108. Ibid., January 7, 1950, p. 2.

109. Ibid., January 14, 1950, p. 2.

110. Ibid., March 21, 1931, p. 1.

111. Editorial, ibid., May 9, 1931, p. 8.

112. Ibid., November 12, 1932, p. 7. The San Antonio Negro Little Theatre, founded in 1931 by J. W. Hemmings, had presented Paul Green's tragedy of the Old

South in May 1931. J. W. Hemmings portrayed the principle role which was played on Broadway by Jules Bledsoe. Ibid., May 14, 1932, p. 8.

113. Editorial, ibid., November 25, 1933, p. 2.

114. Ibid., December 8, 1934, p. 1.

115. Ibid., January 5, 1935, p. 8.

116. James A. Hulbert, "Library Notes," ibid., January 12, 1935, p. 8.

117. Doris Wesley, "Little Theatre Play Shows Fine Talent," ibid., February 23, 1935, p. 1.

118. Ibid., March 30, 1935, p. 11.

119. Ibid., April 20, 1940, p. 8. Participant groups represented Gregory, Crawford, and Emancipation Parks.

120. Ibid., November 22, 1941, p. 13; ibid., December 27, 1941.

121. Ibid., April 12, 1947, p. 4.

122. Ibid., February 28, 1953, sec. 2, p. 9.

123. Ibid., May 30, 1953, sec. 1, p. 6.

124. *Dallas Express,* April 4, 1953, p. 10; May 2, 1953, p. 2.

125. Ibid., September 5, 1953, p. 18.

126. Ibid., January 16, 1954, p. 6.

127. Patrick J. Gilpin, "Charles S. Johnson: Entrepreneur of Harlem Renaissance," in *The Harlem Renaissance Remembered,* Arna Bontemps, ed. (New York: Dodd, Mead & Company, 1972), pp. 236–237.

128. In addition to the author's doctoral research, this conclusion is borne out in Charles Grose, "The Black Press in Texas, 1870–1970" (Ph.D. dissertation, University of Texas, 1972).

The Rise of the NAACP in Texas

MICHAEL L. GILLETTE

Numerous historians have pointed to the fact that in the Dixieland states, black Texans led the struggle for political, educational, and social equality. The most pivotal organization in this civil rights struggle was the National Association for the Advancement of Colored People (NAACP). What is frequently overlooked is that this struggle predated the civil rights movement of the 1950s and 1960s. As Michael Gillette reminds us, the Texas NAACP had a troubled history prior to its successes in the 1940s. Effective locals organized in the teens and worked for black rights during the 1920s, however by the end of the decade and continuing into the 1930s, the NAACP suffered a decline, perhaps in part due to the hardships of the depression. Beginning with the late 1930s, and culminating with the war years, the Texas NAACP recovered from its previous decline and became a formidable agent for change in the Lone Star State. Reasons for its success abounded and included strong leaders, ties to the professional classes, improved economic conditions, World War II generated militancy. One of the most influential accomplishments was the successful challenge of the white primary. As a result of a case begun in Texas, the United States Supreme Court declared the Democratic white primary unconstitutional in Smith v. Allwright, *thus encouraging African American voters and leading to other challenges by black Texans to the unseemly Jim Crow system.*

*

IN THE LATE 1930s an extraordinary group of black Texans began to organize and direct the state's civil rights movement. As they revived the five languid branches of the National Association for the Advancement of Colored People,[1] they built a statewide organization, the Texas State Conference of Branches of NAACP, which ultimately included more than 170 local chapters. Through this structure they mobilized local branches and coordinated their programs with the policies and strategies of the NAACP's national office in New York. They also planned and initiated lawsuits against racial discrimination in the areas of voting rights, jury service, employment, housing, education, and public accommodations.

One man whose vision of a statewide NAACP organization was especially influential was Antonio Maceo Smith. Not only was he instrumental in its development, but he also spearheaded its activities for two decades. A gifted practitioner of the political arts of compromise and consensus, he combined the administrative talents of the bureaucrat with the promotional skills of an insurance executive. Confident and charismatic, he was above all an organizer.[2] He was exactly what the NAACP needed.

Born in Texarkana in 1903, Maceo Smith was educated at Fisk University and New York University, where he received degrees in business. While in New York, he worked as a Red Cap in Grand Central Station and organized an advertising agency in Harlem. Returning to Texas in 1929 after the death of his father, Smith then moved to Oklahoma City in 1932. In January 1933, he came to Dallas to organize a life insurance company. There he rejuvenated the Negro Chamber of Commerce and played a major role in obtaining and directing participation in the Texas Centennial Exposition in Dallas. By 1936 he had become secretary of the Dallas NAACP branch and the Progressive Voters League. Through these activities he developed ties with key African American leaders in Dallas and other cities. Increasingly, he thought in terms of statewide organizations. From Smith's discussions with other black leaders on matters relating to the Texas Centennial, the Negro Chamber of Commerce and the Progressive Voters League came their decision to organize the State Conference of NAACP Branches.[3]

They received encouragement from the NAACP national office, which had promoted the establishment of a state conference since 1935. In that year publisher Roscoe Dunjee, president of the Oklahoma State Conference, and NAACP field secretary William Pickens had toured Texas to stimulate branches and to recommend the formation of a state conference.[4] When NAACP field worker Juanita Jackson came in March 1937 to reorganize the Houston and Dallas chapters, she also suggested establishing a state conference "in order to give the branches something to work towards." She discussed the matter with Waco attorney Richard D. Evans, who told of his plans to tour the state, organizing committees and planning for the Conference. Jackson asked Walter White, NAACP secretary, to write several officers of Texas branches, suggesting plans for the Conference and indicating which member of the national staff would be present. "Urge them to make

preparations at once," she added, and "to get their delegates in line."
On June 1, 1937, Maceo Smith, described by Jackson as the "dynamo
behind the Dallas branch," asked the national office for supplies that
"will enable us to organize new branches and spread the work of the organization throughout the State." Later that week, Evans issued a call
to all Texas branches to attend the Conference and to plan a united approach to the many Texas problems. To Roscoe Dunjee, it appeared
that "Evans has at last awakened."[5]

The State Conference was convened at the Moorland Branch of the
Dallas YMCA on June 18 and 19, 1937. Delegates came from the five
Texas branches: Houston, Dallas, Waco, San Antonio, and Marshall.
Viewing the Conference as an opportunity "to attack statewide problems from statewide angles," the delegates talked of organizing
branches and youth councils in all cities. Their emphasis in discussions
and resolutions was on overturning the white primary and securing
greater educational opportunities. The Conference also established
committees, adopted the NAACP constitution and by-laws, and elected
its officers: Richard D. Evans, president; A. Maceo Smith, secretary; and
Mrs. P. R. Lubin, treasurer.[6]

Despite its optimistic beginning, the State Conference required almost three years to emerge as the organization envisioned by its
founders. Although annual meetings were held in Houston in 1938 and
Tyler in 1939, most of the projects undertaken were local branch activities, lacking the resources, planning, and organization of a statewide
movement. Moreover, establishing new branches and maintaining existing ones proved difficult. Although the number of units increased to
ten, no active branch existed in Austin, while Waco's chapter had become dormant. The Fort Worth branch was also inactive, controlled by
a president who would neither function nor allow the election of a re-
placement.[7]

Meanwhile, in 1939 the Houston chapter experienced one of its pe-
riodic, destructive crises. Presiding over the branch was Clifton F.
Richardson, one of its charter members, a newspaper publisher, and
also leader of the Garner-for-President drive among blacks in Texas. He
had touched off a controversy at the NAACP national convention in
Richmond in 1939 by distributing pro-Garner publicity among the delegates. The other Houston branch officers angrily wrote to Walter
White, disclaiming any connection with Richardson's action.[8]

This rift was only a fraction of the turmoil in Houston that surfaced
after Richardson's death the following month. When NAACP national

THE RISE OF THE NAACP IN TEXAS

office representative Daisy Lampkin arrived in the city in October 1939, she described the branch's situation as "a hornet's nest," and "the worst I have ever seen." The most serious problem involved financial mismanagement by two or three men, who, in Lampkin's words, "have practically made their living off the NAACP." She blamed Richardson and Edward L. Snyder, citing the former's collection of almost $500 to pay for delegates' expenses to Richmond. She reported that Snyder, who as promotional secretary had collected money for a defense fund, had been allowed to pocket 30 percent of his "promotions." Attributing the misconduct partially to the fact that the NAACP branch and the local Negro Chamber of Commerce had the same men as officers, she asserted that "there has been so much stealing and so many irregularities that each man is forced to support the other."[9]

While Daisy Lampkin contemplated resigning from the staff, Walter White considered revoking the Houston branch's charter. Yet Lampkin remained to reorganize the branch, conduct a membership drive, and hold an election of new officers. When she left Houston on November 11, the branch had 1,484 members with a respected minister, Albert A. Lucas, as its new president. Lampkin's reorganization efforts were aided by Richardson's business rival, Carter W. Wesley, and by Lulu B. White. Wesley, who had attended Fisk University and Northwestern University Law School, practiced law with J. Alston Atkins in Oklahoma for five years during the 1920s. After earning a large sum in the Leonard Ingram case involving oil claims, Wesley and Atkins moved to Houston and set up a law firm that included James M. Nabrit Jr. They bought into Richardson's Houston *Informer* and by 1930 had wrested control of the paper from him. After a bitter feud, Richardson withdrew and organized another Houston newspaper, *The Defender*.[10]

Lulu B. White, the Houston branch's acting president after Richardson's death in August 1939, had taken little interest in the NAACP until then. Described by Lampkin as "honest and upright," Lulu White later not only became the driving force behind the Houston chapter, but she also had an enormous impact on the statewide movement.[11]

The Houston chapter was now in a position to rival the Dallas NAACP as Texas's most active branch. With the financial resources of wealthy black businessmen, such as Mack H. Hannah Jr., Hobart T. Taylor Sr., Julius White, and Carter W. Wesley, the Houston branch could generally raise more money than its Dallas counterpart. Yet serious internal strife plagued Houston again and again. Financial mismanagement, the injection of partisan political issues, and conflicts of ideology, strategy, and personality would repeatedly throw the organization into turmoil, requiring intervention by the national office.[12]

The overlapping organizations that Daisy Lampkin thought contributed to the problems in Houston apparently had no adverse effect on the Dallas branch. Ably led by an active group of businessmen and clergy, including Maceo Smith, Maynard H. Jackson, Ernest C. Estell, Charles T. Brackins, and Dr. B. E. Howell, the Dallas NAACP benefited from their affiliations with the Interdenominational Ministerial Alliance, the Negro Chamber of Commerce, and the Progressive Voters League. When the executive committees of these organizations convened, they were practically indistinguishable from each other. On occasion, one meeting would adjourn; the officers would change places, open another set of minute books, and then call to order the meeting of a different organization.[13]

Whatever the auspice, the leadership functioned most often as a political pressure group, presenting grievances to the Dallas City Council and other units of government. In this way, they promoted expansions of educational and recreational facilities, paving of streets, larger salaries, and additional housing projects.[14]

Prior to 1940, the most significant program of the Dallas NAACP was a challenge to the exclusion of blacks from jury service. Following a favorable Supreme Court ruling in one of the Scottsboro cases, the chapter stepped up its activity in the hope of securing a test case. In August 1938, Dr. B. E. Howell, president of the branch, outlined the procedure for blacks to follow when summoned for jury service. He urged them not to disqualify themselves voluntarily, but to take witnesses with them to court. Two months later, an attempt was made by George F. Porter, accompanied by Howell, Reverend Estell, and Charles Graggs. Porter, a sixty-five year old teacher, had previously tried to serve on juries in 1921 and 1936. These earlier efforts had produced a series of hostile threats, including that of lynching, and had ended in Porter's dismissal. When he arrived at the courthouse on September 26, 1938, he was determined to serve. For two days, he sat with the panel of prospective jurors without incident. Then, on September 28, after Porter refused suggestions that he excuse himself, two white men dragged him from the courtroom and threw him down the steps of the building, causing permanent injuries.[15]

Porter's experience dramatized the issue and rallied Dallas NAACP members with an example of courage and sacrifice. It also brought to

Texas for the first time a remarkable black lawyer from the NAACP national office. Thurgood Marshall arrived in Dallas on October 8, 1938, to meet with local branch officials and to conduct an investigation of the Porter incident. Two days later, Judge Paine L. Bush refused to dismiss a juryman named W. I. Dickson. In one court after another, the barriers to jury service were gradually lifted. In 1942, in a case sponsored by the Dallas NAACP, the United States Supreme Court reversed the conviction of Henry Allen Hill on the ground that blacks had been excluded from his jury at the trial level.[16]

By 1940 the leadership of the State Conference was passing from older African Americans to younger officers, many still in their thirties. The first president, Richard D. Evans, was killed in a car-train accident on June 26, 1938, the day before a similar fate befell NAACP national leader James Weldon Johnson. Evans's successor was Clifton F. Richardson, who died only fourteen months after assuming office.[17]

Maceo Smith, who continued to divide his attention among numerous organizations, did not fully devote his considerable energy to the NAACP until after mid-1938. In that year he became employed as the racial relations officer of the Federal Housing Authority. Since the white housing officials did not want to share their new Fort Worth office with a black man, Smith was quartered in a Dallas housing project, assigned a secretary, and allotted travel funds to tour projects throughout the state. Interpreting his assignment liberally, he reasoned that racial relations could be improved by securing equal opportunities for blacks through the work of the NAACP. While Smith's superiors in Washington concurred in his analysis, his white co-workers in Fort Worth were unaware that his Dallas office had become the nerve center for statewide NAACP activity. By conducting a voluminous correspondence with local branch officers and convening frequent executive council meetings, Smith helped to mold a working organization of the state's NAACP leaders. Simultaneously he developed efficient lines of communication with the national office staff. He solicited their advice, informed them of plans and events in Texas, and coordinated the state's NAACP activities with national policies and procedures.[18]

For twenty years, the Texas NAACP branches' most enduring quest had been for the right to vote in the Democratic primary elections. After a series of limited victories and defeats in the 1920s and 1930s, the Association mounted its most determined effort during the election year of 1940.[19] Houston, the center of voting rights activity for the past decade, continued to take the initiative, only to become engulfed by strife. Tied to political, financial, and personal conflicts were three divergent views on how to secure the ballot. One element favored a proposed amendment to the Hatch law eliminating poll tax payment in the election of federal officials. A second faction accepted as the best approach a promise by state Democratic officials to present to the convention a resolution that would open the primary to all loyal Democrats. A third group that included most of the NAACP leadership believed that only a lawsuit would be productive. The most spirited opposition to litigation came from C. W. Rice, E. L. Snyder, W. A. Carr, and other pro-Garner blacks with close ties to the Texas Democratic establishment. Fearful that a Democratic primary suit filed before the party's national convention would embarrass Garner's candidacy by calling attention to discrimination in his home state, they reasoned that such action would result in Texas blacks being excluded from the Democratic convention.[20]

Embarrassing Garner's campaign was also a consideration of Walter White when he suggested, in January 1940, that James M. Nabrit Jr., prepare a "program of action" in Texas. White accurately predicted that the Supreme Court's recent appointees would be more inclined than previous justices to rule against the white primary. Moreover, mindful of the prospect of several hastily prepared suits brought by local branches or independently of the Association, he saw the need for a single case that the NAACP national office "can guide from its very inception to ensure its being properly handled."[21]

In Texas, plans for an Association-supervised suit moved forward while the pro-Garner elements voiced their opposition. In March 1940, various black leaders met in Houston and voted to organize on a statewide basis to raise funds for a primary case. Designating themselves a committee of the Houston NAACP branch until the State Conference could take over the effort at its annual meeting in May, the conferees decided to support the local branch as the sponsor of the suit. Reverend Lucas then called a mass meeting of the Houston chapter the following week to promote plans for litigation. This gathering, held at Olivet Baptist Church and attended by the pro-Garner forces, dramatized the heated rivalries among Bayou City blacks. Carter Wesley seized the opportunity to lambaste the Garnerites, as did Richard R. Grovey, who denounced them as "a sinister force." After efforts to abandon or to postpone the suit were defeated, one of the Garner leaders, Alfonse Mills, whether seeking to disrupt the meeting or simply angered by Wesley's barbs, engaged the publisher in a fistfight. If one is to believe Wesley's subsequent front-page account of the fracas, Mills was "thrashed" and led out of the church "puffing and swelling."[22]

The essential plans for the primary case were formulated at two important meetings later that spring. On May 5 Thurgood Marshall met in Dallas with members of the NAACP State Legal Redress Committee to discuss procedure. The lawyers decided that an announcement of their intention to file suit would precede the Democratic convention. They also agreed that only one case in the state would be prosecuted and that it would be handled under the supervision of the NAACP national office and the Texas State Conference.[23]

In Marshall's opinion, the suit would have to involve some new fact or point of law in order to set it apart from the unsuccessful *Grovey v. Townsend* case, which Carter Wesley and J. Alston Atkins had litigated independently of the NAACP. Marshall later characterized the *Grovey* suit as "one of the biggest mistakes made in the fight for Negroes' rights," for the Court's ruling in 1935 had provided a major precedent for the constitutionality of the white primary. Specifically, the Court had held that the Democratic party was a private association of citizens with the right to determine its own voting membership. So the lawyers in Dallas agreed to search the legislative journals for possible changes in the state law since the *Grovey* decision and to find out about any relevant actions of the Democratic party. After outlining a "defense fund" budget of $8,000, the conferees decided to contact key individuals in various Texas cities to head the fund-raising drive. Attorney William J. Durham of Sherman was appointed resident counsel for the case; his fee was tentatively set at $2,500 plus expenses.[24]

Durham, by 1940, was recognized as the leading black lawyer in Texas. Born on a farm near Sulphur Springs in 1896, he attended Emporia State College in Kansas for one semester.[25] Following military service in France during World War I, he studied law in the office of Bell F. Gafford, a white attorney in Sherman. When Durham passed the Texas bar examination in 1926 after several unsuccessful attempts, he established his practice in Sherman. Despite the fact that a lynch mob in 1930 burned the town's black business district, including his office, he began to take on civil rights cases. Such lawsuits were seldom profitable, but a lucrative practice as legal counsel to an insurance company enabled him to devote part of his time to the struggle for equality. His increasing business ties and NAACP activities in Dallas, together with the wartime shortage of gasoline, caused him to move to Dallas in 1943. There he labored for a quarter of a century until the last years before his death in 1970.[26] He briefed his cases thoroughly before drawing up petitions, and he was particularly adept at pleadings. His skill and diligence he also taught to many young black lawyers who trained under him. Although Durham's irritable temperament and tough money-making instincts made him difficult to get along with, his legal ability and unparalleled dedication in his work made him virtually indispensable to the civil rights movement in Texas.[27]

Several days after the Dallas gathering, Marshall and members of the legal Redress Committee drove to Corpus Christi to present their plans to 1,200 NAACP delegates at the annual meeting of the State Conference. Held at the First Congregational Church on May 10, 11, and 12, the meeting provided a forum for further groundwork on the white primary suit. A fund-raising drive was organized, and each branch was assigned a quota toward the $8,000 goal. Marshall addressed the delegates, promising that the national office would maintain control over the suit. This assurance, he believed, was crucial to bring Texas blacks together after the disheartening defeat in *Grovey v. Townsend*.[28]

The significance of the historic Corpus Christi meeting extended well beyond the white primary case. A new fervor and vision pervaded the State Conference as the delegates defined their goals for the next decade. In addition to challenging the white primary, they also resolved to achieve educational equality and to mount an attack on the entire system of segregation. Not only did the Corpus meeting mark the rise of the movement in Texas, but this fact was immediately apparent to its leaders. Calling the session "the greatest in the history of our State Conference," A. Maceo Smith reported to Walter White that "we laid plans that will realize for the Negroes of Texas a new era in the fight for civil rights." To Marshall, it seemed that the State Conference had been just barely existing since its organization, but "now this Texas group will really go to town." He reassured White that despite any views to the contrary about African Americans in the South, blacks in Texas "are not afraid to fight for their rights."[29]

Fund-raising for the primary case began auspiciously. In the first week, San Antonio raised $300 of its $1,000 goal. Houston followed by pledging $1,000 of its $1,600. Pledges began to exceed actual contributions, however, and by July 1941, only $2,500 of the $8,000 goal had been collected. San Antonio was the only branch to reach its quota. In October 1941, a printing bill of $421 caused Maceo Smith to issue an urgent appeal for contributions. The crisis was averted when Lucas, Wesley, Durham, and Smith contributed most of the money themselves. They also continued to tap the resources of wealthy Texas African Americans, for, as Marshall reported to the national office, "there is really money down there." Even so, the $8,000 goal was never reached. Moreover, the dependence on large contributions from a few individuals reflected a lack of the widespread participation that would later characterize the movement's fund-raising endeavors.[30]

Fortunately, there was no comparable shortage of plaintiffs for the lawsuit. Maceo Smith and other NAACP officials initially decided on Clifton F. Richardson Jr., who had succeeded his father as publisher of *The Defender*. The choice of Richardson as plaintiff infuriated Carter Wesley, who could not reconcile himself to giving "large blotches of publicity to a competitor." After Wesley declared that his *Informer* chain would carry no publicity on the primary suit, Reverend Lucas designated two other plaintiffs. Dr. Lonnie E. Smith, a Houston dentist, went to the county clerk's office on July 15 and requested an absentee ballot for the Democratic primary election on July 27. He was turned away. On the latter date, Sidney Hasgett, a hod carrier, went to the polls to vote, and he was also refused a ballot. Lucas announced that these voting attempts had been made at his direction for the purpose of laying a predicate for a lawsuit. Yet the suit was not filed immediately. The attorneys decided to wait until after an additional attempt had been made on August 24, the date of the run-off primary, so the applicants would have been refused in both primary elections. On the latter date Hasgett, accompanied by a delegation that included Richard R. Grovey, Carter Wesley, and Julius White, presented his poll tax receipt and again requested to vote. Again he was denied a ballot. On Hasgett's behalf the subsequent suit was filed in the United States District Court on January 14, 1941, by Henry S. Davis, a black attorney for the Houston branch. The petition requested a declaratory judgment and $5,000 in damages for the election judges' refusal to permit Hasgett to vote in the Democratic run-off primary on August 24. When the case was tried in the federal district court on April 25, 1941, Marshall and Durham represented the plaintiff. Two weeks later, T. M. Kennerly, the presiding judge, ruled against Hasgett, while offering his own opinion that the democrats' action was invalid. Predictably the case was appealed by the NAACP. The hearing was scheduled for November 1941.[31]

In the interim two crucial factors substantially altered the course of the litigation. In May, 1941, the United States Supreme Court, in *United States v. Classic*, reversed its traditional interpretation of primary elections. Although the case involved corrupt election practices in Louisiana rather than the question of black voting, it contained important implications for the latter. The court ruled that the primary election had become so much a part of the whole electoral process that it could no longer be considered merely a private matter, the standard rationale for excluding blacks. Thus, without a single reference to *Grovey v. Townsend*, the high court in effect reversed it. This decision vastly improved the prospects for victory in a white primary case, but the NAACP lawyers later discovered a serious weakness in the Hasgett suit. Although *Hasgett v. Werner* challenged the exclusion of African Americans from primary elections in which federal as well as state offices were involved, the petition was drawn to apply to the August 24 run-off primary. Yet all of the federal nominations had been determined in the earlier election on July 27. After realizing this discrepancy, the NAACP lawyers decided to abandon the case shortly before its scheduled hearing in the Circuit Court of Appeals in November, 1941.[32]

Now the attorneys had to decide whether to file a new suit based on the July 27 primary or wait until the 1942 election. They concluded that a year's delay would retard the movement in Texas, whereas a case filed immediately might receive a favorable decision before the next election. Nonetheless, Marshall's task of justifying to Texas leaders the dropping of the *Hasgett* case was none too pleasant. His arrival in Dallas on November 5 was preceded by criticism from members of the local branch about his "messing up the case." He spent most of his first day in the city defending his actions. He stressed the difficulties in the case and the advantages in filing another suit.[33]

The next step was to find another plaintiff. The Dallas branch had also sponsored a voting attempt in 1940 and had also been refused. After the leaders assured Marshall that they had a good plaintiff, a new complaint was drafted. Yet the prospective plaintiff, when consulted, could not remember whether he had attempted to vote in the first primary or the run-off primary. A check of the Dallas newspapers revealed it had been the latter. In Marshall's words, "we were right back where we started—out in the street."[34]

From Dallas, Marshall traveled to Houston where he faced additional criticism. The truculent Julius White warned him that he had better win the next case or not return to Texas. Fortunately, the Houston branch still had another prospective plaintiff in Lonnie Smith, since he had attempted to vote in both primaries. Marshall conferred with Smith, checked out his story, drafted a complaint, and filed a new suit. From that point *Smith v. Allwright* began its route to the United States Supreme Court, despite attempts by district court officials to delay the process. Marshall and William Hastie argued the case for the plaintiff before the nine justices on November 10 and 12, 1943, and again on January 12, 1944. In the decision, handed down on April 3, 1944, the Court outlawed the white primary. Subsequent suits were ultimately required to overcome further stratagems of voting discrimination, such as Fort Bend County's Jaybird primary.[35]

Lulu B. White, executive secretary of the Houston branch, heralded "the *Smith v. Allwright* decision as the second emancipation of the Negro." For Mrs. White, the court's ruling also had propitious timing, since she was then engaged in a vigorous membership drive that would make the Houston NAACP the largest chapter in the South. From only a few hundred members in the late 1930s the Houston branch grew to 5,679 members in 1943, then doubled to more than 12,000 by 1945. The State Conference, which ranked as second largest in the nation, expanded from 36 branches to 104, with 23,000 members, during the same period, and averaged almost 30,000 during the postwar years until 1949. Yet the numbers are somewhat misleading. Although the total membership was overwhelmingly urban, most of the branches were in small rural communities and consisted of only a few members. Many of these units were dormant or only sporadically active. In virtually every branch a large majority of the members did nothing other than pay annual dues of a dollar. They did not attend meetings or participate in the Association's activities.[36]

Even so, the wartime growth represented tremendous progress. It reflected not only the aggressive fieldwork involved in visiting African American communities throughout the state but also the organization's greater appeal among black Texans. Moreover, the expansion increased the Association's financial resources and was accompanied by an influx of active new leaders at the branch level.

An assortment of factors contributed to the NAACP's phenomenal growth. Improved economic conditions with almost full employment meant that more blacks could afford to contribute to such causes. The war itself generated a spirit of awareness and militancy among African Americans. If they had an obligation to battle totalitarianism abroad, they should also fight racism at home. Another principal factor was the white primary case itself. In 1940 Marshall had accurately predicted that it would be the means of building up the NAACP in Texas. Not only did the case give the organization an issue with which to rally

Texas African Americans, but the victory provided ample proof of the NAACP's effectiveness.[37]

When the *Smith* suit was filed, the national office agreed to assume financial responsibility for the case, enabling the State Conference to concentrate on enlarging its base. Maceo Smith recognized that soliciting memberships rather than contributions to specific cases was the best way to develop a sustained program. Following this strategy, the State Conference focused on the addition of new branches and the expansion of existing ones. Charles Deo of Lubbock helped to create a number of new chapters in the western part of the state, as did H. M. Morgan of Tyler in East Texas. Smith himself, when touring federal housing projects around the state, took the opportunity to establish NAACP branches along the way. Reverend J. A. Gilliam, a white minister, who had done fieldwork for the NAACP in Oklahoma, was retained by the Texas State Conference for similar activity. Although he organized thirty-four new branches, his services were discontinued in 1945. His health was failing, and the State Conference leaders realized that the financial arrangement allowing Gilliam to receive a portion of each membership fee collected was contrary to the NAACP's national constitution.[38]

The two most successful fieldworkers were Lulu White of Houston and Juanita Craft of Dallas. In late 1946 they were officially designated for the jobs in which they were experienced and able. White was elected director of branches; Craft was appointed state organizer. Working under the direction of Smith as executive secretary, these two remarkable women traveled from town to town, covering most of the state. Whether they went together in Lulu White's car (as they sometimes did) or separately, they were immensely effective in garnering contributions, organizing new branches, and reactivating old ones. Both of these vibrant women were tireless workers, forceful speakers, and superb recruiters for the NAACP.[39]

Lulu B. Madison was born in Elmo, Texas, circa 1900. She attended Butler College and Prairie View A&M, where she received training as a teacher. Her husband, Julius White, had been a long-standing member of the Houston NAACP and had served as the plaintiff in several white primary cases. His business prosperity was such that his wife, not having to supplement his income, could devote her time to the NAACP. As executive secretary of the Houston branch from 1943 until 1949, she became its leading spokesman and omnipresent representative. When local African Americans "reported instances of discrimination,

Lulu White was the one who responded. She developed close friend-ships with Walter White, Daisy Lampkin, Thurgood Marshall, and Roy Wilkins. Like Maceo Smith, she exerted considerable influence on the Association at the national level. Her contribution in Texas, many of her colleagues believe, was second only to that of Smith. Her political radicalism and unconcealed defiance of discrimination were tempered by her cheerfulness and implacable optimism. More than any other in-dividual, Lulu White symbolized the spirit of the civil rights move-ment in Texas.[40]

In Dallas, Juanita Craft read about Lulu White's NAACP activities. After participating in a local membership drive in 1942, she traveled to Houston to meet Mrs. White and work with her. The two quickly be-came allies and went to Chicago in 1944 to attend the NAACP national convention. In the following year Craft directed a massive membership campaign for the Dallas branch, which expanded its membership to 7,000 by 1946. While serving as state organizer, she took on the addi-tional responsibility of director of youth councils in 1947.[41]

Craft's procedure was to write to individuals interested in establish-ing an NAACP chapter in their community. She instructed them to or-ganize a nucleus of prospective members and discuss the objectives of the Association. When fifty people had agreed to join, the group applied for an NAACP charter. They launched the organization with a well-publicized mass meeting, at which Craft was the main speaker. She then traveled to the next community to organize or reactivate another branch. Her visit was "like a blood transfusion to a very weak patient," one local leader reported.[42]

Other events and individuals helped to spark the movement. When the NAACP held its 1941 national convention in Houston, a host of prominent civil rights personalities invaded the city. If the gathering, with its accompanying publicity, stimulated local and statewide inter-est in the Association, the almost simultaneous murder of an NAACP-sponsored defendant in a Conroe courtroom dramatized the need for it. Walter White conducted a well-publicized tour of Texas in 1942. Daisy Lampkin, described by one branch official as "America's great cam-paigner," often participated in the state's annual membership drives, and her presence seemed to guarantee their success.[43] As the most fre-quent visitor from the NAACP national office, Thurgood Marshall, too, played a key role in generating popular support during his numerous trips to Texas for legal strategy sessions and court proceedings.

A succession of respected State Conference presidents in the 1940s increased the organization's prestige. Reverend Lucas, who had helped revive the Houston branch after 1939, was elected state president in 1940. Believing that "prayer without action isn't worth a dip of Scott's snuff," Lucas provided two years of firm leadership. He was succeeded by C. Austin Whittier, a prominent San Antonio physician. John J. Jones, a wealthy Texarkana funeral director elected in 1943, presided for a full decade. Yet each president relied greatly on the services of A. Maceo Smith, Lulu White, and William J. Durham. As the three central figures in the State Conference, they were so vital to the movement that to imagine the organization without them is difficult.[44]

The NAACP leaders in Texas came primarily from the professional class. They were ministers, dentists, executives in black business, housewives, lawyers, labor leaders, and doctors. Although generally not the most affluent blacks in the state, they were successful in business. Their prosperity depended on the support and patronage of the black community, but they were financially independent of whites. For example, black teachers participated to a far lesser extent than other educated groups. Vulnerable to the whims of local school boards, they feared that NAACP affiliation would cost them their jobs, which it sometimes did. By contributing substantial funds through the Colored Teachers State Association and other organizations, they did aid the NAACP's successful lawsuits to equalize teachers' salaries. But few teachers assumed leadership roles, and in 1947, Lulu White contended that "Negro teachers are our biggest foe." Notable exceptions included John H. Clouser, a Galveston teacher, who served as the State Conference's trusted treasurer for more than a decade. Educators at the private college level, particularly men like Dr. Joseph J. Rhoads and James H. Morton, were considerably more active than their counterparts in public secondary and elementary schools.[45]

Appropriately, black ministers constituted a large portion of the leadership of a movement that had a religious tenor. In 1943, for example, nearly seventy-five churches cooperated with a local membership drive conducted by the Houston branch. NAACP meetings, frequently held in churches, were seasoned with prayer, preaching, and hymn-singing. In fact, the entire organization took on a revivalist spirit.[46]

Their political differences have been noted above, although by 1940 many of the leaders had become Franklin D. Roosevelt Democrats. While some later adhered to the state's more conservative Democratic organization, others took up the banner of Henry Wallace in 1948.[47]

Virtually all joined in civic activities besides the NAACP, such as voter registration drives, YMCA, and the Negro Chamber of Commerce. Prominence in the movement automatically brought threats, especially malicious telephone calls, on a regular basis. Yet the recipients were not noticeably embittered, anti-white, or humorless.

Although the significant leaders of the movement number only about forty, most were active for many years. Those who emerged with the State Conference in the late 1930s and early 1940s continued to direct its affairs until the mid 1950s. Maceo Smith, Thurgood Marshall, William J. Durham, Lulu White, Carter Wesley, and other veterans of the white primary litigation were the same activists who subsequently, in 1945, planned a successful lawsuit against the segregated University of Texas.[48] Their long-term commitment to the NAACP's civil rights agenda and their organizational achievements through the Texas State Conference enabled them to overturn much of the state's legal framework of discrimination and segregation.

Notes

1. The NAACP branches in Texas were chartered during the second decade of the twentieth century. After a period of activism, during the 1920s, the organization had declined by the early 1930s. Robert Bagnall to G. F. Porter, February 6, 1923, NAACP Papers (Library of Congress, Washington, D.C.), Box G-201; William Pickens to G. Duke Crawford, July 5, 1935, ibid., Box G-203; C. F. Richardson to Juanita Jackson, February 27, 1937, ibid., Box G-204.

2. Thurgood Marshall to M. L. G., October 31, 1974, interview. Numerous statements regarding Smith's role in the Texas State Conference are printed in its *Twentieth Anniversary Souvenir Booklet* (1956). Thurgood Marshall wrote that Smith's "best training is in the field of business and everything he undertakes is done in a business like manner based on thorough organization." Thurgood Marshall to Walter White, April 8, 1939, NAACP Papers, Box G-201.

3. A biographical sketch of Smith appears in the Texas State Conference, *Twentieth Anniversary Souvenir Booklet* (1956); A. Maceo Smith to M. L. G., March 23, July 21, 1973; February 15, 1975, interviews; *Dallas Express*, April 4, 1936; December 3, 1938; *Informer* (Houston), January 18, 1941; Marshall to White, April 8, 1939, NAACP Papers, Box G-201; Jesse O. Thomas, *Negro Participation in the Texas Centennial Exposition* (Boston, 1938); Dallas *Morning News*, May 3, 1973.

4. *Informer* (Houston), October 5, 1935.

5. Jackson to White, April 22, 1937 (first, second, third, and fourth quotations); Roscoe Dunjee to White, June 9, 1937 (sixth quotation), NAACP Papers, Box G-200; Smith to Dickens, June 1, 1937 (fifth quotation), ibid., Box G-201.

6. Resolutions-State Conference of Branches, Dallas, Texas, June 19, 1937 (quotation); Minutes of the Texas State Conference of Branches, NAACP, June 18, 19, 1937, NAACP Papers, Box G-200. A formal State Conference constitution and by-laws were adopted in 1940. NAACP Papers, Unprocessed Files.

7. The ten branches were Beaumont, Dallas, El Paso, Fort Worth, Houston, Galveston, Guadalupe County, Tyler, San Antonio, Waxahachie. Edward L. Snyder to White, September 7, 1939; Fred Morrow to Richardson, June 9, 1939, NAACP Papers, Box G-200.

8. Unsigned memorandum to Walter White re: NAACP Meeting in the South, September 5, 1939; Sidney Hasgett and others to White, August 15, 1939, NAACP Papers, Box G-204.

9. Daisy Lampkin to White, October 30 (first, second, third, and fourth quotations), November 6, 1939 (fifth quotation), NAACP Papers, Box G-204.

10. Lampkin to White, November 6, 1939; White to Lampkin, November 15, 1939, NAACP Papers, Box G-204; *Informer* (Houston), April 20, 1940; James M. Nabrit Jr. to M. L. G., November 1, 1974, interview; Charles William Grose, "Black Newspapers in Texas, 1868–1970" (Ph.D. dissertation; University of Texas, Austin, 1972), 170.

11. Lampkin to White, October 30, 1939, NAACP Papers, Box G-204.

12. Marshall to M. L. G., October 31, 1974, interview; Carter W. Wesley to Local Branch, NAACP, January 17, 1947; Donald Jones to Gloster Current, July 15, 1950, NAACP Papers, Unprocessed Files.

13. Smith to M. L. G., January 15, 1975, interview.

14. "Dallas Negro Chamber of Commerce, Reviewing 1939," NAACP Papers, Unprocessed Files.

15. *Dallas Express*, July 30, August 13, October 1, 8, 1938. In the second Scottsboro case, *Norris v. Alabama*, the United States Supreme Court overturned the conviction of nine young Alabama African Americans accused of rape because blacks had been habitually prohibited from jury service, *Norris v. Alabama*, 294 U.S. 587 (1935).

16. *Dallas Express*, October 8, 15, 1938; Marshall to M. L. G., October 31, 1974, interview; *Informer* (Houston), June 6, 1942.

17. *Dallas Express*, July 2, 1938; *Informer* (Houston), September 2, 1939.

18. White to Lampkin, November 2, 1939, NAACP Papers, Box G-204; Smith to M. L. G., February 15, 1975, interview.

19. Histories of the white primary include the following: Robert Wendell Hainsworth, "The Negro and the Texas Primaries," *The Journal of Negro History*,

XVVII (October, 1933), 426–450; Thurgood Marshall, "The Rise and Collapse of the 'White Democratic Primary,'" *Journal of Negro Education*, XXVI (Summer, 1957), 249–254; Carter W. Wesley, "Texans Seek Right to Vote," *The Crisis*, XLVII (October, 1940), 312–313, 322; Walter Lindsey, "Black Houstonians Challenge the White Democratic Primary, 1921–1944" (M.A. thesis; University of Houston, 1969); Conrey Bryson, *Dr. Lawrence A. Nixon and the White Primary* (El Paso, 1974); Darlene Clark Hine, "The NAACP and the Destruction of the Democratic White Primary, 1924–1944" (Ph.D. dissertation; Kent State University, 1975); Melvin James Banks, "The Pursuit of Equality: The Movement for First Class Citizenship among Negroes in Texas, 1920–1950" (Ph.D. dissertation; Syracuse University, 1962).

20. Smith to White, March 23, 1940, NAACP Papers, Unprocessed Files; *Informer* (Houston), March 30, 1940.

21. White to William H. Hastie, January 15, 1940 (quotations), NAACP Papers, Unprocessed Files; Wesley, "Texans Seek Right to Vote," 313, 322.

22. *Informer* (Houston), March 16, 23, 30 (quotations), 1940.

23. Minutes of the State Legal Redress Committee, May 5, 1940, NAACP Papers, Unprocessed Files.

24. Ibid. (second quotation); Marshall to Wesley, December 27, 1946 (first quotation), NAACP Papers, Unprocessed Files; *Grovey v. Townsend*, 295 U.S. 45 (1935).

25. The facts of Durham's early life are uncertain. The records of Emporia State College indicate that he was born in April 1896, graduated from high school in 1915, and attended Emporia State College for one semester in the fall of 1917. In later life, Durham contended that the year of his birth was 1904 (which is unlikely since he served in World War I) and that he graduated from the University of Kansas Law School. That institution has no record of his attendance. W. J. Durham to the Board of Legal Examiners, December 1, 1924, State Bar of Texas Files; Francis H. Heller to M. L. G., June 14, 1973.

26. Sherman *Daily Democrat*, May 11, 1930; Ben N. Ramey to M. L. G., July 27, 1973, interview; *Informer* (Houston), May 9, 1942; Durham to John Britton, May 1, 1968, interview, the Civil Rights Documentation Project (Howard University); Dallas *Morning News*, December 25, 1970. Durham's account of the Sherman riot appears in a letter. Durham to Smith, January 17, 1940, NAACP Papers, Unprocessed Files.

27. Harry M. Bellinger to M. L. G., May 27, 1974, interview; C. B. Bunkley Jr. to M. L. G., March 23, 1973, interview; Marshall to M. L. G., October 31, 1974, interview; Nabrit to M. L. G., November 1, 1979, interview; Ramey to M. L. G., July 27, 28, 1973, interviews; Thumas Dent to M. L. G., June 9, 1974, interview; Francis Williams to M. L. G., October 20, 1975, interview.

28. Official Program of the Fourth Annual Session of the Texas Conference of Branches, NAACP, Corpus Christi, Texas, May 10–12, 1940, NAACP Papers, Un-

processed Files; Marshall to White, May 14, 1940, ibid.; *The Crisis*, XLVII (July, 1940), 222.

29. Banks, "Pursuit of Equality," 189–192; Smith to M. L. G., March 23, 1973, interview; Report of Committee on Resolutions of the State Conference of Branches, NAACP, Corpus Christi, Texas, May 11, 1940, NAACP Papers, Unprocessed Files; Smith to White, May 18, 1940 (first and second quotations); Marshall to White, May 14, 1940 (third and fourth quotations), ibid.

30. *Informer* (Houston), August 10, 1940; July 26, October 11, 1941; June 6, 1942; Marshall to White, May 14, 1940 (quotations), NAACP Papers, Unprocessed Files. The wider participation, for instance, enabled the Texas State Conference in 1945 to raise more than $7,000 to finance a lawsuit against the segregated University of Texas, *Informer* (Houston), February 12, 1946.

31. Wesley to Marshall, June 4 (quotation), July 20, September 11, 1940; Wesley to Durham, August 14, 26, 1940, NAACP Papers, Unprocessed Files; *Informer* (Houston), August 10, 1940; January 18, April 26, May 10, November 22, 1941; Wesley, "Texans Seek Right to Vote," 313; Complaint, *Sidney Hasgett v. Theodore Werner and John H. Blackburn*, Civil Docket No. 449, in the United States District Court for the Southern District of Texas, Houston Division, January 14, 1941 (Regional Federal Records Center, Fort Worth).

32. *United States v. Classic et al.*, 313 U.S. 299 (1941); Marshall, "The Rise and Collapse of the 'White Primary,'" 249–254; *Informer* (Houston), November 15, 22, 1941; Marshall to M. L. G., October 31, 1974, interview.

33. Marshall to office, November 17, 1941, NAACP Papers, Unprocessed Files (quotation); *Informer* (Houston), November 22, 1941.

34. Marshall to office, November 17, 1941.

35. Marshall to M. L. G., October 31, 1974, interview; Marshall to office, November 17, 1941; Lulu B. White to Roy Wilkins, July 26, 1948, NAACP Papers, Unprocessed Files; *Smith v. Allwright, Election Judge et al.*, 321 U.S. 649 (1944); *Terry et al. v. Adams et al.*, 345 U.S. 461 (1952); Lindsey, "Black Houstonians Challenge the White Democratic Primary," 76–78; *Informer* (Houston), January 15, 1944.

36. *Informer* (Houston), April 8 (quotation), December 23, 30, 1944; Lulu B. White to Walter White, April 13, 1943; Memorandum, Financing the Regional Offices, December 17, 1946, NAACP Papers, Unprocessed Files; H. M. Morgan to Donald Jones, in *Negro Labor News* (Houston), November 15, 1947; Juanita Craft to M. L. G., May 26, 1973, interview.

37. Address to Louis T. Wright at the 38th Annual Conference of NAACP, Washington, D. C., June 21, 1941; Marshall to White, May 14, 1940, NAACP Papers, Unprocessed Files. A theme of the NAACP's Wartime Conference was "NAACP: For Freedom at Home and Abroad."

38. Marshall to office, November 17, 1941; Minutes of Texas NAACP Board Meeting held in connection with the Regional Leadership Training Institute, Fort Worth, Texas, October 7, 1945; Wesley to Smith, June 11, 1945, NAACP Papers, Unprocessed Files; Smith to M. L. G., February 15, 1975, interview.

39. Smith to M. L. G., March 23, 1973, interview; John H. Clouser to M. L. G., July 28, 1973, interview; Sid Hilliard to M. L. G., June 9, 1973, interview; Moses and Erma LeRoy to M. L. G., June 9, 1973, interview; George T. Nelson to M. L. G., July 15, 1973, interview; Ben and May Ramey to M. L. G., July 28, 1973, interview.

40. Nabrit to M. L. G., November 1, 1974, interview; Heman M. Sweatt to M. L. G., February 10, 1973, interview; Moses and Erma LeRoy to M. L. G., June 9, 1973, interview; Marshall to M. L. G., October 31, 1974, interview; Juanita Craft to M. L. G., May 26, 1973, interview; Clouser to M. L. G., July 28, 1973, interview; Ben and May Ramey to M. L. G., July 28, 1973, interview; Hainsworth, "The Negro and the Texas Primaries," 434, 446; *Informer* (Houston), February 12, December 9, 1944; July 13, 1957.

41. Craft to M. L. G., May 26, 1973, interview; *Informer* (Houston), July 8, 1944; Dallas NAACP Branch Minute Books for 1942, Juanita Craft Papers (Archives, University of Texas, Austin); G. F. Porter to Roy Wilkins, March 1, 1946, NAACP Papers, Unprocessed Files; *Dallas Express*, January 20, 1945. Craft was appointed state organizer in November 1946, and director of youth councils in September 1947. Juanita Craft to Carolyn Mitchell, October 29, 1947; Smith to Craft, October 9, 1947, Juanita Craft Papers.

42. Craft to Smith, May 31, 1949; Craft to J. R. Farris, November 25, 1947; Craft to John W. Sykes, May 2, 1947; Donald Jones to Mrs. Dorothy Robinson, June 3, 1948 (quotation), Juanita Craft Papers.

43. *Informer* (Houston), June 21, 1941; G. F. Porter to Roy Wilkins, March 1, 1946 (quotation), NAACP Papers, Unprocessed Files. After his visit, Walter White wrote: "If the spirit I encountered in Texas is at all an indication, I believe your goal of 100,000 members in Texas is not unobtainable." White to Smith, March 12, 1942, ibid.

44. *Informer* (Houston), June 6, 1942 (quotation); Texas State Conference of Branches, NAACP, Minutes of Annual Meeting, Houston, Texas, June 19–20, 1943, NAACP Papers, Unprocessed Files; Marshall to M. L. G., October 31, 1974, interview.

45. Clouser to M. L. G., July 28, 1973, interview; Donald Jones to Walter White, April 9, 1945; Smith to A. T. Atkinson, November 18, 1948; Lulu White to Marshall, rec'd. November 24, 1947 (quotation), NAACP Papers, Unprocessed Files; Craft to M. L. G., May 26, 1973, interview.

46. Daisy Lampkin to Walter White, April 10, 1943, NAACP Papers, Un-

processed Files. For a discussion of ministers' role in the NAACP, see Minutes of the Eleventh Annual Meeting of the Texas NAACP, Denison, Texas, September 5–7, 1947, Juanita Craft Papers.

47. Minutes of the Committee to Get Wallace on the Ballot in Texas, Files of National Alliance of Postal Employees, Houston; *Negro Labor News* (Houston), March 13, 1948.

48. *Sweatt v. Painter et al.*, 339 U.S. 629 (1950); Smith to Marshall, April 9, 1945, NAACP Papers, Unprocessed Files.

The Elusive Ballot

The Black Struggle against the
Texas Democratic White Primary, 1932–1945

DARLENE CLARK HINE

While Michael Gillette explicates the role of the NAACP in challenging the Democratic white primary, Darlene Clark Hine meticulously depicts the struggle of individual black Texans against the white-only primaries of the Democratic party in order to acquire for themselves that "elusive ballot." As Hine puts it, "the black quest for the elusive ballot reveals the many ways in which local politicians can negate laws and Supreme Court decisions" (296). Such a struggle included internal challenges—acquiring financial support, choosing the right person and the right case, gaining the right combination of attorneys, and keeping supporters continuously involved. Hine looks not only at the backgrounds of the major court challenges—Nixon v. Herndon (1927), Nixon v. Condon (1932), Grovey v. Townsend (1935), Smith v. Allwright (1944), and Terry v. Adams (1952)—but also at changing white tactics and the concomitant black strategies for overcoming white truculence. It was a long struggle, beginning even before the Texas legislature passed a law mandating a Democratic white primary in 1923 to the last primary case in 1952. Hine focuses her inquiry on the special effort taken by black Texans and their allies during the years after the second Nixon case in 1932 to the conclusion of the Smith case in 1945.

*

WHILE THE MAJORITY of Americans sought relief from the miseries of the Great Depression and riveted their hopes for a better future on President Franklin D. Roosevelt and the New Deal, black Texans viewed with increasing dismay the seemingly endless repertoire of disfranchisement schemes white Texas Democrats devised to render them politically impotent. The Democratic white primary as used in Texas was one of the most blatantly discriminatory and, perhaps, most effective techniques employed to keep blacks from voting. In response to and in spite of a black frontal assault on the political system, the Texas white primary received the sanction of the United States Supreme

Court, the United States Department of Justice, and the Division of Investigation (later known as the Federal Bureau of Investigation). On the state level, the attorney general of Texas defended and the Texas Supreme Court upheld the white primary against the frequent attacks of black lawyers, citizens, and the National Association for the Advancement of Colored People (NAACP). By employing a variety of techniques, Texas white politicians on the state and county levels were able to nullify the Supreme Court decisions of 1927 and 1932 that had seemed to benefit the cause of the black voters.[1]

For black Texans the thirties represented no political New Deal. Efforts to gain access to the political system met with frustration and repeated failure. The political ostracism of blacks in Texas was, in a larger view, but one example of the general legal and social plight of black southerners.

After the Civil War and the adoption of the Fourteenth and Fifteenth Amendments, blacks armed with the ballot gained access to political positions and became actively involved in political affairs in Texas. In the 1870s and 1880s, as Reconstruction concluded, whites in the black belt counties of East Texas organized clubs, unions, and associations for the express purpose of ousting blacks from local, county, and state politics. These groups, formed under the banner of the Democratic party, restricted membership to white citizens. They usually held primary elections to select Democratic candidates who then ran without opposition in the fall general elections. During the next quarter century, through fraud, intimidation, and murder, white Democrats in counties such as Grimes, Wharton, Fort Bend, and Harrison achieved their objective, and the political complexion of those counties where blacks were in the numerical majority or, at least, represented sizeable proportions of the total population changed as blacks were eliminated from the political system. By the turn of the century, Texas was a one-party state with the Democratic party reigning supreme. The practice of holding primaries, begun on the local level, had become a statewide phenomenon, and nomination in the Democratic primary was tantamount to election. The general election was little more than a formal acknowledgment of the results of the primary. Therefore, to be excluded from participation in the primaries, where the important decisions were made, constituted disfranchisement.[2]

In an effort to make Texas politics as white as possible, a poll tax amendment was added to the state's constitution in 1902. This measure, however, did not completely eradicate the black vote. In 1903, at the urging of Travis County representative, Alexander W. Terrell, the state legislature adopted a mandatory primary statute. Terrell argued that the adoption of such a measure would ensure against selling of votes. In 1905 the legislature amended the statute to permit county Democratic Executive Committee chairmen to establish voting qualifications. Although the statutes did not mention blacks specifically, it was implicitly understood that blacks would be barred from voting in the party's primaries. Because white Democrats never unanimously agreed upon the effective enforceability of this method of black disfranchisement, many county executive committee chairmen were opposed to the proscription, and white candidates continued to solicit the black vote. The uncertainty surrounding the issue created a climate in which various factions and personalities within the Democratic party intensified agitation for universal black disfranchisement and a law that would remove the question from the political arena altogether.[3]

As a result of pressure from local whites in Bexar County—particularly from the district attorney, D. A. McAskill (who proclaimed that the black vote had to be annihilated because of the degree to which it was manipulated by unscrupulous white and black politicians), with the combined support of prohibitionists and probably many Ku Klux Klan members—the Texas state legislature in 1923 enacted a law that declared: "In no event shall a negro be eligible to participate in a Democratic party primary election held in the State of Texas, and should a negro vote in a Democratic primary election, such ballot shall be void and election officials shall not count the same." Lawrence A. Nixon, a black El Paso dentist, and L. W. Washington, the local El Paso branch president of the NAACP, contacted the national NAACP headquarters in New York and requested assistance to launch a campaign to have the law declared unconstitutional.[4]

Nixon, a fourteen-year resident of El Paso, was born in Marshall, Texas, in 1884. He received his medical training at Meharry Medical College in Nashville, Tennessee, and established his dental practice in El Paso in 1910. Until the 1923 white primary statute, Nixon had regularly voted in Democratic primary and general elections. He agreed to serve as the plaintiff in legal action against the white primary. Washington quickly mobilized the members of the local El Paso NAACP branch to raise funds and financially support the suit. They retained white attorney Fred C. Knollenberg to handle the case on the state level. Under the close supervision of NAACP Legal Committee chairman, Arthur B. Spingarn; the association's president, Moorfield

Storey; and the organization's superb attorney, Louis Marshall; Knollenberg laid the groundwork for the first two white primary cases. The Supreme Court decisions in these two cases seemed to bode well for Texas blacks. In the first case, *Nixon v. Herndon* (1927), the United States Supreme Court in a unanimous decision delivered by Justice Oliver Wendell Holmes declared the Texas statute unconstitutional and a violation of the Fourteenth Amendment. The court found the state of Texas guilty of using its authority to deny blacks ". . . the equal protection of the laws."[5] In sum, the state of Texas could not enact a law barring blacks from participation in Democratic primary elections. However, the question of whether or not blacks could vote in primary elections in the absence of a state law remained unanswered.

Undaunted, the Texas state legislature repealed the offending statute and granted the executive committee of the Democratic party the power to prescribe membership qualifications and voting requirements for its primaries. The executive committee, as expected, declared that only whites could vote in the primaries.[6] The NAACP, again using Nixon as plaintiff, filed another suit to contest this latest action. In the second case, *Nixon v. Condon* (1932), Supreme Court Justice Benjamin Cardozo wrote the majority opinion in a five to four decision. The court held that the state of Texas had simply delegated its responsibility and authority to a quasi-public body and that the action taken by the executive committee was merely an extension of the power of the state. "Delegates to the State's power have discharged their official functions in such a way as to discriminate invidiously between white citizens and black" and in so doing had again abridged the Fourteenth Amendment. The court continued, "The Fourteenth Amendment, adopted as it was with special solicitude for the equal protection of members of the Negro race, lays a duty upon the court to level by its judgment these barriers of color."[7]

The national officers of the NAACP and black Texans were ecstatic about the decision, but white attorney Nathan Margold, who had argued the NAACP case before the Supreme Court, expressed dissatisfaction and advised caution. Although the decision in the particular case had been favorable to the plaintiff, Cardozo had implied that a Texas Democratic Party Convention, as the truly representative body of the Democratic party in the state of Texas, could determine qualifications for voting, even though the executive committee could not. Margold's fears were justified. White Texas Democrats quickly took advantage of the limitations of the decision and devised a new strategy to accomplish black disfranchisement, which would not bruise the constitutional sensibilities of the Supreme Court judges. The chairman of the Harris County Democratic Executive Committee and editor of the Houston *Chronicle*, W. O. Huggins, presented a disfranchisement plan on May 24, 1932, at the annual meeting of the state Democratic Convention. The Huggins Plan, as it was named, called for the repeal of the resolution of the state Democratic Executive Committee and the adoption by the state convention of a new restrictive measure. He convinced his fellow Democrats that the Supreme Court would not rule that the state convention was an agency of the state of Texas and, therefore, any resolution adopted would not be viewed as originating in the mandate of the law. The convention, thus persuaded, adopted the resolution: "Be it resolved that all white citizens of the State of Texas who are qualified to vote under the constitution and laws of the state shall be eligible to membership in the Democratic party and as such to participate in its deliberations."[8]

Black leaders of the Harris County Democratic Club, attorneys James M. Nabrit and Carter W. Wesley (both graduates of Northwestern University Law School and relatively new residents of Houston), attempted to appear before the Resolution Committee before the convention adjourned.[9] They were repeatedly repulsed because—according to the claim of W. O. Huggins, chairman of the Resolution Committee—the vote had already been taken. Incensed over what they considered to be a flagrant disregard of the two Nixon decisions, black Texans filed numerous suits requesting injunctions against local Democratic leaders and organizations in Bexar, Grayson, Tarrant, and Jefferson counties. Black lawyers spearheaded the legal attacks. R. D. Evans of Waco, W. J. Durham of Sherman, and Nabrit and Wesley of Houston quickly prepared individual cases to prohibit white democratic officials from interfering with black voting in the primaries. All of the cases met with defeat in the local courts.[10]

C. A. Booker of San Antonio employed white attorney Carl Wright Johnson to handle his suit. Booker sought an injunction to compel the county Democratic Executive Committee (specifically, John K. Weber, chairman; C. O. Wolfe, secretary; and Adolph Lassner, presiding officer of precinct number seventy-three) to permit him and other qualified black voters to exercise their franchise in the Democratic primaries. Judge T. M. Kennerly ruled against Booker but suggested that there was a possibility that the Democratic Convention's adoption of the resolution was illegal, for if the state could not enact such a restrictive law perhaps the same prohibition applied to the convention.[11]

Booker appealed the ruling and Johnson presented the case before the federal District Court in San Antonio. On July 22, 1932, the day before the first Democratic primary, the court granted Booker's request for an injunction. The District Court based its decision to a large degree on the second Nixon case. Booker was delighted with the ruling and the prospect of voting. His pleasure, however, lasted only hours. Bexar County white Democrats quickly protested the decision and later in the same day, the Fourth Circuit Court of Appeals set aside the injunction. The Appeals Court held that a political party was a voluntary organization and possessed the power to determine its membership. Booker subsequently appealed to the Texas Supreme Court, which dismissed the case and allowed the Appellate Court's decision to stand. Attorney Knollenberg wrote Walter White, executive secretary of the NAACP, that the Supreme Court of Texas had "rendered a decision . . . which virtually denied the right to participate, on account of the fact that they [Booker and Johnson] had not included all of the persons who may have been responsible for passing the resolution that all white citizens are entitled to participate" in Democratic party primaries.[12] Knollenberg's exasperated comments were prompted by the Supreme Court's reliance upon the relatively weak judicial concept that a decree against one official could not be applied to other similar officials.

In the meantime, El Paso blacks desired to file a case but the NAACP advised them against doing so. The national officers closely observed the various proceedings but refrained from entering the fights against the convention's resolution until all the decisions were handed down in the local litigations. Legal Committee chairman Arthur Spingarn and Secretary White reviewed the pleadings and decisions and carefully devised a strategy that they hoped would avoid the mistakes and failures encountered in the other cases. With two victories to their credit the NAACP officials were torn between a desire to avoid tarnishing their record with a defeat and the importance of maintaining a leading role in the white primary fight. Coupled with these considerations, was the organization's lack of adequate financial resources.[13]

By late October 1932, the NAACP was prepared, both from a legal and a financial point of view to venture forth once again into the legal fray. Spingarn, with assistance from attorney Margold, whom the NAACP had retained "to direct its proposed legal campaign under the Garland Fund Appropriations," and James Marshall, son of the late

Louis Marshall, decided to sue the election officials who had denied Nixon the right to vote in the July and August primaries.[14] James Marshall outlined the three arguments that the association would utilize in the third case, *Nixon v. McCann*. First, the statutes of Texas originally set forth the qualifications of voters in primary elections and created and organized the structure of the state convention. Therefore, the state committed an unconstitutional act when it permitted the state convention to modify the qualifications for participation in primaries in such a way as to create a distinction between voters on the grounds of race and color. Second, the state created a quasi-public body to perform a quasi-governmental function and any discrimination by the state convention on the ground of race or color was prohibited by the Constitution. Regardless of whether there were state regulations as to participation in primary elections, any discriminatory resolution passed by this quasi-governmental body (the Democratic State Convention) would be unconstitutional. Finally, the judges of election, acting as election officials, were vested with their power by the state, and they did not have the right to deprive Nixon of his right to vote. When they denied Nixon his ballot because of color, they violated the Fourteenth Amendment of the Constitution.[15]

Fifteen months later, Federal District Court Judge Charles Boynton held Justice Cardozo's decision in *Nixon v. Condon* binding and declared that the resolution of the state Democratic convention unconstitutionally deprived Nixon of his right to vote in the primaries. Boynton decided that the resolution passed by the convention did not exclude blacks from voting but merely established that white persons who were qualified voters could participate in the primaries. Thus, the judge continued, when the executive committee instructed the El Paso County chairman to exclude blacks, it was an action of the executive committee and not the convention. Ben Howell, attorney for the election officials and the Democratic executive committee of El Paso did not appeal the decision. Nixon was awarded five dollars for damages. This was the first victory for the NAACP in a Texas white primary case in a court lower than the United States Supreme Court.[16]

The decision in the *Nixon v. McCann* litigation was little more than a pyrrhic victory. It had almost no effect on the political status of blacks in Texas. Due to the lack of unanimity among white Texans some blacks were allowed to vote in certain counties even before the *Nixon v. Condon* decision and in spite of the Democratic party's resolution.[17] But for the majority of black Texans, voting in Democratic primaries remained just a hope. The constant reminder of their political impotence goaded them into developing community-based political organizations through which they attempted to gain entry into the political process. Working from the outside was never satisfactory, and blacks in Dallas, Houston, and San Antonio continued agitating for their political rights. Because Texas blacks refused to let the question of their voting in primary elections die, it became a perennial issue.[18] All white Democratic aspirants to political office confronted this issue and had to deal with it at one level or another during their election campaigns.

The gubernatorial election year of 1934 served as another setback for black Texans. Their defeats in the local courts in 1932 were compounded by political problems in 1934. There were seven contenders for the gubernatorial office in the 1934 primaries. One candidate, however, occupied a unique position insofar as the issue of black voting in the primaries was concerned. James V. Allred, born on March 29, 1899, at Bowie, Texas, had become the attorney general of the state in 1930. Allred had earned an impressive reputation as a trust-busting attorney general who was not afraid to challenge big business.[19] In 1934, having served two terms, Allred entered the governor's race and was promptly besieged with demands for some definitive statement of his position on black voting in that year's Democratic primaries.

Allred found himself confronted with a dilemma: should he or should he not use his official position for political advantage? As a gubernatorial candidate he was cognizant that many blacks supported one of his opponents, C. C. McDonald, and that any decision he rendered or statement he made regarding white primaries could affect the outcome of the election. His campaign advisers and organizers continually warned him that the black vote was going against him. The chairman of the Allred for Governor Club of Houston, Judge C. A. Teagle, for example, insinuated that one of his opponents was going to buy the black vote: "I know from experience what the negro vote means and that a little money will go a long way with them." Another principal Allred organizer, Jack Todd of Jefferson County, warned the attorney general of the adverse consequences of the black vote. The white primary was a "hot issue" in Beaumont and some blacks had openly endorsed one of his opponents. Todd suggested that if Allred would wire him an endorsement of the white primary, it would "make lots of votes" in Beaumont.[20] In both of these counties blacks composed a sizeable proportion of the total population.

Finally, as a result of the advice from his supporters and his belief that the opposition was using the black vote to his disadvantage, attorney general/gubernatorial candidate Allred issued an official declaration. In his "Opinion" Allred maintained that blacks were prohibited from the Democratic primaries under the resolution adopted in the Houston Convention of 1932: "In view of the resolution passed by the State Convention of the Democratic Party on May 24, 1932 you are respectfully advised that, in our opinion, negroes are not entitled to participate in the primary elections of the Democratic Party...." Furthermore, he added, the legitimacy of the current resolution passed by the state Democratic Convention was based on the *Nixon v. Condon* decision. He found additional support for his "Opinion" in the ruling of the Texas Supreme Court in *County Democratic Executive Committee in and for Bexar County v. C. A. Booker.*[21]

The factionalism within the Texas Democratic party was apparent in the divided and heated reactions of county chairmen and the white press to Allred's "Opinion." Many Democratic county chairmen heartily approved Allred's decree, particularly those who were involved in local power struggles. In Jefferson County the county Democratic chairman, J. R. Edmunds, had unsuccessfully attempted to restrict Jefferson County balloting to white democrats. His actions had created divisions within the county's Democratic party leadership. Allred's ruling according to newspaper accounts, came just in time to unify Jefferson County's party organization. A few county chairmen and editors of major white dailies disagreed with Allred's "Opinion." Chairman Will A. Morriss Jr. of the Bexar County Democratic executive committee decided that he would permit the approximately four to five thousand qualified black voters in Bexar County to vote. Morriss openly stated that the attorney general had acted without full knowledge and that he would not adhere to the ruling.[22] The Dallas *Journal's* editor reportedly criticized the "Opinion" as "mighty poor law." The editor contended that it was "manifestly absurd" for the attorney general to assert, on the one hand, that the party was not the creature of the state and, on the other, that the attorney general, as the servant of the state, had the right to decide who was eligible to vote in the primary.[23] These responses indicated that the efforts to bar blacks were not unanimously supported by all white Democrats in Texas.

Two black men from Jefferson County responded to this latest assault on their franchise rights. W. H. Bell and E. L. Jones, without NAACP assistance, filed a petition for a writ of mandamus against the governor of Texas, the attorney general, the state Democratic executive committee, the members of the Jefferson County Democratic executive committee, and the various election officers in Jefferson County. To guard against the court ruling against them on grounds of faulty pleadings and failure to name the right parties in the suit, Bell and Jones named approximately two hundred individuals as defendants. The object of the suit was to invoke the jurisdiction of the court to require the election officials to permit them to vote in the Democratic primaries on July 28, 1934.

Eight days before the July primary the Texas Supreme Court denied Bell and Jones the mandamus. It held that since no other Democratic convention had revoked the resolution of 1932, it was still valid and was the policy of the Democratic party of the state. The court drew upon the decision in the case of *Bexar County et al. v. Booker* to support its ruling. In that case Special Associate Justice S. S. Searcy had proclaimed that "the Democratic Party of Texas [was] a voluntary political association," and that its convention possessed "the power to determine who shall be eligible for membership in the party, and, as such, eligible for participation in the primaries. A study of the election laws of Texas and their history can lead to no other conclusion." The Supreme Court of Texas concluded that "the Attorney General of this state, in a recent able opinion, has likewise sustained the validity of the resolution passed by the Houston Convention. With the opinion of the Court of Civil Appeals at San Antonio and with that of the Attorney General we are in accord."[24]

An elated Allred immediately issued a statement asking every candidate for governor to request all election officials to follow the opinion of the court. In a speech before a cheering crowd of seven hundred in Longview, Texas, Allred pointed out that when he first released his "Opinion" the campaign manager of one of the candidates took issue with it and two of the "big city newspapers" attacked it. He added emphatically, "I now call upon the newspapers and all the candidates to follow the Supreme Court's opinion and keep the Democratic Party of Texas a white man's party."[25] His timely delivery of the "Opinion" proved to be the right political strategy. It won him the white vote and eliminated the black vote. The Texas Supreme Court's decision in *Bell v. Hill* unquestionably strengthened his candidacy.[26] (Predictably, Allred won the gubernatorial election.)

Ironically, Nixon and his business associate in El Paso were the only two blacks allowed to vote in the July and August primaries.

White Democrats chose not to risk involvement in another court action, so they provided Nixon with a ballot marked "colored," which Knollenberg thought a very "smart trick." The El Paso attorney theorized that this allowed election officials to ignore the ballot once cast and yet give the impression of compliance with the federal law as interpreted by the Supreme Court.[27]

Allred's "Opinion" and the *Bell v. Hill* decision seemingly closed another door on the possibility of blacks voting in Texas Democratic primaries. R. D. Evans of the National Bar Association, the formal organization of black lawyers, and Walter White of the NAACP were not at all satisfied with the turn of events in Texas. Leaders of both organizations, acting independently of one another, filed complaints with the United States Attorney General's Office and requested investigations of election practices in Texas. The National Bar Association's president, E. Washington Rhodes, expressed concern about the *Bell v. Hill* decision while White questioned the legality of Allred's "Opinion." Assistant Attorney General Joseph Keenan promised to give careful consideration to the matter to determine if any federal criminal laws had been violated. He also suggested that White contact Rhodes and assist him in furnishing affidavits from black Texans who were denied ballots in the last primaries.[28]

From his office in Waco, Texas, attorney R. D. Evans alerted black lawyers across the state to the necessity of sending as many affidavits as possible to the attorney general's office. Scores of affidavits from the cities of Waco, Beaumont, and El Paso, and from Harris, Travis, Jefferson, and McLennan counties were forwarded to White to be sent to Keenan.[29] Rhodes and White met to work out other strategies to compliment the affidavits and to increase the pressure on the Department of Justice. To dramatize the role of the black attorneys in the struggle, Rhodes proposed the appointment of a delegation of leading black lawyers who would go to Washington, D.C., to discuss the matter of the white primary directly with the attorney general. Evans enthusiastically supported Rhodes's idea of a delegation, but White disagreed. White recommended that the National Bar Association and the NAACP jointly draft a memorandum brief for the attorney general setting forth not only the legal grounds on "which the Attorney General may act, but citing the grounds on which he must act if the law so indicated."[30]

Keenan forwarded the affidavits and related material to attorneys general S. D. Bennett of the Eastern District at Beaumont, Douglas W.

McGregor of the Southern District at Houston, and W. R. Smith of the Western District at San Antonio. He ordered them to conduct a special investigation to review the allegations of voting discrimination and illegalities in violation of the United States Supreme Court decisions in the two Nixon cases. They were further asked to determine whether criminal prosecution of election officials was warranted under the Civil Rights Statute of Sections 19 and 20 of the Criminal Code.[31] Black lawyers in Texas exerted continuous pressure on the district attorneys general and carefully monitored the progress of the investigations. Smith became defensive and refused to give out any voting information, whereupon blacks suggested to the U.S. attorney general that Smith was remiss in conducting the investigations.[32]

The efforts of the NBA and the NAACP accomplished very little. The district attorneys general all agreed that prosecution of election officials who refused ballots to blacks was inadvisable. McGregor's staff concluded that "no grand jury in Texas would indict these officials, nor would a jury convict them." S. D. Bennett wrote, "I am of the opinion that criminal prosecution under the provisions of the statutes referred to could not be successfully maintained."[33]

Smith, perhaps because of the close attention blacks focused on him, filed a rather detailed report based upon James V. Allred's "Opinion" and the two cases adjudicated in Texas: *Bexar County v. Booker* and *Bell v. Hill.* Smith argued that the Texas Court of Civil Appeals in the case of *Bexar County v. Booker* had upheld the resolution adopted by the Democratic Party Convention on May 24, 1932. In that opinion the court had ruled that the Convention's resolution was in keeping with the expression of the *Nixon v. Condon* decision, which had "strongly indicated that the Convention of the party itself could restrict its membership and determine the qualifications thereof in any way determined upon by the Convention." He concluded that the election officials who refused to allow blacks to cast their ballots were acting in good faith and without any criminal intent in following the decision of the court in the Booker case and in adhering to the "Opinion" of the attorney general of Texas. Furthermore, he added, the Supreme Court of Texas had sustained the Allred "Opinion" in the *Bell v. Hill* litigation.[34]

Shortly before these reports were filed, J. Edgar Hoover, director of the Justice Department's Division of Investigation assigned a special agent from the San Antonio Division Office to look into the issue of voting irregularities. The special agent in charge of the investigation arrived at the same conclusion as Smith. Agent Gus T. Jones informed Hoover that on the basis of preliminary study, no investigation was warranted because "the denial of the negro the right to vote was not a matter of fact but a matter of law." That is, the Texas Supreme Court's decision in *Bell v. Hill* and the resolution of the Democratic Convention provided the legal justification for the disfranchisement of blacks.[35]

Keenan reviewed the reports and informed White that the Department of Justice would not institute criminal proceedings and that the case was closed. He summarized the findings and advised White that it would be difficult if not impossible to prove that the election officials had any criminal intent to break the law or that they had not acted in apparent good faith pursuant to a state statute and its interpretation by the Supreme Court of Texas. Keenan added that the *Nixon v. Condon* decision had not decided that white Democrats violated the constitutional rights of blacks by excluding them from participation in the party's primaries. That, according to Keenan, would have to be decided in a new case by the United States Supreme Court. Until then, the present practice in Texas was constitutional.[36]

By the end of 1934 the NAACP, black lawyers, and local black leaders in Texas had almost reached a dead end. After a decade of obstinateness and legal maneuvering, white Texas Democrats who favored disfranchisement of blacks had seemingly achieved their objective. The Allred "Opinion," the *Bell v. Hill* decision, and the Justice Department's decision not to intercede left blacks virtually defenseless and voteless.

This disheartening situation steadily deteriorated in 1935. In 1934 the black law firm of Atkins, Nabrit and Wesley had filed a suit at the request of Houston barber and political activist, R. R. Grovey, against County Clerk Albert Townsend for denying Grovey an absentee ballot to vote in the Democratic primary of that year. The NAACP disapproved of the suit and the way it was presented and advised the Houston lawyers against pursuing the case. J. Alston Atkins, a Yale University Law School graduate, reasoned that because the county clerk was an elected official of the state of Texas and not an official of the Democratic party he could be charged with violation of the Fourteenth and Fifteenth Amendments for denying Grovey an absentee ballot. Attorney Atkins then, in a striking move, took the case before a justice of the peace court instead of filing it in Houston Federal Court. He asked for ten dollars damage to Grovey for his loss of the voting privilege.

The justice of the peace court ruled against Grovey, whereupon the lawyers asked the United States Supreme Court for a writ of certiorari from the justice of the peace court. By this mechanism Atkins was able to bypass the Appeals Court.[37]

The United States Supreme Court agreed to review the transcript of the case on March 11, 1935, and delivered a devastating decision less than three weeks later on April Fools Day, 1935. Justice Owen J. Roberts wrote a unanimous opinion that was an outright rejection of the black Texan's appeal. The Supreme Court held that "we find no ground for holding that the respondent has in obedience to the mandate of the law of Texas discriminated against the petitioner or denied him any right guaranteed by the Fourteenth and Fifteenth Amendments." The decision rested to a considerable extent on *Bell v. Hill*.[38]

The decision stunned the blacks in Texas and across the country. Under banner headlines Carter Wesley declared in the *Informer*: "In 1935 the Supreme Court of the United States in *Grovey v. Townsend* makes political slavery in Texas and the South constitutional, just as the Dred Scott decision made bodily slavery constitutional seventy-eight years ago." When the Associated Negro Press asked William J. Thompkins in the Recorder of Deeds Office in Washington, D.C., to comment on the decision, he stated: "I regard this decision as being infinitely worse than the Dred Scott decision. . . ." He continued: it "affects directly every colored person in the State of Texas and might eventually affect every adult man and woman in every state in the Union." NAACP executives were equally disturbed by the Grovey decision. Secretary Walter White noted in his autobiography, "It should not be difficult to imagine the gloom we all felt. Years of hard work and heavy expense appeared to have gone for naught."[39]

The *Grovey* decision should not be considered in isolation. The Supreme Court justices who rendered the *Grovey* decision handed down, on the same day, a landmark civil rights decision in a case originating out of the famous Scottsboro trials. Nine black youths were accused of raping two white girls in Alabama. After a hasty trial, amidst an atmosphere of intense racial hostility, the boys had been summarily convicted and sentenced to die. The communists became involved in the case after the initial trials and in two separate instances (1932 and 1935) appealed the convictions to the United States Supreme Court. In 1932 in *Powell v. Alabama* the Supreme Court overturned the convictions on the basis that the defendants "were not accorded the right to counsel in any substantial sense"; thus their constitutional rights to due process had been violated.[40] A retrial resulted in the same verdict and a return to the United States Supreme Court. Chief Justice Charles Evans Hughes on April 1, 1935, delivered the unanimous decision in *Norris v. Alabama* invalidating the convictions on the grounds that blacks were systematically excluded from jury service.[41]

The Norris decision gave blacks back their rights to serve on juries that would, perhaps, mitigate the excesses of southern justice meted out to blacks. In most southern states, however, jurors were selected from the pool of property-owning, poll tax–paying voters. Blacks who could not afford to vote did not serve on juries. The ineffectiveness of the Norris decision was further highlighted by the attitudes and actions of white lawyers who utilized their peremptory challenge to keep off blacks who were called for grand and petit juries.[42]

In another decision delivered the following month, the Supreme Court retreated from ruling upon other civil liberties, some as fundamental as the freedom of speech. On May 20, 1935, the Supreme Court in a six to three decision dismissed Angelo Herndon's appeal. Herndon, a young black communist, was convicted by the Georgia Supreme Court of attempting to incite a communist-led insurrection or conspiracy against the state of Georgia. Before the United States Supreme Court Herndon's defense attorneys presented an eloquent plea for the protection of free speech and other civil liberties and argued that Georgia's insurrection law violated the due process clause of the Fourteenth Amendment. The majority opinion, prepared by Justice George Sutherland, declared that Herndon had failed to raise the correct constitutional questions at the appropriate time and thus the court lacked jurisdiction. The dissenting opinion, written by Justice Benjamin Cardozo with Justices Louis Brandeis and Harlan Fiske Stone concurring, asserted that the court did have jurisdiction and was essentially side stepping the complicated constitutional issues posed.[43] Occurring as they did within a six-week span, these three court cases reflect the United States Supreme Court's ambivalence in regards to the civil rights of blacks. The *Norris* decision was pro–civil rights, although it had limited effect in practice. The *Grovey* decision was blatantly against civil rights, and the *Herndon* decision evaded the issue.

Nine years elapsed before the NAACP and black Texans were again able to challenge the white primary before the United States Supreme Court. During the interim, significant domestic changes and international crises occurred. Only two of the nine justices who had ruled on Grovey remained on the Supreme Court: Owen Roberts and Harlan F.

Stone. The seven justices appointed by Franklin D. Roosevelt were of decidedly more liberal views. The United States' entry into World War II and the rise of Nazism in Germany with its concomitant emphasis on theories of racial superiority had forced many Americans to question the continued denial of basic citizenship rights to blacks. The hypocrisy of fighting a war against Nazism and for the freedom of people external to America while denying the rights of first-class citizenship to the Negro population at home had become obvious. The situation was almost too much for most black Americans to bear. With renewed vigor blacks, during the late thirties and the war years, pushed forward and increased their demands to be treated as equals, particularly in the political arena.

As early as 1936 the NAACP Legal Committee, under the leadership of Thurgood Marshall, began to lay the groundwork for a new white primary case. An acute shortage of funds prevented Marshall and the NAACP from developing a case before the 1938 elections. This did not deter leaders in the Houston branch, however. C. F. Richardson, editor of the Houston *Defender*, William Greene, William M. Drake, a prominent Houston physician, and Julius White, an active leader in the Harris County Negro Democratic Club, filed the case of *C. F. Richardson et al. v. Executive Committee of the Democratic Party for the City of Houston, Harris County*, asking for damages for deprivation of the right to vote and for an injunction to prevent further interference with black voters. The suit focused on whether blacks could be prohibited from voting in municipal primary elections.

Shortly after the hearings, Judge T. M. Kennerly denied the requests for a preliminary injunction and refused to consider any of the other contentions of the plaintiffs. Kennerly maintained that there was no substantial difference between this case and one that had been brought to the court in 1933, in *Drake v. Executive Committee of the Democratic Party for the City of Houston*. In both cases the plaintiffs had requested an injunction against the Democratic party of the city. The decision in the Drake case and the Texas Supreme Court's decision in Bell, according to Kennerly, had fully discussed and settled the laws involved in the whole primary issue. Moreover, he added, the United States Supreme Court had delivered the final word in *Grovey v. Townsend*.[44]

By 1941 the NAACP was ready to move. In January 1941, NAACP attorneys filed suit in behalf of Sidney Hasgett, a black Houston, Texas, hod carrier, against election judges Theodore Werner and John H.

Blackburn. They asked for five thousand dollars in damages for the re-fusal to permit Hasgett to vote in the Democratic run-off primary held on August 24, 1940. District Justice T. M. Kennerly set the trial date for April 14, 1941. After being postponed several times, the case was heard in court on April 25; on May 3 Judge Kennerly ruled against Hasgett.[45] While the *Hasgett v. Werner* litigations were underway, a case dealing with primary elections in Louisiana was making its way up to the United States Supreme Court. Black attorneys in Texas and the NAACP immediately focused their attention on the case of *United States v. Classic.*

Although the *Classic* case was not concerned with questions of race, it was a harbinger of things to come. In the *Classic* case five white commissioners of election including Patrick B. Classic were charged with conducting a primary election under Louisiana law to nominate a candidate of the Democratic party for the United States House of Rep-resentatives in which they willfully altered and falsely counted and certified the ballots cast in the primary election. The United States Supreme Court was called upon to decide whether the right of qualified voters to vote in the Louisiana primary and to have their ballots counted was a right "secured by the Constitution."[46]

Chief Justice Stone delivered the five-to-three opinion. The court held that "the authority of Congress . . . includes the authority to regu-late primary elections when . . . they are a step in the exercise by the people of their choice of representative in Congress." Thurgood Mar-shall termed the decision "striking and far reaching" and after brief consideration persuaded the NAACP and black Texans to drop their ap-peal of the Hasgett decision and begin a new case more in accordance with the *Classic* decision.[47]

On April 20, 1942, Marshall argued the new *Smith v. Allwright* case before the District Court. In his presentation he stressed that the De-mocratic party in Texas possessed few characteristics of a closed organ-ization. He observed that it had no constitution, no by-laws, member-ship rolls, etc. Marshall further asserted that under the facts and laws, the case was almost identical to that of *United States v. Classic.* Nei-ther the District Court nor the Circuit Court of Appeals agreed with Marshall's interpretations. He subsequently petitioned for a writ of cer-tiorari in the United States Supreme Court.

In January 1944, the Supreme Court heard final arguments in *Smith v. Allwright.* After deliberation, Justice Stanley Reed, author of the eight-to-one decision, declared the white primary unconstitutional.

Neither the state nor the Democratic party possessed the power to deny blacks the right to vote in primary elections. The court acknowledged that the primaries were an integral part of the election process and effectively controlled the choice of the officials elected.[48]

White Texans did not immediately cave in to the *Smith* decision. They made yet another attempt to preserve, if not resurrect, the white primary. For sixty years white citizens in Fort Bend County had held preliminary elections under the auspices of the Jaybird Democratic Association. The Jaybirds conducted what amounted to privately financed "pre-primary" primaries to endorse candidates for the Democratic nomination. Of course these pre-primary primaries were open to whites only. In 1952 the United States Supreme Court agreed to hear arguments in *Terry et al. v. Adams et al.*, the last of the white primary cases. The Court ruled that the Jaybird Association was more than a private club and that exclusion of blacks violated the Fifteenth Amendment. Thus sounded the death knell of the Democratic white primary.[49]

It would be incorrect to assert that the 1930s witnessed a steady deterioration in the status of southern blacks. Their status was already fixed on the lowest rung of southern society. While many blacks had made significant strides since the Reconstruction era, during the 1930s the masses were still relegated to an inferior position within America. They remained economically destitute, largely uneducated, socially segregated, and politically powerless. The court cases and legal battles of the thirties reflect the extent of black debasement and concomitantly the lengths to which whites would go to preserve white supremacy. The struggles in the judicial arena then merely lifted the veil and permitted the world to observe the underside of American justice.

Most accounts of the white-primary struggle center around the final and determinative cases heard and ruled upon by the Supreme Court in the 1940s. The impact of Supreme Court decisions was largely contingent upon the political predispositions and social attitudes of the black and white participants in the struggle. To ignore their roles and the events that transpired before a case reached the High Tribunal results in an incomplete understanding of the effects of judicial decisions, the development of political strategies, and the operation of organizations such as the NAACP. The black quest for the elusive ballot reveals the many ways in which local politicians can negate laws and Supreme Court decisions. Against seemingly insurmountable white obstinance and repeated failures, blacks persisted in the white supremacy struggle because somehow, the conviction that justice was ultimately color-blind could not be destroyed. More important, however, was the realization that to be barred from participation in the selection of public officials indicated more than anything else that blacks were only half free.

Notes

1. *Nixon v. Herndon*, 273 U.S. 536–541 (1927); *Nixon v. Condon*, 286 U.S. 73–106 (1932).

2. Alwyn Barr, *Reconstruction to Reform: Texas Politics, 1876–1906* (Austin, 1971), 17, 193–196; J. Morgan Kousser, *The Shaping of Southern Politics: Suffrage Restrictions and the Establishment of the One-Party South, 1880–1900* (New Haven, 1974), 196–200; Lawrence D. Rice, *The Negro in Texas, 1874–1900* (Baton Rouge, 1971), 114–119; Cortez Arthur Ewing, *Primary Elections in the South: A Study in Uni-party Politics* (Norman, 1953), 8–9; Paul Lewinson, *Race, Class and Party: A History of Negro Suffrage and White Politics in the South* (New York, 1932), 112–113; Lawrence C. Goodwyn, "Populist Dreams and Negro Rights: East Texas as a Case Study," *American Historical Review*, LXXVI (December, 1971), 1435–1456.

3. Charles Kincheloe Chamberlain, "Alexander Watkins Terrell, Citizen, Statesman" (Ph.D. dissertation; University of Texas, 1956), 462–468; Rice, *Negro in Texas*, 136; Paul E. Isaac, "Municipal Reform in Beaumont, Texas, 1902–1909," *Southwestern Historical Quarterly*, LXXVIII (April, 1975), 421–422; Conrey Bryson, *Dr. Lawrence A. Nixon and the White Primary* (El Paso, 1974), 12; Harold M. Tarver, "The Whiteman's Primary (An Open Letter to D. A. McAskill, 1922)." A printed copy of this letter from a black resident of San Antonio is in the Library, Barker Texas History Center, University of Texas, Austin. This letter is listed in the library card catalogue under "Tarver."

4. *Texas Revised Civil Statutes*, Article 3107 (1925) (quotation); J. Alston Atkins, *The Texas Negro and His Political Rights: A History of the Fight of Negroes to Enter the Democratic Primaries of Texas* (Houston, 1932), 6–24; Lewis Gould, *Progressives and Prohibitionists: Texas Democrats in the Age of Wilson* (Austin, 1973), 48–49; Alwyn Barr, *Black Texans: A History of Negroes in Texas, 1529–1971* (Austin, 1973), 134–135; Lewinson, *Race, Class and Party*, 113; Charles C. Alexander, *The Crusade for Conformity: The Ku Klux Klan in Texas, 1920–1930*, Texas Gulf Coast Historical Association. Vol. VI, No. 1 ([Houston], 1962), v; Charles C. Alexander, *The Ku Klux Klan in the Southwest* (Lexington, Kentucky, 1966), 121; Kenneth T. Jackson, *The Ku Klux Klan in the City, 1915–1930* (New York, 1967), 71–73; Bryson, *Dr. Lawrence A. Nixon*, 12–13; Arnold S. Rice, *The Ku Klux Klan in*

American Politics (Washington, D.C., 1962), 15; Tarver, "The Whiteman's Primary"; San Antonio *Express*, July 23, 1922, May 11, 1923.

5. *Nixon v. Herndon*, 273 U.S. 536–541 (1927) (quotation); *Nixon v. Herndon*, 47, S.C. 446 (1927); Bryson, *Dr. Lawrence A. Nixon*, 34–51.

6. *House Journal 40th Legislature, First Called Session* (Austin, 1925), 228, 268–271, 328–331; *General and Special Laws of the State of Texas, 40th Legislature, First Called Session* (Austin, 1927), 193; Bryson, *Dr. Lawrence A. Nixon*, 53–55; *Yale Law Review*, XLI (1932), 1212.

7. *Nixon v. Condon*, 286 U.S. 73–106 (1932).

8. Ibid.; Nathan Margold to Felix Frankfurter, May 5, 1932; Carter W. Wesley to Fred C. Knollenberg, May 30, 1932, NAACP Papers (Library of Congress, Washington, D.C.), Box D-63; W. R. Smith, District Attorney General for the Western District at San Antonio, Texas, to the United States Attorney General, care of Joseph Keenan, September 18, 1934, Department of Justice Files (National Archives, Washington, D.C.), Folder 72-100-5; Bryson, *Dr. Lawrence A. Nixon*, 72; "Nixon v. Condon," *Yale Law Review*, IV, No. 8 (June, 1932).

9. James M. Nabrit to D. C. H., April 6, 1974, interview.

10. Wesley to Knollenberg, May 30, 1932, NAACP Papers, Box D-63; Robert Wendell Hainsworth, "The Negro and the Texas Primaries," *Journal of Negro History*, XVIII (October, 1933), 433–435; *White v. Harris County Democratic Executive Committee* 60F (2d) 973 (S.D. Texas, 1932); *Informer* (Houston), July 30, 1932.

11. Knollenberg to Walter White, August 31, 1932, The Lawrence A. Nixon Papers, (Lyndon B. Johnson Library, Austin, Texas); O. Douglas Weeks, "The White Primary," *Mississippi Law Journal*, VIII (December, 1935), 135–153; Hainsworth, "The Negro and the Texas Primary," 434, 436–438; *Informer* (Houston), July 30, 1932.

12. *County Democratic Executive Committee in and for Bexar County et al. v. Booker*, 53 S.W. (2d) 123 (Texas, 1932); *County Democratic Executive Committee in and for Bexar County et al. v. C. A. Booker*, 52 S.W. (2d) 908 (Texas, 1932); Knollenberg to White, August 31, 1932, Nixon Papers (quotation).

13. Nixon to Robert Bagnall, August 3, 1932; White to Nixon, August 8, 1932, NAACP Papers, Box D-63.

14. Margold to Knollenberg, October 21, 1930, Arthur B. Spingarn Papers, Library of Congress (Washington, D.C.), Box 5. Louis Marshall died in October 1929. The Garland Fund, formally known as the American Fund for Public Service, had been established by Charles Garland.

15. Marshall to Knollenberg, April 18, 1933, NAACP Papers, Box D-63.

16. El Paso *Herald Post*, February 7, 1934; NAACP Press Release: "Third Texas Primary Case Won in Federal Court," February 9, 1934, NAACP Papers, Box D-63.

17. NAACP Press Release: "Outcome of Attempts of Negroes to Vote at Demo-

cratic Primaries in Texas on July 25, 1932," August 11, 1932, NAACP Papers, Box D-63; *Informer* (Houston), July 30, 1932.

18. Melvin James Banks, "The Pursuit of Equality: The Movement for First Class Citizenship Among Negroes in Texas, 1920–1950," (Ph.D. dissertation; Syracuse University, 1962), 221–235; *Informer* (Houston), September 10, 1932.

19. Knollenberg to James V. Allred, January 26, 1932, Nixon Papers; Walter B. Moore, *Governors of Texas* (Dallas, 1963), 31; Walter Prescott Webb, H. Bailey Carroll, and Eldon S. Branda (eds.), *The Handbook of Texas* (3 volumes; Austin, 1952, 1976), III, 21–22.

20. C. A. Teagle to Sidney Benhow, Assistant Attorney General, May 17, 1934 (first quotation); Jack Todd to Dick Watters, July 12, 1934, (second and third quotations), James V. Allred Papers (University of Houston, Houston, Texas), Containers 84–85.

21. Allred to D. B. Wood, Williamson County Attorney, June 9, 1934. NAACP Papers, Box D–63.

22. Bay City *Tribune*, July 14, 1934; Fort Worth *Star-Telegram*, July 8, 1934.

23. The Dallas *Journal* as quoted in *Informer* (Houston), July 21, 1934.

24. Tyler *Telegram*, July 21, 1934; *Bell et al. v. Hill, County Clerk, et al.*, 74 S.W. (2d), 113–122 (Texas, 1934) (quotations). The case was argued before Texas Supreme Court, July 19, 1934.

25. Tyler *Telegram*, July 21, 1934.

26. John Speer to Allred, July 30, 1934, Allred Papers, Container 83.

27. Nixon to White, September 8, 1934; Knollenberg to White, September 21, 1934 (quotation), NAACP Papers, Box D-63.

28. E. Washington Rhodes to Attorney General Homer S. Cummings, July 24, 1934; Joseph B. Keenan to Rhodes, July 26, 1934; White to Cummings, July 27, 1934; Keenan to White, July 28, 1934; White to Keenan, July 30, 1934; Department of Justice Files, Folder 72-100-5; White to Arthur Spingarn, Summary of all of the developments concerning the Justice Department and the NAACP, August 7, 1934, NAACP Papers, Box D-63.

29. White to Keenan, August 3, 6, 1934, Department of Justice Files, Folder 72-100-5; White to Rhodes, August 9, 1934, NAACP Papers, Box D-63.

30. Rhodes to White, August 1, 1934; R. D. Evans to Rhodes, August 15, 1934; White to Rhodes, August 9, 21 (quotation), 1934, NAACP Papers, Box D-63.

31. Keenan to S. D. Bennett, U.S. Attorney, Beaumont, Texas, August 11, 1934; Keenan to Douglas W. McGregor, U.S. Attorney, Houston, Texas, August 11, 1934; Keenan to William R. Smith Jr., U.S. Attorney, San Antonio, Texas, August 18, 1934; Keenan to White, August 10, 1934; Bennett to Keenan, August 6, 1934; McGregor to Keenan, August 16, 1934; Smith to Keenan, August 21, 1934, Department of Justice Files, Folder 72-100-5.

32. White to Keenan, September 4, 1934: Keenan to Smith, September 6, 1934; Smith to Keenan, September 13, 1934, Department of Justice Files, Folder 72-100-5.

33. Carlos G. Watson, Assistant to District Attorney General Douglas W. Mc-Gregor to the United States Attorney General, October 6, 1934 (first quotation); Bennett to the United States Attorney General, January 17, 1935 (second quotation), Department of Justice Files, Folder 72-100-5.

34. Smith to the Attorney General, September 18, 1934, Department of Justice Files, Folder 72-100-5.

35. John Edgar Hoover, Director of the Division of Investigation to Keenan, October 17, 1934; Gus T. Jones, Special Agent in Charge of the San Antonio Division Office to Hoover, October 8, 1934 (quotation); McGregor to Jones, October 6, 1934; H. A. Fisher, Attorney, to Keenan, November 16, 1934, Department of Justice Files, Folder 72-100-5.

36. Keenan to White, December 28, 1934, NAACP Papers, Box C-285; Keenan to Hoover, January 9, 1935, Department of Justice Files, Folder 72-100-5.

37. James M. Nabrit to D. C. H., April 6, 1974, interview; Walter White, *A Man Called White: The Autobiography of Walter White* (Bloomington, Indiana, 1970), 88.

38. Bryson, *Dr. Lawrence A. Nixon,* 74–75; Banks, "The Pursuit of Equality," 220–232; *Grovey v. Townsend,* 295 U.S. 45–55 (1935) (quotation); Walter Lindsey, "Black Houstonians Challenge the White Democratic Primary, 1921–1944" (M.A. thesis; University of Houston, 1969), 26–27.

39. *Informer* (Houston), April 6, 1935 (first quotation); William J. Thompkins to Marvin Hunter McIntyre, Assistant Secretary to President Roosevelt, April 23, 1935 (second and third quotations) (Franklin Delano Roosevelt Library, Hyde Park, New York); White, *A Man Called White,* 88 (fourth quotation).

40. *Powell v. Alabama,* 287 U.S. 45–77 (1932).

41. *Norris v. Alabama,* 294 U.S. 587–599 (1935); Dan T. Carter, *Scottsboro: A Tragedy of the American South* (Baton Rouge, 1969), 319–324.

42. Henry J. Abraham, *Freedom and the Court: Civil Rights and Liberties* (2nd ed.; New York, 1972), 331–333; Ralph Bunche, *The Political Status of the Negro in the Age of FDR,* Dewey W. Grantham, editor, (Chicago, 1973), 297.

43. Charles Martin, *The Angelo Herndon Case and Southern Justice* (Baton Rouge, 1976), 108, 149–150; *Herndon v. Georgia,* 295 U.S. 446–455 (1935).

44. C. F. Richardson to Charles Houston, July 25, 1938, NAACP Papers, Box D-92; *Informer* (Houston), October 22, November 5, 1938; *C. F. Richardson et al. v. Executive Committee of the Democratic Party of the City of Houston* 20F (2d) (S.D. Texas, 1938); Memorandum and copy of judge T. M. Kennerly's decision, Legal Files, November 2, 1938, NAACP Papers, Box D-92.

45. Memorandum from Legal Department to members of the National Legal

Committee, Re: Activities and Developments during January and February, 1941, Texas Primary Case, *Hasgett v. Werner,* NAACP Papers, Unprocessed Files; *Informer* (Houston), February 8, March 8, April 5, 19, 26, May 10, 1941.

46. *United States v. Classic* et al., 313 U.S. 299–341 (1941).

47. Ibid. (first quotation); Richard Claude, *The Supreme Court and the Electoral Process* (Baltimore, 1970), 31–36; Thurgood Marshall to Belford V. Larson, December 19, 1941 (second quotation), NAACP Papers, Unprocessed Files; Judge William H. Hastie to D. C. H., November 27, 1973, interview.

48. *Smith v. Allwright,* 321 U.S. 649–670 (1940); *United States v. Classic* 61 S.C. 1031, 85 L. Ed. 867 (1941); Robert E. Cushman, "The Texas 'White Primary' Case—*Smith v. Allwright,*" *Cornell Law Quarterly,* XXX (September, 1944), 66–76; Bryson, *Dr. Lawrence A. Nixon,* 78.

49. *Terry et al. v. Adams et al.,* 345 U.S. 461 (1952); Nina Benware Margraves, "The Jaybird Democratic Association of Fort Bend County: A White Man's Union" (M.A. thesis; University of Houston, 1955), 45–61; Banks, "Pursuit of Equality," 328; Thurgood Marshall, "The Rise and Collapse of the 'White Democratic Primary'," *Journal of Negro Education,* XXVI (Summer, 1957), 249–254.

Black Houstonians
and the "Separate but Equal" Doctrine
Carter W. Wesley versus Lulu B. White

MERLINE PITRE

The African American struggle for civil, educational, and political rights in Texas resulted in a number of astounding gains, but the struggle often came at great personal cost to the activists. Among the casualties of this contest was the loss of friendship between two articulate, visible, able, and committed leaders, Houstonians Carter W. Wesley and Lulu B. White. This break-up is particularly disheartening because it occurred over an issue that perplexes even today's observers: the issue of "separate but equal" or "full integration." In this instance, Merline Pitre affirms, the question was whether to push for full integration at the University of Texas or to accept the state leaders' promise of a separate and equal university. Though he also gave support to the effort to integrate the University of Texas, Wesley especially espoused creating a separate university for blacks. White, on the other hand, together with most prominent NAACP spokesmen, pressed for total integration. In the long run, the NAACP won the Sweatt case, and the state also provided funds for a separate school. Pitre notes that both positions of the two leaders, White and Wesley, undoubtedly arose from their backgrounds and that no one could deny the commitment that each had for racial equality.

*

IRONIC as it may have appeared in the late 1940s and early 1950s, two of Houston's most popular black personalities engaged in continuous warfare over the "separate but equal" doctrine in education. Indeed, the feud between Lulu Bell White, executive secretary of the NAACP, and Carter W. Wesley, editor of the *Houston Informer*, lasted from 1945 to 1957. What seems most baffling is that White and Wesley possessed similar personalities, philosophies, and personal styles and drew their support from similar constituencies. Both were flamboyant, crowd-pleasing prima donnas, who used their theatrical skills to hold center stage. Both stressed independence, sought coalitions, and challenged the white establishment. Moreover, White and Wesley championed the powerless racial and ethnic groups from which they themselves sprang. Their liberal concerns intersected most pointedly on the issue of the integration of the University of Texas vis-à-vis the establishment of Texas Southern University. Yet the feud occurred partly because of their similarities and partly because of the political context from which each individual emerged.

Personal experiences fostered Wesley's commitment to social justice. Born in Houston in 1892, Wesley graduated from the public schools of the city, attended Fisk University, and went on during World War I to become one of the first black officers in the United States military. Upon his return, he pursued and earned a doctorate in jurisprudence from Northwestern University. After four years of legal practice in Oklahoma, Wesley returned to Houston in 1927.[1] Finding his legal practice in Texas limited because of his race, he became a businessman and bought into a newly formed publishing company that owned the *Informer*.[2] Wesley used the *Informer* as a weapon against racism and as a podium to become a spokesman for his people.

Gaining control of the *Informer's* parent company in 1934, Wesley used the paper to publicize the battle against the white Democratic primaries, which dominated Texas politics from 1900 to 1944 and effectively denied blacks the right to vote. The paper, then, became Wesley's platform from which to encourage black men and women to pay their poll taxes, to vote, and to fight for equal rights.[3] Thus, Wesley's story is that of a man not content to fight his own battle against discrimination, but who preferred to fight the battle of blacks everywhere—boycotting, criticizing, raising funds, publicizing or refusing to publicize an issue as his own judgment dictated. So, when he fought the battle for the establishment of Texas Southern University within the context of the "separate but equal" doctrine, he saw it as a battle for all. Undoubtedly his view was influenced by his own experiences as a black man struggling to achieve within mainstream white institutions.

Like Wesley, Lulu White's concern for civil rights stemmed from being born black in Elmo, Texas, in 1898. The small East Texas town was characterized by racial tension and the prevalence of the Ku Klux Klan. Educated in the public schools of Elmo and at Butler College, White moved to Houston in 1925. One year later, she decided to continue her education at Prairie View College where she received a bachelor's degree in English. In Houston she met and married Julius White, a long-standing member of the NAACP, who had served as the plaintiff in several white primary cases.[4] Shortly after her marriage, White became an activist with the NAACP in the struggle to eliminate the white Democratic primary. After teaching school for three years, White resigned her post and devoted herself full time to the NAACP. Her work resulted in her elevation to interim president of the Houston Branch in 1939 and to executive secretary in 1943.[5] Thus Lulu White became the matriarch of the civil rights movement in Texas from 1943 to 1957. Unafraid to speak her mind to powerful whites and differing black factions, she tackled almost any issue. She publicly advocated the right to vote and hold office. She pushed for equal access to jobs and education. She defended the rights of blacks and complained loudly when those rights were infringed upon.

Lulu White's story is that of a driven lady, deeply dedicated to the cause of integration. Her personal attitude toward desegregation was refracted through her perception of democracy and what it entailed. To her, the preservation of democracy and black people's full integration into the benefits and responsibilities of American life were inextricably linked. With this outlook, she worked hard and moved to the forefront of the movement to integrate the University of Texas.

Desegregation of the University of Texas had been a chief objective of the NAACP since the establishment of a statewide organization in 1937. But only after successfully proving itself in the elimination of the white Democratic primary in 1944 did the Texas NAACP decide to tackle the fight for equal education.[6] At that time, both Carter Wesley and Lulu White exhibited ambivalent feelings toward the doctrine of "separate but equal." Forced into a dual identity by the prevailing social order, they alternated between a race-conscious sense of solidarity and a denial of the validity of race. Life in Texas severely circumscribed their alternatives, and their actions had to be weighed against the social, political, and economic consequences.

Almost at the same time that the NAACP decided to make plans to test the dual system of education in Texas, another black group organized—the Southern Negro Conference for the Equalization of Education. At its inception in 1945, this group, founded by Carter Wesley, denounced the dual school system of the South but said nothing about integration. This stance implied that integration could not act as a panacea for the problems blacks faced in education.

The Southern Negro Conference for the Equalization of Education grew out of the Southern Regional Council. The Southern Regional Council had originated with a group of so-called moderate blacks who met in Durham, North Carolina, in October 1942 to discuss World War II and its effects on race relations. Representing for the most part the professional classes—college presidents, school principals, publishers, businessmen, doctors, and social workers—these blacks affirmed their loyalty to the Allies' war policies. But on the other hand, they maintained that such loyalty should not distract blacks from tackling the present problems of poverty, educational inequity, and poll taxes. Although these blacks were fundamentally opposed to the principle and practice of compulsory segregation, they believed that it was more sensible and timely to attack other current problems of racial discrimination.[7]

About a hundred prominent white Southerners met in Atlanta in December 1942 to affirm this position. The meeting resulted in the establishment of the Southern Regional Council in June 1943. While committed to improving race relations and conditions of blacks in the South through education and increased government consideration of black social and economic needs, the Southern Regional Council remained vague and equivocal on segregation. In fact, the priorities set by the Council did not include any direct attack on segregation. This stance, shared by Wesley, would become the main point of contention between him, Lulu White, and the NAACP.[8]

When Wesley formed his organization in 1945, he resolved to work for equalization of education at all levels. Still, he opposed making a frontal attack on segregation—the main obstacle to equal opportunity. Rather, he emphasized the manner in which equal rights should be attained. While he saw the need to use the courts in pursuing equality, he believed that true equality could be accomplished under the "separate but equal" doctrine. He further postulated that a broadly based organization such as his own could realize that objective faster and for a larger number of blacks.[9]

Whatever the tactical wisdom of Wesley's Southern Negro Conference on Equalization of Education, Lulu White was dissatisfied with this view. She sharply rebuked Wesley's organization for its failure to confront the segregation question. She challenged the "separate but equal" alternative that would bring black schools up to parity with those of whites but would allow them to remain separate. That segregation was a violation of the Constitution made it awkward, in her opinion, to pursue true equality in "separate but equal" schools. Wesley demanded equal opportunity under the current segregation law as stated in the Texas Constitution, while White could see no equality in segregation.

To disarm critics who suspected that Wesley's organization was un-progressive and compromising, Wesley insisted in 1945 that it could work hand in hand with the NAACP. Thurgood Marshall, NAACP legal counsel, concurred.[10] Wesley advocated the NAACP's coordina-tion of all court cases involving higher education, while Marshall agreed to defend the Southern Negro Conference if and when the need should arise. In keeping with his policy of cooperation with the NAACP, Wesley provided substantial publicity in his newspaper about the anticipated lawsuit against the University of Texas, resulting in the collection of a huge sum of money to fund the suit. And when the NAACP had not found a plaintiff for the case by September 1945, Thur-good Marshall asked Carter Wesley for advice.[11] The two wrestled with the problem of finding the right person for the case, dismissing five prospective plaintiffs. Then, in October, Lulu White wrote Marshall: "I think I have a plaintiff for the Education Case."[12] The individual was Heman Marion Sweatt, a thirty-three-year-old Houstonian with a B.S. degree from Wiley College, presently employed part time on the *In-former* staff and full time by the post office.

Lulu White along with A. Maceo Smith, executive secretary of the State Branches of the NAACP, and William J. Durham, NAACP resi-dent counsel, encouraged Sweatt to file an application at the University of Texas Law School. Sweatt told them that he could not do so until he had consulted with his employer—Carter Wesley. Wesley approved the idea, assuring Sweatt that his job would always be waiting for him after necessary court absences. White also gave Sweatt moral support in the case.[13]

Despite what appeared to be a congenial relationship between Wes-ley and Marshall and Wesley and White, this cooperation would be short-lived. Conflicts over the issue of integration versus separation, the University of Texas versus Texas Southern University, would de-stroy the apparent friendship in the years to come.

Urged by the NAACP and accompanied by Lulu White, among other supporters, Heman Sweatt attempted to register at the University of Texas in Austin on February 26, 1946. After discussions with Presi-dent Theophilus S. Painter and other university officials, Sweatt left his application at the campus and returned to Houston, hoping for a quick answer. During his stay on the campus, Sweatt made no mention of filing a lawsuit; however, the much publicized intentions of the NAACP alerted university officials to the possibility. It is not surpris-ing, then, that in writing Texas Attorney General Grover Sellers for an opinion on Sweatt's application that Painter said: "This is to be a test case on the question of admission of Negro students in higher education of the state. . . . This applicant is duly qualified for admission to the Law School, save and except for the fact that he is a Negro. [Please advise]."[14] Sellers's ruling did not come until March 16, 1946, at which time he upheld the laws of Texas which said, "No African or persons of African descent should be admitted to the University of Texas." Adding insult to injury, Sellers concluded that Sweatt could apply for legal training at Prairie View, since Senate Bill No. 228 had made it a university (on paper) in 1945.[15]

Sellers's argument set things in motion. It signaled the beginning of a concerted campaign to end segregated education in Texas. Conversely, it stimulated the thinking of some blacks who wanted a separate but equal university. Shortly after Sellers issued his opinion, A. Maceo Smith wrote Wesley that the Sweatt case should be pursued, but "realism dictates that a special university is about all we are going to get . . . the Texas Council of Negro Organizations is the appropriate agency such as that should prepare for negotiation when the time, arises."[16] Wesley countered that "mule" caution should be taken in accepting such an alternative. "The seeming advantage," he reasoned, "that we might have in putting them on the spot might trap us."[17] Wesley proved perceptive. Sweatt's registration attempt mobilized the political establishment to press for a black statutory university.

After Sweatt filed suit against university officials on May 16, 1946, for denial of admission, Dudley K. Woodward Jr., chairman of the University of Texas Board of Regents, began to talk about making provisions for a black university. Woodward's motives were not humanitarian; he took the lead in advancing the cause for a black university in order to make sure that a branch university for colored youths as required by the state constitution would not threaten the Permanent University Fund of the University of Texas. In Woodward's opinion, a black university sharing the endowment would "entail consequences of most destructive character." Therefore, a solution to the problem would be to create another black university by statute. "It is of great importance," Woodward wrote, "that the [constitutional option] be effectually destroyed."[18]

Judge Roy Archer's decision on June 17, 1946, to postpone the issuance of a writ of mandamus to compel the University of Texas to admit Sweatt allowed the state time to provide for a black statutory university that would be substantially "equal to whites."[19] Archer's ruling set December 17, 1946, as the date for final execution of the judgment. Officials from the University of Texas and from Texas A&M College, who had been appointed in 1945 to study Negro education, held a joint meeting to address the issue. Their report concluded that a black institution of higher education should be established, while Prairie View would provide agricultural and mechanical training for blacks on the same order as Texas A&M made available for whites. This group also recommended that the governor appoint a biracial committee to study their report and to make recommendations to the governor that could be presented to the legislature as soon as possible. When White heard about the group, she warned Thurgood Marshall that state education officials planned to establish a separate black university.[20]

On July 25, 1946, the new biracial committee held a meeting at the State Capitol and approved the recommendations of the joint committee on Negro education. The biracial committee also decided to hold a gathering for blacks on August 8 to address and listen to their concerns regarding an institution of higher learning. Realizing that such a meeting might result in a fiasco unless blacks had previously reached a consensus, A. Maceo Smith called together ninety-six black leaders from across the state on August 3 for the purpose of agreeing on a uniform course of action. The eighty-three leaders who attended agreed that they should rest their case on Article 7, Section 14 of the Texas State Constitution, which stated that "The Legislature shall also, when deemed practical, establish and provide for the maintenance of a college or branch university for the instruction of colored youths of the State." Blacks interpreted Section 14 to mean that such a university would share in the endowment fund of the University of Texas but would not preclude the right of blacks to enter the University of Texas. At the conclusion of their meeting, the black leaders selected Carter Wesley and Joseph J. Rhoads, president of Wiley College, to present their views to the biracial committee.[21]

When Wesley and Rhoads made their presentation on August 8, 1946, their demands went further than Governor Coke Stevenson and his cohorts had expected. Black leaders supported the NAACP in the Sweatt case but also demanded that a black university be established that would share equally in an endowment fund with the University of Texas. Further, they made it clear that they had no interest in a legislative arrangement by which a makeshift university would be established.[22] Responding to this group, President Painter asserted that a black statutory university would be established. And, in an attempt to head off integration of other professional areas, Painter told his audience that this university should be located in Houston not only because of the facilities offered the state by the Houston College for Negroes but also because the city's two black hospitals would enable the black university to establish its own medical school.[23] In a heated debate, Lulu White attacked Painter's statement as an insult to black people. She pointed out that the hospitals he referred to were "separate and unequal"; one of them, Jefferson Davis Hospital, had refused to treat some black patients. Painter's suggestion, she charged, was simply a ploy to prevent blacks from attending the University of Texas.[24]

Always skeptical of Wesley's Southern Conference on Equalization of Education, White became incensed when, on September 3, 1946, she discovered that Wesley had written a letter to the Texas Council of Negro Organizations, as well as to other black groups in Texas, inviting them to form a new group to demand equality in segregation; that is, to accept the compromise offered by Painter. Wesley planned to call his group the Texas Conference on Equalization of Education. White's feeling soon turned to bitterness when she discovered that the list of names Wesley used to constitute his new organization came from the NAACP.[25]

White opposed this new group because, in her opinion, "when such an organization takes the members of the same organization that is fighting Jim Crow and [now asks them to maintain segregation], such organization could only cloud the issue."[26] She argued that if blacks wanted to establish a university under the present structure of segregation, they should join the Texas Council of Negro Organizations—which was already charged with pursuing that goal. And, for this reason, she could not see how A. Maceo Smith had allowed himself to be used by supporting the new group.[27] Later, White speculated that Wesley's new organization had a racist intent. Writing Thurgood Marshall, she minced no words: Smith and Wesley "didn't want any white members. They said this was a Negro fight and we must have a Negro organization."[28]

The already heated debate grew hotter after the NAACP chose White as its director of state branches in November 1946. A. Maceo Smith called upon the state branches to endorse Wesley's organization, and White objected that "there was no need for such an organization."[29] Her argument implied that the Texas branches should divorce themselves from Wesley's organization because the NAACP "needs to lead in all programs advancing the Negro in the state."[30] Wesley took this to mean that White and the NAACP wanted the last word on all racial matters affecting blacks. White had the support of the national office of the NAACP. At this point, it appeared that the quarrel between White and Wesley had reached an impasse.

When Wesley had first introduced his organization to blacks of the Lone Star state, Thurgood Marshall warned both Wesley and A. Maceo Smith against allowing the Southern Negro Conference and the NAACP to duplicate each other's efforts."[31] One year later, Wesley found himself under increasing attacks by White for his use of the NAACP's mailing list to establish the Texas Conference on Equalization of Education, and for his favorable stance on Judge Roy Archer's ruling of June 16, 1946. In more forceful language than he had used previously, Marshall cautioned Wesley about the activities of his organization; telling him not to ask for something Marshall found undesirable—segregation.[32] Wesley answered in a scathing four-page letter, sending carbon copies to all black leaders in Texas. Marshall responded in kind, and the battle was on between them as well.[33]

Prior to 1946, Lulu White and Carter Wesley maintained a friendship and collaborated on a number of issues. Julius White, Lulu's husband, also had a cordial relationship with Wesley. Once the educational struggle took center stage in Texas and the issue of integration versus separation became the focus of attention, however, all friendship ceased. After the fight became personal, neither Wesley nor White seemed able to hear what the other had to say. Wesley's *Informer* editorial of December 28, 1946, clearly shows this. He lambasted White's intransigence, which he claimed made it impossible to use any other approach to eradicate inequity in education save for integration. Wesley maintained that the education fight in Texas should be waged on all fronts, by the Texas Conference on Equalization of Education, the Texas Council of Negro Organizations, and the NAACP. He argued that the framework in which the state had to operate made it possible for blacks to have their cake and eat it too—integration of the University of Texas and the establishment of a black university.[34]

In the same editorial, Wesley went on to make unwarranted allegations against White that caused her to tender her resignation from the local branch of the NAACP. Among the charges he leveled at her were: 1) White was a communist, 2) the NAACP wanted a monopoly on racial issues, and 3) White had caused internal strife within the Texas leadership. Of all the allegations, the last carried the most weight. In her letter of resignation, White stated: "If something could be done to prove to Julius that I had not caused internal strife, I would stay on."[35] Apparently something was done. The local branch refused to accept her resignation and instead gave her a vote of confidence. White stayed on with the blessing of Thurgood Marshall, who wrote her: "I have been accused of giving comfort to you in your stand against segregation. I think you are absolutely right."[36] Meanwhile Wesley resigned from all affiliation with the NAACP—the local branch, the State Conference of Branches, and the national membership.[37] This action cleared the way for Wesley to wage a full scale war against Lulu White.

Meanwhile, during the interim between Judge Archer's initial ruling of June 16, 1946, and his final ruling on December 17, 1946, as White and Wesley continued to feud over a constitutional branch university vis-à-vis a statutory one, the state of Texas embarked on a program to create a "black-proof" educational system. In November 1946, the Board of Directors of Texas A&M University, under the authority of Senate Bill No. 228, which had passed in 1945, established a black law school at 409 1/2 Milam Street in Houston.[38] Similarly, on December 17, 1946, when Judge Archer again denied Sweatt's petition for a writ of mandamus, the biracial committee recommended the creation of a statutory university. It made its decision after officials from the University of Texas and Texas A&M reported that their Permanent University Fund would not be sufficient to support a black university in addition to their own.[39]

When the Milam Street Law School opened in February 1947 neither Sweatt nor any other students had applied. Consequently, it closed the same month. In order to safeguard the sanctity of segregation, the legislature decided on March 3, 1947, to pass Senate Bill No. 140, providing for the establishment of a three-million-dollar Negro university, including a law school, to be located in Houston. Thus was born Texas State University for Negroes, later renamed Texas Southern University. Since time was a factor in the Sweatt case, the legislators hurriedly set up the makeshift law school in the basement of a building in Austin.[40]

While Wesley accepted the creation of the new university, White staged a protest, advocated a demonstration against Senate Bill No. 140, and insisted that the state had only raised the stakes in maintaining Jim Crow schools.[41] When Wesley pointed out that he embraced the black institution because he favored taking whatever the state had to "offer in the way of improved education,"[42] both White and Thurgood Marshall took this to mean that he was no longer willing to pursue integration in the courts. This was not the case, however. Wesley never

wavered in his support of the Sweatt case: he saw it as the litmus test
for the law which excluded blacks from state tax-supported professional schools in the absence of any semblance of equal but separate facilities.

From the editor's perspective, the NAACP's strategy focused too
narrowly on one area of discrimination. Because of the limitation of
such a strategy, Wesley argued that an equalization case should
accompany Sweatt's, that the NAACP should attack the makeshift
law school in Austin, and that the NAACP should file suit for the
Permanent University Fund monies and ask for repayment for the
bricks that blacks had given to the Houston College for Negroes.[43]
Similarly, his idealistic notions led him to believe that his own organization could force the state to live up to its responsibility of making
separate equal.

Even though Wesley devoted a great deal of attention to securing
equality under segregation, his role in the civil rights movement
should not be misinterpreted. Clearly, Wesley's response to the doctrine of "separate but equal" reveals much about his approach. However, focusing on "separate but equal" without placing it in the context
of Wesley's activities on the broader issue of race obscures the nature of
his position. While never a separatist, Wesley did have doubts as to
whether or not the efforts of the NAACP for integration, as manifested
through the Sweatt case, would bring about the greatest good for the
greatest number of blacks. But Wesley quarreled with the approach, not
the intent, of the NAACP in seeking to make blacks first-class citizens
and reaping the benefits thereof. The record is replete with his efforts
to achieve this goal.[44]

Meanwhile, A. Maceo Smith, trying to act as a moderating influence between White and Wesley, called upon White once more on August 27, 1947, to embrace Wesley's new organization, saying, "The
NAACP is part of the Texas State Conference on Equalization of Education."[45] White stubbornly refused and accused Smith of "trying to
make the NAACP a puppet organization."[46] Writing in disgust to Thurgood Marshall, White said, "We should let Maceo go to hell with
Carter. . . . I may be called dumb, but I cannot see equality in segregation[.] I hope I die just that dumb."[47]

Without a doubt, Lulu White held strong and well-developed views
about the inequities of segregation. Wisdom born from experience
taught her that "separate but equal" was a contradiction in terms.
Thus, in responding to Wesley's argument, she took the position of the

NAACP—that the only thing blacks could gain from attacking the state on inequality was a rash of Jim Crow schools, and that any attempt to sue for equality admitted the legality of "separate but equal." More than anything else White wanted to destroy the legal basis on which Jim Crow rested.[48] So, despite Wesley's assertion that "we put all whites against us when we attack segregation openly and practically,"[49] White took the opposite view. To her way of thinking, the violation of constitutional rights involved in court cases such as Sweatt's warranted prompt relief. But any relief short of integrated schools and universities necessarily implied the continuing deprivation of these rights.

Throughout 1948, White and Wesley held fast to their respective philosophies and approaches to the doctrine of "separate but equal," and the hostility between the two increased. Wesley continued to allege that White was a communist. Most whites simply refused to believe that local blacks truly wanted integrated education. Given the racist premise that blacks were happy and contented with the status quo, the only reason whites could see for local black protest against segregated schools was because they were misled by outside agitators—the NAACP, said to be linked to communism. White was regarded as a cat's-paw of that organization. White did nothing to discourage such an image. She supported Henry A. Wallace for president of the United States in 1948, and subsequently she was called to appear before the House Un-American Activities Committee.[50] Still, she continued to push for integration against the advice of some blacks and in the face of violent opposition from whites, asserting at the end of 1947, "We are raising hell down here on the educational front."[51]

As White pursued the Sweatt case, she also watched events at Texas Southern University. When two white students tried to enroll at the university in 1948 and found their admission denied because of race, they turned to White and the NAACP. But White feared to do anything she thought might hamper her goal of breaking down segregation through the Sweatt case.[52] Despite White's inaction on the issue of Texas Southern University and Wesley's continued support of the Sweatt case, the war between the two continued into 1949. White continued to attack Wesley's position, while Wesley increasingly aimed to remove White from the local branch of the NAACP through a series of name-calling articles. He succeeded on June 18, 1949, when White tendered her resignation as president of the Houston Branch of the NAACP.[53] Afterward, the diatribes between the two lessened. The feud eventually dissipated when Sweatt won his case on June 5, 1950, but truly ended only with Lulu White's death on July 6, 1957.[54]

The tragedy of this long conflict between the two leaders is that it stemmed from their deep-rooted commitment to racial equality. Because their common goal was so important to both Wesley and White, they considered an "incorrect" approach to that goal to be unforgivably irresponsible. White argued that she found it difficult to believe in the worth of any group whose fundamental ideology consisted of a repressive belief in segregation. White publicly stated that it was a pity that Wesley's group received so much publicity, since it did not support racial democracy. White could not understand how anyone could believe in equality and segregation simultaneously. On the other side, Wesley believed that White's approach would raise blacks' hopes momentarily but would not solve the problems of the majority of black students who would continue to live in black neighborhoods and go to black schools. The personal backgrounds of the two may have helped to shape these different attitudes: Wesley's experiences in the military and at Northwestern University would have shown him firsthand how little could be achieved by integration that included only token blacks, while White's upbringing amid strong racial tensions and organized racism made her a fierce proponent of blacks' rights.

The difference between the two positions was augmented by the difference in personal style between the two leaders. Wesley valued the freedom to speak his mind fearlessly on any subject and so focus attention on wrongs that could be righted, while White preferred to be a team player with the NAACP, cooperating with other black leaders. Interestingly, their preferred styles seem to have compensated to some degree for the weak points in each position. White's emphasis on governmentally mandated opportunities for blacks to enter white society on an equal footing exacted a certain dependence, which to some could have the effect of diluting black culture. Wesley's tactics of gradual reform encouraged blacks to work for improvement but to accept compromises that often frustrated their goals, to accept the existing racial patterns of segregation while asking for favors and exceptions within them.

In sum, both White and Wesley clung to the hope that their approach to the doctrine of "separate but equal" would find vindication in the years to come. However, the ambivalences of both approaches continue to plague institutions of black education such as Texas Southern University. The feud between Carter Wesley and Lulu White highlights questions that have long made the struggle for racial justice painful and perplexing, as blacks strive to attain equality in American society without losing their own sense of identity and solidarity.

Notes

1. Nancy Ruth Bessent, "The Publisher: A Biography of Carter W. Wesley" (unpublished Ph.D. diss., University of Texas, 1981), 27.

2. Bessent, 238–240.

3. *Ibid.*, 240–243.

4. *The 13th Census of the United States, 1910 Population, Kaufman County, Texas,* ed. 36; Johnnie Jordan (niece of Lulu White), interview by author, February 6, 1987; Houston *Informer,* April 1, 1944; Scrapbook of Lulu White, 1926–1928, in possession of Johnnie Jordan.

5. Daisy Lampkin to Walter White, October 30, 1939; Lulu White to Walter White, April 13, 1943; Houston *Informer,* July 28, 1939. Unless otherwise stated, all cited letters are in the NAACP Files, Group 2, Series C, Manuscript Division, Library of Congress, Washington, D.C.

6. Dallas *Express,* March 31 and May 16, 1945; Carter Wesley to A. P. Tureau et. al., May 1, 1945; Wesley to Rufus Clement, July 7, 1945. See also Darlene Hine, *Black Victory: The Rise and Fall of the White Democratic Primary in Texas* (New York, 1979).

7. Thomas A. Kureger, *And Promises to Keep: The Southern Conference for Human Welfare, 1938–48* (Nashville, 1967), 119–121; Morton Sona, *In Search of the Silent South* (New York, 1977), 114–120, 152–167.

8. Kureger, 119–121; Sona, 114–120, 152–167.

9. Houston *Informer,* February 8, June 7, and August 16, 1947.

10. Wesley to Thurgood Marshall, August 11, 1945; Marshall to Wesley, August 21, 1945; Marshall to Wesley, October 10, 1945.

11. Marshall to Wesley, September 26, 1945.

12. Lulu White to Marshall, October 10, 1945. Sweatt volunteered to be a plaintiff after White made a passionate plea to a group of black Houstonians. Coupled with this plea was the longstanding friendship between White and the Sweatt family.

13. Wesley to Marshall, October 8, 1947; Michael Gillette, "Heman Marion Sweatt: Civil Rights Plaintiff" in Alwyn Barr and Robert Calvert, eds., *Black Leaders: Texans for Their Time* (Austin, 1983), 161.

14. Theophilus S. Painter to Grover Sellers, February 1946. This letter was leaked to the press and later published in its entirety in the Houston *Informer,* March 2, 1946.

15. *Texas Attorney General Opinion, No. 0-7126,* March 16, 1946. See also Texas Legislature, *General and Special Laws of the State of Texas Passed by the Regular Session of the 40th Legislature, Austin, 1945.*

16. A. Maceo Smith to Wesley, March 21, 1946. A small group of blacks supported Smith's position with the hope that Prairie View would he transformed from a normal school to a "classical university." See also Lulu White to Marshall, November 26, 1949.

17. Wesley to Smith, March 30, 1946; Wesley to William J. Durham, March 22, 1946. Wesley was in favor of a black "classical" university but was undecided as to whether Prairie View should be converted to one. For the time being, he wanted to have a black board of regents and a black president for Prairie View.

18. Dudley K. Woodward Jr. to Gibb Gilchrist, June 20, 1946, General Files, "Negroes in College, 1939–1954," University of Texas President's Office Record, Barker Texas History Center, University of Texas at Austin. See also Michael Gillette, "Blacks Challenge the White University," *Southwestern Historical Quarterly* 86 (October 1982): 344–384.

19. Houston *Chronicle,* May 17, 1946.

20. Smith to R. L. Carter, August 9, 1946; Mark McGee to Coke Stevenson, December 17, 1946; General Files, President's Office Record: Bi–Racial Commission Report, December 6, 1946; General Files, President's Office Record. The two black members of the committee were Wilette Banks, principal of Prairie View, and Ernest Gavins, a dentist from Austin. See also Lulu White to Marshall, July 30, 1946.

21. Smith to R. L. Carter, August 9 and August 12, 1946; Houston *Post;* August 9, 1946.

22. Smith to R. L. Carter, August 9 and August 12, 1946; "Resolution of the Texas Council of Negro Organizations to the Governor's Bi-Racial Commission," August 8, 1946, NAACP Files.

23. Houston *Post,* August 9, 1946.

24. *Ibid.*

25. Lulu White to Walter White, January 2, 1947; Lulu White to A. A. Lucas, December 31, 1946; Smith to Wesley, September 3, 1946.

26. Lulu White to Walter White, January 2, 1947.

27. Lulu White to Walter White, January 2, 1947; Lulu White to Gloster Current, January 20, 1947; Smith to R. L. Carter, October 16, 1946.

28. Lulu White to Walter White, undated.

29. Lulu White to Lucille Black, November 22, 1946; Lulu White to Walter White, January 2, 1947.

30. Lulu White to Walter White, January 2, 1947; Lulu White to Marshall, December 11, 1946.

31. Marshall to Wesley, August 21, 1945; Wesley to Smith, March 26, 1946.

32. Marshall to Wesley, October 25, 1946.

33. Wesley to Marshall, December 23, 1946; Marshall to Wesley, December 27, 1946.

34. Houston *Informer*, December 28, 1946.

35. Lulu White to A. A. Lucas, December 31, 1946.

36. Marshall to Lucas, January 14, 1947; Lulu White to Lucas, December 3, 1946.

37. Wesley to Marshall, December 27, 1946.

38. Houston *Informer*, December 7, 1946.

39. Bi-Racial Commission Report, December 6, 1946; Mark McGee to Coke Stevenson, December 17, 1946, General Files, President's Office Record; Houston *Post*, February 25, 1947.

40. See Neil Sapper, "The Fall of the NAACP in Texas," *The Houston Review* 7 (no. 2, 1985): 53–68; Senate Bill #140, Texas Legislature; *General and Special Laws of the State Passed by the Regular Session of the 50th Legislature 36-4*; House Bill #82, *Texas House of Representatives Journal, 52nd Legislature.

41. Smith to Leslie Perry, February 21, 1947; Lulu White to Marshall, December 11, 1946.

42. Houston *Informer*, June 7 and August 16, 1947. See also Lulu White to Lucas, December 31, 1946.

43. Houston *Informer*, June 7 and August 16, 1947.

44. Houston *Informer*, June 7 and August 16, 1947.

45. Lulu White to Marshall, August 27, 1947.

46. *Ibid.*

47. *Ibid.*

48. Lulu White to Roy Wilkins, January 14, 1948.

49. Houston *Informer*, June 7 and August 16, 1947.

50. U.S. Congress, House Committee on Un-American Activities, "The American Negro in the Communist Party" (Washington, D.C., 1950), 24. See also *70th Official Government Report 1934–1954*, in Texas NAACP Files, Barker Texas History Center; Lulu White to Weldon Hart, March 24, 1948.

51. Lulu White to Gloster Current, December 22, 1947.

52. Lulu White to Marshall, December 22, 1948.

53. Lulu White to L. H. Simpson, June 18, 1949. See also Houston *Informer*, August 21, 1948; *Ibid.*, June 11 and June 18, 1949. Wesley announced in 1950 that he had broken with A. Maceo Smith, state NAACP leader, Houston *Informer*, November 11, 1950.

54. Houston *Informer*, July 7, 1957.

Direct Action at the University of Texas During the Civil Rights Movement, 1960–1965

MARTIN KUHLMAN

Civil rights successes in Texas, such as those in San Antonio, were less pub-licized and frequently less dramatic than victories in the Deep South, but they nonetheless effectively challenged the status quo of white supremacy and segregation. Sometimes the movement faced precarious odds. While there was little violence, many conservatives opposed integration, and they used various means to voice their opposition, including economic pressure. For example, racist legislators and private contributors held money back from the University of Texas at Austin when they determined that the uni-versity integrated too rapidly and accommodated blacks too readily. Direct action at the university, Martin Kuhlman shows, was a significant part of the national civil rights struggle. Soon after Brown v. Topeka, *the University of Texas, in 1955 and 1956, allowed black graduate and undergraduate stu-dents to attend, but the facilities remained segregated both on and off cam-pus. From 1960 to 1965, University of Texas students, sometimes with sup-port from other colleges in Austin, used direct action such as sit-ins or stand-ins to integrate lunch counters, dormitories, athletic facilities, restaurants, lounges, and theaters. As Kuhlman concludes, "although not as well known as other civil rights battles, the activities on the University of Texas campus represent an important chapter in the story of the struggle for civil rights in America."*

*

While the war against racial segregation was waged most prominently in the Deep South, the University of Texas at Austin was also a signifi-cant site in the national struggle of African Americans for civil rights. As early as the 1940s, an NAACP chapter formed at the university—the first on a segregated campus. After a court case and years of contro-versy, Heman Sweatt, a graduate of all-black Wiley College in Mar-shall, entered the University of Texas law school in 1950, becoming the first African American to integrate a law school in a state of the former

Confederacy. Students at the university had aided in the collection of funds for the *Sweatt* case.

In his article "Blacks Challenge the White University," Michael L. Gillette detailed the continuing struggle to integrate the university, during which some students and faculty members participated in rallies calling for integration. The university accepted black graduate students in 1955 and undergraduates the following year. Nevertheless, as Richard B. McCaslin has pointed out, the university's new black students had little opportunity for extracurricular activities, as the vast majority of recreational events and facilities remained segregated, thus providing a target for continued direct action. Like the better-known sit-ins in Greensboro, North Carolina, the direct-action demonstrations at the University of Texas in the early 1960s did not appear spontaneously but were the outgrowth of these prior years of civil rights activism.[1]

Despite desegregation on the academic front at the University of Texas, Jim Crow continued to ride high on the campus and in Austin. Besides adhering to southern tradition, university officials also opposed desegregation activities that might upset supporters of the university. Direct action had become an important tactic in the struggle for civil rights after the Montgomery bus boycott in 1955. In 1963 the Student Interracial Committee announced that "The Negro at UT has also come to realize his responsibility for direct action in the struggle." The involvement of University of Texas students in direct action, however, occurred at least three years before this statement. Students mirrored much of the civil rights activity in the nation and even initiated some national tactics as they challenged segregation in non-academic areas on the campus and in Austin.[2] On February 1, 1960, a student-led movement of direct action challenging segregated lunch counters began in Greensboro, North Carolina. By the following month University of Texas students had adopted direct action in the struggle against segregation. A biracial group of thirty-two students, twenty-five blacks and seven whites, demonstrated outside the campus on March 11. One protester announced that they wanted to make the student body aware of segregation in university policies. The protesters passed out leaflets pointing out that only one-fifth of the university's dormitories accepted African Americans and that these segregated dormitories were substandard. The printed statement also pointed out that although the Southwest Conference had no rules against black players, the University of Texas, like other schools in the conference, did not allow African Americans to play intercollegiate sports. The university also excluded blacks from stage productions, and a protester carried a sign exclaiming, "All the World's a Stage, but Negroes Can't Participate in Drama at UT." Protest leaders urged activists to avoid "heated discussion" or actions that might be perceived as causing trouble. The picketing lasted for a few days and ended after a meeting between university officials and demonstrating students. Students labeled the meeting unsatisfactory,[3] but turned their attention to demonstrations against Austin's segregated lunch counters.

The Austin Commission on Human Relations initiated negotiations between lunch counter owners and an interracial coalition of student groups in April. When negotiations broke down, University of Texas student Lynn Goldsmith announced that unless the counters were desegregated in a week, the coalition would be forced to utilize other methods "to present the problem effectively and to find a satisfactory solution." A week later, activists from the University of Texas, St. Edwards University, Huston-Tillotson College, and the Episcopal and Presbyterian seminaries picketed Congress Avenue with signs reading "I don't want it 'to go,' I want to sit down," "Why pay for racism?" and "Sit Ins? It's up to you!" The picketing lasted for nine hours, with groups of approximately thirty students walking in one-hour shifts. Some passersby heckled the picketers, while merchants made their intention to refuse service clear. One restaurant owner stated, "If I can't stop them at the door and they sit down, I'm not going to serve them." Representatives of H. L. Green, Kress, and Woolworth announced that they would "follow community practices" in deciding whom to serve. The Austin Commission on Human Relations, however, recognized "the democratic and moral rights of Negroes to equality of service at lunch counters of stores serving the public."[4]

On April 29, seventy-five to one hundred activists launched sit-ins challenging lunch counters at seven locations on or near Congress Avenue. Before the sit-ins began, the participants received written instructions telling them to be courteous, not to laugh out loud, and not to strike back if physically attacked. Merchants responded to the sit-ins by closing counters. H. L. Green and the Continental bus station removed stools, while the Greyhound bus station directed protesters to a separate dining room for African Americans. A few black diners did eat at segregated counters as individuals or in small groups. At Woolworth the first few black students to arrive received service, but after more students appeared, the manager stated he could not "keep it [the counter] open in the face of a demonstration." Although the sit-ins did not desegregate the targeted counters, Bray and Jordan pharmacies subsequently announced their intention to serve all customers.[5]

Students also looked to national figures in their struggle for desegregation. The interracial coalition of student groups sent U.S. Sen. Lyndon Baines Johnson a letter requesting the senator to use his Austin television station, his newsletter, and his influence in the community to "bring into practice the full human rights of all the citizens of Texas." The University of Texas Young Democrats also sent a letter urging Johnson to accept his responsibility.[6]

As students continued to picket and stage sit-ins, Mayor Tom Miller and other Austin community leaders formed a biracial action group to deal with the question of desegregation of counters. Former Texas Supreme Court Associate Justice W. St. John Garwood chaired the group. During the following days individual African Americans received service at a number of lunch counters. By mid-May the situation appeared stable enough that the action group disbanded. Renfro drugstores refused to desegregate their counters, however, and faced additional demonstrations.[7] The action group had only dealt with the question of desegregation in lunch counters while leaving many other facilities segregated.

The University of Texas student assembly proclaimed its support for the sit-ins, as did the University Religious Council (URC), which became a prominent pro-integration group on the campus. At a meeting in the university YMCA in November 1960, members of the URC discussed passing out cards in front of segregated restaurants. URC members would ask the patrons to give the cards, which read, "I will continue to patronize this establishment if it is integrated," to cashiers. The group thus hoped to demonstrate that integration would not lead to financial losses. Resistance to the URC appeared when two university students exploded a homemade bomb outside the YMCA during a URC meeting. The Federal Bureau of Investigation joined the Austin police in investigating the explosion, and the students received sentences of thirty days in jail and $200 fines. The violence did not deter the URC, however, as the group passed out 3,800 cards in less than a month.[8]

On the first anniversary of the sit-in movement, February 1, 1961, the Student Non-Violent Coordinating Committee (SNCC) announced a "second phase" of direct action challenging segregated theaters. Civil rights supporters at the University of Texas had pioneered the new form of direct action, known as stand-ins, three months earlier. Inspired by the sit-in movement, Houston Wade suggested to fellow student and school newspaper reporter Chandler Davidson that students should utilize similar means to desegregate theaters near the campus. Together Davidson and Wade organized an active civil rights group.[9]

Students for Direct Action (SDA) formed on the campus at the end of November 1960. Davidson, the chairperson of the group, said SDA's goals included spotlighting the plight of African Americans, identifying those responsible for segregation, and taking "peaceful, lawful, but definite action to remedy the situation." Although it met under the auspices of the student government's Human Relations Committee, SDA did not want any connection with groups officially recognized by the university. SDA hoped to avoid "the formidable red tape which has hamstrung 'official' groups in the past." Davidson believed that independence from the student government would allow SDA to sidestep "the extreme conservatism" and the "jungle of bureaucratic procedures" that made direct action "virtually impossible." One of the group's first activities was to circulate a petition asking students to patronize at least one integrated restaurant per week. The petition proclaimed that "Now is the time to make your voice heard in favor of civil rights."[10]

On the evening of December 2, 1960, a biracial group of two hundred University of Texas students demonstrated against the Texas Theater, which excluded African Americans. The protesting students stood in line to purchase tickets to the movie, and when they stepped up to the ticket booth asked if all Americans would be admitted. The ticket attendant refused to sell tickets to the black protesters, and although they could purchase tickets and enter the theater, white students refused "until all Americans are sold tickets." The demonstrators then returned to the back of the ticket line to begin the procedure again. Two graduate students and English instructors from the university, Claude Allen and Sandra Cason, joined the stand-ins.[11]

Reaction to the demonstrations came swiftly. The manager of the theater, Leonard Masters, told the protesters he could not sell tickets to black students because of the policy of the chain. The chain had recently reaffirmed its decision to uphold segregation. When the students continued to wait in line, the manager set up another ticket booth inside the theater and forbade the protesters to enter. Masters also threatened to call the police if demonstrations continued. The protesting students did not go into the building but remained in front of the theater urging other patrons to stay out, too. Some moviegoers continued into the theater, and a few patrons and people in passing cars jeered the protesters, but others refused to enter, and some even joined the demonstration.[12]

Stand-ins quickly spread to the Varsity, another theater near campus that excluded African Americans. As in the earlier protests, students stood in line and asked ticket sellers, "Do you still discriminate against Americans?" Picketers also appeared carrying anti-segregation signs, including one that proclaimed, "Your money spent here supports segregation." The manager of the Varsity announced over a public address system that customers should ignore the protesters and continue into the theater. Many patrons did so; a member of SDA reported that moviegoers "just look right through you. When they go into the movie, they put on their blank stare and look embarrassed." The theater's position remained that "The company has a right to refuse service to all it chooses." The Foundation for the Advancement of Conservative Thought distributed newsletters on campus saying that businessmen should have the right to make their own decisions on whom to serve. The refusal of the theaters to negotiate caused SDA leaders to recognize that stand-ins needed to continue at a rate of at least two to three per week in order to disrupt business enough to force the theaters to desegregate. SDA's resolve won national attention.[13]

During winter break, members of SDA spread the word about stand-ins. Sandra Cason, chairperson of the student government's Human Relations Council, met with the executive committee of the National Student Association (NSA). The committee passed a resolution commending the stand-ins and also informed NSA members of an SDA resolution calling for national demonstrations against theater chains that practiced segregation anywhere in the United States. Davidson met with many supportive college groups throughout the country. Eleanor Roosevelt sent Cason a telegram stating, "I admire so much the stand which the students at The University of Texas have taken."[14]

The demonstrations continued and gained momentum when classes convened again. *The Daily Texan*, the campus newspaper, gave favorable coverage to the stand-ins for the first few months, which aided the growth of the movement. Although the protesters remained peaceful, having been told not to retaliate against aggression, the Austin police arrested two youths for assaulting picketers. Eyewitnesses reported that the attackers had "spit on them [the protesters], pushed them, shoved them into the gutter, and threw football blocks" at them. In mid-January SDA sent material to other colleges asking for sympathy demonstrations against all segregated theater chains.[15]

SDA chose the anniversary of Abraham Lincoln's birthday for these demonstrations. The SDA executive board announced that commitments for sympathy demonstrations on February 12 had been received from campuses in San Antonio; Dallas; Houston; Shreveport; New York City; Chicago; Los Angeles; San Francisco; Ann Arbor, Michigan; Cambridge, Massachusetts; Oberlin, Ohio; and Champaign, Illinois. ABC-Paramount, the chain that owned the Varsity, experienced stand-ins on February 12 in New York City, Boston, San Francisco, and Chicago. Stand-ins also appeared in Houston, San Antonio, and Dallas. The largest stand-ins to date occurred in Austin on Lincoln's birthday. Close to 450 people participated in the demonstrations. Students from Huston-Tillotson and Concordia Lutheran colleges and St. Edwards University joined together with SDA members as protesters picketed and sought admission to the two theaters near campus. Rev. Lee Freeman of the University Baptist Church announced to his congregation that he would participate in the stand-ins. Demonstrators denounced the governors of two southern states, Arkansas and Louisiana. They sang, "We are going to hang Orval Faubus to a sour apple tree" and "We're going to send Jimmie Davis to an integrated hell." That night, the stand-ins moved to two downtown theaters, the State and the Paramount, for the first time.[16]

A few segregationists appeared during the demonstrations carrying a sign with a quotation wrongly attributed to Abraham Lincoln's second inaugural address: "I do not believe in the social or political equality of the two races." The quote did correctly paraphrase some of Lincoln's statements in the 1850s. Charles Root, who managed the Interstate chain in Austin, which owned three theaters experiencing stand-ins, stated that the protesters should "go back to Russia" if they believed the rights of minorities could ever overshadow the rights of the majority. Root said that the demonstrators had their rights but added that the theater owners also had rights. State Sen. Frank Owen of El Paso branded the demonstrations as "communist inspired" with views of overthrowing the government. Owen's statement does not appear to be completely racially motivated, as he had participated in a filibuster against newly proposed state segregation laws in 1957. The FBI office in Austin investigated Chandler Davidson for Communist ties.[17]

Opposition also came from official channels at the university. Chancellor Harry Ransom referred to picketing as "gratuitous and silly." The Board of Regents also objected to students participating in demonstrations. Speaking of SDA-led demonstrations a year later,

Chairman Thorton Hardie argued that participating students should be "summarily dismissed." He believed that picketing students showed little interest in acquiring an education and did not belong in the university. Other board members stated that nothing could be done to the students since the protests took place off campus and during the students' free time. The university did investigate Claude Allen because of his pro-integration views and activities. When interviews with his students revealed that Allen did not attempt to influence their opinions, the university dropped the investigation. Allen was nonetheless shifted from working with students to a research assignment. Another volley against SDA came after the Lincoln's birthday marches when Arno Nowotny, dean of student life, proposed at a Board of Regents meeting that all organizations not officially recognized by the university be barred from the campus YMCA. The proposal appeared to be aimed specifically at the SDA, since the university had officially recognized all the other civil rights groups that met at the YMCA. Nowotny added that he had heard rumors that financial support for SDA came from northerners and outsiders, although Davidson vehemently denied the rumors. The YMCA, however, declared that it would protect "free speech and free assembly" and allow SDA to meet there. More support for SDA appeared when 227 faculty members endorsed the stand-ins while condemning "arbitrary barriers that isolate groups of individuals from each other." But not many professors actually joined the stand-ins. One professor warned his graduate students not to participate in the protests because doing so might damage their career opportunities.[18]

Stand-ins continued throughout the spring of 1961. SDA led the campaign in Austin as well as in the rest of the state. Davidson and Wade helped organize a similar campaign in San Antonio. Civil rights activists from Southern Methodist University in Dallas, Texas Christian University in Fort Worth, Trinity and St. Mary's Universities in San Antonio, and Wiley College in Marshall met with SDA to discuss stand-in strategy. In April Davidson wrote ABC-Paramount president Leonard Goldenson and the United States State Department stating that "We seek through persuasion to improve those parts of the American system we deem defective." An open letter in *The Texas Observer* gave Goldenson's address and urged readers to write that they would patronize only integrated theater chains. The letter also solicited funds to purchase a full-page advertisement in the *New York Times* protesting ABC-Paramount's policy of segregation in southern theaters. Ac-

cording to the letter in *The Texas Observer, The Daily Texan* had refused to print a similar letter. SDA received more national publicity
when ABC commentator Edward P. Morgan sympathetically presented
the group's activities. Another sympathy demonstration appeared in
New York when four members of the Young People's Socialist League
acted upon the urging of SDA leaders and staged a thirty-seven-hour
sit-in in Goldenson's office.[19]

University of Texas government student Booker T. Bonner played an
active role in challenging theaters on an individual basis. Although a
member of SDA, he often disagreed with the format of the protests, the
fact that whites made most of the decisions, and the socialist bent of the
organization. Bonner pondered an action that would impress upon
people the seriousness of the situation. He also wanted to prove to members of the African American community that they did not need to be
dependent on white leadership. He decided to hold a one-man vigil and
hunger strike in hope of "bringing attention to what was happening here
and to try to prevail upon a person's mind [about the unfairness of segre-
gation]." In February Bonner sat on a stool in front of the Texas Theater,
foregoing food and sleep for sixty and one-half hours. During the sit-in
Bonner was verbally abused and threatened by segregationists. He
enacted a similar protest in June when he sat in front of the university
theaters for seven days with a sign that read: "Racial segregation (1) a
destroyer of our global prestige, (2) a damnation in our democracy" on
one side and "Racial segregation is an imbecility, a coward's shield, and
an unearned badge of superiority" on the other.[20]

Direct action brought the policy of segregation in Austin theaters
into the public light, but only negotiation could bring about a permanent change. Pressure applied to ABC-Paramount by members of the
Austin Jewish community and the Austin Commission on Human Relations aided in bringing about negotiations. On August 4 representatives from the campus theaters; a faculty member who endorsed the
stand-ins; Rabbi Charles Mintz, president of the Austin Commission
on Human Relations; and Houston Wade met to discuss the situation.
The Texas and Varsity theaters agreed to desegregate, but the managers
reserved the right to cancel integration if it hurt business. SDA also
agreed to call off all other stand-ins in the city. The State and the Paramount refused to integrate, however, until "the rest of the Austin business district is ready." University of Texas students once again demonstrated against segregation at the Paramount and State theaters
beginning in March 1963.[21]

The SDA-initiated stand-in campaign seemed to be more successful than SNCC's campaign. The SDA influenced direct action in three other Texas cities and five cities across the nation. Rev. James Bevel, a civil rights activist in Nashville, reported that only in Nashville had protesters heeded SNCC's call for continuous demonstrating against segregated theaters. The amount of national recognition SDA received must have had at least some influence on SNCC's call for a "second phase."[22]

SDA became involved in other civil rights activities. In February 1961 the group joined the Young Democrats, the Student Party, and URC in soliciting money for black sharecroppers in Somerville, Tennessee, who faced economic retaliation for voting. SDA also challenged segregation on the campus. Houston Wade circulated a petition for the integration of University of Texas athletics and called for all facilities of tax-supported institutions to be opened to all students. Wade submitted the petition with six thousand signatures to the Board of Regents in September 1961. The next month an athletic integration referendum indicated that most students were satisfied with segregation.[23]

The university's dependence on state funds influenced the administration's policies concerning desegregation. The university had lost support in the state legislature because of integration during the 1950s. State Rep. Jerry Sadler of Precilla announced that he had voted against appropriations for the university "because they have Negro undergraduates." Rep. Joe Chapman of Sulphur Springs, another pro-segregation legislator, pointed out that the state legislature controlled the university through appropriations. During appropriations hearings in the late 1950s, university administrators dropped Barbara Smith, an African American, from the cast of an opera. Chapman had told UT President Logan Wilson that casting a black singer would result in bad publicity. Wilson argued that Chapman's call did not influence his decision to dismiss Smith, insisting instead that he had done so to keep the university from "becoming a battleground for extremists on both sides [of the integration question]." Board members rejected the athletic petition in the fall of 1961 because they believed they had gone further in desegregating the campus "than a majority of the citizens of Texas and of the members of the Legislature would approve" and would not be forced to desegregate by an active vocal minority of the student body.[24] The slow pace of integration, however, brought direct action onto campus.

The majority of dormitories on the University of Texas campus continued to exclude African Americans. In 1956 Tom Sealy, chairman of the Board of Regents, stated that the university would integrate for educational purposes but remain segregated for residential purposes. Black women could visit rooms in the hall, but the door had to remain closed. De facto segregation also banned African Americans from drinking fountains, bathrooms, and the lobby. University officials reaffirmed the policy of residential segregation in the fall of 1961. When officials announced that students violating segregation rules would be punished, fifty African Americans staged a sit-in in the lobby of Kinsolving dormitory, a white women's residence hall. Protesting students assembled in the lobby and ignored requests to leave as they sat for an hour talking, studying, or watching television. Soon after the incident, University of Texas President J. R. Smiley released a statement urging all students to keep "the real business of the University, which is the training of the intellect in a wholesome academic community," in mind. Smiley also said that the right to "the orderly expression of your thoughts and opinions" might be jeopardized by incidents such as the one at Kinsolving.[25]

Some regents planned to take steps more drastic than warning students. Chairman Hardie proclaimed:

> It is my thought that if we let these people get away without some punishment that they can understand and feel, we are inviting them to take mob action again, and they will undoubtedly do so whenever it suits them.

The dean called all black students into his office and asked if they had participated in the sit-in. Officials released students answering "no," put twenty-two students answering "yes" on disciplinary probation for the rest of the fall semester, and placed one student who refused to answer on probation until June 1. Officials charged the students with failing to comply with "properly constituted authority." The URC denounced the punishment, and student body president Maurice Olian called the actions "backward, narrow-minded, and hypocritical." Chairman Hardie demanded an apology for the statement, but Olian refused. News of the sit-in also created a stir at other colleges. President Smiley received a telegram from the student council of Brandeis University in Massachusetts protesting the disciplinary action; the council reported sending a similar telegram to U.S. Attorney General Robert Kennedy.[26] Although many university organizations denounced the probation, civil rights activists lost one ally on campus.

The Daily Texan, which had supported integration activities in the past, warned demonstrating students against "further agitation" that might alienate supporters. The pro-integration stand the paper had taken before the Kinsolving incident had brought the daily under the scrutiny of the Board of Regents. Hardie attacked actions of the newspaper in a letter to other board members a month before the Kinsolving sit-in. He specifically referred to editorials that criticized university officials for deciding not to integrate certain facilities. Hardie believed "that those in charge of *The Daily Texan* will, unless proper steps are taken, continuously malign and down grade The University of Texas and Board of Regents." He feared that the paper's attacks would cause the university to lose public support. Hardie suggested that students and faculty members in agreement with university policy should be encouraged to write letters and articles for the paper. In February 1962, the regents took selection of the editor away from the student body and gave a nine-member board the right to appoint the editor. The university claimed to have made the move to better journalism at the school.[27]

The faculty also voiced its opposition to university segregation policies. In May 1961 the general faculty recommended complete desegregation of the university as soon as possible. After the Kinsolving sit-in, the faculty voted 512 to 170 against dormitory segregation. Faculty opinion often conflicted with official university policy, and to some extent the university did lose public support as a result. One private citizen stopped a bequest of $10,000 to the university because of the faculty resolution opposing segregation in dormitory rest rooms. Although President Smiley received a number of letters opposing the probation given to the students involved in the Kinsolving sit-in, the majority of writers supported the action.[28]

The probation, however, did not deter civil rights activists. One hundred students singing "We Shall Not Be Moved" marched in front of Kinsolving and Whitis dormitories a few days after the sit-in and disciplinary actions. The university's Traffic and Security Division and Fire Department took pictures of the protesters for their records. Activists also utilized courts in an attempt to desegregate university dormitories. Three students, Leroy Sanders, Sherryl Griffin, and Maudie Ates, brought a lawsuit against university officials calling for the integration of dormitories. Campus groups supporting civil rights raised more than $2,500 to help finance the suit. The regents fought back by warning law professor Dr. Ernest Goldstein, who had given legal counsel to SDA, attended integration rallies, encouraged the students to file the dormitory lawsuit, and organized a petition calling for the desegregation of dormitories and dining facilities that 832 faculty members approved, not to become involved in the case or risk "disciplinary action." Although the students' lawyers argued that the federal funds borrowed for the building of Kinsolving should have precluded segregation, university officials claimed that dormitories were not part of the "educational process." Frustration over the length of the court's deliberations led to a demonstration in front of Kinsolving in January 1964. The case became moot in May 1964, when the Regents voted to end segregation in all university dormitories.[29]

Segregation hurt the university financially. In 1962 the Peace Corps canceled a $257,513 contract to train volunteers for a project in Brazil. Segregation in the Forty Acre Club, which claimed to be for "the faculty, staff, and friends of The University of Texas," first caused the Peace Corps to rethink giving the contract to the university. The university often utilized the off-campus club for meetings and official visitors. Segregation in the Forty Acre Club led to an investigation of other university practices. A Peace Corps official announced that the university's action on the dormitory integration suit represented "the catalytic agent" in the withdrawal of the contract. SDA challenged the university's association with the club. SDA cited a graduate seminar to be held in the club, the utilization of the club for official university visitors, and the club's use of university property for advertising as evidence of the association, and began to picket the club in August 1962. Four hundred faculty members censured the club, and some members resigned. The club accepted its first African American member in 1965.[30]

University of Texas students also demonstrated against a lounge near campus that remained segregated after passage of the federal Civil Rights Act of 1964. Roy's Lounge avoided compliance with the law by ending the service of food. Under the federal law, bars and taverns that did not serve food did not have to desegregate. Roy's remained segregated out of fear that integration would hurt business. After a nonviolent training session, the Student Interracial Committee (SIC) began protests in April 1965. Countermarchers confronted the activists, however, and strains of "Dixie" mingled with "We Shall Overcome." Opposition to desegregation came not only from blatant segregationists, such as members of the Society for the Prevention of Negroes Getting Everything (SPONGE), but also from students, such as members of

Young Americans for Freedom, who opposed government telling a private business whom to serve."[31]

The university did struggle against some forms of segregation. In the fall of 1962 it canceled ice skating classes at the Austin Ice Palace because of the rink's policy of segregation. Other university policies slowly changed. Darrell Royal, the university's athletic director and head football coach, announced complete desegregation of athletics in November 1963. After the end of the dormitory case in 1964, the university adopted an official policy against discrimination in any part of the university. University students remained active in challenging segregation in Austin, subsequently supporting a city anti-bias ordinance and participating in a parade depicting the burial of Uncle Tom.[32]

University of Texas students utilized direct action to challenge segregation. Of course, only a small minority of university students participated in these demonstrations, and one student referred to them as "red pawns." But demonstrations placed the spotlight on segregated facilities in Austin and often hurt profits of businesses. Although in many cases negotiations put an end to segregation, direct action forced businessmen to negotiate. Direct action also had an impact on university policies. The sit-in at Kinsolving led to the lawsuit against the university. After delivering a speech at the university in 1962, Dr. Martin Luther King Jr. consulted with students about the best strategy to bring about integration.[33] University administrators, however, attempted to censor student direct-action groups so as not to give the university a bad image with the majority of Texas citizens and the state legislature.

The University of Texas had made relatively large strides in integrating educational facilities in the 1950s, yet other non-academic facilities remained segregated, as the university administration attempted to slow desegregation so as not to alienate the powerful Texans who controlled the university's funding. Austin segregationists did respond with some violence and intimidation to civil rights demonstrations, but their reaction proved less violent than in the Deep South. Thus more civil rights activities could take place with less fear of retaliation. The civil rights demonstrations at the University of Texas were integrated protests, although some disagreements between participants of different races did occur.

Although the courts could order the integration of educational facilities, civil rights activists often resorted to direct action to bring about negotiations and lawsuits aimed at desegregating facilities over which the courts had less control. By the early 1960s, when the tactics of direct action spread throughout the south, a limited tradition of civil rights activities already existed on the University of Texas campus. The university YMCA, for example, had sponsored civil rights rallies since the 1940s.[34] This tradition and the integration struggles of the 1950s to some extent aided the introduction of direct action at the university. But University of Texas students not only applied strategies first employed elsewhere; to desegregate public facilities, they also pioneered the use of direct-action tactics which later gained national acceptance. Although not as well known as other civil rights battles, the activities on the University of Texas campus represent an important chapter in the story of the struggle for civil rights in America.

Notes

1. Michael L. Gillette, "Blacks Challenge the White University," *Southwestern Historical Quarterly*, LXXXVI (Oct., 1982), 321–344; Richard B. McCaslin, "Steadfast in His Intent: John W. Hargis and the Integration of the University of Texas at Austin," ibid., XCV (July, 1991), 21–41; William H. Chafe, *Civilities and Civil Rights: Greensboro, North Carolina, and the Black Struggle for Freedom* (New York: Oxford University Press, 1981), 17–55.

2. Release from Student Interracial Committee, Sept. 27, 1963, in Almetris Marsh Duren Papers, Center for American History, University of Texas at Austin (cited hereafter as CAH).

3. Student flyer in ibid.; "Integration-University of Texas," scrapbook, Vertical Files: Subject, CAH.

4. Austin *American*, Mar. 12 (1st quotation), April 21, 1960 (2nd–4th quotations); Dallas *Morning News*, Apr. 28, 1960. Attempts to desegregate Austin eating places began before 1960. In 1952 Sam Gibbs, a UT graduate assemblyman, wrote fifty-three restaurants asking them to drop racial bars. Most owners refused, while others announced a willingness to do so if others desegregated first. UT Chancellor's Office Records, System-Wide, Central Administration Policy and Procedure Files, 1962–64, Desegregation, CAH.

5. Austin *American*, Apr. 30, 1960 (quotation). Four UT students attended the National Student Conference on Sit-Ins in April 1960. *The Daily Texan* (Austin), Apr. 29, 1960.

6. *The Daily Texan* (Austin), Apr. 27 (quotation), 29, 1960.

7. Austin *American*, May 2, 15, 1960.

8. *The Daily Texan* (Austin), May 1, 5, Dec. 20, 1960; Austin *American*, Nov. 30, 1960 (quotation); San Antonio *Register*, Dec. 9, 1960.

9. James H. Lane, *Direct Action and Desegregation, 1960–1962: Towards a Theory of the Rationalization of Protest* (Brooklyn: Carlson Publishing, 1989), 332 (quotation); Chandler Davidson to Martin Kuhlman, Nov. 22, 1992 (interview).

10. *Texas Observer* (Austin), Dec. 9, 1960; "Integration-UT," scrapbook, CAH.

11. Dallas *Morning News*, Dec. 3, 1960 (quotation); *Texas Observer* (Austin), Dec. 9, 1960; San Antonio *Register*, Dec. 2, 1960.

12. *Texas Observer* (Austin), Dec. 9, 1960.

13. Dallas *Morning News*, Dec. 3, 1960 (2nd and 3rd quotations); *Texas Observer* (Austin), Jan. 14, 1961 (1st quotation).

14. *The Daily Texan* (Austin), Jan. 5, 1961.

15. *Texas Observer* (Austin), Jan. 14, 1961 (quotation); *The Daily Texan* (Austin), Jan. 10, 15, 1961.

16. UT Chancellor's Office Records, System-Wide, Central Administration Policy and Procedure Files, 1960–1962, Desegregation, CAH (cited hereafter as UT Chancellor's Office Records, Desegregation, 1960–1962); *The Daily Texan* (Austin), Feb. 13, 1961; Austin *American*, Feb. 13, 1961 (quotations); *Texas Observer* (Austin), Feb. 18, 1961; *New York Times*, Feb. 13, 1961.

17. *The Daily Texan* (Austin), Feb. 13, 1961 (1st and 3rd quotations); *Texas Observer* (Austin), Feb. 18, 1961 (2nd quotation); Davidson to Kuhlman (interview).

18. UT Chancellor's Office Records, Desegregation, 1960–1962 (1st and 2nd quotations); *The Daily Texan* (Austin), Feb. 16, 17, Mar. 17, 1961 (3rd quotation); Davidson to Kuhlman (interview).

19. *The Daily Texan* (Austin), Feb. 3, 28, Apr. 26, 1961 (quotation); *Texas Observer* (Austin), May 20, Sept. 9, 1961.

20. *Texas Observer* (Austin), Mar. 18 (1st quotation), June 10, 1961 (2nd quotation); Booker T. Bonner to Martin Kuhlman, Nov. 11, 1992 (interview). Bonner became an important figure in direct action as he led a civil rights march in Austin in 1963, joined the struggle for a municipal city rights ordinance in Austin, and became a field representative for the Southern Christian Leadership Conference in Texas. Austin *American*, Aug. 29, 1963; Dallas *Morning News*, Apr. 17, 1964; *Texas Observer* (Austin), Aug. 6, 1965.

21. *Texas Observer* (Austin), Sept. 9, 1961 (quotation); "Blacks-Integration," scrapbook, Vertical Files: Subject, CAH. A UT student working as an usher at the Paramount quit his job during the demonstration, saying he could not work in a place opposed to his principles. *The Daily Texan* (Austin), Mar. 10, 1963.

22. Aldon D. Morris, *The Origins of the Civil Rights Movement: Black Communities Organizing for Change* (New York: The Free Press, 1984), 232.

23. UT President's Office Records, Administrative Files, Desegregation, 1960–1966, CAH (cited hereafter as UT President's Office Records, Desegregation, 1960–1966); "Integration-UT," scrapbook, CAH; *The Daily Texan* (Austin), May 8, 1957.

24. Decision of Board, Fall 1961, UT President's Office Records, Desegregation, 1960–1966; "Integration-UT," scrapbook; *The Daily Texan* (Austin), May 8, 1957 (1st and 2nd quotations).

25. Almetris Marsh Duren, *Overcoming: A History of Black Integration at the University of Texas at Austin* (Austin: University of Texas Press, 1979), 6; Dallas *Morning News*, Oct. 22, 1961; Message to Student Body, Oct. 1961, UT President's Office Records, Desegregation, 1960–1966, CAH.

26. Thornton Hardie to Board of Regents Members, Oct. 27, 1961, UT President's Office Records, Desegregation, 1960–1966 (1st quotation); *Texas Observer* (Austin), Oct. 27, 1961. The cited number of students placed on disciplinary probation represents official university figures. The Campus Interracial Committee stated that seventy-five students received probation. Duren Papers.

27. Dallas *Morning News*, Oct. 22, 1961 (1st quotation); Hardie to Board of Regents Members, Oct. 27, 1961, UT President's Office Records, Desegregation, 1960–1966 (2nd quotation); *The Daily Texan* (Austin), July 28, 1961.

28. Duren Papers; UT Chancellor's Office Records, Desegregation, 1960–1962.

29. UT President's Office Records, Desegregation, 1960–1966 (quotations); Duren Papers; "Integration-UT," scrapbook.

30. Duren Papers; Duren, *Overcoming*, 11; *Texas Observer* (Austin), Aug. 3, Sept. 21, 1962 (2nd quotation).

31. "Integration-UT," scrapbook.

32. *The Daily Texan* (Austin), Sept. 20, 1962; UT Chancellor's Office Records, Desegregation, 1962–1964, CAH; "Integration-UT," scrapbook.

33. Duren, *Overcoming*, 11.

34. Gillette, "Blacks Challenge the White University," 339.

The Texas Negro Peace Officers' Association
The Origins of Black Police Unionism

W. MARVIN DULANEY

One of the long-standing issues in black communities nationwide has been the importance of having black officers on the police forces of urban areas. They are needed not only to understand and better serve the black community but also to create a measure of equity. In Houston, black policemen have served steadily since the late nineteenth century; the city council appointed the first black officer in 1870. In the earliest days after being allowed on police forces, African Americans usually worked in limited roles as a "colored police brigade," but over time their responsibilities increased, as did their numbers. As the numbers grew, Texas officers organized a black police union in 1935, the first in the United States. The Texas Negro Police Officers' Association, as Marvin Dulaney asserts, started essentially as a social club but expanded its activities over the years. The efforts of the union and the concerns of the leaders of the emerging civil rights movement in Houston led to changes in the use of black police. The actions led to the ability to arrest whites. At the same time, the behavior of white police in black communities underwent change. They were prevented from some of the most officious racist behavior of the past.

*

IN OCTOBER 1935, the six members of Houston's black police detail organized the Texas Negro Peace Officers' Association (TNPOA), the first organization of black police officers in the United States, founded to "increase the efficiency and cooperative spirit of its members." The TNPOA marked the beginnings of black police unionism. The Houston detail formed the nucleus of the organization and provided its impetus, although the organization later included black police officers from Galveston, Beaumont, and San Antonio. In forming this organization, the officers initiated a movement that attempted to address the precarious status of black police in Texas and the South. But the TNPOA's reach stretched much farther. It also provided a model that black police throughout the nation would use in their efforts to reform the token status of blacks in American police departments and to challenge the racism in American law enforcement.[1]

The conditions that black police unions such as the TNPOA attempted to address began when blacks first integrated American police departments in the nineteenth century. In the South, blacks became police officers almost immediately after the Civil War. Republican-controlled state and local governments in the South appointed blacks as police officers to address the violence of the Reconstruction period, such as the race riots in New Orleans and Memphis in 1866, and the terrorist violence against blacks in Texas. In the North, with the ratification of the 15th Amendment in 1870 and the extension of the franchise to black men, blacks began participating in machine politics and earned patronage jobs as police officers in most big city police departments. In both the North and the South, nineteenth-century black police functioned as essentially token police officers. They usually could not arrest whites, they worked exclusively in the neighborhoods and communities inhabited by other blacks, and they were not eligible for promotions within the police hierarchy. Usually, they did not even wear police uniforms. Only the black police appointed during Republican control in the South deviated from this token status. To quell the violence of the Reconstruction period, black police who served under Republican-controlled state and municipal governments not only arrested white lawbreakers; if necessary, they also used violent force. Indeed, many white southerners cited the presence of black police as one of the most objectionable experiences of the Reconstruction period.[2]

After the end of Reconstruction blacks lost access to police jobs in the South. While blacks in the North retained their token police jobs because of their continued participation in machine politics in most northern cities, violent intimidation and disfranchisement ended significant black political participation in the South. The presence of black police reminded many white southerners of Reconstruction—an era that they wanted to forget. Moreover, the presence of gun-toting, black law enforcement officers challenged the prevailing notions of white supremacy. Thus, by the beginning of the twentieth century, almost every major city in the South had eliminated blacks from police jobs and made police work and other government employment the exclusive preserve of white males.[3]

Unlike other major cities in the South, Houston retained a black presence on its police force. Just as in other southern cities, blacks obtained police jobs in Houston during Reconstruction, and the city council appointed the first black police in the city in 1870. Whites in Houston also objected to the presence of blacks as police officers, but after the end of Reconstruction blacks still retained a token presence on the police force. From 1870 to 1926, Houston maintained a special "colored police brigade," which consisted of at least one and sometimes as many as three black officers. The blacks who served in this "brigade" had a status similar to that of black police in the northern states: they could not arrest whites, they policed only other blacks, and they worked exclusively in Houston's black neighborhoods. Unlike the black police in the North, however, they generally did not wear uniforms, and the white members of the Houston police force did not recognize them as real police officers. Their low status as "special," token, or quasi-police officers and their assignment to handle only black crime problems probably explains why their presence was tolerated in Houston when every other major city in the South had eliminated blacks from police jobs.[4]

In the 1920s Houston police chief Tom Goodson attempted to upgrade the status of black police officers in the city and improve the department's relationship with the city's black community. After his appointment as chief of police in 1923, he issued orders banning police brutality. He chastised several police officers for their brutality against black citizens, and he suspended one white police officer for beating a black citizen on a street car. Beginning in 1925, Goodson moved to improve the status of blacks in the department by appointing nine blacks as police officers over a four-year period. In 1926, he even assigned two blacks to uniform and dismissed three white officers who objected to black officers in uniform and refused to march in a parade with them.[5]

Support for Goodson's reforms came from the Houston *Informer*, the city's largest black newspaper and from the Texas Commission on Interracial Cooperation. Prior to Goodson's appointment as police chief, Clifton F. Richardson, editor of the *Informer*, had editorialized against the crime problems in Houston's black neighborhoods and the mistreatment of Houston's black citizens by the police. In Richardson's opinion, the appointment of more black police officers would solve both problems. In addition, it would "reduce friction between the races to a minimum."[6] With better race relations as its prime objective, the Houston chapter of the Texas Commission on Interracial Cooperation organized in 1920 and began to act on Richardson's proposal to increase the number of black police in the city. While Richardson initially criticized the Commission as a way for whites to use blacks on the Commission to inform on other blacks, the Commission appeared to have had the influence and means to achieve what Richardson could not. Like Richardson, members of the Commission believed that increasing the number of black police in Houston and upgrading their status would improve race relations in the city. Black and white members of the Commission worked to achieve this objective, and in the Commission's annual reports for 1926 and 1928, they took credit for influencing both the mayor and police chief to act on the proposal of hiring additional black police officers in the city of Houston. The reports also indicated that the new black police had improved race relations and that the new men were "giving perfect satisfaction."[7]

Richardson's agitation in *The Informer* and the work of the Commission resulted in a net increase in the number of black police in Houston from two in 1923 to six by 1931. From 1929 to 1948, six became the quota for black police in the city. During that time period, the department appointed only one black police officer—after the accidental death of one member of the black police detail in 1938. Blacks in Houston would break the quota for black police in the city in 1948 by securing thirteen appointments as a payoff for their political support in the city council election of 1946. But the quota of six remained until that year. Despite this small quota for black police in Houston, only the upper South city of Louisville, Kentucky, employed more black officers. In the 1930s, all other cities in the lower South employed only one, two, or none.[8]

The increase in the size of Houston's black police detail and the fact that some began to wear uniforms, did not change their status as police officers. They still could not arrest whites. They still worked in predominantly black neighborhoods and communities in Houston. They remained ineligible for promotion in the Houston police department. Their status was similar to that of black police throughout the United States. Only the black police officers in large, northern cities such as Chicago and New York differed from this norm: the officers in these two cities could arrest whites and had received promotions above patrolman.

When blacks in fields such as law and medicine confronted racial discrimination and occupational restrictions earlier in the century, they responded by creating their own organizations such as the National Bar Association and the National Medical Association. Through these race organizations, they established their own professional standards and fought discriminatory policies in their professions. By the 1930s, black police in Houston had the numbers and leadership to start such an organization among black police officers in Texas.[9]

In 1934 Houston's black police detail took the first step toward organization. In that year they organized a ball to raise money for the police burial fund. Police officers mutual and benevolent associations throughout the nation held these fundraisers, but racial segregation in Houston mandated that black police officers in the city have a separate ball in order to contribute to a fund that benefited all police officers. The black police detail not only appealed to Houston's black community to support the ball, but they also invited other black police officers in South Texas to participate. Thus, black police officers from Galveston, Beaumont, and San Antonio also attended the ball.[10]

With the success of this first ball, Houston's black police detail organized a second ball the following year. Again, they extended an invitation to black police officers from Galveston, Beaumont, and San Antonio. But they used this social event as an opportunity to organize the TNPOA as well. The group elected Houston police officer James A. Ladd as the first president.[11]

No existing records reveal the initial purpose of the TNPOA in its first year. Nor is it clear why black police officers in South Texas decided to organize at this particular time. Retired Galveston police officer LeRoy "Buster" Landrum, who was present at the first organizational meeting in 1935, stated that in the beginning their purpose was more social than professional. According to Landrum, a fraternal spirit existed among the black police officers in South Texas. Black officers from Houston visited Galveston to attend social functions with him, and he in turn visited Houston to attend social functions sponsored by black police there. He also noted that black police in Texas had limited options: they could not socialize with white police officers because of racial segregation, but their police role was often a barrier to socializing extensively among other blacks. Past and recent studies of the relationship of black police officers to other blacks confirm Landrum's observations. While middle-class, educated blacks treated police officers with respect and some esteem, they still did not regard them as their social equals. Lower-class blacks did not hold them in high esteem and felt that black police inhibited and prevented their illegal and extralegal activities. Given their marginality in both the police culture and among other blacks, initially black police chose to organize both because they had common interests as police officers and in order to socialize with each other.[12]

The purpose of TNPOA, however, soon expanded to promote the hiring of black police officers throughout Texas and to make the TNPOA into a statewide organization. In 1936 members of the year-old TNPOA agreed to march in the Negro Day parade at the Texas State Fair's Centennial celebration in Dallas, in response to an invitation from the Dallas Negro Chamber of Commerce. This parade became the "coming out party" for the TNPOA. The TNPOA's first president, James A. Ladd of Houston, saw their appearance in Dallas as an opportunity to publicize the organization's existence throughout the state and to assist the Dallas Negro Chamber of Commerce in building support in that city for the appointment of blacks to the Dallas police force. Since the city had no black police officers to participate, the Dallas police chief assigned two police station orderlies uniforms for the parade to represent Dallas. Members of the TNPOA led the parade and the Dallas *Express*, the city's largest black newspaper, lauded the officers for bringing to Dallas "one of the most thrilling features" ever seen in the history of the city. Despite the impressive showing of the TNPOA's members from Houston, San Antonio, Austin, Galveston, Beaumont, and Port Arthur in the Negro Day parade, the Dallas police chief removed the two orderlies from uniform after the parade, and the Negro Chamber's effort to integrate the Dallas police force failed.[13]

The Dallas Negro Chamber of Commerce invited the members of the TNPOA to participate in the Texas State Fair's Negro Day parade on two more occasions, in 1937 and 1938. The Negro Chamber tried on both occasions to use the TNPOA as an example of the professionalism and efficiency of black police officers in order to convince Dallas city officials to integrate the city's police force. The meetings helped the Negro Chamber to raise the issue of appointing blacks as police officers in the city, but the effort again failed. Meanwhile, members of the TNPOA used the two trips to Dallas to strengthen their organization. In the 1937 visit, the TNPOA called a convention of black police officers in Texas and Oklahoma to "further the cause of Negro peace officers." A new organization, the "Texas and Oklahoma Association of Negro Peace Officers," emerged from the 1937 meeting, uniting black police officers in the two states. Prior to the 1938 visit to Dallas, the Texas and Oklahoma Association of Negro Peace Officers called for a national convention of black police officers. The Dallas Negro Chamber of Commerce hosted the three-day event, and forty black police officers attended as delegates. But "a squad of detectives" from Kansas City were the only officers outside of the states of Texas and Oklahoma to attend the event. Prior to this convention, TNPOA president James A. Ladd had announced plans to form a "national Negro police association." The poor attendance at the 1938 convention forestalled such plans.[14]

The TNPOA's attempt to organize a national black police officers association was subsequently echoed elsewhere in the country. In 1941 black police officers from ten states met in Atlantic City, New Jersey, to lay the groundwork for a national organization, but they also failed. In 1943 black police officers in New York City began holding informal meetings for what became the Black Guardians Association. In 1944 the city of Miami, Florida, appointed its first six black police officers; two years later they organized the Miami Colored Police Benevolent Association (MCPBA). Also in 1946, a racial incident involving a black police officer in Cleveland, Ohio, motivated black police in that city to organize the Shield Club.[15]

At its annual convention in 1949, the TNPOA again discussed the issue of a national organization. A year later, Houston police officer Henry Breed even traveled to Los Angeles in an attempt to interest black police in that city in a national organization, but he proved unsuccessful.[16] With the exception of the statewide TNPOA in Texas, only local efforts by black police to organize succeeded. Black police just did not have the numerical strength or the job security to organize a national group that could withstand reprisals from their white superiors. Reprisals were a serious concern, since the motivations that led black police outside of Texas to organize were not primarily social. In New York City, Miami, and Cleveland, black police organized to confront racial discrimination and departmental policies that prevented them from exercising their full authority as police officers. In the 1940s, black police officers in Texas began to develop a similar rationale for the TNPOA.

After the 1938 convention in Dallas, the TNPOA concentrated its efforts on building a strong black police organization in Texas. The organization met in Tulsa, Oklahoma, in 1939, but the Texas and Oklahoma Association of Negro Police Officers dissolved shortly afterward, and black police officers in Texas held no more meetings with those in Oklahoma. Beginning in 1940, the TNPOA held all of its annual conventions in Texas cities. The agendas of these conventions included topics that affected all police officers, such as the proper use of firearms and tear gas, proper arrest procedures, relationships with the FBI, marksmanship, and crime prevention.[17] Other issues on the agenda focused on the specific experiences and concerns of black police officers in Texas. The conventions themselves offered an opportunity to become more visible; through the 1940s and the 1950s, the TNPOA met in every major city of Texas in order to advertise the organization and to introduce the members of the TNPOA to white police officials throughout the state. This important concern merited frequent discussions at several TNPOA conventions because white police in Texas and throughout the South would arrest black police found carrying guns outside of their jurisdiction. The TNPOA met with white police officials throughout Texas in an attempt to promote courtesy and acknowledgement of common ground with white officers.[18]

Despite the meetings, the TNPOA members did not achieve any significant improvement in their status during the 1940s and 1950s. Racial discrimination continued to limit the police powers of black police officers throughout the South. Ironically, as the TNPOA sought to improve the status of black police in Texas, cities throughout the South that had no black police began to appoint black officers *with* restrictions on their police powers. Dallas and Savannah each appointed their first black police in 1947, Atlanta in 1948, New Orleans in 1950, and Fort Worth in 1953. All of these cities limited the police powers of black officers, and Atlanta even wrote the racial proscriptions into law.[19] Despite these restrictions, most southern cities claimed that the appointment of black police officers would deter and control crime in black neighborhoods. But as the appointment of thirteen blacks as police officers in Houston in 1948 indicated, southern politicians also made such appointments to satisfy the patronage demands of the black communities newly enfranchised by the invalidation of white primaries. White politicians wanted the black vote, but they would not give black officers the full authority to arrest whites and thus challenge the prevailing norms of white supremacy in the South. Thus, even in the 1940s and 1950s black police throughout the South had limited police powers and remained essentially token police officers.[20]

In the South, the TNPOA was one of only two black police organizations that attempted to address the question of how to protect the limited police authority of black police officers. (The other organization was the MCPBA in Miami.) The 1949 constitution of the TNPOA addressed this issue in its preamble and in a by-law providing for a defense fund for members. Given the nature of legal segregation throughout the state of Texas and the ever-present possibility that a black police officer would have an unfortunate encounter with a white lawbreaker, the TNPOA's defense fund served as the only source of legal support. Unlike white police officers, black police officers in Texas and throughout the South could not rely on their department's rank and file organizations to defend them if they were charged with dereliction of duty—especially if they violated the written or unwritten codes of racial etiquette in the performance of their duties. The TNPOA provided black police officers in Texas some insurance to protect their limited police powers and their jobs in the hostile, racially segregated environment in which they had to work. Southern police departments would also support black officers in some instances. But both the department's and TNPOA's support of black police officers still depended upon the circumstances and nature of their violation of the racial code in the performance of their duty. As a veteran black officer told Alvin V. Young when he joined the Houston police force in 1949, if he exercised police authority over whites, "you might beat the rap, but you won't beat the riot."[21]

In addition to protecting the limited police powers of black police in Texas, the TNPOA also sought to improve the relationship between black police officers and black citizens. In this endeavor the TNPOA was the forerunner in establishing the position that black police organizations adopted in the 1960s on police-black community relations. In the 1940s and 1950s, members of the TNPOA not only invited black citizens to participate in the public meetings and social events at its annual conventions, they also sought to end the adversarial relationship that some black citizens had with black police. In 1950, for example, Marshall Jenkins, president of the local TNPOA chapter in Houston, addressed the Fifth Ward Civic Club and the Knights of Peter Claver and stated that "the old time, untrained Negro police officer is being replaced by intelligent well-trained men." He also stated that the "old, Negro officers with no training" had been hired to use violence in the black community, to "whip heads and use whatever force necessary" to control the behavior of black citizens. According to Jenkins, the new black police officer was "carefully selected and highly trained, not only in handling prisoners, but in methods of treating the public."[22] Jenkin's assessment of the "new" black police officer's role in the black community represented a redefinition of the role. Black officers in the TNPOA believed that they could prove their professionalism as police officers by raising the standard of policing in the black community.[23]

From the inception of the TNPOA, its leadership had worked to develop a positive relationship between black police and black citizens.

As the first president and the chief spokesman of the TNPOA, Houston's James A. Ladd began this effort by appealing to the city's black community to support the police balls held in 1934 and 1935, by showcasing the organization in the 1936 Negro Day parade in Dallas, and by attempting to heighten professionalism through forming a national organization for black police. After Ladd's accidental death in 1938, the TNPOA's second president, Brown L. Brackens of San Antonio, opened the TNPOA's meetings to black citizens, promoted police work as a career for blacks, and involved the TNPOA in public service activities among black citizens outside of police work. Brackens served as president of the TNPOA for twenty years, and under his leadership the TNPOA received its first organizational charter in 1947, recruited new members from Dallas and Fort Worth, and helped to organize a similar black police association in Louisiana. Under Bracken's leadership the TNPOA also dropped "Negro" from its name in order to open the organization to all police officers and to bring the organization in line with the emerging civil rights movement across the South to end segregation.[24]

The status and background of black police officers changed greatly over these decades. The "new breed of black police officer" that Jenkins described in 1950 was better educated than earlier black officers and most white police officers. Most police departments did not require a college education for employment and few police officers attended college in this period. In the 1930s, this was true for blacks as well as for whites. Among six black officers in Houston who founded TNPOA in 1935, only one had attended college—William Stevenson, who attended Wiley and Huston Colleges.[25] Many of the black police officers recruited in southern cities in the 1940s and 1950s, however, had attended college. Indeed, black leaders throughout the South encouraged the most qualified young black men to join the police department. Black leaders wanted to ensure that the men chosen as police officers would do a good job and negate whites' claims that employing blacks as police officers was a risky experiment. In addition, racial discrimination in the private sector of the job market made police work attractive to young, college-educated blacks because of its civil service status and relative job security. For many black men, police work was the best that they could get, in spite of discrimination and restrictions associated with the job. As a result, it was no accident that both of the blacks appointed as police officers in Dallas in 1947 had attended college. Five of the eight black police officers appointed in Greensboro, North Carolina, in 1943 had attended college. At least five of the blacks appointed to the Houston force in the 1948–1949 group had attended college; among them was Alvin V. Young, a Prairie View A&M graduate and a World War II veteran.[26]

When Young joined the Houston police force in 1949, the status of black police had changed very little. As Young recalled, black police officers could not arrest whites, they worked exclusively in Houston's Third and Fifth Wards, and no black officer had ever achieved promotion above patrolman. Young's college degree did not open any new opportunities for him in the Houston Police Department. A dual system of law enforcement existed in Houston: one for blacks and one for whites, in which the same crimes were treated seriously depending on the race of the person involved. This hindered the police powers and advancement of black police officers and caused some black citizens not to respect them. In 1961 Henry Bullock of the Mayor's Negro Law Enforcement Committee also maintained that the dual law enforcement system in Houston caused the city's high homicide rate, since it taught citizens to ignore the law.[27] Young learned how to negotiate the dual enforcement system because veteran black officers on the force recruited him into the TPOA and he became an active member. He learned the organization's history and discerned how the organization attempted to protect the limited police powers of black officers in the state. Young became president of the TPOA in 1961 and led the group in its transition from a fraternal organization to a police union working to improve the status of black police officers throughout Texas and especially in Houston.[28]

Young became state president of the TPOA concurrently with the national civil rights movement in which black Americans sought to win the citizenship rights accorded other Americans. One of the issues raised by the movement was that of the brutality that some police had used in black communities throughout the United States. Opposition to police brutality and other unfair police practices united citizens and black officers against police departments and unions such as the Fraternal Order of Police and the Police Benevolent Association. As black officers were increasingly estranged from much of the rest of the police force and its predominantly white organizations, the role of black police groups expanded to combat discrimination both in the community and in the American police departments. Thus, in the 1960s, organizations such as the TPOA became unions and pressure groups that attempted to improve the policing that black communities received, to defend other blacks from police brutality, and to end the discrimination that limited the number of blacks in the profession and prevented their advancement.[29]

Young and the TPOA began to challenge the overt segregation in the Houston Police Department, especially the policy of separate patrols for black police officers and their exclusive assignment to patrol areas in Houston's black communities. The TPOA received support in this endeavor from black citizens in Houston and from black newspapers such as the Houston *Forward Times*; the *Forward Times*, in particular, publicized and challenged department policies that discriminated against black police officers. Along with other black organizations in Houston, such as the NAACP and the Harris County Council of Organizations, the *Forward Times* pressured the Houston Police Department to hire more black officers and to upgrade the status of those already on the force.[30] The pressure had some effect. A 1969 survey of black police deployment in Texas cited Houston as "the most progressive department in the state in the assignment of black officers." While it reported correctly that the Houston police department had begun to "integrate" by pairing black and white police officers in patrol cars and assigning them in all parts of the city on a nonracial basis, the survey failed to note that such reforms had occurred because of pressure from black police officers and black citizens. Furthermore, the survey provided incorrect information on several points. The most glaring error was in its statement that black police in Houston had been "promoted to supervisory positions and employed in every division of the department."[31] In fact, the Houston Police Department did not promote a black police officer to a supervisory role until 1974, thus becoming one of the last major cities in the United States to promote a black officer above patrolman. Even San Antonio and Dallas, two cities that had approximately one-third and one-half of the fifty-four black police officers that Houston employed in 1970, respectively, promoted blacks to supervisory positions earlier than did Houston. Dallas had a black deputy police chief in 1973, before Houston had its first black sergeant. The failure of the Houston Police Department to promote blacks to supervisory roles led to two lawsuits against the department in 1973 and 1976.[32]

Young was one of the plaintiffs in the 1976 lawsuit and his participation indicated the different strategies and tactics that black police officers and their organizations used in the 1960s and 1970s to seek redress for their grievances. No longer did black police officers accept discrimination and token roles without challenging them. They used their police organizations and unions to represent their claims, and they often clashed with the older rank-and-file police associations. For example, immediately after the filing of the 1976 lawsuit the Houston Police Association threatened to file a countersuit to prevent the black police officers' suit from blocking the promotion of white police officers in Houston. This incident was indicative of the difference between the old-line organizations, which sought to preserve the privileges that white police officers had, and black police organizations, which emerged as unions to upgrade the status of black police officers in American law enforcement.[33]

By the time that the TPOA made the successful transition from a fraternal organization to a police union advocating the rights of black police officers and working to improve their status, such groups had emerged in every major American city. Many new black police organizations had joined the TPOA, the Shield Club of Cleveland, the MCPBA of Miami, and the Black Guardians of New York City in the struggle to upgrade black police positions. In 1972, thirty-three of these organizations met in St. Louis to form the National Black Police Association, finally realizing the vision of James A. Ladd, Brown L. Brackens, Leroy Landrum, and the other black police officers who met in Houston in 1935 to lay the groundwork for the movement.[34]

Notes

1. There is very little scholarly work on the formation of black police organizations and unions. Chapter 9 of Hervey A. Juria and Peter Feuille, *Police Unionism, Power and Impact in Public Sector Bargaining* (Lexington, Massachusetts, 1973), discusses black police unions, but it does not address the origins of black police unionism and why black police unions are different from the typical rank-and-file police organizations and associations. Richard L. Bolden's "A Study of the Black Guardian Association in the New York City Police Department from 1943–1978" (Ph.D. diss., Columbia University, 1980), is the only other study that addresses thoroughly the phenomenon of black police unionism. The founding date for the Texas Negro Peace Officers' Association and the quote are found in the *Constitution of the Texas Negro Peace Officers' Association* (Beaumont, 1949), 1, and the *Texas Peace Officers' Association Golden Anniversary Annual State Conference Souvenir Program* (San Antonio, 1983), respectively.

2. Howard N. Rabinowitz, "The Conflict Between Blacks and Police in the

Urban South, 1865–1900," *The Historian* 39 (November 1976): 62–76; Rabinowitz, *Race Relations in the Urban South, 1865–1890* (New York, 1978), 31–60; W. Marvin Dulaney, "Black Shields: A Historical and Comparative Survey of Blacks in American Police Forces" (Ph.D. diss., The Ohio State University, 1984), 12–15; and Vernon L. Wharton, *The Negro in Mississippi, 1865–1890* (New York, 1963), 168. For the violence against blacks in Texas during Reconstruction, see Barry Crouch, "A Spirit of Lawlessness: White Violence, Texas Blacks, 1865–1868," *Journal of Social History* 18 (Winter 1984), 217–232; Record of Criminal Offenses Committed in the State of Texas, September, 1865–December, 1868, Roll 32, Records of the Assistant Commissioner for the State of Texas, Bureau of Refugees, Freedmen and Abandoned Lands, 1865–1868, National Archives, Washington, D.C.

3. Dulaney, 14–18. Two articles by Dennis C. Rousey illustrate how two southern cities maintained a black presence on the police force after Redemption, but both cities eliminated them by the early twentieth century. See Rousey, "Yellow Fever and Black Policemen in Memphis: A Post Reconstruction Anomaly," *Journal of Southern History* 51 (August 1985): 357–374; Rousey, "Black Policemen in New Orleans During Reconstruction," *The Historian* 49 (February 1987): 223–243. The following sources indicate how blacks lost police jobs in the South: Cleveland *Gazette*, September 27, 1884, and March 5, 1890; New Orleans *Daily Picayune*, April 4, 1889, and "New Orleans Gets Two Negro Police," Press Release, June 19, 1950, Associated Negro Press Clipping File, Claude A. Barnett Papers, Chicago Historical Society (hereafter cited as ANP Clipping File).

4. For the black police in Houston, see the Houston *Telegraph*, December 11, 1870; Marion E. Merseberger, "A Political History of Houston, Texas, During the Reconstruction Period As Recorded by the Press, 1868–1873" (M.A. thesis, Rice Institute, 1950), 108; and Louis Marchiafava, *The Houston Police, 1878–1948*, Rice University Studies 63 (Houston, 1977), 11–13. For reference to the "colored police brigade," see a 1910 clipping entitled "Police Time Book Entries" in Mrs. Patrick H. Campbell, "Scrapbook of Clippings, 1900–1923," vol. 2, Texas and Local History Department, Houston Public Library. The presence of blacks on the Houston police force can also be followed in Morrison and Fourmy's *Houston City Directories, 1870–1926*, which listed every police officer on the force and identified the black police by (c), (col'd), or (col). Some of the black police officers in Houston during Reconstruction were also members of the Texas State Police. See Ann Patton Baenziger, "The Texas State Police During Reconstruction," *Southwestern Historical Quarterly* 72 (April 1969): 470–491; and the Houston *Forward Times*, June 15, 1963.

5. Houston *Informer*, January 20, 1923, and June 5 and 12, 1926.

6. *Ibid.*, February 19, 1921, and June 20, 1923.

7. *Ibid.*, November 11, 1922. *Texas Commission on Interracial Cooperation—Miscellaneous Publications* (Houston, 1925–1926); Minutes of the Annual Meeting

of the Texas Commission on Interracial Cooperation, Houston, Texas, November 6, 1926; *Condensed Reports of the Conditions in Texas Affected By the Texas Commission on Interracial Cooperation, November, 1925–February, 1928* (Houston, 1928). All of the Commission documents are located in the Texas Commission on Interracial Cooperation Records, Houston Metropolitan Research Center, Houston Public Library. For a critical analysis of the 1920s Interracial Commission movement in the South, see John H. Stanfield, "Northern Money and Southern Bogus Elitism: Rockefeller Foundations and the Commission on Interracial Cooperation Movement, 1919–1920," *Journal of Ethnic Studies* 13 (Summer 1987): 1–22.

8. Houston *Informer*, June 5, 1926, March 10, 1928, September 21, 1929, and April 7, 1948; Dallas *Express*, November 12, 1938; Mrs. James S. Crate, "Texas Commission Works for Human Rights," *New South* (October 1948), 14, 20; Chandler Davidson, *Biracial Politics: Conflict and Coalition in the Metropolitan South* (Baton Rouge, 1972), 121. The City of Houston, *Annual Reports: Police Department, 1925–1931*, also listed the black police appointments in this period. Monroe N. Work, ed., *Negro Year Book*, 1921–1922, 1925–1926, 1931–1932, 1937–1938 (Tuskegee, Alabama), listed the cities in the South that employed at least one black police officer for the years given. Work reported that outside of three cities in Florida, only Houston, San Antonio, Austin, Galveston, and Beaumont employed black police officers in the lower South.

9. Dulaney, 34–39. For the status of black police in Chicago, see Harold F. Gosnell, *Negro Politicians: The Rise of Negro Politics in Chicago* (Chicago, 1935), 244–279; and for New York, James I. Alexander, *Blue Coats, Black Skin: The Black Experience in the New York City Police Department Since 1891* (Hicksville, New York, 1978). For the origins of the National Bar Association and the National Medical Association, see August Meier, *Negro Thought in America, 1880–1915: Racial Ideologies in the Age of Booker T. Washington* (Ann Arbor, Michigan, 1971), 127, 262. For a discussion of the need for race organizations, such as the NBA and NMA, by Houston publisher and editor Carter Wesley, see his editorials in the Dallas *Express*, September 1 and 8, 1951.

10. Houston *Informer*, February 17 and 24, 1934, and March 24, 1934; Leroy "Buster" Landrum, interview by author, January 7, 1987, Galveston, Texas.

11. Landrum interview; Dallas *Express*, September 3, 1949; *Constitution of the Texas Negro Peace Officers' Association*, 8.

12. Landrum interview. Several studies analyze the relationship of black police to black citizens and the dichotomy between the feelings of lower and middle class blacks toward black police. A partial listing: James Ball III, "A Study of Negro Policemen in Selected Florida Municipalities" (M.A. thesis, Florida State University, 1954); Elliott M. Rudwick, "The Negro Policeman in the South," *Journal of Criminal Law, Criminology and Police Science* 31 (July–August, 1960): 273–276; William

M. Kephart, *Racial Factors and Urban Law Enforcement* (Philadelphia, 1957); Nicholas Alex, *Black in Blue: A Study of the Negro Policeman* (New York, 1969); Dulaney, Ch. 5. Jon J. Daykin, "A Study of Negro Police Officers in Eleven Selected Major Mid-South Cities" (M.A. thesis, University of Mississippi, 1963), 28, advanced the thesis that black police officers were "marginal men" since they could not be a part of the police culture because of their race, nor a part of the black community because of their jobs as police officers.

13. Landrum interview; Dallas *Express*, October 17 and 31, 1936; Alvin V. Young, interview by author, November 10, 1977, Houston, Texas; "Dallas Gets Negro Policemen," Press Release, October 23, 1936, ANP Clipping File.

14. Dallas *Express*, September 2, 1937, October 2 and 30, 1937, August 6, 1938, September 10 and 24, 1938, and October 1, 8, 15, and 22, 1938.

15. *Ibid.*, September 6, 1941; Bolden, 35–36; Atlanta *World*, September 3, 1944; Robert Ingram, "Brother Man," in *The Officer Victor Butler Souvenir Program* (Miami, 1971), 4; Cleveland (Ohio) *Call and Post*, September 28, 1946, and October 5, 1946; Dallas *Express*, September 3, 1949.

16. Los Angeles *Sentinel*, July 13, 1950; Dulaney, Ch. 3.

17. Dallas *Express*, July 29, 1939, and September 9, 1939. For examples of the issues addressed by the TNPOA in the 1940s, see the Dallas *Express*, August 30, 1946, and the Houston *Informer*, August 21, 1948. For a comparison with the overall police unionization movement in the period, see Robert M. Fogelson, *Big-City Police* (Cambridge, Massachusetts, 1977), Ch. 3.

18. Dallas *Express*, August 23 and 30, 1947, August 28, 1948, August 20, 1949, and September 3, 1949; Houston *Informer*, May 1, 1954, and September 3, 1955. Alvin V. Young discussed this problem with the author in the November 10, 1977, interview. Examples of the problems that black police had outside their jurisdiction can be found in the Dallas *Express*, August 7, 1948; Houston *Informer*, August 21, 1948, and January 30, 1954; "Negro Cop's Arrest Fought by Milwaukee—City Lawyer to Defend Him in Tennessee," Press Release, June 16, 1959, ANP Clipping File.

19. Atlanta *World*, May 6, 1947; Dallas *Morning News*, March 25, 1947; Atlanta *World*, April 3, 1948; "New Orleans Gets Two Negro Police"; Dallas *Express*, January 10, 1953; City of Atlanta, *Council Minutes* XLV, December 1, 1947, 86–88.

20. The *Smith v. Allwright* case, which ended the white primary in Texas and in other parts of the South, was instrumental in opening up the political process to blacks and their acquiring police jobs. Houston *Informer*, April 17, 1948. For examples of the political nature of black police appointments in the South, see Herbert T. Jenkins, "Police Progress and Desegregation in Atlanta," *New South* (June 1962): 10–13; Elliott M. Rudwick, "Negro Police Employment in the Urban South," *Journal of Negro Education* 30 (Spring 1961): 102–108; Harold C. Fleming, "How Negro

Police Worked Out in One Southern City," *New South* (October 1947): 3–5, 7; Dulaney, 40–41. For an analysis of the subordinate position of black police in the
South, see Gunnar Myrdal, *An American Dilemma: The Negro Problem and Modern Democracy* (New York, 1944), 542–545.

21. Alvin V. Young, interview by author, January 6, 1987, Houston, Texas. Juris
and Feuille in *Police Unionism* discuss the defense funds maintained by organizations such as the Police Benevolent Association and the Fraternal Order of Police.
The TNPOA's defense fund is cited in the 1949 *Constitution*, 2, 5. The TNPOA's
charter, "Charter of the Texas Negro Peace Officers' Association," No. 90976, filed
in Bexar County, Texas, April 10, 1947, also listed the organization's purpose and
objectives. An exception to the rule was the Houston Police Association's defense of
Officer H. G. Mackey after he was arrested for carrying his gun in Madisonville,
Texas. Dallas *Express*, August 7, 1948. For an assessment of how black police in
Houston felt about their limited arrest powers and the support that the Houston police department would provide them, see the Dallas *Morning News*, October 30,
1946.

22. Dallas *Express*, November 5, 1950.

23. Rudwick, "Negro Policeman in the South," 276; Kephart, 122. Jenkin's assessment of the role of black police officers in black communities is an important
counterpoint to that of a black police officer in Chicago who justified the use of the
"old methods"—beating and killing black offenders. See Sylvester, "Two Gun Pete"
Washington, "Why I Killed 11 Men," *Ebony* (January 1950): 51–57.

24. For Ladd's activities as the leader of the TNPOA, see the Houston *Informer*,
February 24, 1934; Dallas *Express*, October 30, 1937, October 1, 8, and 15, 1938.
Ladd was struck by a bus and killed in 1938. Dallas *Express*, November 12, 1938.
For references to Bracken's leadership, see the *Express*, August 30, 1947, and September 3, 1949; Houston *Informer*, May 1, 1954, August 28, 1954, May 7, 1955, and
September 3, 1955; *Golden Anniversary Souvenir Program*. Bracken's efforts to recruit members for the TNPOA are documented in the *Express*, August 15, 1953, and
in his letter to A. Maceo Smith of the Dallas Negro Chamber of Commerce, July 20,
1949, Correspondence, Dallas Negro Chamber of Commerce Collection, Texas-
Dallas Collection, Dallas Public Library. The influence of Brackens and the TNPOA
on the formation of the Louisiana Magnolia State Peace Officers Association is
noted in an interview with Chief Julius Guillory of Opelousas, Louisiana, by Harry
Gardner, May 15, 1977, and in the Houston *Informer*, May 1, 1954. For the
TNPOA's name change to Texas Peace Officers' Association, see "Domestic
Amendment of the Texas Negro Peace Officers' Association," No. 17-90976, filed in
Galveston County, May 31, 1955. For an example of the involvement of the TNPOA
in public service activities, see the Dallas *Express*, April 19, 1947.

25. Houston *Informer*, May 15, 1948.

26. Rudwick, "Negro Policeman in the South," 274; Atlanta *Constitution,* April 4, 1948; Dallas *Express,* February 8, 1947; Young interview, November 10, 1977; Houston *Chronicle,* March 9, 1969.

27. Henry A. Bullock, Chairman of the Mayor's Negro Law Enforcement Committee, *Report to the Honorable Lewis Cutrer, Mayor, City of Houston: The Houston Murder Problem: Its Nature, Apparent Causes, and Probable Cure* (Houston, 1961), 69–84, available in the Texas and Local History Department, Houston Public Library.

28. Young interviews, November 10, 1977, August 25, 1978 (Chicago), and January 5, 1987; Houston *Chronicle,* August 12, 1959.

29. Fogelson, Ch. 10; Alex, 209; Alexander, 80–108; Bolden, 60–74; Dulaney, 68–76.

30. Houston *Forward Times,* February 16, 1963, April 22, 1967, and February 28, 1970; Davidson, 121; Houston *Chronicle,* January 24, 1961, and March 9, 1969; Houston *Post,* February 3, 1970, and April 16, 1970.

31. Donald A. Cole, George G. Kellinger, Charles M. Friel, and Hazel B. Kerper, *The Negro Law Enforcement Officer in Texas,* vol. 1, Criminal Justice Monograph (Huntsville, Texas, 1969), 67.

32. City of Houston, Civil Service Department, *Affirmative Action Report* (Houston, January, 1974), 107. For the first promotions in Houston, see the Houston *Post,* April 15, 1974. The Dallas *Post Tribune,* June 26, 1982, and John J. Grimes, "The Black Man in Law Enforcement: An Analysis of the Distribution of Black Men in Law Enforcement Agencies and the Related Recruitment Problems" (M.A. thesis, John Jay College of Criminal Justice, 1969), 112, provide the information on black police promotions in other major cities up to 1970. For the two lawsuits, see the Houston *Chronicle,* October 30, 1973; Houston *Post,* October 23, 1976.

33. Houston *Post,* October 26, 1976. For a more comprehensive study of the conflict between black and white police associations, see Leonard Ruchelman, *Police Politics: A Comparative Study of Three Cities* (Cambridge, Massachusetts, 1974), and Edward Palmer, "Black Police in America," *The Black Scholar* 5 (October 1973): 19–27.

34. For the origins and purpose of the National Black Police Association, see Norman Seay, Coordinator of the First National Conference of Black Policemen, to Colonel Delbert Miller, president, St. Louis Board of Police Commissioners, July 18, 1972, Correspondence of the St. Louis Ethical Police Society, and a news release issued by Norman Seay, August 29, 1972, announcing the formation of the National Black Police Association. The author has copies of both documents.

Black Texas History:
A Selected Bibliography

BRUCE A. GLASRUD

Abernethy, Francis E., Carolyn Fiedler Satterwhite, Patrick B. Mullen, and Alan B. Govenar, eds. *Juneteenth Texas: Essays in African-American Folklore.* Denton: University of North Texas Press, 1996.

Abramowitz, Jack. "John B. Rayner—A Grass-Roots Leader." *The Journal of Negro History* 36 (1951): 160–193.

Addington, Wendell C. "Slave Insurrections in Texas." *Journal of Negro History* 35 (1950): 408–434.

Ainslie, Ricardo C. *Long Dark Road: Bill King and Murder in Jasper, Texas.* Austin: University of Texas Press, 2004.

Akers, Monte. *Flames after Midnight: Murder, Vengeance, and the Desolation of a Texas Community.* Austin: University of Texas Press, 1999.

Alexander, Charles C. *Crusade for Conformity: The Ku Klux Klan in Texas, 1920–1930.* Houston: Texas Gulf Coast Historical Association, 1962.

———. "Secrecy Bids for Power: The Ku Klux Klan in Texas Politics in the 1920's." *Mid-America* 46 (1964): 3–28.

Alyn, Glen. *I Say Me for a Parable: The Oral Autobiography of Mance Lipscomb, Texas Bluesman.* New York: Da Capo Press, 1993.

Amin, Julius. "Black Lubbock: 1955 to the Present." *West Texas Historical Association Year Book* 65 (1989): 24–35.

Ashburn, Karl E. "Slavery and Cotton Production in Texas." *Southwestern Social Science Quarterly* 14 (1933): 257–271.

Atkins, J. Alton. *The Texas Negro and His Political Rights: A History of the Fight of the Negro to Enter the Democratic Primaries of Texas.* Houston, Tex.: Webster Publishing Company, 1932.

Bailey, Anne J. "A Texas Cavalry Raid: Reaction to Black Soldiers and Contrabands." *Civil War History* 35 (June 1989): 138–152.

———. "Was There a Massacre at Poison Spring?" *Military History of the Southwest* 20 (Fall 1990): 157–168.

Bailey, Herbert J. "Charles Bellinger and Jim Crow in San Antonio, Texas,

1905–1937." *South Texas Studies* 4 (1993): 75–88.

Baker, T. Lindsay, and Julie P. Baker, eds. *Till Freedom Cried Out: Memories of Texas Slave Life*. College Station: Texas A&M University Press, 1997.

Banks, Melvin James. *The History of the New Hope Baptist Church: A Century of Faith*. Dallas: New Hope Baptist Church, 1967.

———. "The Pursuit of Equality: The Movement for First Class Citizenship among Negroes in Texas, 1920–1950." Ss.D. dissertation, Syracuse University, 1962.

Barker, Eugene C. "Influence of Slavery in the Colonization of Texas." *Mississippi Valley Historical Review* 11 (June 1924): 3–36.

———. "The African Slave Trade in Texas." *Texas Historical Association Quarterly* 6 (1902): 145–158.

Barr, Alwyn. "African Americans in Texas: From Stereotypes to Diverse Roles." In *Texas Through Time: Evolving Interpretations*, edited by Walter L. Buenger and Robert A. Calvert, 50–80. College Station: Texas A&M University Press, 1991.

———. "Black Migration into Southwestern Cities, 1865–1900." In *Essays On Southern History: Written In Honor of Barnes F. Lathrop*, edited by Gary W. Gallagher, 15–38. Austin: General Libraries of University of Texas, 1980.

———. "The Black Militia of the New South: Texas as a Case Study." *Journal of Negro History* 63 (July 1978): 209–219.

———. "Black Texans." In *A Guide to the History of Texas*, edited by Light Townsend Cummins and Alvin R. Bailey Jr., 107–121. Westport, Conn.: Greenwood Press, 1988.

———. "Black Legislators of Reconstruction Texas." *Civil War History* 32 (1986): 340–352.

———. *Black Texans: A History of African Americans in Texas, 1528–1995*. Second edition. Norman: University of Oklahoma Press, 1996.

———. "The Right to Vote." In *Reconstruction to Reform: Texas Politics, 1876–1906*, 193–208. Austin: University of Texas Press, 1971.

———. "The Texas 'Black Uprising' Scare of 1883." *Phylon* 41 (1980): 179–186.

———. "The Impact of Race in Shaping Judicial Districts, 1876–1907." *Southwestern Historical Quarterly* 108 (2005): 423–439.

Barr, Alwyn, and Robert A. Calvert, eds. *Black Leaders: Texans for Their Times*. Austin: Texas State Historical Association, 1981.

Barr, Alwyn, and Robert L. Foster. "Black Lubbock." *West Texas Historical Association Yearbook* 54 (1978): 20–31.

Beeth, Howard. "A Black Elite Agenda in the Urban South: The Call for Political and Racial Economic Solidarity in Houston during the 1920s." *Essays in Economic and Business History* 10 (June 1922): 41–55.

———. "Houston & History, Past and Present: A Look at Black Houston in the 1920s." *Southern Studies* 25 (Summer 1986): 172–186.

Beeth, Howard, and Cary D. Wintz, eds. *Black Dixie: Afro-Texan History and Culture in Houston.* College Station: Texas A&M University Press, 1992.

Beil, Gail K. "Dr. James Leonard Farmer: Texas' First Black Ph.D." *East Texas Historical Journal* 36.1 (1998): 18–25.

———. "Melvin Tolson—Texas Radical." *East Texas Historical Journal* 40.1 (2002): 26–36.

———. "Sowing the Seeds of the Civil Rights Movement: Dr. Leonard J. Farmer and Wiley College, Marshall, Texas, as Case Studies of the Educational Influence on Modern Civil Rights Leaders." Master's thesis, Stephen F. Austin State University, 1999.

Bernstein, Patricia. *The First Waco Horror: The Lynching of Jesse Washington and the Rise of the NAACP.* College Station: Texas A&M University Press, 2005.

Blackwelder, Julia Kirk. *Styling Jim Crow: African American Beauty Training During Segregation.* College Station: Texas A&M University Press, 2003.

Boone, Theodore Sylvester. *Feet Like Polished Brass.* Fort Worth, Tex.: Masonic Printing Department, 1933.

———. *"Old Chief," Alexander Lorenza Boone, D.D., LL.D.; A Biography By His Son.* Houston, Tex.: Western Star Publishing Company, 1927.

———. *The Philosophy of Booker T. Washington: The Apostle of Progress, The Pioneer of the New Deal.* Fort Worth, Tex.: Manney Printing, 1939.

———. *Paramount Facts in Race Development.* Chicago: Hume, 1921.

———. *From George Lisle to L. K. Williams: Short Visits to the Tombs of Negro Baptists.* Detroit: A. P. Publishing Company, 1941.

Boswell, Angela. *Her Act and Deed: Women's Lives in a Rural Southern County, 1837–1873.* College Station: Texas A&M University Press, 2001.

Botson, Michael R., Jr. *Labor, Civil Rights, and the Hughes Tool Company.* College Station: Texas A&M University Press, 2005.

Branch, Hettye Wallace. *The Story of "80 John": A Biography of One of the Most Respected Negro Ranchmen in the Old West.* New York: Greenwich Book Publishers, 1960.

Brandenstein, Sherilyn. "Prominent Roles of Black Women in *Sepia Record*, 1952–1954." Master's thesis, University of Texas at Austin, 1989.

———. "*Sepia Record* as a Forum for Negotiating Women's Roles." In *Women and Texas History: Selected Essays,* edited by Fane Downs and Nancy Baker Jones, 143–157. Austin: Texas State Historical Association, 1993.

Brewer, J. Mason. *An Historical Outline of the Negro in Travis County [Texas].* Austin, Tex.: Samuel Huston College, 1940.

———. *Negro Legislators of Texas and Their Descendants: A History of the Negro in Texas Politics from Reconstruction to Disfranchisement.* Dallas, Tex.: Mathis Publishing, 1935.

———. *Aunt Dicy Tales: Snuff-Dipping Tales of the Texas Negro.* Austin, Tex.: J. Mason Brewer, 1956.

———. *Dog Ghosts and Other Texas Negro Folk Tales.* Austin: University of Texas Press, 1958.

———, ed. *Heralding Dawn: An Anthology of Verse by Texas Negroes.* Dallas, Tex.: June Thomason Printing, 1936.

———. "Juneteenth." In *Tone the Bell Down*, edited by J. Frank Dobie, 9–54. Austin: Texas Folklore Society, 1932.

———. *Negrito.* San Antonio, Tex.: Naylor, 1933.

———. "Old Time Negro Proverbs." In *Spur-of-the-Cock*, edited by J. Frank Dobie, 101–105. Austin: Texas Folklore Society, 1933.

———. *The Word on the Brazos: Negro Preacher Tales from the Brazos Bottoms of Texas.* Austin: University of Texas Press, 1953.

Britten, Thomas A. *A Brief History of the Seminole-Negro Indian Scouts.* Lewiston, N.Y.: Mellen Press, 1999.

———. "The Dismissal of the Seminole-Negro Indian Scouts, 1880–1914." *Fort Concho and the South Plains Journal* 24 (1992): 54–77.

———. "The History of the Seminole-Negro Indian Scouts." Master's thesis, Hardin-Simmons University, 1990.

———. "The Seminole-Negro Indian Scouts in the Big Bend." *Journal of Big Bend Studies* 5 (1993): 67–77.

Brophy, William J. "Black Business Development in Texas Cities, 1900–1950." *Red River Valley Historical Review* 6 (Spring 1981): 42–55.

———. "The Black Texan, 1900–1950: A Quantitative History." Ph.D. dissertation, Vanderbilt University, 1974.

———. "Black Texans and the New Deal." In *The Depression in the Southwest*, edited by Donald W. Whisenhunt, 117–133, 153–154. Port Washington, N.Y.: Kennikat, 1980.

———. "Active Acceptance—Active Containment: The Dallas Story." In *Southern Businessmen and Desegregation*, edited by Elizabeth Jacoway and David R. Colburn, 137–150. Baton Rouge: Louisiana State University Press, 1982.

Bryan, Marilyn T. "The Economic, Political and Social Status of the Negro in El Paso." *Password* 13 (1968): 74–86.

Bryant, Ira B. "The Need for Negro History in the Schools of Texas." *Negro History Bulletin* 20 (January 1957): 77–78.

———. *The Texas Negro Under Six Flags.* Houston, Tex.: Houston College for Negroes, [1936].

———. *Barbara Charline Jordan: From the Ghetto to the Capitol.* Houston, Tex.: D. Armstrong Company, 1977.

———. "Administration of Vocational Education in Negro High Schools of Texas." Ed.D. dissertation, University of Southern California, 1948.

————. *The Development of the Houston Negro Schools.* Houston, Tex.: Webster Publishing Company, 1935.

————. *Texas Southern University: Its Antecedents, Political Origin, and Future.* Houston, Tex.: D. Armstrong Company, 1975.

————. "Vocational Education in Negro High Schools in Texas." *The Journal of Negro Education* 18 (Winter 1949): 9–15.

Bryson, Conrey. *Dr. Lawrence A. Nixon and the White Primary.* Southwestern Studies Monograph no. 42. El Paso: Texas Western Press, 1974.

————. "El Paso and the Poll Tax." *Password* 4 (1959): 46–52.

Bugbee, Lester E. "Slavery in Early Texas." *Political Science Quarterly* 13 (September–December 1898): 398–412, 648–668.

Bullard, Robert D. "The Black Family: Housing Alternatives in the 80s." *Journal of Black Studies* 14 (March 1984): 341–351.

————. "Black Housing in the Golden Buckle of the Sunbelt." *Free Inquiry* 8 (November 1980): 169–172.

————. "Dispute Resolution and Toxics: Case Studies." In *Dumping in Dixie: Race, Class, and Environmental Quality,* second edition, 37–74. Boulder, Colo.: Westview Press, 1994.

————. "Endangered Environs: The Price of Unplanned Growth in Boomtown Houston." *California Sociologist* 7 (Summer 1984): 84–102.

————. *Fear of Crime, Fear of Police and Black Residents' Endorsement of Crime–Reduction Strategies.* Houston: Texas Southern University, 1981.

————. "Housing Problems and Prospects in Contemporary Houston." In *Black Dixie: Afro-Texan History and Culture in Houston,* edited by Howard Beeth and Cary D. Wintz, 236–252. College Station: Texas A&M University Press, 1992.

————. *Invisible Houston: The Black Experience in Boom and Bust.* College Station: Texas A&M University Press, 1987.

————. "Solid Waste Sites and the Black Houston Community." *Sociological Inquiry* 53 (1983): 273–288.

Bullard, Robert D., and Odessa L. Pierce. "Black Housing in a Southern Metropolis: Competition for Housing in a Shrinking Market." *Black Scholar* 11 (November/December 1979): 60–67.

Bullard, Robert D., and Donald L. Tryman. "Competition for Decent Housing: A Focus on Housing Discrimination in a Sunbelt City." *Journal of Ethnic Studies* 7 (Winter 1980): 561–563.

Bullock, Henry Allen. *Pathways to the Houston Negro Market.* Ann Arbor, Mich.: J. N. Edwards, 1957.

————. *Profile of Houston's Negro Business Enterprises: A Survey and Directory of Their Attitudes.* Houston, Tex.: Negro Chamber of Commerce, 1962.

————. "The Availability of Education in the Texas Negro Separate School." *The Journal of Negro Education* 16 (1947): 425–432.

———. "Racial Attitudes and the Employment of Negroes." *American Journal of Sociology* 56 (March 1951): 448–457.

———. "Some Readjustments of the Texas Negro Family to the Emergency of the War." *Southwestern Social Science Quarterly* 25 (September 1944): 100–117.

———. "Expansion of Negro Suffrage in Texas." *Journal of Negro Education* 26 (Summer 1957): 369–374.

———. "Significance of the Racial Factor in the Length of Prison Sentences." *Journal of Criminal Law, Criminology, and Police Science* 52 (1961): 411–417.

———. "Urban Homicide in Theory and Fact." *Journal of Criminal Law, Criminology, and Police Science* 45 (1955): 565–575.

Bundy, William Oliver. *Life of William Madison McDonald, Ph.D.* Fort Worth, Tex.: Bunker Printing and Book Company, 1925.

Burran, James A. "Violence in an 'Arsenal of Democracy': The Beaumont Race Riot, 1943." *East Texas Historical Review* 14.1 (1976): 39–51.

Campbell, Randolph B. *An Empire for Slavery: The Peculiar Institution in Texas, 1821–1865.* Baton Rouge: Louisiana State University Press, 1989.

———. *Grass-Roots Reconstruction in Texas, 1865–1880.* Baton Rouge: Louisiana State University Press, 1997.

———. "Intermittent Slave Ownership: Texas as a Test Case." *The Journal of Southern History* 51 (1985): 15–23.

———. "Local Archives as a Source of Slave Prices: Harrison County, Texas, as a Test Case." *The Historian* 36 (August 1974): 660–669.

———. "'My Dear Husband': A Texas Slave's Love Letter, 1862." *The Journal of Negro History* 65 (Fall 1980): 361–364.

———. "Slave Hiring in Texas." *American Historical Review* 93 (1988): 107–114.

———. "Human Property: The Negro Slave in Harrison County, 1850–1860." *Southwestern Historical Quarterly* 76 (1973): 384–396.

———. "The End of Slavery in Texas: A Research Note." *Southwestern Historical Quarterly* 88 (July 1984): 71–80.

———. "Planters and Plain Folk: Harrison County, Texas, as a Test Case, 1850–1860." *Journal of Southern History* 40 (August 1974): 369–398.

———. "Planters and Plain Folk: Harrison County, Texas, as a Test Case, 1850–1860." *Journal of Southern History* 40 (August 1974): 369–398.

———. "The Burden of Local Black Leadership During Reconstruction: A Research Note." *Civil War History* 39 (June 1993): 148–153.

———. "Carpetbagger Rule in Reconstruction Texas: An Enduring Myth." *Southwestern Historical Quarterly* 97 (1994): 587–596.

———. "The End of Slavery in Texas: A Research Note." *Southwestern Historical Quarterly* 88 (July 1984): 71–80.

————. "Statehood, Civil War, and Reconstruction, 1846–76." In *Texas through Time: Evolving Interpretations*, edited by Walter L. Buenger and Robert A. Calvert, 163–196. College Station: Texas A&M University Press, 1991.

Cantrell, Gregg. *Feeding the Wolf: John B. Rayner and the Politics of Race, 1850–1918*. Wheeling, Ill.: Harlan Davidson, 2001.

————. "Racial Violence and Reconstruction Politics in Texas, 1867–1868." *Southwestern Historical Quarterly* 93 (1990): 333–355.

————. "'Dark Tactics': Black Politics in the 1887 Texas Prohibition Campaign." *Journal of American Studies* 25 (April 1991): 85–93.

————. "John B. Rayner: A Study in Black Populist Leadership." *Southern Studies* 24 (Winter 1985): 432–443.

————. *Kenneth and John B. Rayner and the Limits of Southern Dissent*. Urbana: University of Illinois Press, 1993.

Cantrell, Gregg, and D. Scott Barton. "Texas Populists and the Failure of Biracial Politics." *Journal of Southern History* 55 (November 1989): 659–692.

Carhart, John Wesley. *Under Palmetto and Pine*. Cincinnati, Ohio: Editor Publishing Company, 1899.

Carlson, Paul H. *"Pecos Bill": A Military Biography of William R. Shafter*. College Station: Texas A&M University Press, 1989.

————. *The Buffalo Soldier Tragedy of 1877*. College Station: Texas A&M University Press, 2003.

————. "William R. Shafter, Black Troops, and the Finale to the Red River War." *Red River Valley Historical Review* 3 (Spring 1978): 247–258.

————. "William R. Shafter Commanding Black Troops in West Texas." *West Texas Historical Association Yearbook* 50 (1974): 104–116.

————. "William R. Shafter, Black Troops, and the Opening of the Llano Estacado, 1870–1875." *Panhandle-Plains Historical Review* 47 (1974): 1–18.

Carnathan, W. J. "The Attempt to Re-Open the African Slave Trade in Texas, 1857–1858." *Southwestern Political and Social Science Association* 6 (1925): 134–144.

Carrigan, William D. *The Making of a Lynching Culture: Violence and Vigilantism in Central Texas, 1836–1916*. Urbana: University of Illinois Press, 2004.

Christian, Garna L. *Black Soldiers in Jim Crow Texas, 1899–1917*. College Station: Texas A&M University Press, 1995.

————. "The El Paso Racial Crisis of 1900." *Red River Valley Historical Review* 6 (Spring 1981): 28–41.

————. "The Violent Possibility: The Tenth Cavalry at Texarkana." *East Texas Historical Journal* 23 (Spring 1985): 3–15.

————. "The Ordeal and the Prize: The 24th Infantry and Camp MacArthur." *Military Affairs* 50 (April 1986): 65–70.

———. "Rio Grande City: Prelude to the Brownsville Raid." *West Texas Historical Association Yearbook* 57 (1981): 118–132.

———. "The Brownsville Raid's 168th Man: The Court-Martial of Corporal Knowles." *Southwestern Historical Quarterly* 93 (1989): 45–59.

———. "The Twenty-fifth Regiment at Fort McIntosh: Precursor to Retaliatory Racial Violence." *West Texas Historical Association Year Book* 55 (1979): 149–161.

———. "Adding On Fort Bliss to Black Military Historiography." *West Texas Historical Association Year Book* 54 (1978): 41–54.

Cohen-Lack, Nancy. "A Struggle for Sovereignty: National Consolidation, Emancipation, and Free Labor in Texas, 1865." *Journal of Southern History* 58 (February 1992): 57–98.

Cole, Thomas. *No Color Is My Kind: The Life of Eldrewey Stearns and the Integration of Houston.* Austin: University of Texas Press, 1997.

Cotton, Walter, comp. *History of Negroes of Limestone County from 1860 to 1939.* Mexia, Tex.: J. A. Chatman and S. M. Merriwether, 1939.

Crouch, Barry A. *The Freedman's Bureau and Black Texans.* Austin: University of Texas Press, 1992.

———. "Black Dreams and White Justice [Texas, 1865–1868]." *Prologue* 6 (1974): 255–265.

———. "A Spirit of Lawlessness: White Violence, Texas Blacks, 1865–1868." *Journal of Social History* 18 (Winter 1984): 217–232.

———. "Self-Determination and Local Black Leaders in Texas." *Phylon* 39 (1978): 344–355.

———. "'All the Vile Passions': The Texas Black Code of 1866." *Southwestern Historical Quarterly* 97 (July 1993): 13–34.

———. "The 'Cords of Love': Legalizing Black Marital and Family Rights in Postwar Texas." *Journal of Negro History* 79 (Fall 1994): 334–351.

———. "Hidden Sources of Black History: The Texas Freedmen's Bureau Records as a Case Study." *Southwestern Historical Quarterly* 83 (1980): 211–226.

———. "Seeking Equality: Houston Black Women during Reconstruction." In *Black Dixie: Afro-Texan History and Culture in Houston,* edited by Howard Beeth and Cary D. Wintz, 54–73. College Station: Texas A&M University Press, 1992.

———. "Freedmen's Bureau Records: Texas, a Case Study." In *Afro-American History: Sources for Research,* edited by Robert L. Clarke, 74–94. Washington, D.C.: Howard University Press, 1981.

———. "'Unmanacling' Texas Reconstruction: A Twenty-Year Perspective." *Southwestern Historical Quarterly* 93 (1989): 275–302.

———. "The Freedmen's Bureau and the 30th Sub-District of Texas: Smith County and Its Environs during Reconstruction." *Chronicles of Smith County, Texas* 11 (Spring 1972): 15–30.

———. "Hesitant Recognition: Texas Black Politicians, 1865–1900." *East Texas Historical Journal* 31.1 (1993): 41–58.

———, ed. "View from Within: Letters of Gregory Barrett, Freedmen's Bureau Agent." *Chronicles of Smith County, Texas* 12 (Winter 1973): 13–28.

Crouch, Barry A., and Larry Madaras. "Reconstructing Black Families: Perspectives from the Texas Freedmen's Bureau Records." *Prologue* 18 (Summer 1986): 109–122.

Crouch, Barry A., and L. J. Schultz. "Crisis in Color: Racial Separation in Texas During Reconstruction." *Civil War History* 16 (March 1970): 37–49.

Cunningham, Roger D. "'A Lot of Fine, Sturdy Black Warriors': Texas's African American 'Immunes' in the Spanish-American War." *Southwestern Historical Quarterly* 108 (2005): 345–367.

Curlee, Abigail Scott (Holbrook). "The History of a Texas Slave Plantation, 1831–1863." Master's thesis, University of Texas, 1922.

———. "A Study of Texas Slave Plantations, 1822–1865." Ph.D. dissertation, University of Texas, 1932.

———. "A Glimpse of Life on Antebellum Slave Plantations in Texas." *Southwestern Historical Quarterly* 76 (1973): 361–383.

———. "The History of a Texas Slave Plantation, 1831–1863." *Southwestern Historical Quarterly* 26 (1922): 79–127.

Curtin, Mary Ellen. "Reaching for Power: Barbara C. Jordan and Liberals in the Texas Legislature, 1966–1972." *Southwestern Historical Quarterly* 108 (October 2004): 211–231.

Maceo C. Dailey, Jr., and Kristine Navarro, eds. *Wheresoever My People Chance to Dwell: Oral Interviews with African American Women of El Paso.* Baltimore: Black Classic Press, 2000.

Davidson, Chandler. *Biracial Politics: Conflict and Coalition in the Metropolitan South.* Baton Rouge: Louisiana State University Press, 1972.

———. *Race and Class in Texas Politics.* Princeton: Princeton University Press, 1990.

Davies, Nick. *White Lies: Rape, Murder and Justice, Texas Style.* New York: Avon Books, 1993.

Davis, William R. *The Development and Present Status of Negro Education in East Texas.* New York: Columbia University Teachers College, 1934.

Dodgen, Mary. "The Slave Plantations as an Educational Institution." Master's thesis, University of Texas, 1932.

Dulaney, W. Marvin. "Long Ride to Blue." *Our Texas* (Summer 1992): 14–15.

———. "The Progressive Voters League." *Legacies: A History Journal for Dallas and North Central Texas* 3 (Spring 1991): 27–35.

———. "The Texas Negro Peace Officers' Association: The Origins of Black Police Unionism." *Houston Review* 12 (1990): 59–78.

———. "Whatever Happened to the Civil Rights Movement in Dallas, Texas?" In

Essays on the American Civil Rights Movement, edited by W. Marvin Dulaney and Kathleen Underwood, 66–95. College Station: Texas A&M University Press, 1993.

———. "The Black Church: An Agent of Social and Political Change." *Texas Journal of Ideas, History and Culture* 10 (Fall/Winter 1988): 8–10.

Duren, Almetris Marsh, and Louise Iscoe. *Overcoming: A History of Black Integration at the University of Texas at Austin.* Austin: University of Texas at Austin, 1979.

Elliott, Claude. "The Freedmen's Bureau in Texas." *Southwestern Historical Quarterly* 56 (1952): 1–24.

Emmons, Martha. *Deep Like the Rivers: Stories of My Negro Friends.* Austin, Tex.: Encino Press, 1969.

Engelking, Johanna Rosa. "Slavery in Texas." Master's thesis, Baylor University, 1933.

Faust, Drew Gilpin. "Trying to do a Man's Business: Gender Violence and Slave Management in Civil War Texas." In *Southern Stories: Slaveholders in Peace and War,* edited by Drew Gilpin Faust, 174–192. Columbia: University of Missouri Press, 1992.

———. "African Americans in West Texas: A Selected Bibliography." *Journal of Big Bend Studies* 18 (2006): 191–212.

Fontaine, Jacob, III, and Gene Burd. *Jacob Fontaine: From Slavery to the Greatness of the Pulpit, the Press, and Public Service.* Austin: University of Texas Press, 1983.

Fornell, Earl W. "Agitation in Texas for Reopening the Slave Trade." *Southwestern Historical Quarterly* 60 (October 1956): 245–259.

———. "The Abduction of Free Negroes and Slaves in Texas." *Southwestern Historical Quarterly* 60 (1957): 369–380.

Foster, Robert L. "Black Lubbock: A History of Negroes in Lubbock, Texas, to 1940." Master's thesis, Texas Tech University, 1974.

Fowler, Manet Harrison. "History of the Texas Association of Negro Musicians." *The Negro Musician* (August 1929): 114–116.

Franklin, J. E. *"Black Girl": From Genesis to Revelations.* Washington, D.C.: Howard University Press, 1973.

Gillette, Michael L. "Blacks Challenge the White University." *Southwestern Historical Quarterly* 86 (October 1982): 321–344.

———. "Heman Marion Sweatt: Civil Rights Plaintiff." In *Black Leaders: Texans for Their Times,* edited by Alwyn Barr and Robert A. Calvert, 157–188. Austin: Texas State Historical Association, 1981.

———. "The NAACP in Texas, 1937–1957." Ph.D. dissertation, University of Texas at Austin, 1984.

——. "The Rise of the NAACP in Texas." *Southwestern Historical Quarterly* 81 (1978): 393–416.

Glasrud, Bruce A. ed. *African Americans in the West: A Bibliography of Secondary Studies.* Alpine, Tex.: SRSU Center for Big Bend Studies, 1998.

——. "African Americans in West Texas: A Selected Bibliography." *Journal of Big Bend Studies* 18 (2006): 191–212.

——. "Blacks and Texas Politics During the Twenties." *Red River Valley Historical Review* 7 (Spring 1982): 39–53.

——. "Black Texas Improvement Efforts, 1879–1929: Migration, Separatism, Nationalism." *The Journal of South Texas* 14 (2001): 204–222.

——. "Black Texans, 1900–1930: A History." Ph.D. dissertation, Texas Tech University, 1969.

——. "Child or Beast? White Texas' View of Blacks, 1900–1910." *East Texas Historical Journal* 15 (Fall 1977): 38–44.

——. "Early Black Nationalist Movements in Texas." *Journal of Big Bend Studies* 11 (1999): 159–169.

——. "Enforcing White Supremacy in Texas, 1900–1910." *Red River Valley Historical Review* 4 (Fall 1979): 65–74.

——. "From Griggs to Brewer: A Review of Black Texas Culture, 1899–1940." *Journal of Big Bend Studies* 15 (2003): 195–212.

——. "Nixon *vs.* Condon, 286 US 73 (1932)." In *Encyclopedia of African-American Civil Rights: From Emancipation to the Present,* edited by Charles D. Lowery and John F. Marszalak, 405. Westport, Conn.: Greenwood Press, 1992.

——. "Jim Crow's Emergence in Texas." *American Studies* 15 (1974): 47–60.

——. "The Harlem Renaissance in Texas and the Southwest." In *Encyclopedia of the Harlem Renaissance,* edited by Cary D. Wintz and Paul Finkelman, 2 volumes, 521–525. New York: Routledge, 2004.

——. "William M. McDonald: Business and Fraternal Leader." In *Black Leaders: Texans for Their Times,* edited by Alwyn Barr and Robert A. Calvert, 83–111. Austin: Texas State Historical Association, 1981.

Glasrud, Bruce A., and Laurie Champion, eds. *Exploring the Afro-Texas Experience: A Bibliography of Secondary Sources about Black Texans.* Alpine, Tex.: SRSU Center for Big Bend Studies, 2000.

——. "African Americans in the West: A Short Story Tradition." *Journal of Big Bend Studies* 10 (1998): 221–242.

——. "Texas as a Foil: Racism in Chester Himes' 1940s Writings." *Southwestern American Literature* 27 (Fall 2001): 9–19.

Glasrud, Bruce A. , and James M. Smallwood. "The Texas Tech School of Black History: An Overview." *West Texas Historical Association Year Book* 82 (2006).

Goldberg, Robert A. "Racial Change on the Southern Periphery: The Case of

San Antonio, Texas, 1960–1965." *Journal of Southern History* 49 (1983): 349–374.

Govenar, Alan. *Living the Blues.* Dallas: Dallas Museum of Art, 1985.

———. *Portraits of Community: African American Photography in Texas.* Austin: Texas State Historical Association, 1996.

Govenar, Alan, and Jay Brakefield. *Deep Ellum and Central Track: Where the Black and White Worlds of Dallas Converged.* Denton: University of North Texas Press, 1998.

Govenar, Alan, and Benny Joseph. *The Early Years of Rhythm and Blues: Focus on Houston.* Houston, Tex.: Rice University Press, 1990.

Green, Ely. *Ely: Too Black, Too White.* Amherst: University of Massachusetts Press, 1970.

Griffin, Marvin C. *Texas African-American Baptists: The Story of the Baptist General Convention of Texas.* Austin, Tex.: Publisher's Marketing House, 1994.

Griggs, Sutton E. *Imperium in Imperio.* 1899. New York: Arno Reprints, 1969.

———. *The Story of My Struggle.* Memphis, Tenn.: n.p., 1914.

Hagood, Louise Wimberley. "Negroes in Northeast Texas, 1850–1875." Master's thesis, North Texas State University, 1966.

Hainsworth, Robert W. "The Negro and the Texas Primaries." *Journal of Negro History* 18 (1933): 426–451.

Hales, Douglas. *A Southern Family in White and Black: The Cuneys of Texas.* College Station: Texas A&M University Press, 2003.

———. "Black Cowboy: Daniel Webster '80 John' Wallace." In *The Cowboy Way: An Exploration of History and Culture,* edited by Paul H. Carlson, 33–43. Lubbock: Texas Tech University Press, 2000.

Hall, Frank. *The Burning Walls.* Amarillo, Tex.: Russell Stationery, 1934.

Hall, Josie Briggs. *Hall's Moral and Mental Capsule for the Economic and Domestic Life of the Negro, as a Solution of the Race Problem.* Dallas, Tex.: Rev. F. S. Jenkins, 1905.

Hall, Martin Hardwick. "Negroes with Confederate Troops in West Texas and New Mexico." *Password* 13 (1968): 11–12.

Hare, Maud Cuney. *Norris Wright Cuney: A Tribune of the Black People.* New York: Crisis, 1913.

Harper, Cecil, Jr. "Slavery without Cotton: Hunt County, Texas, 1846–1864." *Southwestern Historical Quarterly* 88 (1985): 387–405.

Hawkins, Marjorie Brown. "Runaway Slaves in Texas." Master's thesis, Prairie View Agricultural and Mechanical College, 1952.

Haynes, Robert V. *A Night of Violence: The Houston Riot of 1917.* Baton Rouge: Louisiana State University Press, 1976.

———. "The Houston Mutiny and Riot of 1917." *Southwestern Historical Quarterly* 76 (1973): 418–439.

————. "Unrest at Home: Racial Conflict between White Civilians and Black Soldiers in 1917." *Journal of the American Studies Association of Texas* 6 (1975): 43–54.

————. "Black Houstonians and the White Democratic Primary, 1920–45." *Black Dixie: Afro-Texan History and Culture in Houston,* edited by Howard Beeth and Cary D. Wintz, 192–210. College Station: Texas A&M University Press, 1992.

Heintze, Michael R. *Private Black Colleges in Texas, 1865–1954.* College Station: Texas A&M University Press, 1985.

Henson, Margaret Swett. "Development of Slave Codes in Texas, 1821–1845." Master's thesis, University of Houston, 1969.

Hickman, R. C. *Behold the People: R. C. Hickman's Photographs of Black Dallas, 1949–1961.* Austin: Texas State Historical Association, 1994.

Hine, Darlene Clark. *Black Victory: The Rise and Fall of the White Primary in Texas.* Millwood, N.Y.: KTO Press, 1979.

————. "Blacks and the Destruction of the Democratic White Primary, 1932–1944." *Journal of Negro History* 62 (1977): 43–59.

————. "The Elusive Ballot: The Black Struggle against the Texas Democratic White Primary, 1932–1945." *Southwestern Historical Quarterly* 81 (1978): 371–392.

Holbrook, Abigail Curlee. "A Glimpse of Life on Antebellum Slave Plantations in Texas." *Southwestern Historical Quarterly* 76 (1973): 361–383.

Holland, Ada Morehead, and C. C. White. *No Quittin' Sense.* Austin: University of Texas Press, 1969.

Holloway, Harry. "The Negro and the Vote: The Case of Texas." *Journal of Politics* 23 (1961): 526–556.

————. "The Texas Negro as a Voter." *Phylon* 24 (Summer 1963): 135–145.

Hornsby, Alton, Jr. "The 'Colored Branch University' Issue in Texas—Prelude to *Sweatt v. Painter.*" *Journal of Negro History* 61 (1976): 51–60.

————. "The Freedmen's Bureau Schools in Texas, 1865–1870." *Southwestern Historical Quarterly* 76 (April 1973): 397–417.

————. "Negro Education in Texas, 1865–1917." Master's thesis, University of Texas, 1962.

Ivy, Charlotte. "Forgotten Color: Black Families in Early El Paso." *Password* 35 (1990): 5–18.

Jackson, A. W. *A Sure Foundation and A Sketch of Negro Life in Texas.* Houston, Tex.: A. W. Jackson, 1940.

Jackson, Bruce, ed. *Wake Up Dead Man: Afro-American Worksongs from Texas Prisons.* Cambridge, Mass.: Harvard University Press, 1972.

Jackson, Charles Christopher. "A Southern Black Community Comes of Age: Black San Antonio in the Great Depression, 1930–1941." Master's thesis, Texas A&M University, 1989.

Jackson, James Thomas. "The Burning of the Books." In *Waiting in Line at the*

Drugstore and Other Writings of James Thomas Jackson, collected by June Acosta, 78–84. Denton: University of North Texas Press, 1993.

———. "Houston's Fourth Ward." In *Juneteenth Texas: Essays in African-American Folklore,* edited by Francis E. Abernethy, Carolyn Fiedler Satterwhite, Patrick B. Mullen, and Alan B. Govenar, 41–47. Denton: University of North Texas Press, 1996.

———. "Once Upon a Time in Houston." In *Waiting in Line at the Drugstore and Other Writings of James Thomas Jackson,* collected by June Acosta, 7–10. Denton: University of North Texas Press, 1993.

Jackson, LaVonne Roberts. "Freedom and Family: The Freedmen's Bureau and African-American Women in Texas in the Reconstruction Era." Ph.D. dissertation, Howard University, 1996.

Jackson, Susan. "Slavery in Houston: The 1850's." *The Houston Review* 2 (Summer 1980): 66–82.

Jones, Carolyn. *Volma, My Journey: One Man's Impact on the Civil Rights Movement in Austin, Texas.* Austin, Tex.: Eakin Press, 1998.

Jordan, Barbara, and Shelby Hearon. *Barbara Jordan: A Self-Portrait.* Garden City, N.J.: Doubleday, 1979.

Junkins, Enda. "Slave Plots, Insurrections, and Acts of Violence in the State of Texas, 1828–1865." Master's thesis, Baylor University, 1969.

Kealing, H. T. *History of African Methodism in Texas.* Waco, Tex.: C. F. Blanks Publisher, 1885.

Kellar, William Henry. *Make Haste Slowly: Moderates, Conservatives, and School Desegregation in Houston.* College Station: Texas A&M University Press, 1999.

Keir, Scott S. "Middle Class Black Families in Austin, Texas: An Exploratory Analysis of Husbands and Wives." Ph.D. dissertation, University of Texas at Austin, 1987.

Kirven, Lamar L. "A Century of Warfare: Black Texans." Ph.D. dissertation, Indiana University, 1974.

Kosary, Rebecca A. "Regression to Barbarism in Reconstruction Texas: An Analysis of White Violence Against African-Americans From the Freedmen's Bureau Records, 1865–1868." Master's thesis, Southwest Texas State University, 1999.

Kossie-Chernyshev, Karen. "A 'Grand Old Church' Rose in East Texas: The Church of God in Christ (COGIC) in East Texas." *East Texas Historical Journal* 41.2 (2003): 26–36.

———. "Constructing Good Success: The Church of God in Christ and Social Uplift in East Texas, 1910–1935." *East Texas Historical Journal* 44.1 (2006): 49–55.

Kuhlman, Martin. "The Civil Rights March on Austin, Texas, 1963." In *Bricks Without Straw: A Comprehensive History of African Americans in Texas,* edited by David A. Williams, 153–166. Austin, Tex.: Eakin Press, 1997.

———. "The Civil Rights Movement in Texas: Desegregation of Public Accommodations, 1950–1964." Ph.D. dissertation, Texas Tech University, 1994.

———. "Direct Action at the University of Texas During the Civil Rights Movement, 1960–1965." *Southwestern Historical Quarterly* 98 (1995): 550–566.

Lack, Paul D. "The Black Texans and Slavery in Revolution and War." In *The Texas Revolutionary Experience: A Political and Social History, 1835–1836*, by Paul D. Lack, 238–252, 309–311. College Station: Texas A&M University Press, 1992.

———. "Dave: A Rebellious Slave." In *Black Leaders: Texans for Their Times*, edited by Alwyn Barr and Robert A. Calvert, 1–18. Austin: Texas State Historical Association, 1981.

———. "Slavery and the Texas Revolution." *Southwestern Historical Quarterly* 89 (1985): 181–202.

———. "Slavery and Vigilantism in Austin, Texas, 1840–1860." *Southwestern Historical Quarterly* 85 (July 1981): 1–20.

———. "Urban Slavery in the Southwest." Ph.D. dissertation, Texas Tech University, 1973.

———. "Urban Slavery in the Southwest." *Red River Valley Historical Review* 6 (1981): 8–27.

Laine, Alice K. "An In-Depth Study of Black Political Leadership in Houston, Texas." Ph.D. dissertation, University of Texas at Austin, 1978.

Lane, Ann J. *The Brownsville Affair: National Crisis and Black Reaction.* Port Washington, N.Y.: Kennikat Press, 1971.

Lay, Shawn. *Revolution and the Ku Klux Klan: A Study of Intolerance in a Border City.* El Paso: Texas Western Press, 1985.

Leckie, William H. "Black Regulars on the Texas Frontier, 1866–1885." In *The Texas Military Experience: From the Texas Revolution through World War II*, edited by Joseph G. Dawson, 86–96, 219–221. College Station: Texas A&M University Press, 1995.

Ledbetter, Billy D. "White Over Black in Texas: Racial Attitudes in the Ante-Bellum Period." *Phylon* 34 (1973): 406–418.

Lede, Naomi. *Precious Memories of a Black Socialite.* Houston: D. Armstrong, 1991.

Leicker, James N. *Racial Borders: Black Soldiers along the Rio Grande.* College Station: Texas A&M University Press, 2002.

Lewis, J. Vance. *Out of the Ditch: A True Story of an Ex-Slave.* Houston, Tex.: Rein & Sons, 1910.

Lightfoot, Billy Bob. "The Negro Exodus from Comanche County, Texas." *Southwestern Historical Quarterly* 56 (January 1953): 407–416.

Lockhart, W. E. "The Slave Code of Texas." Master's thesis, Baylor University, 1929.

Logan, Rayford W. "Estevanico, Negro Discoverer of the Southwest: A Critical Reexamination." *Phylon* 1 (1940): 305–314.

Lucko, Paul M. "Dissertations and Theses Relating to African American Studies in

Texas: A Selected Bibliography, 1904–1990." *Southwestern Historical Quarterly* 96 (1992): 547–573.

McDaniel, Vernon. *History of the Teachers State Association of Texas.* Washington, D.C.: National Education Association, 1977.

———. "Negro Publicly Supported Higher Institutions in Texas." *Journal of Negro Education* 31 (1962): 349–353.

McQueen, Clyde. *Black Churches in Texas: A Guide to Historic Congregations.* College Station: Texas A&M University Press, 2000.

Mardis, Jas., ed. *KenteCloth: Southwest Voices of the African Diaspora, The Oral Tradition Comes to the Page.* Denton: University of North Texas Press, 1997.

Marten, James. "Slaves and Rebels: The Peculiar Institution in Texas, 1861–1865." *East Texas Historical Journal* 28 (Spring 1990): 29–36.

Mason, Kenneth. *African Americans and Race Relations in San Antonio, Texas, 1867–1937.* New York: Garland Publishing, 1998.

Massey, Sara R., ed. *Black Cowboys of Texas.* College Station: Texas A&M University Press, 2000.

Mathis, Annie Maie. "Negro Public Health Nursing in Texas." *Southern Workman* 56 (July 1927): 302–303.

Maxwell, Louise Passey. "Freedmantown: The Evolution of a Black Neighborhood in Houston: 1865–1880." Master's thesis, Rice University, 1993.

Miles, Merle Yvonne. "'Born and Bred' in Texas: Three Generations of Black Females: A Critique of Social Science Perceptions on the Black Female." Ph.D. dissertation, University of Texas at Austin, 1986.

Miller, Vickie Gail. *Doris Miller: A Silent Medal of Honor Winner.* Austin, Tex.: Eakin Press, 1997.

Minton, John. "Houston Creoles and Zydeco: The Emergence of an African American Urban Popular Style." *American Music* 14 (1996): 480–526.

Moneyhon, Carl H. "George T. Ruby and the Politics of Expediency in Texas." In *Southern Black Leaders in the Reconstruction Era,* edited by Howard N. Rabinowitz, 363–392. Urbana: University of Illinois Press, 1982.

———. "Public Education and Texas Reconstruction Politics." *Southwestern Historical Quarterly* 92 (1989): 393–416.

———. *Republicanism in Reconstruction Texas.* Austin: University of Texas Press, 1980.

———. *Texas after the Civil War: The Struggle of Reconstruction.* College Station: Texas A&M University Press, 2004.

Muir, Andrew Forest. "The Free Negro In Jefferson and Orange Counties, Texas." *Journal of Negro History* 25 (April 1950): 183–206.

———. "The Free Negro in Harris County, Texas." *Southwestern Historical Quarterly* 46 (January 1943): 214–238.

———. "Free Negro in Fort Bend County, Texas." *Journal of Negro History* 33 (January 1948): 79–85.

———. "The Free Negro in Galveston County, Texas." *Negro History Bulletin* 22 (1958): 68–70.

Obadele-Starks, Ernest. *Black Unionism in the Industrial South.* College Station: Texas A&M University Press, 2000.

Oliphant, Dave. "Eddie Durham and the Texas Contribution to Jazz History." *Southwestern Historical Quarterly* 96 (1993): 490–525.

Parks, Katie. *Remember When? A History of African Americans in Lubbock, Texas.* Lubbock: Friends of the Library/Southwest Collection, 1999.

Pemberton, Doris. *Juneteenth at Comanche Crossing.* Austin, Tex.: Eakin Press, 1983.

Pennington, Richard. *Breaking the Ice: The Racial Integration of Southwest Conference Football.* Jefferson, N.C.: McFarland, 1987.

Phillips, Edward Hake. "The Sherman Courthouse Riot of 1930." *East Texas Historical Journal* 25.2 (1987): 12–19.

Pitre, Merline. *In Struggle Against Jim Crow: Lulu B. White and the NAACP, 1900–1957.* College Station: Texas A&M University Press, 1999.

———. "The Evolution of Black Political Participation in Reconstruction Texas." *East Texas Historical Journal* 26.1 (1988): 36–45.

———. "A Note on the Historiography of Blacks in the Reconstruction of Texas." *Journal of Negro History* 66 (Winter 1981): 340–348.

———. "Richard Allen: The Chequered Career of Houston's First Black State Legislator." In *Black Dixie: Afro-Texan History and Culture in Houston,* edited by Howard Beeth and Cary D. Wintz, 74–83. College Station: Texas A&M University Press, 1992.

———. "Black Houstonians and the 'Separate But Equal' Doctrine: Carter W. Wesley versus Lulu B. White." *Houston Review* 12 (1990): 23–36.

———. *Through Many Dangers, Toils, and Snares: Black Leadership in Texas, 1868–1900.* Austin, Tex.: Eakin Press, 1985.

Porter, Kenneth W. "Negroes and Indians on the Texas Frontier, 1834–1874." *Southwestern Historical Quarterly* 53 (1949): 151–163.

———. "Negroes and Indians On the Texas Frontier, 1831–1876: A Study in Race and Culture, I." *Journal of Negro History* 41 (July 1956): 185–214.

———. "Negroes and Indians On the Texas Frontier, 1831–1876: A Study in Race and Culture, II." *Journal of Negro History* 41 (October 1956): 285–310.

———. "The Seminole Negro-Indian Scouts, 1870–1881." *Southwestern Historical Quarterly* 55 (1952): 358–377.

———. "Negro Labor in the Western Cattle Industry, 1866–1900." *Labor History* 10 (Summer 1969): 346–374.

Prather, Patricia Smith, and Jane Clements Monday. *From Slave to Statesman: The Legacy of Joshua Houston, Servant to Sam Houston.* Denton: University of North Texas Press, 1993.

Pruitt, Bernadette. "Exodus, the Movement: People of African Descent and Their Migrations to Houston, 1914–1945." Ph.D. dissertation, University of Houston, 2004.

———. "'For the Advancement of the Race': The Great Migrations to Houston, Texas, 1914–1919." *Journal of Urban History* 31 (May 2005): 435–478.

Purcell, Linda Myers. "Slavery in the Republic of Texas." Master's thesis, North Texas State University, 1982.

Rabe, Elizabeth R. "Slave Children of Texas: A Qualitative and Quantitative Analysis," *East Texas Historical Journal* 42.1 (2004): 10–24.

Ramsdell, Charles W. "The Natural Limits of Slavery Expansion." *Mississippi Valley Historical Review* 16 (September 1929): 151–171.

———. "Presidential Reconstruction in Texas." *Quarterly of the Texas State Historical Association* 11 (April 1908): 288–294.

———. *Reconstruction in Texas.* New York: Columbia University Press, 1910.

Redwine, W. A. "Brief History of the Negro in Five Counties." *Chronicles of Smith County [Texas]* 11 (Fall 1972): 13–70. Originally published as a book (Tyler, Tex.: privately printed, 1901).

Reese, James V. "Negroes in Texas." In *The Handbook of Texas: A Supplement*, edited by Eldon Stephen Branda, 643–645. Austin: Texas State Historical Association, 1976.

Reich, Steven A. "Soldiers of Democracy: Black Texans and the Fight for Citizenship, 1917–1921." *Journal of American History* 82 (1996): 1478–1504.

Reynolds, Donald E. "Reluctant Martyr: Anthony Bewley and the Texas Slave Insurrection Panic of 1860." *Southwestern Historical Quarterly* 96 (1993): 344–361.

Rice, Lawrence D. *The Negro In Texas, 1874–1900.* Baton Rouge: Louisiana State University Press, 1971.

Richter, William L. "The Army and the Negro During Reconstruction, 1865–1875." *East Texas Historical Journal* 10 (Spring 1972): 7–13.

———. *The Army in Texas During Reconstruction.* College Station: Texas A&M University Press, 1987.

———. *Overreached on All Sides: The Freedmen's Bureau Administrators in Texas, 1865–1868.* College Station: Texas A&M University Press, 1991.

Roberts, Randy. "Galveston's Jack Johnson: Flourishing in the Dark." *Southern Historical Quarterly* 87 (1983): 37–56.

———. *Papa Jack: Jack Johnson and the Era of White Hope.* New York: Free Press, 1983.

Robinson, Charles F., II, "Legislated Love in the Lone Star State: Texas and Miscegenation." *Southwestern Historical Quarterly* 108 (2004): 65–84.

Robinson, Dorothy Redus. *The Bell Rings at Four: A Black Teacher's Chronicle of Change.* Austin, Tex.: Madrona Press, 1978.

Rodenberger, Lou Halsell. "A Developing Tradition: African-American Writers." In *Texas Women Writers: A Tradition of Their Own,* edited by Sylvia Ann Grider and Lou Halsell Rodenberger, 247–252. College Station: Texas A&M University Press, 1997.

Rogers, Mary Beth. *Barbara Jordan: American Hero.* New York: Bantam Books, 1998.

Romero, Francine Sanders. "'There Are Only White Champions': The Rise and Demise of Segregated Boxing in Texas." *Southwestern Historical Quarterly* 108 (2004): 27–42.

Sackler, Howard. *The Great White Hope.* New York: Bantam, 1969.

Sample, Albert Race. *Racehoss: Big Emma's Boy.* Austin, Tex.: Eakin Press, 1984.

Sapper, Neil G. "Aboard the Wrong Ship in the Right Books: Doris Miller and Historical Accuracy." *East Texas Historical Journal* 18 (January 1980): 3–11.

———. "The Fall of the NAACP in Texas." *The Houston Review* 7 (Summer 1985): 53–68.

———. "Black Culture in Urban Texas: A Lone Star Renaissance." *Red River Valley Historical Review* 6 (1981): 56–77.

———. "A Survey of the History of the Black People of Texas, 1930–1954." Ph.D. dissertation, Texas Tech University, 1972.

Sayre, Harold Ray. *Warriors of Color.* Fort Davis, Tex.: privately printed, 1995.

Schaffer, Ruth C. "The Health and Social Functions of Black Midwives on the Texas Brazos Bottom, 1900–1985." *Rural Sociology* 56 (Spring 1991): 89–105.

Schoen, Harold R. "The Free Negro in the Republic of Texas." Master's thesis, University of Texas, 1933.

———. "The Free Negro in the Republic of Texas." Ph.D. dissertation, University of Texas, 1938.

———. "The Free Negro in the Republic of Texas: Origin of the Free Negro in the Republic of Texas." *Southwestern Historical Quarterly* 39 (April 1936): 292–308.

———. "The Free Negro in the Republic of Texas: The Free Negro and the Texas Revolution." *Southwestern Historical Quarterly* 40 (July 1936): 26–34.

———. "The Free Negro in the Republic of Texas: Manumission." *Southwestern Historical Quarterly* 40 (October 1936): 85–113.

———. "The Free Negro in the Republic of Texas: Legal Status." *Southwestern Historical Quarterly* 40 (January 1937): 169–199.

———. "The Free Negro in the Republic of Texas: The Law in Practice." *Southwestern Historical Quarterly* 40 (April 1937): 267–289.

———. "The Free Negro in the Republic of Texas: The Extent of Discrimination and Its Effects." *Southwestern Historical Quarterly* 41 (July 1937): 83–108.

Schutze, Jim. *The Accommodation: The Politics of Race in an American City.* Secaucus, N.J.: Citadel, 1986.

Searles, Micheal N. "The Black Cowboy—Yesterday and Today: A Hard Won Reputation." *Augusta Today Magazine* 4 (January/February 1997): 20–24.

———. "The Black Cowboy—Yesterday and Today: A Hard Won Reputation." *Texas Illustrated: A Magazine of History and Folklore* 1 (February 1997): 5, 8–10.

———. "Taking Out the Buck and Putting in a Trick: The Black Working Cowboy's Art of Breaking and Keeping a Good Cow Horse." *Journal of the West* 44 (Spring 2005): 53–60.

———. "Addison Jones: The Most Noted Negro Cowboy That Ever 'Topped Off' a Horse." In *Black Cowboys of Texas,* edited by Sara R. Massey, 193–205. College Station: Texas A&M University Press, 2000.

Shabazz, Amilcar. *Advancing Democracy: African Americans and the Struggle for Access and Equity in Higher Education in Texas.* Chapel Hill: University of North Carolina Press, 2004.

Sharpless, Rebecca. *Fertile Ground, Narrow Choices: Women on Texas Cotton Farms, 1900–1940.* Chapel Hill: University of North Carolina Press, 1999.

Sheeler, J. Reuben. "Negro History Week in the Houston Area." *Negro History Bulletin* 19 (October 1955): 2, 21.

Silverthorne, Elizabeth. *Plantation Life in Texas.* College Station: Texas A&M University Press, 1986.

Simond, Ada. "A History of African-American Catholicism in Texas." In *Bricks Without Straw: A Comprehensive History of African Americans in Texas,* edited by David A. Williams, 309–322. Austin, Tex.: Eakin Press, 1997.

Simpson, Julie. *The Clever Leader: Dr. L. H. Simpson, D.D.* Houston, Tex.: privately printed, 1963.

Sitton, Thad, and James H. Conrad. *Freedom Colonies: Independent Black Texans in the Time of Jim Crow.* Austin: University of Texas Press, 2005.

Smallwood, James M. *A Century of Achievement: Blacks in Cooke County, Texas.* Gainesville, Tex.: American Revolution Bicentennial Committee, 1975.

———. *The Struggle for Equality: Blacks in Texas.* Boston: American Press, 1981.

———. "The Black Community in Reconstruction Texas: Readjustments in Religion and the Evolution of the Negro Church." *East Texas Historical Journal* 16 (Fall 1978): 16–28.

———. "Black Education in Reconstruction Texas: The Contributions of the Freedmen's Bureau and Benevolent Societies." *East Texas Historical Journal* 19.1 (1981): 17–40.

———. "Black Freedwomen after Emancipation: The Texas Experience." *Prologue* 27 (1995): 303–317.

———. "Black Texans During Reconstruction: First Freedom." *East Texas Historical Journal* 14 (Spring 1976): 9–23.

———. "Charles E. Culver: A Reconstruction Agent in Texas: The Work of Local Freedman's Bureau Agents and the Black Community.".*Civil War History* 27 (December 1981): 350–361.

———. "Blacks In Antebellum Texas: A Reappraisal." *Red River Valley Historical Review* 2 (Winter 1975): 443–466.

———. "Texas." In *The Black Press in the South, 1865–1979*, edited by Henry Lewis Suggs, 357–377. Westport, Conn.: Greenwood Publishers, 1983.

———. "The Woodward Thesis Revisited: The Origins of Social Segregation in Texas." *Negro History Bulletin* (1984): 6–9.

———. "Early 'Freedom Schools': Black Self-Help and Education in Reconstruction Texas: A Case Study." *Negro History Bulletin* 41 (1978): 790–793.

———. "Emancipation and the Black Family: A Case Study in Texas." *Social Science Quarterly* 57 (1977): 849–857.

———. "The Freedman's Bureau Reconsidered: Local Agents and the Black Community." *Texana* 11 (1973): 309–320.

———. "From Slavery to Freedom: Smith County's Black Community in 1870; A Statistical Overview." *Chronicles of Smith County, Texas* 18 (Summer 1979): 58–61.

———. "G. T. Ruby: Galveston's Black Carpetbagger in Reconstruction Texas." *Houston Review* 5 (Winter 1983): 24–33.

———. "Perpetuation of Caste: Black Agricultural Workers in Reconstruction Texas." *Mid-America* 61 (1979): 5–23.

———. *Time of Hope, Time of Despair: Black Texas During Reconstruction.* Port Washington, N.Y.: Kennikat Press, 1981.

Smallwood, James M., Barry A. Crouch, and Larry Peacock. *Murder and Mayhem: The War of Reconstruction in Texas.* College Station: Texas A&M University Press, 2003.

Smith, C. Calvin. "The Houston Riot of 1917, Revisited." *Houston Review* 13 (1991): 84–102.

Smith, Dick. "Texas and the Poll Tax." *Southwestern Social Science Quarterly* 35 (September 1955): 167–173.

Smith, Robert Lloyd. "Elevation of Negro Farm Life." *Independent* 1 (August 30, 1900): 2103–2106.

———. "The Farmers' Improvement Society of Texas." *AME Review* (January 1909): 289–296.

———. "An Uplifting Negro Cooperative Society in Texas." *The World's Work* 16 (July 1908): 10462–10466.

———. "Village Improvement Among the Negroes." *Outlook* 64 (March 31, 1900): 733–736.

SoRelle, James M. "The Darker Side of 'Heaven': The Black Community in Houston, Texas, 1917–1945." Ph.D. dissertation, Kent State University, 1980.

———. "'An De Po Culled Man Is In De Wuss Fix Uv Awl': Black Occupational Status in Houston, Texas, 1920–1940." *The Houston Review* 1 (Spring 1979): 15–26.

———. "The 'Waco Horror': The Lynching of Jesse Washington." *Southwestern Historical Quarterly* 86 (1983): 517–536.

———. "The Emergence of Black Business in Houston, Texas: A Study of Race and Ideology, 1919–1945." In *Black Dixie: Afro-Texan History and Culture in Houston*, edited by Howard Beeth and Cary D. Wintz, 103–115. College Station: Texas A&M University Press, 1992.

———. "Race Relations in 'Heavenly Houston', 1919–1945." In *Black Dixie: Afro-Texan History and Culture in Houston*, edited by Howard Beeth and Cary D. Wintz, 175–191. College Station: Texas A&M University Press, 1992.

Spurlin, Virginia Lee. "The Conners of Waco: Black Professionals in Twentieth Century Texas." Ph.D. dissertation, Texas Tech University, 1991.

Stimpson, Eddie, Jr. *My Remembers: A Black Sharecropper's Recollections of the Depression*. Edited by James W. Byrd. Denton: University of North Texas Press, 1996.

Strong, Donald S. "The Poll Tax: The Case of Texas." *The American Political Science Review* 38 (August 1944): 693–709.

———. "The Rise of Negro Voting in Texas." *The American Political Science Review* 42 (1948): 510–522.

Sturdevant, Paul E. "Black and White with Shades of Gray: The Greenville Sign." *East Texas Historical Journal* 42.1 (2004): 25–33.

Terrell, John Upton. *Estevanico the Black*. Los Angeles: Westernlore Press Publishers, 1968.

Terrell, Suzanne. *This Other Kind of Doctors: Traditional Medical Systems in Black Neighborhoods in Austin, Texas*. New York: AMS Press, 1990.

Terry, William E. *Origin and Development of Texas Southern University, Houston, Texas*. Houston, Tex.: W. E. Terry, 1978.

Thomas, Jesse O. *Negro Participation in the Texas Centennial Exposition*. Boston: Christopher Publishing House, 1938.

Thomas, Matt. *Hopping on the Border (The Life Story of a Bellboy)*. San Antonio, Tex.: Naylor, 1951.

Thompson, Erwin N. "The Negro Soldiers on the Frontier: A Fort Davis Case Study." *Journal of the West* 7 (1968): 217–235.

Tyler, Ronnie C. "Slave Owners and Runaway Slaves in Texas." Master's thesis, Texas Christian University, 1966.

———. "Fugitive Slaves in Mexico." *The Journal of Negro History* 57 (1972): 1–12.

Tyler, Ronnie C., and Lawrence R. Murphy, eds. *The Slave Narratives of Texas*. Austin, Tex.: Encino Press, 1974.

Walker, May. *The History of the Black Police Officers in the Houston Police Department, 1878–1988*. Dallas, Tex.: Taylor Publishing Company, 1988.

Watley, Sarah Beal. "The Power Structure in the Negro Sub-Community in Lubbock, Texas." Master's thesis, Texas Tech University, 1970.

Watson, Dwight David. *Race and the Houston Police Department, 1930–1990*. College Station: Texas A&M University Press, 2005.

Weaver, John D. *The Brownsville Raid*. New York: W. W. Norton, 1970.

Weeks, O. Douglas. "The White Primary, 1944–1948." *American Political Science Review* 42 (June 1948): 500–510.

Westbrook, Johnnie Mae. "The Sweatt Case: A Study in Minority Strategy in Texas." Master's thesis, Prairie View A&M University, 1953.

White, William W. "The Texas Slave Insurrection of 1860." *Southwestern Historical Quarterly* 52 (1949): 259–285.

Wiggins, Bernice Love. *Tuneful Tales*. El Paso, Tex.: privately printed, 1925.

Williams, David A., ed. *Bricks Without Straw: A Comprehensive History of African Americans in Texas*. Austin, Tex.: Eakin Press, 1997.

———. "A History of Higher Education for African-American Texans, 1872–1977." Ed.D. dissertation, Baylor University, 1978.

Williams, Joyce E. *Black Community Control: A Study of Transition in a Texas Ghetto*. New York: Praeger, 1973.

Williams, L. V. "Teaching Negro Life and History in Texas High Schools." *The Journal of Negro History* 20 (1935): 13–18.

Williams, Milton H., III, "Romeo M. Williams: Tuskegee Airman and Civil Rights Lawyer." *East Texas Historical Journal* 43.1 (2005): 7–13.

Wilson, William H. *Hamilton Park: A Planned Black Community in Dallas*. Baltimore: Johns Hopkins University Press, 1998.

Winegarten, Ruthe. *Black Texas Women: 150 Years of Trial and Triumph*. Austin: University of Texas Press, 1994.

———. *Black Texas Women: A Sourcebook: Documents, Biographies, Time Line*. Austin: University of Texas Press, 1996.

———, ed. *I Am Annie Mae; An Extraordinary Woman in Her Own Words: The Personal Story of a Black Texas Woman*. Austin, Tex.: Rosegarden Press, 1983.

———. "Texas Slave Families." *Texas Humanist* 7 (March–April 1985): 29–30, 33.

Winegarten, Ruthe, and Sharon Kahn. *Brave Black Women: From Slavery to the Space Shuttle*. Austin: University of Texas Press, 1996.

Wintz, Cary D. "Blacks." In *The Ethnic Groups of Houston*, edited by Fred R. von der Mehden, 9–40. Houston: Rice University Studies, 1984.

———. *Blacks in Houston*. Houston: Center for Humanities, 1982.

———. "The Emergence of a Black Neighborhood: Houston's Fourth Ward, 1865–1915." In *Urban Texas: Politics and Development*, edited by Char Miller and Heywood T. Sanders, 96–109, 194–196. College Station: Texas A&M University Press, 1990.

Wood, Roger, and David Fraher. *Down in Houston: Bayou City Blues.* Austin: University of Texas Press, 2003.

Woolfolk, George R. *The Free Negro in Texas, 1800–1860: A Study in Cultural Compromise.* Ann Arbor, Mich.: University Microfilms, 1976.

———. *Prairie View: A Study in Public Conscience, 1878–1946.* New York: Pageant Press, 1962.

———. "Sources of the History of the Negro in Texas, With Special Reference to Their Implications for Research in Slavery." *Journal of Negro History* 42 (1957): 38–47.

———. "Turner's Safety Valve and Free Negro Westward Migration." *Pacific Northwest Quarterly,* 56 (July 1965): 125–130.

Wooster, Ralph A. "Notes on Texas' Largest Slaveholders, 1860." *Southwestern Historical Quarterly* 65 (1961): 72–79.

Work, Monroe N., comp. "Some Negro Members of Reconstruction Legislatures: Texas." *Journal of Negro History* 5 (1920): 111–113.

Yates, Rutherford B. H., and Paul L. Yates. *The Life and Efforts of Jack Yates.* Houston: Texas Southern University Press, 1985.

Contributors

ALWYN BARR, Professor of History and former history department chair at Texas Tech University, received his B.A., M.A., and Ph.D. degrees from the University of Texas at Austin. He is the author of many articles, reviews, and books on southern and African American history. Two of his books, *Black Texans: A History of African Americans in Texas, 1528–1995* and *Reconstruction to Reform: Texas Politics, 1876–1906*, have recently been reissued in second editions. Barr also co-edited the important *Black Leaders: Texans for Their Times* and published the well-received *Texas in Revolt: The Battle for San Jacinto.* He wrote invaluable historiographical articles on black Texans and published articles on black history topics in journals such as *Phylon, The Houston Review,* and *Civil War History.* A Fellow in the Texas State Historical Association, he also has served as president of the TSHA. He has earned university-wide teaching and academic achievement awards during his career at Texas Tech University.

RANDOLPH B. "MIKE" CAMPBELL is Regents Professor of History at the University of North Texas. Campbell received his Ph.D. in history at the University of Virginia; his particular research interests are in nineteenth-century Texas and the early national period of United States history. Among his numerous publications are *Sam Houston and the American Southwest; An Empire for Slavery: The Peculiar Institution in Texas, 1821–1865; Grass-Roots Reconstruction in Texas, 1865–1880; A Southern Community in Crisis: Harrison County, Texas, 1850–1880,* several other books, and numerous scholarly articles and book reviews. He has won many awards, including the Charles W. Ramsdell Award of the Southern Historical Association, the Coral Horton Tullis Memorial Award of the Texas State Historical Association, and twice the Carroll Award from the TSHA. A Fellow of the Texas State Historical Association, Campbell also served as President of the TSHA in 1993–1994.

GREGG CANTRELL has written extensively on the history of Texas and the South. Cantrell received his Ph.D. from Texas A&M University. He is the author of several books and articles, including *Stephen F. Austin, Empresario of Texas* (1999); *Feeding the Wolf: John B. Rayner and the Politics of Race* (2000); and *The History of Texas* (3rd ed.), co-authored with Robert A. Calvert and Arnoldo De Leon. His books and articles have won numerous awards, including the Bates, Tullis, and Carroll Awards of the Texas State Historical Association, the T. R. Fehrenbach Award, and the Presidio La Bahia Award. He has taught at Sam Houston State University, Hardin-Simmons University, and the University of North Texas and is currently professor of history at Texas Christian University.

PAUL H. CARLSON is Professor of History at Texas Tech University. Carlson received a B.A. degree from Dakota Wesleyan University, an M.A. from Mankato State University, and a Ph.D. from Texas Tech University. A specialist in the American West and Native American Studies, he has published many articles on frontier history and Texas history as well as *Texas Woollybacks: The Range Sheep and Goat Industry*, *"Pecos Bill": A Military Biography of William R. Shafter*, *Empire Builder in the Texas Panhandle: William Henry Bush*, and *The Cowboy Way: An Exploration of History and Culture*. Carlson was series editor of Double Mountain Books, Classic Reissues of the American West.

GARNA L. CHRISTIAN was born in Houston, Texas, and currently is Professor of History at the University of Houston–Downtown. He obtained a B.A. in history from Mexico City College and an M.A. in history from Texas Western College. He received a Ph.D. in history at Texas Tech University (1977) for the dissertation "Swords and Plowshares: The Symbiotic Development of Fort Bliss and El Paso, Texas, 1849–1917." Christian has also taught at the University of Houston central campus, Texas Tech University, Texas Woman's University in Houston, Houston Community College, and El Paso Community College. He is the author of *40,000 Window Panes: The Story of the Merchants and Manufacturers Building* and numerous articles on Texas music and the black military in Texas. His articles have appeared in *Southwestern Historical Quarterly, Military Affairs, Houston Review, East Texas Historical Journal, West Texas Historical Association Year Book, Red River Valley Historical Review*, and *Password*. Texas A&M University Press published *Black Soldiers in Jim Crow Texas, 1899–1917* in 1995, which won the T. R. Fehrenbach Award of the Texas Historical Commission and awards from the American Association of State and Local History and the Gustavus Myers Center for the Study of Human Rights in North America in 1996.

W. MARVIN DULANEY is Chair of the History Department and Executive Director of the Avery Research Center at the College of Charleston. An Alabama native, Dulaney received his bachelor's degree from Central State University in Wilberforce,

Ohio, and his M.A. and Ph.D. degrees from Ohio State University. He has published articles and reviews in numerous publications, including *Journal of Negro History, Civil War History, Southwestern Historical Quarterly*, and *The Historian*. He is editor of *The Avery Review*, co-editor of *Essays on the American Civil Rights Movement*, and author of *Black Police in America*. His career has achieved distinctions and awards: the Carter G. Woodson Award for teaching of African American History from the Dallas Independent School District's African American Cultural Heritage Center, Fellow for the National Council of Black Studies Administrative Institute, and president of the Southern Conference on Afro-American Studies (1994–1995). Prior to moving to Charleston, for a number of years he directed the annual "African American History in Texas" Conference for the Dallas Museum of African American Life and Culture.

ROBERT C. FINK received his doctorate from Texas Tech University where he specialized in African American history and twentieth-century cultural history. He also received his M.A. degree from Texas Tech University, where he wrote his master's thesis "African-American Baseball in Texas, 1900–1950." Fink has an article scheduled for publication in *The Journal of the West* and has published several book reviews, including ones for *Southern Historian* and *Western Historical Quarterly*. He has delivered papers at professional meetings such as the West Texas Historical Association, Southern Historical Association, Southwestern Social Science Association, and the Texas State Historical Association. He teaches in the Abilene, Texas, ISD.

MICHAEL L. GILLETTE is Director of the Texas Council for the Humanities; his previous post was Director of the Center for Legislative Archives at the National Archives in Washington, D.C. Prior to that he directed the LBJ Library's Oral History Program. He also directed the Presidential Election Study at the LBJ School of Public Affairs. Gillette has served on the board of directors of the Everett McKinley Dirksen Congressional Leadership Center and the advisory board of the Law Library of Congress' National Digital Library Program. Gillette received his Ph.D. in history from the University of Texas at Austin, where he wrote his dissertation "The NAACP in Texas, 1937–1957." He is the author of *Launching the War on Poverty: An Oral History*, published by Twayne Publishers in 1996. He has also published numerous articles on politics and the civil rights movement.

BRUCE A. GLASRUD is Professor Emeritus of History at California State University, East Bay, and retired Dean, School of Arts and Sciences, at Sul Ross State University. He earned his B.A. degree from Luther College, his M.A. degree from Eastern New Mexico University, and his Ph.D. degree from Texas Tech University. A specialist in peoples of color in the western United States, Glasrud especially focuses on the black experience in Texas. He has authored or coauthored seven books, including *The African American West: A Century of Short Stories* (Colorado) and *Exploring the Afro-Texas Experience: A Bibliography of Secondary Sources About Black Texans* (SRSU Center for Big Bend Studies), fifty articles, and more than twenty-five book reviews.

DARLENE CLARK HINE is John A. Hannah Distinguished Professor of American History at Michigan State University and has been President of the Organization of American Historians (2001–2002). Professor Hine received her B.A. degree from Roosevelt University and her M.A. and Ph.D. degrees from Kent State University. She is the author and editor of several books, including *Black Victory: The Rise of the White Primary in Texas*, *Black Women in White: Racial Conflict and Cooperation in the Nursing Profession, 1890–1950*, and co-author of *The African American Odyssey* and *A Shining Thread of Hope: A History of Black Women in America*. Most recently she is co-editor of *The Harvard Guide to African-American History*. Her book *The Black Professional Class: Physicians and Lawyers and the Origin of the Civil Rights Movement (1890–1955)* was published by the University of Illinois Press in 2002.

MARTIN KUHLMAN is Professor of History at West Texas A&M University. He earned B.B.A., B.A., and M.A. degrees at West Texas State University and received his Ph.D. in history from Texas Tech University in 1994, where he completed his dissertation "The Civil Rights Movement in Texas: Desegregation of Public Accommodations, 1950–1964." A specialist in the Old South, Civil War and Reconstruction, and the Civil Rights Movement, he focuses on the civil rights struggle in Texas. Among his articles are several dealing with the 1963 civil rights march in Austin and on the West Texas Chamber of Commerce; one of these is in *Bricks Without Straw: A Comprehensive History of African Americans in Texas*. He received a faculty excellence award at West Texas A&M University in 2000.

PAUL D. LACK, formerly Professor of History and Vice President for Academic Affairs at McMurry University, currently is Executive Vice President at Villa Julie College. Lack received his bachelor's degree from McMurry College and his M.A. and Ph.D. in history from Texas Tech University. A specialist in the Texas revolutionary period and in urban slavery in the Southwest, he has published articles in *Southwestern Historical Quarterly*, *Texas Through Time*, and *Black Leaders*, among other works. His books include *The Diary of William Fairfax Gray: From Virginia to Texas, 1835–37* and the award-winning *Texas Revolutionary Experience: A Social and Political History, 1835–1836*. For the latter, Lack received six awards, including best book on Texas history and best researched work from the Texas State Historical Association; he is also a Fellow in the TSHA.

ERNEST OBADELE-STARKS is Associate Professor of History at Texas A&M University at College Station. He received a B.A. from Northern Illinois University, an M.A. from Texas Southern University, and a Ph.D. in history from the University of Houston, where he wrote his dissertation "The Road to Jericho: Black Workers, the Fair Employment Practices Commission, and the Struggle for Racial Equality on the Upper Texas Gulf Coast, 1941–1947." A specialist in African American history as well as United States labor history, Obadele-Starks has published articles in journals such as *The Houston Review, Southwestern Historical Quarterly,* and *East Texas Historical Review* as well as a book entitled *Black Unionism in the Industrial South.* He currently is working on a second book manuscript, "The Wages of Wickedness: Slave Trafficking in the American Southwest, 1803–1861."

MERLINE PITRE is Professor of History and Dean of the College of Arts and Sciences at Texas Southern University. She received a Ph.D. degree from Temple University, where she wrote her dissertation entitled "Frederick Douglass: A Party Loyalist, 1870–1895." Pitre has published numerous articles in scholarly and professional journals. Her most noted works are *Through Many Dangers, Toils and Snares: The Black Leadership of Texas, 1968–1900* (a book which was reissued in 1997 and used in a traveling exhibit on black legislators by the State Preservation Board in 1998) and *In Struggle against Jim Crow: Lulu B. White and the NAACP, 1900–1957* (Texas A&M University Press, 1999). Pitre has been the recipient of grants from the Fulbright Foundation, the Texas Council for the Humanities, and the National Endowment for the Humanities. She is a former board member of the Texas Council for the Humanities. Currently, she is a member of the Speakers Bureau for the Texas Council for the Humanities and serves on the Harris County Historical Society.

NEIL SAPPER is Professor of History at Amarillo College, where he has taught for thirty years. Sapper received his M.A. from Eastern New Mexico University and his Ph.D. from Texas Tech University. One of the pioneers from the Texas Tech School of Black History, he wrote a dissertation entitled "A Survey of the History of the Black People of Texas, 1930–1954." He has published articles in *East Texas Historical Review, Texas Military History, The Houston Review,* and *Mississippi Quarterly,* among other journals.

MICHAEL N. SEARLES is Assistant Professor of History at Augusta State University (Georgia), where he teaches African American History. Currently enrolled in the Ph.D. program at The Union Institute, he received a B.A. in history from Southern Illinois University and an M.A. in history from Howard University. Searles has created a persona, Cowboy Mike, to help his audiences understand the western experience of the black cowboy. His publications on the black cowboy have appeared in works including *Black Cowboys of Texas*, edited by Sara R. Massey, and *American National Biography*. Searles chairs the W. Turrentine Jackson Awards Committee for the Western History Association and is on the Membership Committee for the Western Writers of America.

JAMES M. SMALLWOOD is Professor Emeritus of History at Oklahoma State University. Smallwood received his bachelor's and master's degrees from East Texas State University and his Ph.D. from Texas Tech University. He is the author or editor of more than twenty books, including *Time of Hope, Time of Despair: Black Texans During Reconstruction; A Century of Achievement: Blacks in Cook County, Texas; The Struggle for Equality: Blacks in Texas;* and *Born in Dixie: The History of Smith County, Texas* (2 vols.). Smallwood's articles have been published in journals including *Civil War History, Social Science Quarterly, Mid-America, Journal of the West,* and *The Houston Review*. His *Time of Hope, Time of Despair: Black Texans During Reconstruction* won the Texas State Historical Association Coral H. Tullis Award for the best book of the year on Texas history.

JAMES M. SORELLE is Professor of History and Chair of the History Department at Baylor University. SoRelle received his Ph.D. from Kent State University; his dissertation was entitled "The Darker Side of 'Heaven': The Black Community in Houston, Texas, 1919–1945." He taught at Ball State University, where he served as acting director of the Afro-American Studies Program before accepting an appointment on the faculty at Baylor. SoRelle's specialties are in African American history and American urban history. His published work has appeared in *The Houston Review, Southwestern Historical Quarterly, The Oxford Companion to Politics of the World,* and *Black Dixie: Essays in Afro-Texan History in Houston*. He also is the co-editor of *Taking Sides: Clashing Views on Controversial Issues in American History,* a two-volume reader published by Dushkin/McGraw-Hill. He is currently at work on a book-length study of the African American community in Houston in the years between the two world wars, and he has begun an exploration of the use of humor as a form of protest within the black community, using Houston as a case study.

Credits

The editors are grateful to the following contributors and to their previous publishers for allowing these articles to be reissued, sometimes with minimal editing, in this collection.

Barr, Alwyn. "Black Urban Churches on the Southern Frontier, 1865–1900." *Journal of Negro History* 82 (1997): 368–383. Reprinted by permission of the *Journal of Negro History* and the author.

Campbell, Randolph B. "Human Property: The Negro Slave in Harrison County, 1850–1860." *Southwestern Historical Quarterly* 76 (1973): 384–396. Reprinted by permission of the author and courtesy of the Texas State Historical Association. All rights reserved.

Cantrell, Gregg. "John B. Rayner: A Study in Black Populist Leadership." *Southern Studies* 24 (Winter 1985): 432–443. Reprinted by permission of *Southern Studies* and the author.

Carlson, Paul H. "William R. Shafter Commanding Black Troops in West Texas." *West Texas Historical Association Year Book* 50 (1974): 104–116. Reprinted by permission of the West Texas Historical Association and the author.

Christian, Garna L. "The El Paso Racial Crisis of 1900." *Red River Valley Historical Review* 6 (Spring 1981): 28–41. Reprinted by permission.

Dulaney, W. Marvin. "The Texas Negro Police Officers' Association: The Origins of Black Police Unionism." *The Houston Review* 12 (1990): 59–78. Reprinted by permission of the author and *The Houston Review*.

Fink, Robert C. "Semi-Professional African American Baseball in Texas before the Great Depression." Unpublished manuscript, printed by permission of the author.

Gillette, Michael L. "The Rise of the NAACP in Texas." *Southwestern Historical Quarterly* 81 (1978): 393–416. Reprinted by permission of the author and courtesy of the Texas State Historical Association. All rights reserved.

Hine, Darlene Clark. "The Elusive Ballot: The Black Struggle against the Texas Democratic White Primary, 1932–1945." *Southwestern Historical Quarterly* 81 (1978): 371–392. Reprinted by permission of the author and courtesy of the Texas State Historical Association. All rights reserved.

Kuhlman, Martin H. "Direct Action at the University of Texas During the Civil Rights Movement, 1960–1965." *Southwestern Historical Quarterly* 98 (1995): 550–566. Reprinted by permission of the author and courtesy of the Texas State Historical Association. All rights reserved.

Lack, Paul D. "Urban Slavery in the Southwest." *Red River Valley Historical Review* 6 (Spring 1981): 8–27. Reprinted by permission.

Obadele-Starks, Ernest. "Black Labor, the Black Middle Class, and Organized Protest along the Upper Texas Gulf Coast, 1883–1945." *Southwestern Historical Quarterly* 103 (1999): 53–65. Reprinted by permission of the author and courtesy of the Texas State Historical Association. All rights reserved.

Pitre, Merline. "Black Houstonians and the 'Separate but Equal' Doctrine: Carter W. Wesley versus Lulu B. White." *The Houston Review* 12 (1990): 23–36. Reprinted by permission of the author and *The Houston Review*.

Sapper, Neil. "Black Culture in Urban Texas: A Lone Star Renaissance." *Red River Valley Historical Review* 6 (Spring 1981): 56–77. Reprinted by permission.

Searles, Michael N. "In Search of the Black Cowboy in Texas." Unpublished manuscript, printed by permission of the author.

Smallwood, James M. "Emancipation and the Black Family: A Case Study in Texas." *Social Science Quarterly* 57 (1977): 849–857. Reprinted by permission of the Southwestern Social Science Association and the author.

SoRelle, James M. "The 'Waco Horror': The Lynching of Jesse Washington." *Southwestern Historical Quarterly* 86 (1983): 517–536. Reprinted by permission of the author and courtesy of the Texas State Historical Association. All rights reserved.

Index

Mellory Steamship Company of Georgia, 204
Mescalero (Apache), 132
Mexia, Texas, 223
Mexican Americans, 154
Mexican troops, 133
Mexicans, 42–43, 154
Mexico, 1, 9, 97, 130–131, 133, 164, 219, 234; black cowboys in, 86–87
Mexico City, 133
Miami, Florida, 341–342
Michigan, 4, 324
Midland, Texas, 93
Milan Street Law School for Blacks (Houston), 311
Miller Brothers 101 Ranch Real Wild West Show, 90, 95, 97–98
Miller, George, 97
Miller, Joe, 97
Miller, Tom, 321
Miller, Zack, 90, 97
Mills, Alfonso, 264–265
Mills, Jennie V., 247
Mills, Tom, black cowboy, 88
Mintz, Charles, 326
Misery index, 180
Missionaries, 26
Mississippi, lynching in, 183; 10, 110
Mississippi River, 40, 87, 103
Mitchell County, Texas, 94
Mobile, Alabama, slave population in, 46–47
Mob violence, 183–184
Monahans Sand Hills, 128
Monroe, Lee, 96
Montana, 90–91, 99, 160
Montgomery, Alabama, racial incident in, 158; bus boycott in, 319
Morehouse College (Atlanta, Georgia), 248
Morgan, Edward P., 326
Morgan, H. M., 270
Morgan, Joe, 228
Morocco, 23
Morriss, Will A., Jr., 287
Morrow, Ralph E., 59, 67
Morton, James H., 272
Moten, Etta, 239
Mulattos, 1

Munroe, Richard L., 187–189, 191–192
Museum of Fine Arts, in Houston, 242–243
Music, 10

Nabrit, James M., 261, 264, 283
Nashville, Tennessee, 281, 337
Nation, 194
National Association for the Advancement of Colored People, Rise of in Texas, 258–278; and the fight for black voting rights in Texas, 302–315; 175–179, 183–184, 191–193, 196–198, 205–206, 238–239, 259–263, 265, 270–271, 280, 318
National Association of Colored Women's Business Clubs, 206
National Association for the Study of Negro Life and History, 233
National Bar Association, 338
National Negro Baseball League, 228
National Cowboy Hall of Fame (in Oklahoma City), 98
National Editorial Association, 97
National Labor Relations Board, 208
National Medical Association, 338
National Negro Business League, 206, 223–224, 226
National Student Association, 323
National Urban League, 205, 234
Navarro, County, Texas, 94
Nazism, 294
Negrito (poetry), 244
Negro(es): Negro American League (baseball), 227; Negro Business Association, 210; Negro Day, at the Texas State Fair, 178–179; Negro Education Day (at Texas Centennial of 1936), 235; Negro Health Week, 241; Negro History Night (at Samuel Huston College), 237; *Negro Labor News*, 209–210, 212; Negro Hall of Life (at Texas Centennial of 1936), 231; *Negro History*